THE KNOWLEDGE-BASED ECONOMY: MODELED, MEASURED, SIMULATED

Loet Leydesdorff

Universal Publishers
Boca Raton

The Knowledge-Based Economy: Modeled, Measured, Simulated

Cover design: Franz Hoegl (Nürnberg)
Copyediting: Gene Moore

Universal Publishers
Boca Raton, Florida
USA • 2006

ISBN: 1-58112-937-8

www.universal-publishers.com

Includes bibliographical references and indices.

Subject headings:
   knowledge, economy, Triple Helix, innovation, system, anticipation, incursion

To learn more about this book visit the home page of the author at www.leydesdorff.net

Table of Contents

Preface

How can an economy be based on something as volatile as knowledge? The urgency of improving our understanding of a *knowledge-based economy* provides the context and necessity of this study. In a previous study entitled *A Sociological Theory of Communications: The Self-Organization of the Knowledge-based Society,* I specified knowledge-based systems from a sociological perspective. In this book, I take this theory one step further and demonstrate how the knowledge base of an economic system can be operationalized, both in terms of measurement and by providing simulation models.

How does a knowledge-based economy differ from a market-based or political economy? Markets and political (e.g., national) systems can be considered as providing different kinds of subdynamics to the social system. Markets, for example, function mainly to clear imbalances in the system, while political systems, among other things, regulate markets. My thesis is that organized knowledge production and control adds yet a *third* subdynamic to the social system (Schumpeter, [1939] 1964; cf. Hanneman and Collins, 1986; Whitley, 1984). Innovations in the technologies upset the equilibrium-seeking dynamics of the market.

The interactions among three subdynamics can be expected to lead to a non-equilibrium dynamics (Li and Yorke, 1975). This complex dynamics evolves in terms of trajectories and regimes changing the system in which they emerge (Nelson and Winter, 1982; Dosi, 1982). In a complex dynamics, however, the independent (steering) variables at one moment in time may become dependent at a next moment. In other words, the complex dynamics can become self-organizing because the incentives for change are distributed. Consequently, the economic and political mechanisms do not control, but provide a feedback mechanism to enable and constrain the development of scientific and technological knowledge.

Technologies develop in terms of generations along the time axis, while selection environments (e.g., the market) operate at each moment of time. In general, the dynamics of the market at each moment are tangential to the recursive dynamics of a historically evolving system. When three subdynamics interact, the model requires a third axis. This model of three subdynamics will be introduced and micro-founded in Chapter One. It is elaborated empirically into the Triple Helix model in Chapter Seven. The events can have different meaning along the three axes of the system, and also when projected on the planes which can be spanned between each two of them. The knowledge base will be modeled in this study as a second-order interaction term among (first-order) interactions between each two of these three subdynamics.

Each two subdynamics may act upon each other selectively, and thus co-evolve under certain conditions along an emerging axis in a process of mutual shaping (McLuhan, 1964). Such a stabilization can be made meta-stable when a third subdynamic is added. A meta-stabilized system can also be globalized. Reflexively, the various stabilizations can be made the subject of positive theories, while globalization can be specified only as an expectation or an emerging order. In other words, globalization and a knowledge-based order can be considered as an *analytical* possibility, while the observables inform us about the phenotypical retention mechanism or the footprints of a complex dynamics that evolves in terms of fluxes. The crucial question is whether entertaining this hypothesis of a knowledge-based order is fruitful for the explanation of the phenomena. Are the knowledge-based transformations of national systems of innovation and international politics perhaps elusive? (Skolnikoff, 1993). Are the emergence of a knowledge-based economy and globalization merely political buzzwords (Godin, 2006), or can these concepts also be elaborated into relevant theories and indicators? (European Commission, 2000; OECD, 1996a and b). How can a knowledge-based system be made the subject of empirical studies and simulations, and how might one thus be able to generate a research agenda?

The function of scientific and technological developments in socio-economic processes of change has been central to my research interests since the time of my Ph.D. thesis concerning employees and processes of technological innovation (Leydesdorff, 1984). In this project, I worked with trade-union representatives in a high-tech (chemical) industry in the Amsterdam region (Leydesdorff and Zeldenrust, 1984; Leydesdorff and Van den Besselaar, 1987a).[1] The creation of the Amsterdam Science Shop in 1977/1978 provided me with access to work processes in and among R&D departments, pilot plants, and the industrial floor of knowledge-intensive manufacturing (Leydesdorff, 1980; Leydesdorff, Ulenbelt, and Teulings, 1984; Zaal and Leydesdorff, 1987; Leydesdorff and Ward, 2005). Technology assessments of new production processes in the chemical industry taught me that

---

[1] In previous projects we had focused on the informal division of labour in solid state physics between the Philips Research Laboratories and the Dutch university system. In this context, I was astonished by the lack of socio-economic considerations in the decision-making processes about R&D despite the industrial contexts of these efforts (Leydesdorff *et al.*, 1980; Leydesdorff and Van Erkelens, 1981).

the relations between knowledge-intensive processes of technological innovation and the social impacts of the consequent reconfigurations are mediated by management to a varying extent. A careful reconstruction of how corporations structure these processes in terms of strategic and operational planning was required in order to appreciate the various moments at which decisions might be open to external influence (Lewy, 1976; Newman and Logan, 1981).

For example, what appears at the work floor to be a management decision may sometimes be mainly a constraint driven by changes in technologies and markets. In other cases there may be more room for negotiations with the unions and local authorities. In planning cycles economic considerations are matched with new technological perspectives (R&D management) and with geographic considerations. Interactions and frictions among the various perspectives give rise to new problems and puzzles. In the implementation stage, however, one deals with the consequences of managerial decisions about how these puzzles can best be solved. At the lower ends, trade unions—and even national governments—cannot distinguish clearly between the techno-economic environment at the global level and the firm's decisions about these variables (Leydesdorff and Van den Besselaar, 1987b). The resulting practices reflect several rounds of negotiations in which a wealth of analytical considerations had to be optimized from the perspective of management and control.

The reconstruction of decision cycles enabled us to improve our advice to the unions to such an extent that in some cases jobs could be saved. For example, relevant questions could be raised in the enterprise council at the right moments, that is, before decisions had already been made definitive. In the longer run, however, these interventions alienated us from the union's base at the work floor. (Our reports were sometimes appreciated by management.) Increasingly, an asymmetry became manifest between our interests in studying the social influences on knowledge production processes and the union's interests in the social consequences of the new technologies. When the *Science and Society* groups managed to organize an interfaculty department of *Science and Technology Dynamics* at the University of Amsterdam in the early 1980s, I decided to make the methodological question of how to measure scientific knowledge and its communication the focus of my research.

If the subdynamics of 'organized knowledge production and control' (Whitley, 1984) are *analytically* independent from the two other sources of variance (markets and institutions), one needs instruments for measuring these 'elusive' dynamics. At that time, Studer and Chubin (1980) had raised the question of a baseline for measurement in science and technology studies in an appendix to their evaluative study of the cancer mission as a government priority program in the U.S.A. during the 1970s. They formulated the methodological problem as follows:

> Relationships among journals, individuals, references, and citations can be analyzed in terms of their structural properties. But can one be used as a baseline to calibrate our understanding of another? Does it make sense to attempt to "control" for one relationship while studying others? What would be meant by "controlling for ideas" or "controlling for cocitations?" If disparate dimensions of science are not carefully analyzed in their own terms, the possibility of relating their respective contributions is nil. (*ibid.*, at p. 269)

Another crucial step had been to consider the development of the sciences not only in terms of its social contexts (as Studer and Chubin had done in the aforementioned study) but as discourses (Gilbert and Mulkay, 1984). Mulkay *et al.* (1983) had claimed priority for the communication-theoretical approach of discourse analysis in science and technology studies: the sciences develop as systems of *discursive* knowledge. However, these authors did not raise the follow-up question of whether the study of communications would require a statistics different from the parametric statistics prevailing in the social sciences.

Can the dynamics of science and technology be measured in terms of scientific communications? In Leydesdorff (1995a), I argued that the mathematical theory of communication provides a basis for developing a non-parametric (entropy) statistics for knowledge-based systems. These systems are *specific* in terms of their selections from the variations. Specific selections produce and reproduce skewed distributions (Brookes, 1979). Furthermore, systems which develop reflexively, that is, with reference to both their previous states and the incoming (e.g., experimental) information, add a selection mechanism over time to the structural selections at each moment. The expected information content of the resulting distributions and the meaning of the uncertainty can then be evaluated within the system as signals with reference to the two (or more) co-evolving systems and at different levels. For example, one can improve on the quality of the communication by controlling for error in the measurement. Thanks to this process of codification within the (sub)systems, a knowledge base is increasingly developed. I return to these process of codifications below, but let me here first trace the historical line of my intellectual development.

After elaborating the methodological apparatus during the 1980s, I returned in the early 1990s to the more complex issues of innovation at interfaces. How do knowledge-based innovations over the longer term restructure social systems with a dynamics different from economic rationality and political or managerial decision-making (Leydesdorff, 1992; Leydesdorff and Van den Besselaar, 1994)? Discussions with evolutionary economists rapidly taught me that the controversy between evolutionary economists and neo-classical economics had blocked the understanding of the economy as a complex system composed of different and interacting subdynamics (Anderson *et al.*, 1988). While evolutionary economists are fascinated with the non-equilibrium dynamics of (co-)evolutions over time, the neo-classical approach emphasizes the continuous operation of the equilibrium-seeking market mechanism as a problem-solver at each moment of time.

A complex-systems approach legitimizes the specification of knowledge production and control as a *third* subdynamic analytically different from and potentially orthogonal to economic and political systems of communication and control. In the sociological tradition, Niklas Luhmann argued for the advantages of analyzing society as a complex and composed ('functionally differentiated') dynamics. His work is perhaps best known for the proposal to consider human agents as the environment of the self-organization of social systems of communication (Luhmann, 1984/1995). These two systems (society and agency) would then operate independently—that is, along their respective axes—but they remain structurally coupled through the exchange of meaning. I use this theory as a heuristics: my focus is on the systemic character of the exchange of meaning as distinct from the exchange of information (Maturana, 1978). Knowledge can then be considered as a meaning that is further codified (see Chapter Two).

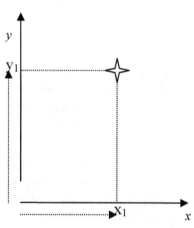

Figure 1. The interaction informs the interacting systems asymmetrically.

The analytical independence of two subdynamics (x and y) presumes that these axes are considered orthogonal (Figure 1). The interaction terms between them—indicated in Figure 1 as a star—are provided with a value using the operations (x_1 and y_1) along the respective axes. I consider providing an event with a value as a reflection. Note that this changes the common notion of reflection, which assumes the metaphor of a mirror reflecting with 180 degrees. Reflections at ninety degrees do not use a next level, but generate only another perspective.

The systems perform their own *autopoiesis*—that is, self-organization—along their respective axes, but they disturb each other's self-referential operations at interfaces.[2] The resulting system is complex because it contains both interactions (at specific moments of time) and recursion (over time). This complex dynamics can be expected to change endogenously, that is, through the operations of the interacting subdynamics upon one another. In the *Wissenschaft der Gesellschaft*—that is, *The Science of Society*—Luhmann (1990a) formulated the research program implied as follows:

> The differentiation of science in society changes also the social system in which it occurs, and this can again be made the subject of scientific theorizing. [...] Developing this perspective, however, is only possible if an accordingly complex systems theoretical arrangement is specified. [3] (Luhmann, 1990a, at p. 340)

In a special issue of *Social Science Information* devoted to this theory, I quoted this statement as a concise formulation of my program of research (Leydesdorff, 1996a, at p. 299). How can a knowledge base emerge in a system as a result of a recursive interaction, and how does the emerging subdynamic feedback and potentially reorganize the system from which it is emerging?

For example, technologies can be expected to develop at interfaces between the sciences and the economy; interface systems can be updated from both sides, that is, by selecting upon each other's variations. Innovation patterns may then

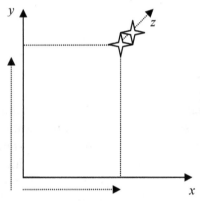

Figure 2. The development of a co-evolution on the basis of a recursive co-variation.

result as a third subdynamic (z) from the interactions along the axis of an emerging co-evolution (Figure 2). Additionally, this mutual shaping of markets and techno-

[2] The subsystems of a self-organizing system can be expected to self-organize themselves to a variable degree, namely, to the extent that this self-organization is functional for the system's development (Leydesdorff, 1993b, 1994a).
[3] 'Die Ausdifferenzierung verändert auch das System der Gesellschaft, in dem sie stattfindet, und auch dies kann wiederum Thema der Wissenschaft werden. [...] Das allerdings ist nur möglich, wenn man ein entsprechend komplexes systemtheoretisches Arrangement zugrundelegt.'

sciences in a positive feedback loop can be 'locked-in' (David, 1985; Arthur, 1988 and 1989).

At the time (Leydesdorff, 1992 and 1993a), my concern was twofold: first, the lack of empirical operationalization and methodological rigour in Luhmann's sociology, and secondly, the failure in social systems theory more generally to bridge the gap with the modeling of complex systems in terms of simulations, as had become common in evolutionary economics (Leydesdorff, 1995b; 2001a; Leydesdorff and Van den Besselaar, 1994). From my perspective, 'an accordingly complex systems theoretical arrangement' should combine the perspective of non-linear dynamics with the study of systems which process meaning in addition to and in interaction with (Shannon-type) information exchange. Thus, the systems are composed both horizontally and vertically of different subdynamics.

It turned out that such elaboration was not a single task. The relationship between the simulation models and the empirical studies required also a further development of the theorizing. For example, the frictions among the subsystems were not appreciated by Luhmann (1984, 1997a) as Shannon-type information. (This will be elaborated in Chapter Two.) In scientific reasoning, however, 'empirical evidence' containing an external reference is crucial for the production of novelty (Fry, 2006). The uncertainty in the communication provides the basis for the production of novelty (Leydesdorff, 1996a).

Two branches of research have been further developed after the specification of these problems at interfaces. In collaboration with Henry Etzkowitz, I developed the Triple Helix of university-industry-government relations into a model of technological innovation (Leydesdorff and Etzkowitz, 1998). A series of workshops, conferences, and special issues of journals has provided me with a wealth of empirical materials that have significantly informed my theorizing about the different modes in which a composed dynamics can operate. This perspective is elaborated in the empirical chapters of this study. An instrument for measuring the Triple Helix-dynamics will be proposed and tested. The knowledge base is measured both at the level of the global system (Chapter Eight) and more specifically for the Dutch and German economies (Chapters Nine and Ten, respectively).

In collaboration with Peter van den Besselaar and Daniel Dubois I have elaborated simulation models for knowledge-based innovations (Leydesdorff and Van den Besselaar, 1998a and 1998b; Leydesdorff, 1995b, 2000a, 2000b, 2001a, 2002a, 2005a; Leydesdorff and Dubois, 2004). A European project entitled 'The Self-Organization of the European Information Society' (SOEIS) provided a context for collaboration with Japanese colleagues of similar interests (Fujigaki and Leydesdorff, 2000; Leydesdorff and Heimeriks, 2001). The series of conferences on 'Computing Anticipatory Systems' (CASYS) organized by Daniel Dubois in Liège (Belgium) and my continuous participation in his program committee have provided the stimulus to study knowledge-based systems as *anticipatory systems* (Leydesdorff, 2000a, 2005a, 2006e). I am grateful to him for providing the proofs of some of the algorithms discussed in Chapter Four (Leydesdorff and Dubois, 2004).

An anticipatory system can be defined as a system which accommodates a model of the system itself (Rosen, 1985). Anticipatory systems reduce uncertainty locally within the system by using the time axis as a degree of freedom (Coveney and Highfield, 1990; Leydesdorff, 1994c; Raju, 2003). In other words, the modeling subroutine of an anticipatory system runs ahead upon the system which is modeled and provides the latter with a prediction about the state of the system at a future moment in time—that is, by looking backward from the position at that future moment in time. Dubois (1998) has called this 'incursion' in order to distinguish it from 'recursion' which follows the arrow of time. At the level of the social system, however, a prediction remains also discursive.

For example, in scientific discourse one can investigate future events in terms of 'what if' questions. Thus, the clocks of the modeled system and the modeling systems are differentiated in the time dimension by codifying the two discourses— the historical one following the participants along the axis of time, and the analytical one—differently. This generates a 'double hermeneutics' (Giddens, 1978). For example, a scientific discourse enables us to discuss future states of systems in the present on the basis of an analysis of examples from the past independently of the participants who experienced these situations historically. In my opinion, reflexivity about this difference in perspectives provides the *differentia specifica* of the sociological perspective (Giddens, 1984; Leydesdorff, 1997a, 2001b, 2006b).

Within the social system the differentiation which occurs along the time axis can interact with the differentiation in the codification at each moment of time (for example, between science and the economy) and thus a strongly anticipatory system can additionally be shaped (Chapter Four). Unlike a weakly anticipatory system, which only entertains a prediction of its future state(s), a strongly anticipatory one can also reconstruct its next state (Dubois, 2003). I shall explain in Chapter Five how this restructuring may lead to techno-economic co-evolutions which change the 'natural' environment by operating at the supra-individual level, that is, beyond the control of individuals or any aggregated group agency. The co-constructing agents are enrolled in the knowledge-based system, and this enrollment transforms them from economic agents with 'natural preferences' to informed places of decision-making. Decisions can be codified into decision-rules (e.g., in organizations).

I shall argue that contrary to biological evolution, cultural evolution restructures the past to the extent that the past can be overwritten by the interactions that occur among anticipatory subdynamics. In a Dutch polder landscape, for example, one can consider the polder vegetation as 'natural' or wish 'to return to nature' by flooding the country. This overwriting of the previous state by a techno-economic co-evolution at the supra-individual level is possible because the functional differentiation in the coding provides the social system with a second updating mechanism in addition to anticipation in the structural coupling between agency and social structures. The communication of information can be codified into meaning at one interface, and meaning can further be codified into knowledge at a next one. Knowledge can be considered as a meaning which makes a difference. However, the codification of the expected information content of a distribution remains always uncertain at the level of the social system because the social system operates in terms of exchanges; distributions are changed by the exchanges, but the distributions can be expected to contain an uncertainty. Consequently, the knowledge-based systems remain emergent and incomplete. Yet, they can be distinguished analytically from their historical realizations.

Because more complexity can be processed when a knowledge base is constructed within the system, the emerging dynamics of expectations may increasingly take control by operating in the present with reference to the future given the system's historical conditions. This idea of a 'rewrite' on the basis of an inversion along the historical axis was first expressed in Joseph Schumpeter's (1939) concept of 'creative destruction.' It can also be related to Edmund Husserl's (1929) notion of 'intersubjectivity' as a system (a 'monade') other than 'subjectivity.' Husserl wrestled with the question of how 'intersubjectivity' can contain 'intentionality' differently from subjective intentionality (Chapter Eleven). The intentionality of the social system is contained in the distribution and is therefore different from (and even orthogonal to) those of human beings. However, the two types of intentionality remain interwoven because of the structural coupling between communications and the carriers of communication.

In other words, the historical stabilization of a system (along the axis of time) can be meta-stabilized if the stabilization is reflected in the present as one among possible representations. Meta-stabilizations create the possibility for globalization.

Globalization occurs with reference to a next-order system. Thus, the social system can be brought into a new regime of knowledge-based development. However, this happens *within* history, and thus the transition towards a knowledge-based economy cannot be completed. A globalizing system is structurally coupled to its manifest (that is, stabilized) layer. The operations of the virtual system remain trade-offs between stabilizations and globalization, but control tends to shift towards the knowledge-based end of the emerging system.

The reflexive systems operate on top of the reflected ones (using ninety degrees for the reflection), but the layers remain dependent on each other in an autocatalytic loop because of the various couplings. The processing of information (uncertainty generation) can then be slowed down or accelerated by the processing of meaning and the processing of knowledge. Information theory enables us to study information-processing, meaning-processing, and next-order knowledge-processing as different subdynamics, but these processes have first to be distinguished analytically and then operationalized. When the differences are clearly specified and the operationalizations independent, one can study the extent to which, why, and in which respects a development is increasingly knowledge-based.

The expectation is that the interacting subdynamics tend towards 'near decomposability' along the different axes, since increasing the spanning of the multi-dimensional space allows the system to process more complexity (Simon, 1969, 1973). The events can differently be projected and provided with meaning along the various axes and planes. However, the mutual information is by definition smaller than the information contained in each of the interacting systems. The reflecting system thus builds upon the reflected ones, but by using an orthogonal axis for the reflection. The systems are reconstructed from a tangential perspective: only the mutual information is available as a window on the other systems (Casti, 1989, at pp. 219 ff. and 1990; Luhmann, 1990b). Since the room for *in*-struction (steering) in the ongoing re-*con*-struction during the self-organization is limited, unintended consequences of interventions can be expected to prevail (Callon, 1998).

The signals received through the windows of interaction provide external references which can be observed, deconstructed, and reconstructed if the receiving systems/subdynamics contain reflexivity. However, each subsystem of the social system is expected to perform its respective internal operations concurrently. Consequently, the mechanisms to reduce uncertainty, such as providing meaning to the (Shannon-type) information—and organizing the various meanings into discursive knowledge—can under certain (e.g., autocatalytic) conditions develop at speeds higher than that of the underlying (since historical) proliferation of uncertainty. When this occurs, the representations no longer have to be materialized at each step, and thus the development of the system tends to become knowledge-based, that is, steered by expectations generated internally at a speed higher than their realizations. In other words, the system henceforth can operate on the basis of discursively codified expectations which have to be confirmed only as instantiations with a frequency sufficient for carrying the inference (Quine, 1953). The disturbance terms, however, remain the source of novelty production. Novelty production can be considered as the goal and purpose of the scientific enterprise. Because of this continuous influx, the system tends to become increasingly knowledge-based.

For the participants, the non-linear dynamics generates an elusive transformation because the agents of change are no longer clearly identifiable. The social system operates in terms of distributions. A specific identification can be deconstructed as a reflexive network effect or, in other words, an attribution by the social system. The historical manifestations fail to inform us sufficiently about the order of expectations. We need a reflexive turn for this. The knowledge base of an economy thus remains in a domain of informed hypotheses. The process is limited and sometimes 'bottlenecked' by the availability of reflexive capacity for the reconstruction, e.g., in scientific discourses and professional practices among human resources. The systems under study remain operational and in transition. Therefore, this perspective on knowledge-based systems can no longer claim to be based in an ontology. Derivatives from the Latin verb *esse* (to be) like 'ontology' and 'essential' give way to derivatives of *frangere* (to break) such as 'fractals,' 'fragments,' and 'fragile.'

In a fragmented reality comprised of different angles of reflection, one can expect more than a single perspective to become codified. The perspectives focus on potentially different subdynamics. Reflections in the scientific discourses provide us with codifications in increasingly orthogonal and therefore potentially incommensurable windows for the appreciation (Kuhn, 1962). The perspective of science and technology studies has reflexively produced as one of its main contributions that the scientific discourses generate epistemic objects by providing specific meaning to otherwise uncertain phenomena. In a knowledge-based order, epistemic objects can be considered as genotypical of the observable phenomena. The discourses provide us with heuristics for competing explanations—that is, provisional stabilizations of understanding—in an order which tends towards globalization because of next-order interactions among the various understandings.

Formalization is required for abstracting from the empirical domain of observables to the epistemic domain of expectations. The expectations remain fallible (albeit theoretically informed) hypotheses. However, a change in the epistemological order is also implied. A knowledge-based system is grounded in reflexivity and discourse. Knowledge operates by translating *a priori* hypotheses into *a posteriori* ones. The foundations of these constructs remain constructs. As Deleuze and Guattari (1987, at p. 15) once noted, in Amsterdam the foundations are also constructed (by driving pillars into the underlying sediment without the hope of a rock bottom). The foundations of knowledge-based systems have analogously been constructed over longer periods of time. A grounding in existential premises might lead to the erronic inference that something could exist because it can be imagined. Individual imaginations are needed for the production of knowledge claims, but communication is needed for the validation of results as a social phenomenon. Existence remains a necessary, but different and therefore increasingly tangential subdynamic; historical manifestations can be considered as the cases that happened to occur among other possible ones given the hypothesized system of reference.

In the final chapter I return to the philosophical implications of these reflections for the empirical studies and simulations presented in the other chapters. The reflections can be considered second-order because the scientific discourses needed for the constructions provided us already with first-order reflections containing substantive knowledge in different paradigms. For example, the biological metaphor of evolution is used throughout this study as a heuristics for the specification of a cultural evolution. However, a second-order perspective is generated by abstracting from the specifically biological content of the (first-order) theorizing. This formalization will enable me to specify mechanisms (like cultural evolution) other than biological ones. This operation is very similar to Husserl's (e.g., 1929, 1939) *epoché* in transcendental phenomenology as an abstraction from empirical psychology. However, the elaboration of the mathematical theory of communication provided us with a set of tools for studying intersubjectivity and communication as a non-linear dynamics grounded in interactions *among* subjective intentionalities: the structure and the dynamics of interhuman communications transcend individual contributions, but they can be reflected in a sociological discourse which is methodologically guided (Leydesdorff, 1997a, 2001b, 2006b).

Furthermore, the operationalization of reflection as a recursion of selection along a different axis allows me to formalize reflexivity without reifying it. The various reflections stand in orthogonal relation and not 'meta' or at a next-order level. The reflexive perspective along an orthogonal dimension remains 'epi' (nearby). One can no longer assume a one-to-one relationship between simulation results and empirical data. Empirical data exhibit states in a phase space of possible states. The bridge between the two perspectives is constructed reflexively by using relevant theories. The task remains eventually to explain and demonstrate why and how a knowledge-based or strongly anticipatory system constructs and continuously reconstructs its own basis in potentially self-reinforcing loops. These loops at the supra-individual level enable us increasingly to reorganize the underlying variation, that is, the limits of our own understanding.

Acknowledgements

This book integrates a number of previous projects. Some of the chapters have been written on the basis of articles and reports with coauthors. The original communications are listed below. I thank for the various coauthorship relations: Wilfred Dolfsma, Daniel Dubois, Henry Etzkowitz, Michael Fritsch, Iina Hellsten, Andrea Scharnhorst, Peter van den Besselaar, Gerben van der Panne, and Paul Wouters. I am also grateful to Gretchen Dee, Franz Hoegl, and Caroline Wagner for their long-term commitment to this project and their comments on previous drafts of the manuscript. I am indebted to Gene Moore for patiently correcting my English and the Amsterdam School of Communications Research for providing a stimulating environment. Can this also be a proper place to thank Margaret Traudes for our life-long project?

List of original communications

Chapter 1: "The Knowledge-Based Economy and the Triple Helix Model." Pp. 42-76 in Wilfred Dolfsma and Luc Soete (Eds.), *Understanding the Dynamics of a Knowledge Economy*, Cheltenham: Edward Elgar, 2006.

Chapter 2: "The Construction and Globalization of the Knowledge Base in Inter-human Communication Systems," *Canadian Journal of Communication* 28(3), 2003, 267-289.

Chapter 3: "Anticipatory Systems and the Processing of Meaning: A Simulation Inspired by Luhmann's Theory of Social Systems," *Journal of Artificial Societies and Social Simulation*, 8(2), 2005, Paper 7, at http://jasss.soc.surrey.ac.uk/8/2/7.html

Chapter 4:
- Loet Leydesdorff and Daniel Dubois, "Anticipation in Social Systems," *International Journal of Computing Anticipatory Systems*, 15, 2004, 203-216;
- "Meaning, Anticipation, and Codification in Functionally Differentiated Social Systems," in: Thomas Kron, Uwe Schimank, and Lars Winter (Eds.), *Luhmann Simulated – Computer Simulations to the Theory of Social Systems*. Münster, etc: Lit Verlag, 2006 (in preparation).

Chapter 5:
- "Technology and Culture: The Dissemination and the Potential 'Lock-in' of New Technologies." In D. M. Dubois (Ed.), *Journal of Artificial Societies and Social Simulation*, 4(3), 2001, Paper 5, at http://jasss.soc.surrey.ac.uk/4/3/5.html;
- "Hyper-incursion and the Globalization of a Knowledge-Based Economy," *American Institute of Physics Proceedings of the Seventh International Conference on Computing Anticipatory Systems CASYS'05*, Liège, Belgium, August 8-13, 2005 (forthcoming).

Chapter 7: "The Evaluation of Research and the Evolution of Science Indicators," *Current Science*, 89(9), 2005, 1510-1517.

Chapter 8: "The Mutual Information of University-Industry-Government Relations: An Indicator of the Triple Helix Dynamics," *Scientometrics* 58(2), 2003, 445-467.

Chapter 9: Loet Leydesdorff, Wilfred Dolfsma, and Gerben van der Panne, "Measuring the Knowledge Base of an Economy in terms of Triple Helix Relations among 'Technology, Organization, and Territory'," *Research Policy*, 35(2) (2006) 181-199.

Chapter 10: Loet Leydesdorff and Michael Fritsch, "Measuring the Knowledge Base of Regional Innovation Systems in Germany in terms of a Triple Helix Dynamics," *Research Policy* (In print).

Chapter 11: "Luhmann's Communication-Theoretical Specification of the 'Genomena' of Husserl's Phenomenology." In: Edmundo Balsemão Pires (Ed.), *Public Space, Power and Communication*, University of Coimbra, Portugal (In print).

Chapter 1

The Knowledge-Based Economy

Few concepts introduced by evolutionary economists have been more successful than that of a 'knowledge-based economy' (Foray and Lundvall, 1996; Abramowitz and David, 1996; OECD, 1996a). This assumption of a qualitative transition in economic conditions has become commonplace among policy-makers and mainstream economists. For example, the European Summit of March 2000 in Lisbon was specifically held "to agree a new strategic goal for the Union in order to strengthen employment, economic reform and social cohesion as part of a knowledge-based economy" (European Commission, 2000). The findings of this meeting concluded that, among other things, "the shift to a digital, knowledge-based economy, prompted by new goods and services, will be a powerful engine for growth, competitiveness and jobs. In addition, it will be capable of improving citizens' quality of life and the environment."[4]

The metaphor of a 'knowledge-based economy' has raised a number of hitherto unanswered questions. For example, can such a large impact on the real economy be expected from something as poorly defined as the knowledge base of an economy? Should one consider this concept merely as a rhetorical reflection of the optimism regarding the potential impact of ICT and the Internet during the 1990s (Godin, 2006)? How would a knowledge-based economy be expected to differ from a market economy or a political economy?

In this study, I shall argue that one can expect a knowledge-based economy to exhibit dynamics different from those of a market-based or political economy. The systematic organization of knowledge production and control (Merton, 1973; Whitley, 1984) provides a third coordination mechanism to the social system in addition to the traditional mechanisms of economic exchange and political decision-making. From the perspective of complex systems and evolution theory, the interactions among these three coordination mechanisms can be expected to generate a knowledge base which is endogenous to the system.

---

[4] See the Conclusions of the EU Presidency at
http://europa.eu.int/comm/research/era/pdf/com2000-6-en.pdf (European Commission, 2000 and 2005).

1.1   What is the knowledge base of an economy?

In an introduction to a special issue on this topic, David and Foray (2002) voiced a caveat against using the metaphor of a knowledge-based economy. These authors cautioned that the terminology was coined recently, and noted that "as such, it marks a break in the continuity with earlier periods, more a 'sea-change' than a sharp discontinuity" (*ibid.*, p. 9). The authors argue that the transformations can be analyzed at a number of different levels. Furthermore, 'knowledge' and 'information' should be more carefully distinguished by analyzing the development of a knowledge-based economy in terms of codification processes (Cowan and Foray, 1997; Cowan, David and Foray, 2000).

The focus of most economic contributions to the topic has hitherto been on the *consequences* of knowledge-based developments, such as the impact of globalization on the relationships among competitors and among labor markets. The emergence of a knowledge-based economy is invoked as a factor to explain historical developments and changes. However, the evolutionary dynamics of the knowledge base itself remain unexplained by these historical analyses. I do not wish to deny the social relevance of the historical transition to a knowledge-based economy and its impacts; on the contrary, my argument implies that knowledge-based dynamics can be expected to provide a coordination mechanism that is qualitatively different from the hitherto prevailing dynamics of politics and market-driven economics. The dynamic of knowledge production and control adds a degree of freedom to the complex system of social relations and coordination that needs to be explained. In other words, I focus on the knowledge base as an *explanandum* rather than as an *explanans* for its economic implications.

Under what conditions can a knowledge-based dynamics be expected to emerge in socio-economic systems? In order to operationalize, model, and eventually also measure the knowledge base of a system, one must first flesh out the meaning of the concept. After the specification of the organization and codification of knowledge as an evolutionary mechanism, one is able to specify, among other things, why the emergence of a knowledge-based economy can be expected to induce 'globalization.' Why and how can a knowledge-based economy be considered a driving force of this transformation? Furthermore, what can function as an indicator of the knowledge base of a system?

First, I will consider the theoretical side and focus on the specification of knowledge-based innovation systems. Thereafter, I turn to the question of how the knowledge base can be operationalized, and whether this knowledge base can be measured and/or simulated. The concept of the knowledge base of an economy is elaborated, and this analysis results in an apparatus which provides a heuristics for empirical research and simulation studies.

1.2   The emergence of a knowledge base

Knowledge enables us to codify the *meaning* of information. Information can be more or less meaningful given a perspective. However, meaning is provided from a system's perspective and with hindsight. Providing meaning to an uncertainty (that is, Shannon-type information) can be considered as a first codification. Knowledge enables us to discard some meanings and retain others in a second layer of codifications. In other words, knowledge can be considered *as a meaning which makes a difference*. Knowledge itself can also be codified, and codified knowledge can, for example, be commercialized. Thus, a knowledge-based system operates in recursive loops that one would expect to be increasingly selective in terms of the information to be retained.

The knowledge base of a social system can be further developed over time by ongoing processes of theoretically informed deconstructions and reconstructions (Cowan *et al.*, 2000; Foray, 2004). Knowledge operates by informing expectations in the present on the basis of previous operations of the system. Informed expectations open the discourse towards future events and possible reconstructions. A knowledge-based economy is driven more by codified anticipations than by its historical conditions (Lundvall and Borras, 1997). In other words, science-based representations of possible futures (e.g., 'competitive advantages') feed back on historically manifest processes (Nonaka and Takeuchi, 1995; Biggiero, 2001).

This reflexive orientation towards the future inverts the time axis locally. However, a local inversion of the arrow of time may increasingly meta-stabilize a historically stabilized system. While stabilization and destabilization are historical processes, meta-stabilization potentially changes the dynamics of the system. A meta-stabilized system can under certain conditions also be globalized (Coveney and Highfield, 1990; Mackenzie, 2001; Urry, 2000). I return to these issues of codification and the inversion of the time dimension in later chapters, but let us first follow the construction of a knowledge base from the historical perspective (Figure 1).

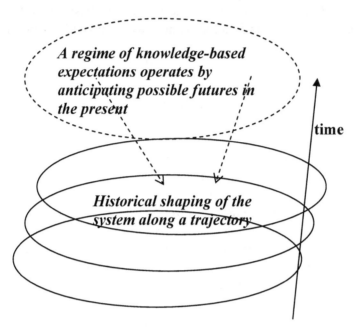

Figure 1.1: A technological trajectory follows the axis of time, while a knowledge-based regime operates within the system in terms of expectations, that is, against the axis of time.

Before the emergence of a knowledge-based economy, the economic exchange of knowledge was first developed as distinct from the exchange of commodities within the context of a market economy. For example, the patent system can be considered as a typical product of industrial competition in the late nineteenth century (Van den Belt and Rip, 1987). Patent legislation became crucial for regulating intellectual property when knowledge markets emerged increasingly in chemistry and later in electrical engineering (Noble, 1977). Patents package scientific knowledge so that new knowledge can function at the interface of science with the economy and be incorporated into knowledge-based innovations (Granstrand, 1999; Jaffe and Trajtenberg, 2002). Patents thus provide a format for codifying knowledge contents for purposes other than the internal requirements of quality control in scientific communication.

The production and control of organized knowledge itself has existed as a subdynamic of the socio-economic system in advanced capitalist societies since approximately 1870 (Braverman, 1974; Noble, 1977). Schumpeter ([1939], 1964) is well-known for his argument that the dynamics of innovation upset the market mechanism (Nelson and Winter, 1982). While market forces seek equilibrium at each moment of time, novelty production generates an orthogonal subdynamic along the time axis. This has been modeled as the difference between factor substitution (the change of input factors along the production function) and technological development (a shift of the production function towards the origin; Sahal, 1981a and b; Figure 1.2). Technological innovations enable enterprises to reduce factor costs in both labor and capital (Salter, 1960).

Innovative change *over time* (novelty production) and economic substitution at each *moment of time* can thus be considered as two analytically independent subdynamics. However, these subdynamics can be expected additionally to interact in the case of innovation.

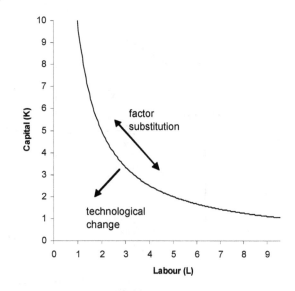

Figure 1.2: Using the production function (Q = c.K.L), factor substitution and technological change can be distinguished as perpendicular subdynamics.

Improving a system innovatively presumes that one is able to handle the system purposefully. When this reflection is further refined by organizing knowledge, the innovative dynamic can be reinforced. This reinforcement will occur at some *places* more than at others. Thus, a third dimension pertinent to our subject can be specified: the geographical—and potentially national—distribution of whatever is invented, produced, traded, or retained. Nation-states, for example, can be expected to differ in terms of the relationship between their respective economy and its knowledge base (Lundvall, 1992; Nelson, 1993). Different fields of science are organized nationally and/or internationally to varying degrees (Wagner and Leydesdorff, 2003; Walsh and Bayma, 1996).

Geographical units of analysis, economic exchange relations, and novelty production cannot be reduced to one another. However, they can be expected to interact to varying extents (Storper, 1997). Given these specifications, one can create a model of the three dimensions and their interaction terms as follows:

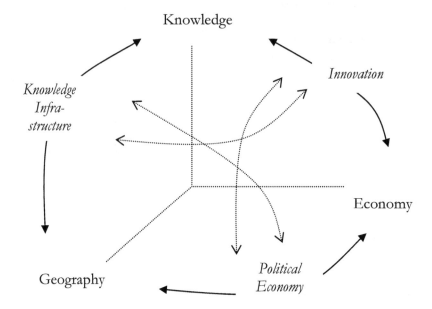

Figure 1.3: Three dimensions of the social system with their three interaction terms.

The three dimensions will provide us below with different micro-operations of the social system because people (1) are differently positioned, (2) can maintain exchange relations, and (3) learn from these relations with reference to their local positions. Figure 1.3 furthermore elaborates the conceptualization by situating each of the interaction terms between two of the three dimensions.

In a pluriform society, the various interactions are no longer synchronized *ex ante*, and thus they may begin to interact among themselves. In general, two interacting subdynamics can be expected to co-evolve along trajectories when the third dynamic is kept relatively constant. Over time, two subdynamics can lock-in into each other in a process of mutual shaping in a co-evolution (Arthur, 1994; Callon *et al.*, 2002; McLuhan, 1964). For example, during the formation of political economies in national systems during the nineteenth century, knowledge production was at first considered as an exogenous given (List, 1841; Marx, 1848, 1867).[5] Under

---

[5] Marx (1857) closely observed the *technological* condition of industrial capitalism, noting, for example, that: "Nature does not build machines, locomotives, railways, electric telegraphs, self-acting mules, etc. These are the products of human industry; natural resources which are transformed into organs of the human control over nature or one's practices in nature. (…) The development of fixed assets shows the extent to which knowledge available at the
continued >

the condition of constitutional stability in the various nation-states after 1870, *national systems of innovation* could gradually be developed among the axes of economic exchange and organized knowledge production and control (Noble, 1977; Rosenberg, 1976a, 1982).

Interactions among three subdynamics generate an evolutionary dynamics of transition within the system (Schumpeter, [1939] 1964). A knowledge-based economy is continuously disturbed by interactions at various interfaces and is never at rest. Stabilities developed between two subdynamics can be de-stabilized by a third. Historically, a hitherto stable context may begin to change. For example, the erosion of relative stability in nation-states because of globalization has changed the conditions of innovation systems. A previously stabilized co-evolution between production and diffusion capacities within a national system can be increasingly subjected to the conflicting conditions of local production and the world market. Alternatively, the new feedback term may globalize a historically stabilized trajectory of technological innovations into a technological regime (Dosi, 1982; Leydesdorff and Van den Besselaar, 1998). I return to these issues from a systems-theoretical perspective below, but let us first follow the historical order of the development of the argument.

When Lundvall (1988) proposed that the nation be considered as a first candidate for the *integration* of innovation systems, he formulated this claim carefully in terms of a heuristics:

> The interdependency between production and innovation goes both ways. [...] This interdependency between production and innovation makes it legitimate to take the national system of production as a starting point when defining a system of innovation. (Lundvall, 1988, at p. 362)

The idea of integrating innovation into production at the *national* level has the analytical advantage of providing us with an institutionally demarcated system of reference. If the market is continuously upset by innovation, can the nation then

---

level of society is transformed into immediate productive force, and therefore, the extent to which the conditions of social life have themselves been brought under the control of the general intellect and have been transformed accordingly. Crucial is the degree to which the socially productive forces are produced not only as knowledge, but as immediate organs of social practice, that is, of the real process of living" (Marx, 1857, at p. 594; my translation). Thus, Marx remained focused on the historical state of the development of science and technology, and on the integration of this condition into the political economy.

perhaps be considered as another, albeit institutionally organized equilibrium (Aoki, 2001)? The specification of this relatively stable system of reference would enable an analyst to study, for example, the so-called 'differential productivity growth puzzle' which is generated by the different speeds of development among the various industrial sectors (Nelson and Winter, 1975). The problem of the relative rates of innovation cannot be defined properly without the specification of a system of reference that integrates different sectors of an economy (Nelson, 1982, 1993, 1994). The solutions to this 'puzzle' can accordingly be expected to differ among nation-states.

The historical progression varies among countries, and integration at the national level still plays a major role in systems of innovation (Skolnikoff, 1993). However, the emergence of transnational levels of government like the European Union, together with an increased awareness of regional differences within and across nations, have changed the functions of national governments (Braczyk *et al.*, 1998). 'Government' has evolved from a hierarchically fixed point of reference into the variable 'governance' that spans a variety of sub- and supranational levels. Larédo (2003) argued that this polycentric environment of stimulation has become a condition for innovation policies in the European Union.

1.3   Interactive knowledge production and control

While a political economy can be indicated in terms of only two subdynamics (for example, as a 'dialectics' between production forces and production relations), a complex dynamics can be expected when three subdynamics are free to operate upon one another (Li and Yorke, 1975; Leydesdorff, 1994b). It will be argued here that the configuration of three possible degrees of freedom—markets, governance, and knowledge production—can be modeled in terms of a Triple Helix of university-industry-government relations (Etzkowitz and Leydesdorff, 1997; Leydesdorff and Etzkowitz, 1998). Governance can be considered as the variable that instantiates and organizes systems in the geographical dimension of the model, while industry is the main carrier of economic production and exchange. Thirdly, universities can play a leading role in the organization of the knowledge-production function (Godin and Gingras, 2000).

In this (neo-)evolutionary model of interacting subdynamics, the institutional dimensions cannot be expected to correspond one-to-one with the functions in the network carried by and between the agencies. Each university and industry, for example, also has a geographical location and is therefore subject to regulation and legislation. In a knowledge-based system, functions no longer develop exclusively at the local level, that is, contained within their institutional settings. Instead, the interactions generate evolutionary dynamics of change in relations at the network level. In other words, university-industry-government relations develop in terms of institutional arrangements that recombine three functions of the socio-economic system: (1) wealth generation and retention, (2) novelty production, and (3) control at the interfaces of these subdynamics. The functions provide a layer of development that is analytically different, but historically coupled to the institutional arrangements.

The first two functions (economy and science) can be considered as relatively open since 'universal' (Parsons, 1951; Luhmann, 1984, 1990a). The third function of normative control bends the space of possible interactions reflexively back to the *position* of the operating units (e.g., the firms and the nations) in the marketplace and at the research front, respectively. In this dimension, the question of what can be retained locally during the reproduction of the innovation processes becomes crucial. The system of reference for this question is the political economy. The advantages of entertaining a knowledge base can additionally be incorporated if the knowledge produced by the interacting fluxes can also be retained. In other words, the development of a knowledge base is dependent on the condition that knowledge production be socially organized.

The interfaces between institutions and functions can be expected to resonate into co-evolutions in some configurations more than in others. However, the resonances remain incomplete because the co-evolving subdynamics are continuously disturbed by the third one. Therefore, the knowledge base cannot be developed without destabilization and reconstruction. A destabilizing dynamics should not be reified reflexively. It remains an order of expectations pending as selection pressure upon the local configurations. The expectations can be further codified through the use of knowledge. Knowledge can be codified in textual practices, for example, as 'scientific knowledge.' Thus, the third subdynamic can increasingly become a driver of change.

For example, Dosi (1982) distinguished between the stabilization of innovations along *technological trajectories* and the knowledge base as a next-order *regime* that remains emergent as a paradigm. As innovations are further developed along trajectories, a knowledge base becomes reflexively available as an evolutionary mechanism for restructuring the historical trajectories on which it builds. The next-order perspective of the regime rests as an additional selection environment on the trajectories. In terms of the previous figure, this second-order system can be added as in Figure 1.4.

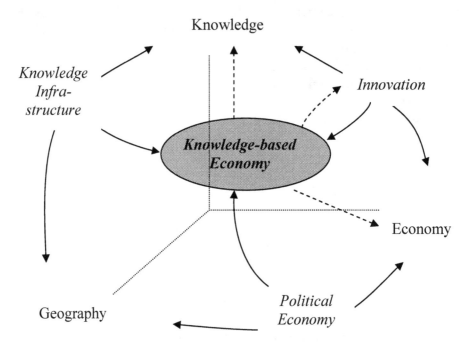

Figure 1.4: The first-order interactions generate a knowledge-based economy as a next-order system.

In summary, the carriers of a knowledge-based system entertain a dually layered network: one layer of institutional relations in which they constrain each other's, behavior and one layer of functional relations in which they shape each other's expectations with reference to the future. The second-order interaction term (the knowledge base) remains a historical result of the first-order interactions in the knowledge infrastructure. An evolving knowledge base can be developed under the condition that the various interactions find their own resonances, that is, in a self-organizing mode. This *self-organization* among the functions exhibits a dynamics potentially different from the *organization* of relations among the institutions.

1.4   The operation of the knowledge base

Interacting expectations can provide a basis for changes in the behavior of the carrying agents. These behavioral changes differ from the institutional imperatives and market incentives that have driven the system previously. While institutions and markets develop historically, that is, with the arrow of time, the knowledge-based structure of expectations drives the system in an anticipatory mode. Future-oriented planning cycles can be expected to become more important than current trends in the market. Thus, informed anticipations increasingly change the dynamics of the system from an agent-based perspective towards a more abstract knowledge-based one.

The organization of knowledge production and control in R&D programs has reinforced this knowledge-based subdynamic in the last century. While markets select at each moment of time, knowledge refines the communication by adding codification as another selection mechanism over time. Furthermore, institutional dynamics develop along historical trajectories, but the knowledge base can be expected to function evolutionarily as the technological regime of the same system. The emerging regime remains pending as anticipated selection pressure generated and reproduced by the interactions among the lower-level subdynamics. The three subdynamics—which continue to develop recursively along their respective axes— are expected to interact in the complex dynamics of a knowledge-based economy.

The availability and growth of a knowledge base reinforces the capacity of the system to develop solutions that improve on combinations developed hitherto. It self-organizes in terms of innovations under the conditions of the organizations upon which it is created as a second-order layer. However, the second-order interaction terms can be expected to reflect changes as the first-order interaction terms change. Thus, a knowledge base may be replaced when the organizations change dramatically during periods of historical transition, such as in Eastern Europe after the demise of the Soviet Union. The horizon of expectations then changes.

Under the current conditions, the knowledge-based economy can be expected to continue to expand and grow using the ICT revolution as its main medium. The knowledge-based subdynamic operates by reconstructing the past in the present on the basis of representations that contain informed expectations (e.g., curves and functions on sheets of paper and computer screens). As the intensity and speed of communication among the carrying agencies increases, the codification of knowledge becomes a functional means to reduce the complexity in the communication. This emerging order of expectations remains accessible to reflexive agents with a capacity to learn. The expectations can be refined as they become more theoretically informed.

When the operation of a knowledge base is assumed, both participants and analysts are able to improve their understanding of the restructuring of the expectations at interfaces within the systems under study, which allows the codifications in the expectations to be further developed. For example, in a knowledge-based economy the price-mechanism of a market-based economy can increasingly be reconstructed in terms of price/performance ratios based on expectations about the life-cycles of technologies (Galbraith, 1967; Heertje, 1973). Thus, more abstract and knowledge-intensive criteria are increasingly guiding economic and political decision-making.

The dynamics of a complex system of knowledge-based innovations are by definition non-linear (Allen, 1994). This non-linearity is a consequence of interaction terms among the subsystems and the recursive processes operating within each of them simultaneously. In the long run, the non-linear (interaction) terms can be expected to outweigh the linear (action) terms because of the higher exponents in the equations. For example, the *interaction* effects between 'demand pull' and 'technology push' can over time be expected to become more important for the systemic development of innovations than the sum of the linear action terms (Kline and Rosenberg, 1986; Mowery and Rosenberg, 1979, 1989).

As noted, trajectories can be stabilized when two of the three subdynamics co-evolve in a process of mutual shaping. For example, when a sector undergoes technological innovation, a 'lock-in' into a market segment may first shape a specific trajectory of innovations (Arthur, 1994). Learning curves can be steep following such a breakthrough and the stabilization of a trajectory in the marketplace (Arrow, 1962; Rosenberg, 1982). The third subdynamic, however, potentially meta-stabilizes a knowledge-based innovation system. Under meta-stable condition the system can move from one (globalized) regime into another. From the perspective of a regime, it is possible to compare different trajectories. However, the regime can only be hypothesized by using a theoretical model (Scharnhorst, 1998). The model provides a basis for discussing alternatives beyond what has become available historically.

Analogously, when a science-based technology locks into a national state (e.g., in the energy or health sector), a monopoly can be immunized against market forces for considerable periods of time. Over longer periods of time, however, these lock-ins can be expected to erode because of the ongoing processes of 'creative destruction' (Schumpeter, 1943). Such creative destruction is based on recombinations of market forces with new insights (Kingston, 2003). Interaction effects among negative feedbacks, however, may lead to global crises that require the restructuring of the carrying layer of institutions (Freeman and Perez, 1988).

Historically, interactions among the subdynamics were first enhanced by geographical proximity (for example, within a national context or the context of a single corporation), but as the economic and technological dimensions of the systems globalized, dynamic scale effects became more important than static ones for the retention of wealth. Such dynamic scale effects through innovation were first realized by multinational corporations (Galbraith, 1967; Granstrand *et al.*, 1997; Brusoni *et al.*, 2000). They became a concern of governments in advanced, industrialized countries after the (global) oil crises of the 1970s (OECD, 1980). Improving the knowledge base in the economies of these nations became a priority as science-based innovations were increasingly recognized as providing the main advantages to these economies (Rothwell and Zegveld, 1981; Freeman, 1982; Irvine and Martin, 1984; Porter, 1990).

In other words, the relatively stabilized arrangements of a political economy endogenously generate the meta-stability of a knowledge-based system when the geographical units begin to interact and exchange more intensively in the economic and technological dimensions. Under the condition of globalization, the institutional make-up of the national systems must be restructured: the national and the international perspectives induce an 'oscillation' of a system between its stabilized and globalized states. The oscillating system uses its resources (among which its innovative capacities) for the continuation of this 'endless transition' (Etzkowitz and Leydesdorff, 1998). From this perspective, the stimulation programs of the European Union may have functioned as catalysts in reinforcing interactions among universities, industries, and governance at a trans-national level (Frenken and Leydesdorff, 2004).

The knowledge base emerges by recursively codifying the expected information content of the underlying arrangements (Berger and Luckman, 1966; Maturana and Varela, 1980; Fujigaki, 1998; Leydesdorff, 2001b; Luhmann, 1984). A previously stabilized system globalizes with reference to its next-order or regime level. However, the latter remains an order of expectations. Innovations can be considered as the historical carriers of this emerging system because they reconstruct, reorganize, and thus restabilize the relevant interfaces. Innovations instantiate the innovated systems in the present and potentially restructure existing interfaces in a competitive mode. In an innovative environment, the existing arrangements have to be reassessed continuously. For example, if one introduces high-speed trains, the standards and materials for constructing railways and rails may have to be reconsidered.

Once in place, a knowledge-based system thus feeds back on the terms of its construction by offering comparative improvements and advantages to the solutions found hitherto, that is, on the basis of previous crafts and skills. Knowledge-intensity drives differentiation at the global level by providing us with alternative possibilities. However, the emerging system continues to operate locally in terms of institutions and solutions that organize and produce observable integration across interfaces. The production facilities provide the historical basis—that is, the knowledge infrastructure and the other constructions—for further developing the knowledge-based operations. The complex knowledge-based system tends to resonate into a regime as a basin of attraction along one historical trajectory or another. This trajectory is evolutionarily shaped as a series of solutions to puzzles.

The expectations are heavily structured and invested with interests in finding solutions to puzzles. Some authors (e.g., Gibbons *et al.*, 1994; Nowotny *et al.*, 2001) have claimed that the contemporary system exhibits de-differentiation among policy-making, economic transactions, and scientific insights due to the mutual 'contextualization' of these processes. These authors posit that a new mode of operation ('Mode 2') should have emerged at the level of the social system because of the dynamics of incorporating scientific knowledge. Indeed, the perpetual restructuring of the system which is guided by the knowledge base can be expected to induce new institutional arrangements. Such rearrangements may include the temporary reversal of traditional roles between industry and the university, e.g., in interdisciplinary research centers (Etzkowitz *et al.*, 2000). Among codified expectations, however, exchanges can be expected to remain highly structured (Figure 1.5) and continue to reproduce differentiation also for evolutionary reasons (Shinn, 2002). A differentiated system of communications can process more complexity than an integrated one.

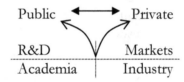

Figure 1.5: Vertical and horizontal interfaces allow for functional and institutional reorganization

Complex systems need both the *integration* of the various subdynamics into organizational formats (stabilization) and *differentiation* (globalization) in order to enhance further developments. This tension allows for meta-stabilization as a transitory state that can sustain both innovation and retention. In such systems, functions develop in interactions with one another and along their own axes, and thirdly in interaction with the exchanges among the institutions. At the interfaces between the economics of the market and the heuristics in R&D processes, translation mechanisms can be further developed that structure and codify these interactions over time. I cited the example of developing the price mechanism into the (bivariate) price/performance criterion, but in innovative environments one can expect all criteria to become multivariate. For example, knowledge-based corporations organize a sophisticated interface between strategic (long-term) and operational (medium-term) planning cycles in order to appreciate and to update the different perspectives (Galbraith and Nathanson, 1978).

Since social coordination, communication, and control in a knowledge-based system no longer provide a single frame of reference, integration and differentiation can be expected to operate concurrently at the various interfaces, but without *a priori* synchronization at the systems level. In terms of the dynamics of the system, differentiation and integration can thus be considered as two sides of the same coin: integration may take different forms, and differentiations can be relatively integrated (as subsystems). From an evolutionary perspective, the question becomes: where in the network can the relevant puzzles be solved and hence competitive edges be maintained? Thus, one can expect both geographically confined innovation systems and technological systems of innovation (Carlsson, 2002, 2006; Carlsson and Stankiewicz, 1991; Edqvist, 1997). The horizontal and vertical overlapping of systems and subsystems of innovation can be considered a hallmark of the knowledge-based economy.

In other words, the definition of a system of innovations becomes itself increasingly knowledge-based in a knowledge-based economy, since the subsystems are differently codified, yet interacting (at different speeds) in the reproduction of the system. Governance of a knowledge-based economy can only be based on a set of assumptions about the relevant systems. These assumptions are predictably in need of more informed revisions because one expects new formats to be invented at the hitherto stabilized interfaces.

1.5   Niches

While the market can be considered in a first approximation as an open network seeking equilibrium, innovation requires closure of the network in terms of the relevant stakeholders (Callon, 1998). Innovations are generated and incubated by locally producing units such as scientific laboratories, artisan workshops, and communities of instrument makers, but in interaction with market forces. This provides innovation with both a market dimension and a technological dimension. The two dimensions are traded off at interfaces: what can be produced in terms of technical characteristics encounters what can be diffused into relevant markets in terms of service characteristics (Lancaster, 1979; Saviotti, 1996; Frenken, 2001).

Thus, a competitive edge can be shaped locally. Such a locally shielded network density can also be considered as a *niche* (Kemp *et al.*, 1998).

Systems of innovation can be considered as complex systems because they are based on maintaining interfaces in a variety of dimensions. Problems at interfaces may lead to costs, but they can be solved more easily within niches than in their surroundings. Unlike organizations, niches have no fixed delineations. They can be considered as densities of interfaces in an environment that is otherwise more loosely connected. Within a niche, competitive advantages are achieved by reducing transaction costs (Biggiero, 1998; Williamson, 1985). Niches can thus be shaped, for example, within the context of a multinational and diversified corporation or, more generally, within an economy. In another context, Porter (1990) proposed analyzing national economies in terms of *clusters* of innovations. Clusters may span vertical and horizontal integrations along business columns or across different types of markets. They can be expected to act as systems of innovation that proceed more rapidly than their relevant environments and thus are able to maintain a competitive edge.

Sometimes, the geographical delineation of systems of innovation in niches is straightforward, as in the case of the Italian industrial districts. These comprise often only a few valleys (Beccatini *et al.*, 2003; Biggiero, 1998). For political reasons one may wish to define a system of innovation as national or regional (Cooke, 2002). However, an innovation system evolves, and its shape is therefore not fixed (Bathelt, 2003). While one may entertain the *hypothesis* of an innovation system, the operationalization and the measurement remain crucial for the validation (Cooke and Leydesdorff, 2006). For example, Riba-Vilanova and Leydesdorff (2001) were *not* able to identify a Catalonian system of innovations in terms of knowledge-intensive indicators such as patents and publications despite references to this regional system of innovation prevalent in the literature on the basis of employment statistics (Braczyk *et al.*, 1998).

'National systems of innovation' have been posited for a variety of reasons, for example, because of the need to collect statistics on a national basis and in relation to national production systems (Lundvall, 1988; Nelson, 1993). In the case of Japan (Freeman, 1988), or in comparisons among Latin American countries (Cimoli, 2000), such a delineation may provide heuristics more than in the case of nations participating in the common frameworks of the European Union (Leydesdorff, 2000a and c). Systems of innovation can be expected to vary in terms of their strengths and weaknesses in different dimensions. For example, one would expect a system of innovations in the Cambridge (UK) region to be science-based (Etzkowitz *et al.*, 2000), while the system of innovations in the Basque country is industrially based and reliant on technology centers that focus on applied research rather than on universities for their knowledge base (Moso and Olazaran, 2002). The evaluation of a 'system of innovation' can also vary according to the different perspectives of policy making. While the OECD, for example, has focused on comparing national statistics, the EU has had a tendency to focus on changes in the interactions among the member states, for example, in trans-border regions.[6]

Belgium provides an interesting example of regional differentiation. The country has been regionalized to such an extent that one no longer expects the innovation dynamics of Flanders to be highly integrated with the francophone parts of the country. In general, the question of which dimensions are relevant to the circumstances of a given innovation system requires empirical specification and research (Carlsson, 2006). However, in order to draw conclusions from such research efforts, a theoretical framework is required. This framework should enable us to compare across innovation systems and in terms of relevant dimensions, but without an *a priori* identification of specific innovation systems. The systems under study provide the evidence, while the analytical frameworks carry the explanation of the differences.

Three such frameworks have been elaborated in innovation studies during the 1990s:

1. the approach of comparing (national) systems of innovation (Lundvall, 1988 and 1992; Nelson, 1993; Edqvist, 1997);
2. the thesis of a new 'Mode 2' in the production of scientific knowledge (Gibbons *et al.*, 1994; Nowotny *et al.*, 2001); and
3. the Triple Helix of University-Industry-Government relations (Etzkowitz and Leydesdorff, 1997, 2000; Leydesdorff and Etzkowitz, 1998).

I submit that the Triple Helix can be elaborated into an *evolutionary* model that accounts for interactions among three dimensions (Lewontin, 2000; Ulanowicz, 1996; Jakulin and Bratko, 2004). This generalized model enables me to integrate three approaches: the 'Mode 2' thesis of the new production of scientific knowledge, the study of systems of innovation in evolutionary economics, *and* the neo-classical

---

[6] The Maastricht Treaty (1991) assigned an advisory role to the European Committee of Regions with regard to economic and social cohesion, trans-European infrastructure networks, health, education, and culture (Council of the European Communities, 1992). This role was further strengthened by the Treaty of Amsterdam in 1997, which envisaged direct consultations between this Committee of Regions and the European Parliament and extended its advisory role to employment policy, social policy, the environment, vocational training, and transport.

perspective on the dynamics of the market. The three micro-operations will first be distinguished and then recombined. However, before generalizing to a *three-dimensional* dynamics, I first elaborate the concept of *bi*lateral co-evolution and its expected (sub)dynamics. In a next step, the three micro-foundations that can interact are specified.

1.6   Co-evolutions and structural changes

In addition to the problems of defining and delineating an innovation system, the dynamics of innovation can change previous system boundaries in a variety of ways. Institutional arrangements can be reorganized from the perspective of functional requirements and/or the functional tasks of an institution can be redefined. In a knowledge-based economy, one expects interaction terms among the functions and the institutional carriers of these functions. The layers of functionality and institutionalization may couple vertically (as when there is a correspondence between functions and the carrying institutions) or horizontally (as in university-industry-government relations). However, the horizontal coupling among institutions could be specified above as containing a dynamic different from the horizontal coupling among functions. Functions couple evolutionarily as differently codified expectations, while institutions couple historically. Both interactions can be relevant for the innovative reorganization of a system.

Variation emerges as a result of interactions and frictions among the various mechanisms. The disturbance terms provide the requisite variation (Ashby 1958). The subdynamics operate as selection mechanisms upon one another by using a recursive reference to their previous states. While selection is deterministic (given the specification of a selection mechanism), variation is expected to contain randomness. The frictions thus prevent the complete consolidation of the systemic structures in one direction or another. Innovation systems can be expected to remain in transition although rigidities can prevail over long periods of time.

Under what conditions can the variation (that is produced as disturbance because of the ongoing interactions) lead to structural change at the systems level? The system is resilient against change because it has been made to 'fit' during its historical evolution; it can be expected to contain resonances. Two mechanisms are important for understanding the potential for structural change despite the resilience of a prevailing system: (1) the possibility of lock-in between subsystems leading to a co-evolution over time, and (2) the possibility of bifurcation between two co-evolving subdynamics. A bifurcation generates an interface (for example, between the subdynamics of production and diffusion), while a lock-in tends to dissolve an interface, for example, by fixing specific relations between a technology and a market. A locked-in system may bifurcate in a next stage, but the two mechanisms are analytically very different.

'Lock-in' was modeled by Arthur (1988, 1989) in terms of the Polýa urn model, but the principle was well-known from the historical work of David (1985) on the QWERTY keyboard (cf. Liebowitz and Margolis, 1999). A system can be locked into suboptimal technologies when the volume of a specific technology has generated network effects that feedback on the adoption of the technology. Instead of decreasing marginal returns, this can lead to increasing marginal returns. Information technologies exhibit the latter type of economy to a larger extent than the industrial technologies of the previous period (Arthur, 1994; Arthur *et al.*, 1997). In the case of lock-in, the system fixes an interface and thereby loses a degree of freedom. For example, the choice among technologies may no longer be available. The fix, however, may lead to the competitive advantage of one of the technologies which can further develop in a co-evolution with its specific market conditions.

While this rigid coupling between dimensions (in case of a lock-in) results in the loss of a degree of freedom at the systems level, the reaction-diffusion mechanism makes it possible to gain degrees of freedom at newly emerging interfaces. In an early stage of the development of a new technology, the processes of invention, production, and marketing may still be small-scale and intensively coupled, for example, within a corporation or a geographical region. It can be shown that when the diffusion parameter becomes larger than half of the rate of the production process, the two hitherto co-evolving mechanisms tend to bifurcate (Turing, 1952; cf. Rosen, 1985, at pp. 183f.).[7] This bifurcation can be expected to lead increasingly to a differentiation of subsystems. Thus, a new interface is generated and consequently a degree of freedom can be gained at the systems level. Once the diffusion of a technological artifact is uncoupled from its production, the former may feedback on the local production, as when the internationalization of a corporation leads to disinvestments in the country of origin.

In summary, the two evolutionary mechanisms of lock-in and bifurcation provide us with a potential for structural change within innovation systems which were

---

[7] Technically, in this case the matrix of the two equations (for production and diffusion) contains two eigenvalues with opposite signs, and consequently the steady state becomes a saddle point. The two trajectories are then expected to diverge. See Chapter Five for the further elaboration and formalization of this argument.

previously stabilized in niches or along trajectories. On the one hand, lock-in leads to a recombination into a new co-evolution along which a trajectory can be expected to develop. This occurs at the cost of sacrificing a degree of freedom. Bifurcation, on the other hand, provides a mechanism for gaining a degree of freedom, but with reference to the dimension that emerged from the co-evolution along a trajectory. Via the trajectory the system can move from one regime to another. For example, economic production is attracted by environments in which diffusion is enhanced. A trajectory can thus have an evolutionary function in addition to a historical one of retaining innovations.

1.7 Micro-foundation in terms of analytically different operations

The trajectory approach has been central to evolutionary economics from its very beginning. In their seminal study entitled 'In search of useful theory of innovation,' Nelson and Winter (1977) formulated their research program as follows:

> Our objective is to develop a class of models based on the following premises. First, in contrast with the production function oriented studies discussed earlier, we posit that almost any nontrivial change in product or process, if there has been no prior experience, is an innovation. That is, we abandon the sharp distinction between moving along a production function and shift to a new one that characterizes the studies surveyed earlier. Second, we treat any innovation as involving considerable uncertainty both before it is ready for introduction to the economy, and even after it is introduced, and thus we view the innovation process as involving a continuing disequilibrium. [...] We are attempting to build conformable sub-theories of the processes that lead to a new technology ready for trial use, and of what we call the selection environment that takes the flow of innovations as given. (Of course, there are important feedbacks.) (Nelson and Winter, 1977, at pp. 48f.)

These two premises led these authors to a programmatic shift in the analysis from a focus on the specification of expectations to observable firm *behavior* and the development of industries along historical trajectories (Andersen, 1994). Thus, a 'heterodox paradigm' was increasingly generated (Casson, 1997; Storper, 1997).

This shift in perspective has epistemological consequences. Both the neo-classical hypothesis of profit maximization by the operation of the market and Schumpeter's hypothesis of the upsetting dynamics of innovations were formulated as analytical perspectives. These theories specify expectations. However, the theory of the firm focuses on observable variation. The status of the model thus changed: analytical idealizations like factor substitution and technological development cannot be expected to develop historically in their ideal-typical forms.

Nelson and Winter's first premise proposed focusing on the observables not as an *explanandum*, but as *variation* to be selected in selection environments (second premise). Innovation is then no longer to be explained, but trajectory formation among innovations serves as the *explanandum* of the first of the two 'conformable theories.' Trajectories enable enterprises to retain competences in terms of routines. Under evolutionary conditions of competition, one can expect the variation to be organized by firms along trajectories. Thus, the knowledge base would remain completely embedded in the institutional context of the firm. The relations between the evolutionary and the institutional perspective were thus firmly engraved in this research program (Nelson, 1994).

The supra- and inter-institutional aspects of organized knowledge production and control (e.g., within scientific communities) are considered by Nelson and Winter (1977, 1982) as part of the selection environment. However, science and technology develop and interact at a global level with a dynamics different from institutional contexts. In the Nelson and Winter models, the economic uncertainty and the technological uncertainty cannot be distinguished other than in institutional terms (e.g., market versus non-market environments). These otherwise undifferentiated selection environments generate 'uncertainty' both in the phase of market introduction and in the R&D phase. Thus, the two sources of uncertainty are not considered as a consequence of qualitatively different selection mechanisms which use different codes for the selections. The potentially different selection environments—geography, markets, knowledge—are not specified as selective subdynamics that may interact in a non-linear dynamics (including co-evolutions in organizational frameworks).

In other words, the models elaborated by Nelson and Winter were based on a biological model of selection operating blindly. Dosi (1982) added the distinction (and the potential coupling mechanism) between 'technological trajectories' and 'technological regimes,' but his theory otherwise remained within the paradigm of Nelson and Winter's theory due to its focus on innovative firm behavior, that is, variation. Others have elaborated these models by using aggregates of firms, for example, in terms of sectors (e.g., Pavitt, 1984). However, the units of analysis (e.g., an industry) remained institutionally defined.

In a thorough reflection on this 'post-Schumpterian' model, Andersen (1994) noted that firms (and their aggregates in industries) cannot be considered as the evolving units of an economy. He formulated his critique as follows:

> The limitations of Nelson and Winter's (and similar) models of
> evolutionary-economic processes are most clearly seen when they are
> confronted with the major alternative in evolutionary modeling which may
> be called 'evolutionary games.' […] This difference is based on different
> answers to the question of "What evolves?" Nelson and Winter's answer is
> apparently 'organisational routines in general' but a closer look reveals that
> only a certain kind of routines is taken into account. Their firms only
> interact in anonymous markets which do not suggest the playing of strategic
> games—even if the supply side may be quite concentrated. (Andersen, 1994,
> at p. 144).

In summary, Nelson and Winter's models are formulated strictly in terms of the
biological metaphor of variation and selection (Nelson, 1995). Variation is
organized along trajectories using a set of principles which is—for analytical
reasons—kept completely separate from selection. The selection environments are
not considered as differentiated (and thus at variance). The various selection
mechanisms do not interact. Technological innovation is considered as endogenous
to firm behavior. The technological component in the selection environments is
consequently not appreciated as a global effect of the interactions among firms.

It is argued here that the knowledge base can be considered as an attribute of the
economy. Although selection environments cannot be observed directly, they can
be hypothesized as structural (sub)dynamics. This hypothesis is theoretically
informed, but the model then becomes more abstract than an institutional one.
While an institutional model begins with observables (and is thus 'history friendly';
Malerba *et al.*, 1999), studies about evolutionary games begin with highly stylized
starting points (Andersen, 1994). These abstract assumptions can be made
comparable with and traded-off (e.g., in simulations) against other hypotheses, such
as the hypothesis of profit maximization prevailing in neo-classical economics. For
example, one can ask to what extent an innovation trajectory can be explained in
terms of the operation of market forces, in terms of its own internal dynamics of
innovation, and/or in terms of interactions among the various subdynamics.

If selection mechanisms other than market choices can be specified—for example,
in the case of organized knowledge production and control—the interactions
among these different selection mechanisms can be made the subject of simulation
studies. In other words, the selection mechanisms span a space of possible events.
From this perspective, the observables and the trajectories can be considered as the
historically stabilized results of selective structures operating upon one another. The
evolutionary progression is a result of continually solving puzzles at the interfaces

among the subdynamics. Thus, the routines and the trajectories can be explained from a systems-theoretical perspective as potentially special cases among other possible solutions.

1.7.1 User-producer relations in systems of innovation

In an evolutionary model one can expect mechanisms to operate along a time axis different from the one prompted by the neo-classical assumption of profit maximization at each moment of time. While profit maximization remains pervasive at the systems level, this principle cannot explain the development of rigidities in the market like trajectories along the time axis (Rosenberg, 1976b). In an evolutionary model, however, the (potentially stabilizing) subdynamic has to be specified in addition to market clearing. Thus, a second selection environment over time is defined in an evolutionary model.[8] (In a later section, I shall specify a third selection mechanism as operating against the axis of time.)

In general, the number of selection mechanisms determines the dimensionality of the model. Innovations take place at interfaces, and the study of innovation therefore requires the specification of at least two systems of reference (e.g., knowledge production and economic exchanges). It has been argued above that the emergence of a knowledge base requires the specification of three systems of reference. Before the three dynamics can interact, however, each selection mechanism has to be 'micro-founded' in theoretical terms as an analytically independent operation of the complex system.

In his study of 'national systems of innovation' Lundvall (1988) argued that the learning process in interactions between users and producers provides a (second) *micro-foundation* for the economy different from the neo-classical basis of profit maximization by individual agents. He formulated this as follows:

> The kind of 'microeconomics' to be presented here is quite different. While traditional microeconomics tends to focus upon decisions, made on the basis of a given amount of information, we shall focus upon a *process of learning*, permanently changing the amount and kind of information at the disposal of the actors. While standard economics tends to regard optimality in the allocation of a given set of use values as the economic problem, *par*

---

[8] The comparison among different states (e.g., using different years) can be used for comparative static analysis, but the dynamics along the time axis are then not yet specified.

préférence, we shall focus on the capability of an economy to produce and diffuse *use values with new characteristics*. And while standard economics takes an atomistic view of the economy, we shall focus upon the *systemic interdependence* between formally independent economic subjects. (Lundvall, 1988, at pp. 349f.)

After arguing that interactions between users and producers belonging to the same national system may work more efficiently for reasons of language and culture, Lundvall (1988, at pp. 360 ff.) proceeded by proposing the nation as the main system of reference for innovations. Optimal interactions in user-producer relations enable developers to reduce uncertainties in the market more rapidly and over longer stretches of time than in the case of less coordinated economies (Hall and Soskice, 2001; Teubal, 1979). I have discussed this above when defining the function of niches.

Lundvall's theory about user-producer interactions as a micro-foundation of economic wealth production at the network level can be considered as a contribution beyond his original focus on national systems. The relational system of reference for the micro-foundation is different from individual agents with preferences. The concept of 'systems of innovation' was generalized to cross-sectoral innovation patterns and their institutional connections (Carlsson and Stankiewicz, 1991; Edqvist, 1997; Whitley, 2001). However, user-producer relations contribute to the creation and maintenance of a system as one of its subdynamics. In an early stage of the development of a technology, for example, a close relation between technical specifications and market characteristics can provide a specific design with a competitive advantage (Rabehirosoa and Callon, 2002).

In other words, proximity can be expected to serve the incubation of new technologies. However, the regions of origin do not necessarily coincide with the contexts that profit from these technologies at a later stage of development. Various Italian industrial districts provide examples of this flux. As local companies develop a competitive edge, they have tended to move out of the region, generating a threat of deindustrialization. This treat has continuously to be countered by these industrial districts (Dei Ottati, 2003; Sforzi, 2003).

Analogously, this mechanism is demonstrated by the four regions designated by the EU as 'motors of innovation' in the early 1990s. These four regions—Catalonia, Lombardia, Baden-Württemberg, and Rhône-Alpes—were no longer the main loci of innovation in the late 1990s (Krauss and Wolff, 2002; Laafia, 1999; Viale and Campodall'Orto, 2002). Such observations indicate the occurrence of bifurcations resulting when the rate of diffusion becomes more important than the local production. Diffusion may reach the level of the global market, and thereafter the globalized dimension can feed back on local production processes, for example, in terms of deindustrialization (Beccatini *et al.*, 2003). Given the globalization of a dominant design, firms may even compete in their capacity to destroy knowledge bases from a previous period (Frenken, 2001).

In summary, a system of innovation defined as a localized nation or a region can be analyzed in terms of the stocks and flows contained in this system. Control and the consequent possibility of appropriation of the competitive edge emerge from a recombination of institutional opportunities and functional requirements. In some cases and at certain stages of the innovation process, local stabilization in a geographic area may prove beneficial, for example, because of the increased puzzle-solving capacity in a niche. However, at a subsequent stage this advantage may turn into a disadvantage because the innovations may become increasingly locked into these local conditions. As various subdynamics compete and interact, the expectation is a more complex dynamics. Therefore, the institutional perspective on a system of innovation has to be complemented with a functional analysis.

1.7.2 'Mode 2' in the production of scientific knowledge

The 'Mode 2' thesis of the new production of scientific knowledge (Gibbons *et al.*, 1994) implies that the contemporary system has more recently gained a degree of freedom under the pressure of globalization and the new communication technologies. What seemed institutionally rigid under a previous regime (e.g., nation-states) can be made flexible under the 'globalizing' regime of communications. In a follow-up study, Nowotny *et al.* (2001) specified that the new flexibility is not to be considered only as 'weak contextualization.' The authors argue that a system of innovation is a construct that is continuously undergoing reconstruction and can be reconstructed even *in the core of its operations*. This 'strong contextualization' not only affects the selections themselves, but also the structures in the selections over time. The possibilities for novelty and change are limited more in terms of our capacity to reconstruct expectations than in terms of historical constraints.

How does one allocate the capacities for puzzle-solving and innovation across the system when the system boundaries become so fluid? The authors of the Mode-2 thesis answered as follows:

> There is no longer only one scientifically 'correct' way, if there ever was only one, especially when—as is the case, for instance, with mapping the

human genome—constraints of cost-efficiency and of time limits must be taken into account. There certainly is not only one scientifically 'correct' way to discover an effective vaccine against AIDS or only one 'correct' design configuration to solve problems in a particular industry. Instead, choices emerge in the course of a project because of many different factors, scientific, economic, political and even cultural. These choices then suggest further choices in a dynamic and interactive process, opening the way for strategies of variation upon whose further development ultimately the selection through success will decide. (Nowotny *et al.*, 2001, at pp. 115f.)

The perspective, consequently, is changed from interdisciplinary—that is, based on careful translations among different discourses—to *transdisciplinary*—that is, based on an external management perspective. The global perspective provides us with more choices than were realized hitherto. The model is that reflexive communications add another dimension to the reflection by individual agents (cf. Beck *et al.*, 2003; Latour, 2003).

While Lundvall (1988) had focused on interaction and argued that communications can stabilize the local innovation environment for agents, these authors argue that communications enable us to entertain a global perspective on the relevant environments. In other words, communications can be expected to develop an internal dynamics between local interactions and global perspectives. The global perspective adds a dynamic that is different from the historical one which follows the time axis. While the latter focuses on the opportunities and constraints of a given unit (e.g., a region) in its historical context, the discourse enables us to redefine the system of reference by contextualizing and analyzing the subjects under study from the perspective of hindsight. Thus, the focus shifts from the historical reconstruction of a system by 'following the actors' (Latour, 1987) to the functional analysis of an innovation system operating in the present. The robustness of this construct depends not on its historical generation, but on the present level of support that can be mobilized from other subsystems of society (e.g., the economy or the political systems involved).

What does this model add to the model of 'national innovation systems' in terms of providing a different micro-foundation? Lundvall's micro-economics were grounded in terms of communication and interaction between users and producers rather than in terms of the individual preferences of agents. The authors of 'Mode 2' define another communication dynamic relevant to the systems of innovation. This other perspective is possible because a network contains a dynamic both at the level of the nodes and at the level of the links. While agency can be considered as a source of communication—and can be expected to be reflexive, for example, in terms of learning and entertaining preferences—an agent necessarily has a position at a node in the network (Burt, 1982). The links of a communication system operate differently from the nodes in the network. The systems of reference are different. Nodes represent agents and the links represent the relations among them.

Categories like reflexivity and knowledge can be expected to have different meanings from one layer of the network to another. For example, agents entertain preferences, but the structure of communication provides some agents with more access than others. In addition to actions which generate the variations, the dynamics of communications, that is, at the level of the links, are able to generate changes at the systems level, that is, in terms of changes in the structural selection mechanisms. These changes are endogenous to the system because they can be the result of non-linear interactions among previously stabilized aggregates of actions. Recursion and interaction add non-linear terms to the aggregations of micro-actions.

Luhmann (1984) was the first to propose that communication be considered as a system of reference distinct from agency. He emphasized the analytical advantages of this hypothesis (e.g., Luhmann, 1996). The two systems of agency and communication are 'structurally coupled' in events like the columns and rows of a matrix. An interaction can be attributed as an action to an actor, while it can be expected to function as a communication within a distributed communication system (Maturana, 1978; Leydesdorff, 1993a, 2001b). In addition to communicating in terms of first-order exchange relations, social systems communicate reflexively by providing meaning to communications from the perspective of hindsight.

Global perspectives can be focused when the communications are increasingly codified. For example, scientific communications may enable us to deconstruct and reconstruct phenomena in ever more detail. I gave the example above of the price mechanism which could be further refined in terms of more abstract price/performance ratios. The differentiation of communication into various functions enables the social system to process more complexity than in a hierarchically controlled mode. However, under this condition one can expect to lose increasingly a central point of coordination. The interacting (sub)systems of communication can become increasingly differentiated in terms of their potential functions for the (uncoordinated) self-organization of the system. This communication regime reshapes the existing communication structures as in a cultural evolution. In other words, selection mechanisms other than 'natural' ones begin to reconstruct the system from various perspectives.

For example, in scientific communications 'energy' has a meaning different from its meaning in political discourse. While economists and politicians are able to worry about 'shortages of energy,' 'energy' is defined as a conserved quantity in physics. Words may have different meanings in other contexts. Thus, the evolutionary dynamics of social communication adds another layer of complexity to the first-order dynamics of the exchange. Institutionalization and organization stabilize the communication structures historically, but by providing meaning to the communication one is able to generate a global perspective (Husserl, [1929] 1973; Urry, 2003).

In summary, the communicative layer provides society with a selection environment for historical institutions. Unlike variation, selection remains deterministic, albeit that in the case of communication systems selections operate probabilistically. Thus, the selection mechanisms cannot be observed directly. However, they can be specified as hypotheses about the systems of reference. The specification of these expectations guides the observations. Furthermore, the communication structures of the social system are complex because the codes of the communication have been differentiated historically. Communications develop along the various axes, but they can additionally be translated into each other by using the different codes at the interfaces reflexively. Thus, systems of translation are generated. A translation reinforces an interface of the translated system.

For example, interaction terms among codes of communication emerged as a matter of concern within knowledge-based corporations when interfaces between R&D and marketing had increasingly to be managed (Galbraith, 1967). In university-industry-government relations three types of communications are interfaced. Frictions at the interfaces between the institutional layers and the dynamics of mutual expectations produce noise that can sometimes be locked-in and thus provide a competitive advantage. The systems thus generated can regain a degree of freedom, which was previously locked into a co-evolution, in a later stage using the third dimension. Let me now turn to my thesis that the utilization of the degrees of freedom between institutions and functions among the three subsystems interacting in a Triple Helix increasingly generates knowledge-based advantages in the economy.

1.7.3 *A Triple Helix of university-industry-government relations*

The systems-of-innovation approach defined innovation systems in terms of (aggregates of) institutional units of analysis. 'Mode 2' analysis defined innovations exclusively in terms of reconstructions on the basis of emerging perspectives in communication. The Triple Helix approach combines these two perspectives as different subdynamics of the systems under study. However, this model enables us to include the dynamics of the market as a third perspective with the micro-foundation of neo-classical economics in natural preferences. Thus, one can assume that innovation systems are driven by various subdynamics to varying extents. Consequently, the discussion shifts from a philosophical one about what an innovation system 'is,' or the question of how it should be defined, to the methodological question of how one can study innovation systems in terms of their different dimensions and subdynamics.

In the Triple Helix model, the main institutions of the knowledge-based economy have first been defined as university, industry, and government (Etzkowitz and Leydesdorff, 1995). These institutional carriers of an innovation system can be expected to entertain a dually layered network: one layer of institutional relations in which they constrain each other's behavior, and another layer of functional relations in which they shape each other's expectations. Three functions have to be recombined and reproduced at the systems level: (1) wealth generation in the economy, (2) novelty generation by organized science and technology, and (3) control of these two functions locally for the retention and reproduction of the system. These layers can be expected to feed back onto each other, thus changing the institutional roles, the selection environments, and potentially the evolutionary functions of the various stakeholders in each subsequent round.

Within this complex dynamic, the two mechanisms specified above—user-producer interactions and reflexive communications—can be considered as complementary to the micro-foundation of neo-classical economics. First, each agent or aggregate of agencies is positioned differently in terms of preferences and other attributes. Second, the agents interact, for example in economic exchange relations. This generates the network perspective. Third, the arrangements of positions (nodes) and relations (links) can be expected to contain information because not all network positions are held equally and links are selectively generated and maintained. The expected information content of the distributions can be *recognized* by relevant agents at local nodes. This recognition generates knowledge within these agents and their organizations. Knowledge, however, can also be processed as discursive knowledge in the network of exchange relations. Knowledge that is communicated can be further codified, for example, as discursive knowledge in the sciences. Figure 1.6 summarizes this configuration.

With this visualization I intend to make my argument epistemologically consistent by relating the various reflections (Cowan *et al.*, 2000; Lundvall and Borras, 1997) to the underlying dimensions of the Triple Helix model. The three analytically independent dimensions of an innovation system were first distinguished in Figure

1.3 (above) as (1) the geography which organizes the positions of agents and their aggregates; (2) the economy which organizes their exchange relations; and (3) the knowledge content which emerges first with reference to either of these dimensions (Archer, 1995). Given these specifications, we were able to add the relevant interaction terms. The second-order interaction among these interactions then provide us with the possibility of the development of a knowledge base endogenous to the system under study.

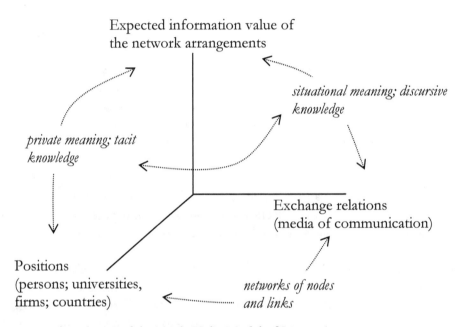

Figure 1.6: Micro-foundation of the Triple Helix Model of Innovations

Figure 6 specifies this as an interaction between discursive and tacit knowledge. This second-order interaction may generate configurational knowledge as an order of expectations. The three different micro-foundations (preferences of agents, learning in interaction, anticipation in the learning through codification) can thus be distinguished reflexively with reference to the analytically distinguished dimensions.

1.8   Empirical studies and simulations

Unlike biological models that focus on observable realities as variation with reference to 'natural' selection mechanisms, the Triple Helix model focuses primarily on the specification of the selection mechanisms. Three helices are sufficiently complex to understand the social reproduction of the dynamics of innovation (Leydesdorff, 1994b; Leydesdorff and Etzkowitz, 1998; Lewontin, 2000). What is observable can be specified as relative equilibria at interfaces between different selection mechanisms operating upon each other. When repeated over time, a *co*-variation can be developed into a *co*-evolution, and a next-order, that is, more complex, system can be generated in a process of 'mutual shaping' (McLuhan, 1964).

I have argued that the Triple Helix can be elaborated into a neo-evolutionary model which enables us to recombine sociological notions of meaning processing, economic theorizing about exchange relations, and insights from science and technology studies regarding the organization and control of knowledge production. The further codification of meaning in scientific knowledge production can add value to the exchange (Foray, 2004; Frenken, 2006). This model can serve as heuristics, but should not be reified. Its abstract and analytical character enables us to explain current transitions towards a knowledge-based economy as a new regime of operations.

The differentiation in terms of selection mechanisms can be both horizontal and vertical. Vertically the fluxes of communications are constrained by the institutional arrangements that are shaped in terms of stabilizations of previous communications. Horizontally, these communications are of a different nature because they can use different codes. For example, market transactions are different from scientific communications. Market transactions can also be cross-tabled with organizational hierarchies (Williamson, 1985). While the control mechanisms at interfaces can be considered as functional for the differentiation among communications, the hierarchy in the organization provides us with a multi-level problem within the institutional dimension.

In summary, the functional perspective is different from the institutional one. Functional communications evolve; institutional relations function as retention mechanisms which respond to functional incentives. The specification of functions in the socio-economic analysis requires reflexivity. All reflections can again be made the subject of communication. Thus, one can study a Triple Helix at different levels and from different perspectives. For example, one can study university-industry-government relations from a (neo-)institutional perspective (e.g., De Rosa Pires and De Castro, 1997; Etzkowitz *et al.*, 2000; Gunasekara, 2006) or one can focus on the relations between university science and the economy in terms of communications (e.g., Langford *et al.*, 1997; Leydesdorff, 2003a). Different interpretations of the Triple Helix model can be at odds with each other and nevertheless inform the model. Each metaphor stabilizes a geometrical representation of an otherwise more complex dynamics.

Competing hypotheses derived from different versions of the Triple Helix can be explored through formal modeling and appreciated through institutional analysis. The case studies inform the modeling efforts about contingencies and boundary conditions, while the simulation model enables us to relate the various perspectives. Such translations potentially reinforce the research process by raising new questions, for example, by comparing across different contexts, yet with reference to emerging phenomena. Innovation can be considered as the reflexive recombination at an interface, such as between a technological option and a market perspective. Specification of the different contexts, however, requires theorizing. For the purpose of innovation, the perspectives have to be translated into each other, for example, in terms of a plan. In summary, the Triple Helix model is sufficiently complex to encompass the different perspectives of participant observers (e.g., case histories) and, from an analytical perspective, to guide us heuristically in searching for options newly emerging from the interactions.

What is the contribution of this model in terms of providing heuristics to empirical research? First, the neo-institutional model of arrangements among different stakeholders can be used in case study analysis. Given the new mode of knowledge production, case studies can be enriched by addressing the relevance of the three major dimensions of the model. This does not mean to disclaim the legitimacy of studying, for example, academic-industry relations or government-university policies, but one can expect more interesting results by observing the interactions of the three subdynamics. Secondly, the model can be informed by the increasing understanding of complex dynamics and simulation studies from evolutionary economics (e.g., Malerba *et al.*, 1999; Windrum, 1999). Thirdly, the second-order perspective adds to the meta-biological models of evolutionary economics the sociological notion of meaning being exchanged among the institutional agents (Luhmann, 1984; Habermas, 1987; Leydesdorff, 2000d).

Finally, on the normative side of developing options for innovation policies, the Triple Helix model provides us with an incentive to search for mismatches between the institutional dimensions in the arrangements and the social functions carried by these arrangements. The frictions between the two layers (knowledge-based expectations and institutional interests), and among the three domains (economy, science, and policy) provide a wealth of opportunities for puzzle solving and innovation. The evolutionary regimes are expected to remain in transition because they are shaped along historical trajectories (Etzkowitz and Leydesdorff, 1998). The knowledge-based regime continuously upsets the political economy and the market equilibria as different subdynamics. Conflicts of interest can be deconstructed and reconstructed, first analytically and then perhaps also in practice in the search for solutions to problems of economic productivity, wealth retainment, and knowledge growth.

The rich semantics of partially conflicting models reinforces a focus on solving puzzles among differently codified communications reflexively. While the lock-ins and the bifurcations are systemic, i.e., largely beyond control, further developments require variety and self-organization of the interactions among the subsystems. New resonances among selections can shape trajectories in co-evolutions, and the latter may recursively drive the system into new regimes. This neo-evolutionary framework assumes that the processes of both integration and differentiation remain under reconstruction. While Neurath's (1932/33, at p. 206) metaphor that 'the ship is repaired on the open sea' focused at that time exclusively on science, a knowledge-based society has internalized the new dynamic of knowledge production and control into the economy at both the micro- and the macro-level.

Chapter 2

Knowledge, Information, and Globalization

In the previous chapter, I argued that organized knowledge production and control adds a coordination mechanism to the social system with dynamics different from those induced by economic exchange relations or geographic constraints. In this chapter, I discuss the dynamics of the knowledge base of a social system from a communication-theoretical perspective. This perspective enables me to explain how a knowledge base can be constructed in terms of exchange relations among agents which are increasingly codified over time. The relationship between the 'knowledge base' and the 'globalization' of communication systems will be explained in terms of these processes of codification.

Inter-human communication takes place at two (interacting) levels. At the first level information is exchanged and provided with meaning, and at a second level meaning can be communicated reflexively. The processing of meaning is structurally coupled to the processing of information as in a co-evolution. At each moment in time this coupling generates meaningful information in the mutual information between the layers. In the literature the definition of 'information' has sometimes been restricted to this 'meaningful information,' that is, 'a difference which makes a difference' (Bateson, 1972, at p. 453; Luhmann, 1984, at p. 103). A difference which makes a difference implies already a selection from the Shannon-type information, that is, the uncertainty contained in the distribution or, in other words, the first difference. The latter can also be considered as variation, while distinguishing the difference in the difference implies making a selection.

How can a difference operate upon a difference? Can the hypothesized selection mechanism be specified? The hypothesis of meaning-processing in social systems as an operation distinct from (but interactive with) information-processing enriches our thinking about these systems. The processing of meaning, for example, invokes a horizon of possible meanings. In other words, the dynamics of meaning-processing are different from the dynamics of information-processing. Some meanings can be more meaningful than others. I shall argue that hypotheses about these selection mechanisms can be operationalized by specifying the next-order codes that provide meaning to the underlying layer of communication. This operation is recursive: knowledge can then be considered as a meaning which makes a difference.

The codification of knowledge in scientific communication is one mechanism of codifying meaning among others. Local markets can be globalized by using next-order markets such as capital markets. The selection mechanisms can further be specified substantively and in terms of how they operate if the various dynamics are first distinguished analytically. Hence, the purpose of this chapter is to define and organize the relevant categories into what might—perhaps too ambitiously—be developed into a mathematical theory of meaning.

2.1 Information, uncertainty, and meaning

Although both sociology and the mathematical theory of communication have focused on distributed systems (e.g., networks), words like 'information,' 'uncertainty,' or 'communication' mean different things from one intellectual tradition to another. Furthermore, the distributions in social systems develop at various levels at the same time. The sociological research design requires methodological guidance because of this variety of levels and perspectives (Monge and Contractor, 2003). However, the mathematical theory of communication has been discredited in the social sciences with the argument that Shannon (1948) defined 'information' as uncertainty (e.g., Bailey, 1994). This definition appears counter-intuitive, since one associates 'information' with a message that 'in-forms' a system receiving the signal (Varela *et al.*, 1991). From the perspective of a receiving system, information can be defined only as meaningful information or 'a difference that makes a difference.'

Shannon detached himself from the implications of his counter-intuitive definition of information as uncertainty by stating that the 'semantic aspects of communication are irrelevant to the engineering problem' (Shannon and Weaver, 1949, at p. 3). However, the use of two concepts of 'information' in the literature has led to considerable confusion (Hayles, 1990). Let us therefore first specify the difference between information as uncertainty and information that is meaningful to a system receiving this information.

The Shannon-type information precedes the information formed within a system. At the level of mathematical theorizing, the system of reference is thus deliberately *not yet* specified (Theil, 1972). The message informs us only that an event (or a series of events) has happened, but does not tell us anything about the nature of the event. The unit of measurement of the uncertainty thus generated (bits of information) remains formal and therefore dimensionless.[9] The measurement instruments and the (entropy) statistics of information theory can be applied to any system that operates in terms of distributions (that is, any set of differences).

When a system receives this (Shannon-type) information, it may be disturbed and therefore initially become more uncertain (about its environment for example). By processing the uncertainty internally, the receiving system can sometimes—that is, if it contains other (e.g., substantive) dimensions—discard part of the incoming information as noise. The remainder is then selectively designated as meaningful information. After this de-selection, the meaningful information potentially reduces the uncertainty. Following Schrödinger (1944), Brillouin (1962) formalized this reduction in the uncertainty as 'negentropy.' Negentropy adds to the redundancy of a system. (By definition, the uncertainty plus the redundancy in a system of communication are equal to the system's maximum information content.)

Despite the confusion regarding these two concepts of information found in the literature, the biological theory of autopoietic systems (e.g., Maturana and Varela, 1984) and the information-theoretical approach (e.g., Abramson, 1963; Theil, 1972) have been consistent in excluding each other's definitions of 'information' for analytical reasons (Boshouwers, 1997). Biological systems can be considered as given 'naturally,' and therefore the biologist is inclined to begin with the specification of an observation rather than the uncertainty of an expectation. As Maturana and Varela (1980, at p. 90) formulated it:

> Notions such as coding and transmission of information do not enter in
> the realization of a concrete autopoietic system because they do not refer
> to actual processes in it.

While these authors insisted on the biological realization of 'actual processes,' Shannon's co-author Weaver (1949, at pp. 116f.) noted the problem of defining 'meaning' from the abstract perspective of a mathematical theory of communication:

> The concept of information developed in this theory at first seems
> disappointing and bizarre--disappointing because it has nothing to do with
> the meaning, and bizarre because it deals not with a single message but

---

[9] Shannon (1948) defined the uncertainty or information as equal to the probabilistic entropy of the communication system. Thermodynamic entropy, however, is different from probabilistic entropy because the former is measured in terms of Joule/Kelvin, while the specification in terms of bits of information is dimensionless.

rather with the statistical character of a whole ensemble of messages, bizarre also because in these statistical terms the two words *information* and *uncertainty* find themselves to be partners.

I think, however, that these should be only temporary reactions; and that one should say, at the end, that this analysis has so penetratingly cleared the air that one is now, perhaps for the first time, ready for a real theory of meaning.

Let us follow this intuition of Weaver and ask whether it is possible to define meaning as abstractly as information, that is, without reference to any specific (e.g., biological or sociological) realization. I submit that *meaning can be defined as the operation which is generated when a system of reference is specified.* This definition precedes the operationalization in terms of a specific system of reference. and is in this sense mathematical.

In general, the analytical specification of a system of reference itself provides the information with system-specific meaning. The meaning of (Shannon-type and therefore meaningless) information can be defined only with reference to a system that is able to organize information. The generation of meaning assumes a system operating over time. A system contains a substance in which information is communicated. This substance can also be considered as the medium of the communication. Shannon-type information, or equivalently probabilistic entropy, is generated whenever the communication system is operating since the medium is then being redistributed. This redistribution generates the probabilistic entropy. Thus, Shannon-type information can be measured when the substance that is redistributed during the communication is specified. The measurement results (in bits) can be provided with an interpretation in terms of the specific system of communication under study.

Note that before the observation of the substance in terms of a redistribution taking place in a system of reference, the specification of the category has the epistemological status of an expectation. Observations can inform the expectations. For example, information theory can be elaborated into a formal statistics for the study of economic transaction processes (Theil, 1972) or for the study of biological evolution (Brooks and Wiley, 1986). Substantive theorizing is needed for the specification of the relevant system(s) of reference (MacKay, 1956) so that a *special* theory of communication—such as one concerning economic exchange relations—can be generated (Steinmueller, 2002). The mathematical theory of communication provides only a formal methodology for studying the non-linear dynamics of systems thus substantively specified. Furthermore, the analytical specification can remain reflexive upon whether the theorizing involved is formal or substantive. The relation between the two can be controlled in the research design.

2.2   Communication, meaning, and codification

The processes of inter-human communication are differentiated: some pieces of information are more meaningful than others, and not all meanings provided are also communicated. The communication of meaning adds value to the first-order communication of information. Value, however, can be defined differently in the various domains of communication. For example, goods can be exchanged in the economy and provided with value in the market. The communication is then symbolically mediated by the price mechanism. In political communication, however, other mechanisms such as power are more important than price for guiding the communication. Language can thus be further codified into symbolically generalized media of communication like power and money (Parsons, 1963a and b). The symbolically generalized media of communication organize the differentiation of the social structure over time (Künzler, 1989; Luhmann, 1975a and b).

Human language can be considered as an evolutionary achievement which enables us to use the two channels of information exchange and meaning processing simultaneously. One can further organize the interaction between these two layers by using processes of codification. Providing meaning from the perspective of hindsight is itself a recursive operation: a meaning that makes a difference can be considered as knowledge. If the production of knowledge is *socially* organized as discursive knowledge (e.g., in the sciences), the perspective of hindsight is reinforced. A globalizing dynamic may thus be added as a feedback on previously stabilized patterns of communications.

Globalization adds *another* subdynamic to the previously stabilizing dynamics. Some stabilizations can be selected for globalization, since the selective operation is recursive. As the globalizing subdynamic becomes increasingly important, globalization can be expected to transform the communications into another evolutionary mode. The self-organization of a knowledge-based society at the global level, however, remains an expectation because unlike stabilizations, globalizations cannot be observed directly. Epistemologically, the status of the knowledge base therefore remains also a hypothesis. As noted, entertaining this hypothesis enriches our thinking about the emerging system because we no longer focus on what can be observed, but on what can be expected.

In general, a knowledge base can be generated within communication when another (that is, global) dimension is added to previously stabilized patterns of communication. Globalization of the communication operates selectively upon stabilizations in the communication that are first shaped historically. In other words, the generation of the global knowledge base of a social system is no longer agent-based, but communication-based. While the agents continue to interact in communications, they generate and reproduce patterns of communication. The interactions of agents and communications can co-evolve into a knowledge-based system when the quality of the communication is improved by the communications operating upon one another selectively. In knowledge-based systems, meaning can be communicated with increasing precision, and thus more complexity can be processed.

The generation of knowledge within the system remains to be considered as one of the subdynamics. First, the communications among agents (context of discovery) provide the knowledge claims as variations that can then be made the subjects of a next-order selection (context of justification). A next-order subdynamic of expectations can co-evolve with the previous-order layer of communications as a feedback term. The feedbacks operate as selection mechanisms upon the variation produced at the other levels. However, which subdynamics provide the variation and which the selection is not preordained. Thus, the subdynamics operate upon one another selectively and disturb each other continuously. The degree of stabilization, however, can vary historically as can the order of the expectations.

An order of expectations is constructed and continuously reconstructed on the basis of the communications that have previously been organized in terms of their meaning. A knowledge-based order remains historical, but at each moment it can be considered as an emergent property because of its selective operation in the present on what was constructed hitherto. The knowledge-based reconstruction is oriented towards possibilities other than those previously given. The codification of communication as knowledge thus provides us with an anticipatory base for a reconstruction of the social system that is different from its historical construction. The historical constructions can be considered as the observable variation. The selection mechanisms, however, are not given historically; they have to be hypothesized on theoretical grounds. The knowledge-based reconstructions can then be considered as instantiations of the selection mechanisms. These reconstructions provide us with options other than those that have been constructed hitherto.

In biological evolution theory, selection is presumed to occur 'naturally.' Communication theory, however, provides us with a knowledge base for the specification of selection mechanisms other than natural ones. The focus of this discourse is on how some information is selectively provided with meaning while other information is not. As knowledge production and control have become increasingly organized in scientific discourses over the past two centuries (e.g., Stichweh, 1984), the knowledge-based perspective has become an institutionalized subdynamic of the social system (Whitley, 1984).

The institutionalization of scientific practices has provided stability for generalizing the codes of these scientific communication systems at the global level. From this perspective, the historical configurations of institutions provide the communication systems with observable stabilities needed for meta-stabilized and potentially globalized competition in a next-order layer. One may in this context, for example, use the distinction between the local context of discovery and the global context of justification (Popper, 1935). The next-order layer, however, can only be accessed through a knowledge-based representation, that is, as a hypothesis that can always be further informed.

2.3   Observations and observational reports

Communication systems can be expected to process information differently from human action systems. Therefore, they can be expected to provide events with another kind of meaning. Whereas Parsons's (1937) theory of social systems focused on actions at the nodes of the network, Luhmann's (1984) sociological theory of communication, in contrast, focused on the links that coordinate the network into an evolving system. In general, the links can be considered as the operators of a network (Barabási, 2002). Coordination among these operators may indicate the presence of a communication *system* (as different from a communication channel). The links provide momentary structure to the network. In social network analysis, for example, this structure can be examined in terms of latent dimensions or eigenvectors. Communication *systems* can be expected to reproduce communication structures over time.

In the social sciences, actors and their actions are often considered as units of *analysis*. In communication theory, however, one focuses on communications as units of *operation*. Unlike units of analysis, units of operation cannot be observed without further reflection. Since communicative operations may also feedback on and change the units of analysis, the specification of units of operation can be expected to enrich our understanding of how networks develop. Observables can be analyzed as traces of previous communications, but only if the communicative operations are first properly specified. For example, an institution may have been shaped as the result of a social conflict. It follows and develops a historical trajectory.

Luhmann (1984, at p. 226 [1995, at p. 164]) already emphasized that *"communication cannot be observed directly, only inferred"* (italics in the original).[10] Some authors have followed him in calling this reflexive inference a 'second-order' observation (Baecker, 1999; Luhmann *et al.*, 1990). Because one needs theoretical guidance to make an inference, a 'second-order observation' can also be considered as the specification of an expectation. Expectations are, in important respects, different from observations by observing agents. For example, expectations operate in terms of uncertainties, while observations can serve the observer by reducing uncertainty.

Because of this difference in its epistemological status, a network system of communications cannot be expected to 'observe' like a human being. The use of the anthropomorphic metaphor of an 'observer' (Maturana, 1978; Von Foerster, 1982) may easily lead to misunderstandings: it is not human observers themselves, but their observations and more particularly observational reports that play a key role in the communication. The systems of reference are different (Matsuno, 2003). When an observation is reported, this information can contribute to updating the expectations entertained at the network level. As noted, this second-order exchange cannot be analyzed without a theoretical perspective. By using a discourse observational reports can be appreciated in relation to one another.

In summary, expectations operate as the substance of communication at the level of social systems (Stichweh, 2000, at p. 241; cf. Luhmann, 1984, at pp. 364 ff.; 1995, at pp. 267 ff.). The next question is how such a volatile system—which is no longer agent-based—can also be reproduced. In order to answer this question, we need to elaborate Shannon's more abstract concept of the expected information value of a distribution into a theory about the evolution of expectations. The model needs to be mathematical in order to abstract from specific expectations. The empirical observation of specific expectations can then inform us about how one system of expectations operates differently from another system of expectations. For example, expectations on the market can be different from expectations in science.

---

[10] Luhmann (1984, at p. 226): 'Die wichtigste Konsequenz dieser Analyse ist: *daß Kommunikation nicht direkt beobachtet, sondern nur erschlossen werden kann.*'

The layer of meaning exchanges can be modelled after our understanding of the layer of the information exchange, but *mutatis mutandis*. At this level the model remains formal: one expects the dynamics created when exchanging meaning or (Shannon-type) information to be very different because *what* is communicated is different. Meaning is not information, and Shannon-type information is not yet meaningful information. Providing meaning to information is a selective operation. The expectations operate on the expected information content of the distributions.

Although this elaboration was not Shannon's intention, the concept of 'expectation' is fundamental to the abstraction in his theory. In information theory, a distribution (e.g., of links and nodes in a network system) contains an uncertainty that can be communicated as the *expected* information of the message that this configuration has occurred as an event. While the definitions at the level of a mathematical theory remain formal, the specification of the systems of reference requires substantive theorizing, for example, about the role of expectations in inter-human communication.

In other words, let us first specify how meaning is generated, communicated, and reproduced in communication at an abstract level. Subsequently, we can provide this specification with meaning at the level of the social system reflexively, that is, by bringing the specification into the discourse as a hypothesis.[11] The operation of the social system in terms of expectations forces us to take this detour: this system develops in terms of expectations and is therefore difficult to observe directly. If one were to try to specify expectations on the basis of empirical experience, one would no longer be able to distinguish sufficiently between expectations at the individual level and those at the level of the social system. One might be inclined to consider the social level as an aggregate of individual expectations or as a macro-actor (e.g., the Leviathan; cf. Callon and Latour, 1981). In order to keep the distinction between the individual and the social dynamics clear—because we will account below also for the function of interactions terms between these two dynamics—one first has to understand how expectations can be codified and updated by observations in information-theoretical terms and at the different levels.

Unlike a social system, an individual, for example, is at the same time a biological system, and therefore performs a life-cycle. The need for performative action and survival enhances *integration*. The social system can tolerate a more differentiated

---

[11] In science studies, this is also called a knowledge claim which has yet to be validated in a process of scientific communication (Myers, 1985; Amsterdamska and Leydesdorff, 1989).

form of operation. While a social system may also have an origin, it is not likely to be 'born' physically (although one may wish to use this metaphor). By first abstracting from the system of reference, we will be able to distinguish between biological evolution and cultural evolution because the selection mechanisms involved can then be provided with different meanings in the respective discourses.

2.4   The sociological theory of communication

Both social and psychological systems were specified by Luhmann (1986a) as substantively different from biological systems to the extent that they are able to process expectations by providing meaning to observations. However, when they receive signals, these two types of systems can be expected to use different dynamics for their respective updates because the concept of 'observation' has a different status in these two contexts. The social system can only process information and meaning in a distributed mode; that is, by communicating the uncertainty as the *expected* information content of a communication. At the level of the social system—because of its inherent distributedness—the uncertainty cannot be resolved. The observations remain uncertain among agents, and therefore the subjects under study can only be specified as expectations.

The exchange of expectations provides us with a second-order domain. Although reflexive, this domain can be specified as an empirical expectation. One expects the social system to operate by providing meaning to the information exchanges. The operation at this level, however, remains an expectation, but this expectation can be updated by providing a theoretical interpretation to first-order observations. Thus, the second-order domain emerges within the first order and remains referential to it. If the domains are properly specified, one is able to infer from observations not only what the observers in question are observing, but also how these observers are providing meaning to their observations and communicating about this. However, when observations can be attributed as one type or the other, this attribution can be expected to remain uncertain. The attributions can be de-constructed and reconstructed by further improving upon the communication.

The distinction between the exchange of expectations and the observations enables us to redefine the relationship between autopoietic systems theory and information theory at the level of social systems. The exchange relations take place at two levels or, in other words, in different dimensions of the communication. These dimensions may additionally interact. Giddens (1979) has called this duality a *double hermeneutics*, but he juxtaposed the two hermeneutics in terms of participant observers and external observers. When one appreciates the two levels as dimensions of the communication, the interaction terms can also be specified.

These different roles can be expected to remain flexible because the differentiation in the communication is not hard-wired (Geertz, 1973). The distinctions (like that between 'emic' and 'etic') are analytical. When both meaning and information are communicated, uncertainty is generated in more than a single dimension and there can be an interaction term. (Using information theory, the uncertainties in different dimensions can be measured as multi-variate probability distributions; the interaction term is then the mutual information between the dimensions.) As noted, understanding the meaning of the results requires that the systems of reference be specified properly. This theoretical specification has to be complex enough to account for the information contained in the messages in the various dimensions. If there are two dimensions, one can analyze both of them *and* their co-variation. In the case of three (or more) dimensions, one expects more complex configurations to become possible. I shall return to mutual information in three dimensions as an indicator of the knowledge base in later chapters.

The specification of uncertainty in terms of a (second-order) system of expectations easily becomes abstract because a discourse about expectations no longer refers exclusively to first-order observables or units of analysis, but also to the meanings attributed to these observables. This meaning may differ in various contexts, and therefore the measurement may not lead to a single (e.g., mean) value. Furthermore, a social distribution of expectations can be provided with meaning recursively. Recognizing meaning as one among a number of possible meanings opens a horizon of expectations (Husserl, 1939; Luhmann, 1984, pp. 114ff.). However, this next-order relationship of meaning to other possible meanings can be distinguished from the historical generation of meaning.

2.5   Stabilization and globalization

The attribution of meaning to information requires an operation over time by a receiving system. However, this system does not have to be stable for any period longer than this single operation. A communication system may also be volatile. In order to be identified as a system, it is assumed that the system under study updates by *repeatedly* distinguishing between signals and noise. In this model, a time axis representing selections diachronically stands perpendicular to the selections made by the system at each moment of time (Figure 2.1).

Meaning reduces the uncertainty by selecting from the incoming information over time. Change over time can be considered as a diachronic outcome of the interactions between variation and selection at different moments in time. Selection is a recursive operation. Meaning-processing systems can be expected to select some of the previous selections for stabilization. Since selections reduce uncertainty, stabilization can be expected to reduce uncertainty at a next order of magnitude. At a next round, stabilizations can further be selected for globalization.

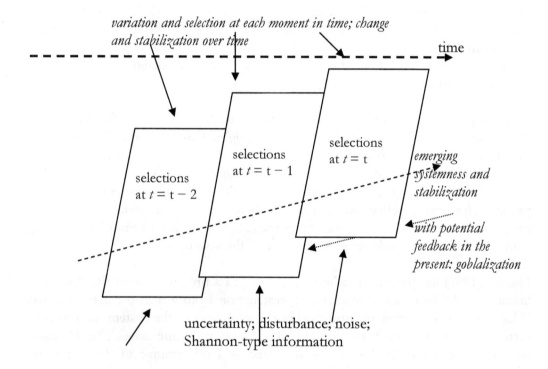

Figure 2.1: *Selection* of variation at each moment in time; *stabilization* of change over time; *globalization* as a feedback mechanism in the present.

Potentially different stabilizations can again be considered as observable variation, but this would imply the perspective of a next-order selecting system. That is, the distinction between variation and stabilization can be made recursive. The next-order (that is, globalizing) system is able to select among the results of the first-order stabilizations. Globalization can thus be considered as a second-order selection process. The next-order system builds upon the lower-level ones by selecting among them and by potentially rewriting the previously attributed meanings in terms of their relative weights within the distribution of possible meanings.

The recursivity of the operation of providing meaning by a next-order system adds another axis to the system as a degree of freedom. The frequencies of the updates of the communicating systems can be expected to have different values. However, this globalization of the system cannot be completed, but remains under construction on top of the previous stabilizations. *Globalization is not a state, but an operation.* Stabilization and globalization can be considered as different subdynamics operating on each other and on underlying selections. Thus, the self-organization of the constructing system comes under the selection pressure of its global dimension as specific constructions are historically realized and stabilized from among all possible constructions.

As a system is shaped historically along the time dimension in a forward mode, global meaning can be attributed only with hindsight. This is achieved by comparing the historical system with other envisioned possible systems. This operation is knowledge-based because the alternatives were not yet necessarily realized. The next-order selection operates upon the temporarily stabilized representations in the present. However, a reflection operating with reference to an instance invoked in the present (x_t) can be distinguished from the recursive update of meaning operating with reference to a historically previous state of the system (x_{t-1}).

Dubois (1998) has proposed calling a recursion to a present state of the system an 'incursion.' An incursion evaluates a representation from a next-order perspective. While the operation remains historical in the evolution of the system, an incursive system can be expected to develop also along the time axis. The incursive subdynamic can thus be historically stabilized as a subdynamic of the system on which it reflects. But this subdynamic cannot be directly observed in terms of historical instantiations because it remains an *operation* in the present state of the system. 'Incursion' occurs *within* systems under historical conditions, that is, as an empirical relation to recursively constructed and reconstructed trajectories.

An incursive system is able to select among its current representations of the past in terms of its future 'survival value' in a next-order selection environment. Thus, the incursive subsystem provides a model of the system itself and thereby provides the system with an anticipatory capacity (Rosen, 1985). In the case of an individual, the modelling is localized and integrated (e.g., in the brain). However, in the social system incursion and recursion can be expected to intertwine as distributed modes of communication. This system tends to differentiate because it operates in a subsymbolic (networked) mode. Under certain conditions, it can increase its capacity to process complexity if it is no longer restricted by the condition of synchronization among its subdynamics. Language enables us to intertwine these operations over time: each statement can be expected (*ex ante*) to contain information and the meaningful information is selected and separated from the noise *ex post*. Thus, incursion provides the system with a subdynamic that is analytically different from historical recursion. The social system can exploit this degree of freedom by differentiating along the time axis between the modelling or meaning-processing system and the modelled communication or information-processing systems.

The incursive system operates on a representation of the system in the present, while recursion operates with reference to the previous state. Because of the ability to select among a variety of possible representations of the system, an incursive system can learn to 'anticipate' possible further developments and thereby become increasingly 'self-organizing.' A meaning-processing system can construct (knowledge-based) representations that compete with those previously generated. Unlike artificial systems, however, social systems remain historical and thus referential to first-order events. Thus, new uncertainty can be used to generate new meaning. The various dimensions of the system, including the virtual operation of the global dimension, can be expected to continue to interact. Because of this interaction with its history, the meaning-processing system can be expected to *fail* empirically to self-organize because it contains no 'self' which has to be reproduced. The capacity of the social system to tolerate tensions and differentiations is greater than that of individuals who face the need to perform and act along a life-cycle.

The social system can be expected to exhibit a mixture of the contingencies of its construction in history and the next-order incursions upon these manifestations. In this evolving context, self-organization can be only a subdynamic of the historical system. Thus, the system develops historically along a trajectory and at the same time can develop an evolutionary regime. The regime remains pending as selection pressure. Analytically, however, a double-layered structure sustaining the exchange of both information and meaning is required before the 'globalization' of a system of expectations can become historically important. At the first level, variation is selected and then selections can be chosen for stabilization so that the structural advancements of the networks can also be retained historically. The stabilizations function evolutionarily as retention mechanisms that have been shown to provide 'survival value' for the configurations that were realized. At a second level, these historical configurations can be selected upon further as second-order variations by another (next-order) dimension of the system. This globalizing operation of the system remains 'virtual' from a first-order perspective (Giddens, 1984) because globalization incurs on the observable instantiations of the system using another dimension of that system. The additional dimension is disbursed in terms of the *distribution* of observable instances.

2.6   Codification and the change of meaning

Whereas positive theories are able to specify and study observable variation at each moment in time and changes over time, selection is a negative operation. One is not able to observe selections directly, but one can observe the distributional effects of selections and then make an inference. The inference specifies the selection mechanism as a hypothesis. This specification of the selection mechanisms is needed when selection can no longer be taken for granted as 'natural selection.' A negative operation cannot be observed directly; therefore, a theoretical inference is needed. Stabilizations can again be observed. The negative sign of the selection can be expected to lead alternately to 'observable' and 'expected' events with each consequent turn.

Observable stabilizations can be distinguished analytically from lower-level variations when the selections that co-evolved into the former have first been specified analytically. Stabilizations, however, cannot be expected to occur randomly. Globalization operates as a second-order selection mechanism on this second-order variation. A relatively stabilized system can be expected to develop along an observable trajectory, while remaining under selection pressure from a global regime (Dosi, 1982). For example, one can ask with hindsight whether an identified unity has remained the same despite ongoing processes of change under next-order selection pressure (Allen, 1994).

The next-order regime remains pending as a latent form of selection pressure on the systems and subsystems upon which it rests. By attributing an analytical identity to this next-order regime an analyst can reduce its complexity and then choose a specific perspective. The self-organization of the *social* system, however, cannot be identified empirically because it can be expected to remain uncertain, and other (and potentially incommensurable) appreciations are always possible. [12] Thus, the identification of a global system is analytical: the self-organization of a social system

---

[12] An identity can perhaps be defined as a codified and, therefore, symbolically stabilized system that is able to entertain its relation to its own next-order system reflexively without loosing stability.

can be specified only as an expectation. The question which becomes crucial is whether entertaining this hypothesis contributes to our theoretical understanding.

In other words, the self-organization of the social system beyond its stabilization is an intrinsically knowledge-based assumption. What is observable provides us with fragments of the global system, which can only be appreciated as instantiations on the basis of entertaining the hypothesis of other options. In this context, Luhmann (1975b, 1984, 1997) proposed distinguishing among three representations of the social system relevant for this analysis: *society* as the global system of communication, the historical *organization* of communication, and concrete *interactions*.

By using social network analysis, *interactions* can be analyzed as being *organized* by latent dimensions (Burt, 1982; Lazarsfeld and Henry, 1968). This organization of the interactions can be made the subject of a discourse because the representation can (provisionally) be stabilized. However, the further selection of the interactions by a next-order level of *self-organization* assumes that another dynamic is operating. The flux in the latent dimensions may be experienced as counter-intuitive by informed and reflexive actors.

Only then is the interpretation knowledge-based, as for example in the case of a child who knows that its parents entertain a level of communication to which it has no access. The child may know that this next-order level of communication can be expected to redefine its own situation beyond its control or understanding. Whether the family is stabilized or destabilized by the communication between the parents remains structurally beyond the child's control. However, the situation can later be reflected in a therapeutic setting despite its counter-intuitiveness.

A globalized system of communications self-organizes the interactions and organizations subsumed under it by selecting in the present using an (hypothesized) degree of freedom for the next-order reflection. By specifying and entertaining this hypothesis, one is able to distinguish analytically between a system developing its complexity historically, that is, along a trajectory, and a self-organizing system that has one more degree of freedom for adjusting to its environments from the perspective of hindsight. When this additional degree of freedom is used reflexively within the system as a dimension of uncertain communication, a meaning-processing system is generated on top of the information-processing one on which it reflects.

In a meaning-*processing* system, meaning can be changed by being communicated. An interaction term is generated among the meaning-providing agents. The resulting meaning is situational and contingent upon the distribution of meanings provided by the communicating agents. However, this next-order meaning may provide feedback on the definitions entertained by the individual agents. Whereas Shannon-type information provided us only with distributions and differences, 'the difference that makes a difference' can then be communicated as 'meaningful information,' i.e., as an interaction term between meaning processing and information processing. The first-order exchange of information is provided with meaning that can further be exchanged at a next-order layer. This additional subdynamic changes the system.

2.7   Language and culture

I submit that human language can be considered as the evolutionary achievement that enables us to attach meaning to the exchange of information and to exchange meaning at the same time (Luhmann, 1984, at p. 208 [1995, at p. 152]). Analytical distinctions are continuously blurred in observable practices because language enables us to operate informally and in an uncertain mode. A message can be provided with meaning, and the meaning can be distinguished from the expected information contained in the message. Thus, through linguistic competence, communication processes are doubled into two interacting layers within the exchange. This occurs, however, in a networked and therefore uncertain mode. Furthermore, the interaction between the layers also generates uncertainty.

The differentiation between the two channels of communication—uncertain information and meaning—is not hard-wired. Inter-human communication can therefore be expected to remain prone to failure. The coding remains flexible and open to reinterpretation (Quine, 1962; Hesse, 1980). Codifications help us to keep the various meanings separate. The uncertainty introduced by this 'double hermeneutics' (Giddens, 1976) allows both for formalization and for informal communication. However, the two layers can be expected to interact continuously. In other words, one can always consider meaningful what has been previously communicated as uncertainty, and one can discuss and deconstruct discursively what previously was codified. The exchanges of meaning and uncertainty co-vary in the communication of 'meaningful information.' The various exchange processes can be expected to generate uncertainty (i.e., introduce new variation) by interacting.

Participants and observers are able to take part both in the historical construction and in the recursive feedback of providing meaning to the reconstructions. This occurs at potentially different times, in different places, and to different degrees. When linguistic capacities enable agents to counteract natural constraints at the supra-individual level by constructing and maintaining a specific codification as a cultural feedback loop, a double hermeneutics is implicated. The possibility of alternating perspectives between the role of participant-observer and external observer provides a basis for improving one's analytical understanding of the reflexive operation of interaction (Parsons, 1968). Two (or more) perspectives for the selection can then be entertained and traded-off. The third-person perspective of a non-participating observer ('a public') is thus generated as an analytical option in the discourse (Stryder, 1999).

In other words, this double contingency in social system communication is based on a differentiation between two relevant selection environments: one selects on observable manifestations and the other on possible ones. A biological system has to adapt—at the risk of extinction—because the selection pressure is 'natural.' Selection environments, however, can already vary among ecological niches. Biological exchange relations can therefore experience additional selection pressure. However, the two types of selection pressures cannot be distinguished by the animals living in these niches unless these agents have the reflexive capacity to entertain concepts for mapping their situation. When these concepts can be communicated, a semantic domain is generated operationally on top of the consensual domain (in which the agents relate structurally; Maturana, 1978). The system of communications can become self-organizing and autopoietic (in the sense of increasingly controlling its own reproduction) when it is able to develop a linguistic domain within the semantic domain as another reflection. This happens in biological cultures like insect populations. However, the insects are not able to develop their 'language' further into a knowledge base because of biological constraints.

Human language extends the biological concept of a linguistic domain because order is not constructed in a biological environment and then stabilized as 'natural,' but remains flexible and under construction *as an expectation of order.* Linguistic denotations can be generalized and used symbolically. The constructed order can then be changed at a next moment in time or by a next-order system, i.e., by adding reflexively a new dimension to the system. What was 'far apart' can be brought into relation to each other using symbolic mediation. Note that 'reproduction' in this case no longer means reproduction in the biological sense, but rather the further development of the communication through the system's previously organized retention mechanisms. The lower-level systems upon which the next-level systems build can be innovatively reconstructed given the additional degree of freedom provided by linguistic exchanges. The represented and the representing systems may thus begin to co-evolve.

The number of reflexive couplings maintained between the layers can be considered as an evolutionary variable because it limits the complexity that can be processed by the communication. A meaning-processing system, for example, can be expected to evaluate its options also in an anticipatory mode because it can entertain and exchange different representations of itself. A knowledge-processing system, like a scientific communication system, can sometimes reconstruct the system under study—to the extent that one is also able to intervene technologically in what is represented. The technological intervention changes the system at the supra-individual level.

2.8   Translation and knowledge generation

The globalizing processes of self-organization at the next-order level remain latent; as a selection mechanism they operate with the resilience of a regime. The complex system can be represented only in terms of its instantiations or equivalently—along the time dimension—its trajectories. The codes of the communication at the level of these subsystems tend to close the operation by attributing specific meaning to the uncertainty (that is, Shannon-type information), but this closure can be altered when exchanges among different codes become historically possible at a next-order level. The changes in meaning due to exchanges at the level of the codes can be considered as 'translations' of the information. Translations enable us to change the meaning of an uncertainty from one system of reference to another.

Through translation, *discursive* knowledge is generated because one has to distinguish among possible meanings in different contexts. In Chapter One, I used the example of discussing energy shortages in political or economic contexts. A physicist would first have to translate the concept of a potential shortage of 'energy' as a shortage of energy carriers (e.g., oil or gas), because in physics 'energy' is defined as a conserved entity, and in the context of physics there cannot be a shortage of energy. Thus, the word 'energy' can be provided with various meanings in different contexts. Yet, if one is knowledgeable about the differences among the codifications, translation becomes possible.

The differentiation of the codes of communication has the evolutionary function of potentially furthering the development of communication systems. Translation of meaning within the system from one code to another provides an internal mechanism for the regeneration and updating of meaningful expectations. The translation mechanism can thus be made 'functional' to the 'reproduction' of the knowledge base of the social system. Novelty is generated when new representations emerge from these (potentially innovative) recombinations of codes. For example, technological innovation can first be considered as the successful generation of new combinations of 'demand' and 'supply.' While 'demand' is codified in terms of markets and users, the 'supply' side is organized in terms of technologies—and the latter may in turn be based on specific combinations of insights from different specialties. The stabilization of innovation into a new system potentially reorganizes the systems from which the innovation was generated. The emergence of the Internet can be studied in these terms (Abbate, 1999), as can the development of the railway systems in the nineteenth century (Urry, 2000).

Whereas mutation prevails as a stochastic mechanism for generating variation in biological systems, selective and reflexive interactions among (sub)systems of the social system generate second-order variations. Historical stabilization within an evolving system will continuously disturb other parts of the system because the stabilization can be expected to function as a constraint on the other fluxes. When disturbances can be provided with meaning at various systemic levels, the historically embedded codes are expected to change gradually. The recursivity in this process of reflexive refinement improves the system locally and generates knowledge endogenously. Meanings which are functional can be distinguished from those which are not (or no longer) functional for the reproduction of the communication. Solutions to puzzles can first be communicated as potential innovations and then selectively codified in a next round (Kuhn, 1962).

Using a paraphrase of Bateson's (1972) definition of information as 'a difference that makes a difference,' this endogenous generation of discursive knowledge can perhaps be defined as the exchange of 'meaning which makes a difference.' When repeated over time, the different selections generate couplings both horizontally and vertically within the knowledge base of the system (Simon, 1973). Some couplings (and not others) are stabilized along trajectories and thus temporarily locked-in, forming communication channels that can be considered as codifications and path-dependencies of previous communications. Communication along a provisionally constructed and stabilized channel can be received as signals by specific systems, whereas higher-order languages, such as scientific discourses, enable us to refine the distinction of signals from noise (Luhmann, 1990b).

When a coupling is provisionally stabilized, a next round of discursive reflection and deconstruction may enable us to reconstruct the system under study and perhaps renew it by searching for a solution to the current puzzle that is different from the ones generated 'naturally' or at previous moments in time. In Holland, for example, polder vegetation can be considered 'natural' even though the polder as a technical system of water management remains artificial. The social system is increasingly able to replace its historically given base with an evolving knowledge base whose operations are *analytically* independent of the historical organization of meaning. The discursive reconstruction of codification in relevant exchange processes (e.g., at markets, in scientific discourses, etc.) enables us to deconstruct an interface in terms of its composing (sub)dynamics—that is, in terms of the relevant selection environments—and then sometimes reconstruct this interface more efficiently by shaping technological artefacts. This technological reconstruction of the natural base can be reinforced at the global level and therefore develop beyond the control of individual or group intentions (Bhaskar, 1998; Marx, 1857).

(Sub)systems shape one another historically along the time axis by providing meaning selectively to their mutual disturbances. The reconstructions increasingly invert the time axis from within, because they have to be updated under selection pressures. Updates operate from the perspective of hindsight. In other words, this process uses another ('incursive') dynamic of the communication. As the interactions gain systemic momentum, the emerging patterns guide the selections with hindsight because the constructs become structured as yet another network layer. The global perspective, although emerging evolutionarily, may under certain conditions begin to drive the historical development of the system into a self-organizing mode. The 'phase space' of alternatives provided by globalization offers new possibilities for restructuring the organization in the reflected systems. This development is knowledge-based and selective because sets of envisioned possibilities are no longer 'naturally given.'

The globalized system can be hypothesized as selecting upon historical manifestations that are recognized in the present. The representations refer to expectations that can be entertained about other ('adjacent'; cf. Kauffman, 2000) possibilities. Globalization can be considered as an evolutionary process that inverts the time axis by opening and then also organizing a space of envisioned possibilities from which one is able to select incursively (Van Lente and Rip, 1998). The theoretical representations remain constrained by historical manifestations because one cannot select upon that which has not yet been envisioned.

2.9   Regimes and identities

Globalization provides an additional mechanism to the social system, one which can be accessed by the individual reflexively, that is, by providing new or restated meaning to previously stabilized systems of communication. The individual in an increasingly knowledge-based society, has the opportunity to trade-off between observable stabilization and hypothesized globalization. At moments when the two operations can be mapped onto each other, an identity can be maintained temporarily. At other moments, one interacts with the social system, and a next-order selection may remain external to the individual. Thus, next-order selection by the social environment and internal reflection at the individual level compete in providing meaning. Both autonomy and inclusion are part of one's personal development in these complex dynamics (Weinstein and Platt, 1969).

The two systems (the individual and the social) can be considered as structurally coupled, since they provide complexity to each other (Luhmann, 1986a; Maturana and Varela, 1980). However, the axes of these systems stand perpendicular to each other because they are substantially different. This difference can be made the subject of reflections within both systems. Whereas an individual agent has a conscious interest in maintaining identity, uncertainty can be expected to prevail in the network mode of communication. The network can improve its knowledge base by developing *discursive* knowledge, whereas the individual can feel alienated from ongoing processes of codification in subsystems of social communication in which he or she is not or is only partially included. The networks generate meanings and discursive knowledge at the supra-individual level, whereas the individual seeks to reflect on these meanings from an identifiable perspective.

The social system reflects the complex dynamics of each individual, but in a distributed mode. The interactions among mutual expectations add another dynamic to the aggregate of individual expectations. When the interaction terms become more important than the aggregation, the dynamics can change from an integrated system to an evolutionarily differentiating one.[13] Differentiation can then be added to the social system at the structural level as a mechanism different from integration. As the human carriers continue to communicate freely in terms of information *and* meaning, this communication system becomes increasingly shaped to enable the communicating agents to process two or even more dimensions of the communication at the same time continuously becoming confused. Thus, the development of the communicative capacities of the carriers promotes the further

---

[13] In a model, the interaction terms can be measured as the between-group variance and the aggregation terms as the weighted sum of the within-group variances (Leydesdorff, 1995a, 2005b).

differentiation within, and codification of, the social (sub)systems, and *vice versa* (Leydesdorff, 2001b).

As long as the actors were operating on the basis of a single (e.g., cosmologically integrated) meaning at the level of the social system, this system could still be considered as an identity. When the actors feel free to deconstruct and reconstruct meanings within communication, the differences between the communication of uncertainty and meaning can be reinforced by codification. When this differentiation can further be stabilized (e.g., by codifying communication in terms of different, symbolically generalized media) the social system obtains one more degree of freedom and therewith the option of globalization. As a historical phenomenon, however, the globalization of the social system remains one of its subdynamics. The super-system fails to exist in terms of a physical or biological reality, since it is *functionally* defined as a knowledge-based operation on this (human) reality, one that has the effect of changing what can be observed. It can only be considered as 'real' in the sense of 'critical realism,' while it exhibits itself in terms of its contingent instantiations (Bhaskar, 1997; Sayer, 2000).

Globalization can thus be considered as yet another subdynamic—one that modulates local communications—in terms of, for example, their symbolic value (Leydesdorff, 1993a). In other words, modernization cannot be completed because it remains a reflexive operation (Habermas, 1968, 1981; Beck *et al.*, 2003). For analytical reasons, however, the reflecting communication must be distinguished from the communication on which it reflects. Thus, the social system is in need of a medium that enables us to communicate both in terms of information exchanges and in terms of the meanings of these exchanges. These two dimensions have not been considered here as different systems, but as differentiations of the linguistic operator: the two layers are not 'hard-wired,' but the quality of the communication can be improved when the two dimensions are clearly specified. The distinctions remain reflexively constructed, although such distinctions (about what certain information means) can be codified historically and stabilized for considerable periods of time.

For example, social meaning can be codified at the supra-individual level, as in the case of the development of a scientific paradigm. The differentiation between common-sense knowledge and scientific (that is, potentially counter-intuitive) knowledge can be made functional to the further development of the individual and/or the society, but again along different axes. In a scientific discourse, for example, the two dimensions (embeddedness in a social group as an individual and cognitive participation in a scientific development as a contributor) are no longer expected to coincide as systems of reference (Gilbert and Mulkay, 1984).

Thenceforth, the problems of differentiation and integration increasingly become puzzles for social coordination and for individuals living in a knowledge-based society (Bernstein, 1995).

Meaning at the level of the social system has a status different from that of meaning at the level of the individual. The social level can be considered an outcome of the *interactions* among individuals. This emergence of social meaning has also been called 'situational meaning' in symbolic interactionism (Blumer, 1969; Knorr-Cetina and Cicourel, 1981). Human carriers are able to distinguish reflexively between the social meaning of a communication and their own personal meaning. This differentiation can be reinforced as the difference between personal (or tacit) knowledge and discursive (i.e., potentially counter-intuitive) knowledge (Leydesdorff, 2000d). Social order can then be seen as an order of expectations that is informed by the manifest institutionalizations of the system (Giddens, 1984).

Social order consists of a reference to expectations exchanged among individuals realizing their life-cycles in interaction with the contingencies of their biological bodies. Within the life-cycles of individuals, certain problems have to be solved: real-life conditions place constraints on the differentiation between possible meanings and the distribution of events (Habermas, 1981, 1987). At the level of a social system, this constraint can be relaxed: different solutions can be achieved by various subsystems. The function of differentiation can be expected to remain uncertain and in flux, more than in the case of a biological system, and the need to perform a life-cycle sets constraints on the degrees of freedom of an individual. As the social system becomes further differentiated into various subsystems, discourses, and codes (such as between an economy, scientific discourses, health care systems, etc.) the carriers are burdened with making translations among the functional domains by means of specific languages. Furthermore, exchange media can be developed and potentially globalized in each of these subsystems. Reflexive discourses enable the carriers to make these translations of meanings in various ways. As they are able to communicate about their respective solutions, for example, using public and/or symbolic media, they may subjectively identify themselves with their historical solutions as a global solution. With hindsight, however, each solution at the level of the social system can be recognized as the globalization of a specific medium (e.g., a television channel like CNN). Each specific organization implies a reduction of complexity in the self-organization, or, in other words, a relative equilibrium in a non-equilibrium dynamics (Aoki, 2001).

Globalization of the social system can be expected to be differentiated into a range of local solutions that have been relatively stabilized. The social system continuously loops back into itself (e.g., between the local and global dimensions), since no informal transgressions are intrinsically forbidden. A globalization represented at a specific moment in time will be perceived in the future as an instantiation of this subdynamic because the globalization itself remains dynamic. The dynamics contain more complexity than one is able to observe at any discrete instant. This more complex system of communications builds on its subdynamics by selecting from them, but not in any order described *a priori*. In addition to institutions, the observable manifestations include rules and regulations as the dynamic counterparts of the institutions (Giddens, 1979, 1984). The observable units of analysis can be considered as footprints of the communications that have served us hitherto. The organization of communications develops along trajectories that have been institutionalized and codified for historical reasons.

Institutionalization and stabilization are historically observable, whereas codification can be considered as providing meaning to some meanings but not to others. Therefore, the latter operation is part of an incursive process of *cultural* evolution. As noted, this process inverts the time axis and highlights the construction of meaning within the system as a future-oriented operation that takes place in the present. By providing new meaning to its previous instantiations, the system is increasingly able to rewrite its history by making new selections from the perspective of hindsight on the basis of socially constructed codifications. As the new meanings are increasingly science-based, the rewritings can become increasingly technology-based. The systematic organization of knowledge production (e.g., in R&D laboratories) thus drives the social system into its globalization.

2.10   The science-society-technology cycle

I have followed Luhmann (1984) in defining the social system as structurally coupled to human agency. Whereas the social system is generated from and based in the network layer among the carriers at the nodes, the links themselves are not initially stable. However, they can be stabilized by the nodes. The network system, however, can be meta-stabilized because the links are operators that induce change. Virtual communications among machines can then also be constructed using specific media of communication as next-order codifications—for example, into scientific and technical discourses. However, these virtual communications have to be provided with meaning locally, since otherwise they would lose their historical significance. While machines can be relatively stabilized along the time axis, the human contexts embed the machines so that a next generation of the technique can be envisioned discursively.

Thus, the evolutionary metaphor and the historical metaphor are two sides of the same coin in the operation of the social system. Historical structuration breaks the symmetry and generates a non-linear dynamics. The self-organization of the communication is constrained by its manifestation. This co-evolution of incursive and recursive subroutines drives the development of the knowledge base from an emerging dimension of the social system into a techno-economic evolution that can become increasingly knowledge-based. While the system is constructed bottom-up, control tends to become top-down. However, each stabilization, including that of control, remains provisional. The social system is unique in this extreme capacity for flexibility and reconstruction.

Man-machine systems, for example, remain historical, and the limits of their evolution are contextually given (Latour, 1988). Human beings are able to reconstruct their history and their environment, but they are not able individually to reconstruct the environment technologically, that is, without invoking and instantiating the transformative capacities of the social system. This system can thus operate increasingly as the pump in a science-society-technology cycle depicted in Figure 2.2.

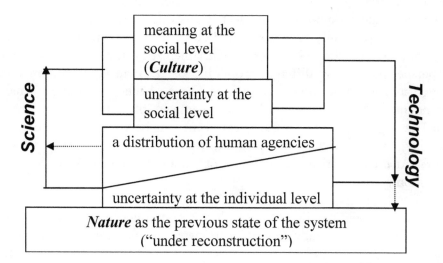

Figure 2.2: The Science-Society-Technology Cycle of Knowledge-Based Reconstructions

At the interface of the mind and the body, perceptions can be codified into language and language can further be codified into science. At the supra-individual level, the sciences are increasingly interfaced with technologies. The latter in turn change their environments. Other agents may be affected by these technologies, and they are equally able to reflect on what happens in their environment and subsequently to propose other solutions. Biological evolution is thus enrolled in a cultural evolution as a next-order level of control.

Discourses enable us to organize communications into representations. These discursive representations can be communicated using geometrical metaphors (Shinn, 1987). Geometrical metaphors reduce the algorithmic complexity in the systems under study by providing us with perspectives that can provisionally be stabilized. The codes of the communication span a universe that processes complexity, while the interfaces between the social and the individual ground the communication. This structural coupling sets the discursive stage for what can historically be considered as 'natural,' 'social,' or 'virtual.' The capacity to channel information selectively continuously challenges the social (sub)systems and their interactions to explore innovative recombinations of meaning.

Methodologically, one is able to measure communications in terms of changes in the distributions of *what* is exchanged. By definition, an exchange generates a probabilistic entropy. Using the abstract concept of 'probabilistic entropy,' 'variation' and 'selection' can be considered as two metaphors for the study of the same (algorithmic) process: the observable variation provides us with a historical description of the evolutionarily deselected cases. In other words, the concepts of probability and probabilistic entropy provide us with a common denominator for 'selection' and 'variation' when using the mathematical theory of communication. This perspective is very different from that of (Darwinian) evolution theory in biology, where these two operations have been considered analytically independent. [14] The two operations, however, can be considered as structurally coupled in a given event. An empirical event can be expected to occur (with a probability); yet the occurrence of events remains uncertain because of selection pressure. At each instance, randomness, or variation, interacts with determination (or selection).

In mathematics, one may be able to deduce a consequence by making an abstract inference. However, in studying empirical operations, one can no longer expect to

---

[14] Ulanowicz (1997, at pp. 33f.) follows the so-called 'Grand Synthesis' in neo-Darwinism which assumes that change occurs from the periphery (Depew and Weber, 1994). The reflexive model developed here locates change in the frictions among the relevant levels and subsystems. Innovation is thus endogenized in this model as a cultural event, and is therefore to be distinguished from mutation.

be completely certain (nor completely uncertain). The theoretical specification of the substances of the communication enables us to select the relevant dimensions from an abstract phase space of possible dimensions. A specific theory of communication can consequently be generated in each dimension that can be specified as relevant. The mathematical concepts are thus provided with substantive meaning. For example, when meaning is communicated, psychology and sociology provide us with relevant discourses (Luhmann, 1986a). When it is assumed that atoms are exchanged among molecules, chemistry can be developed as a discourse that reflects upon these exchanges (Mason, 1992). When molecules are exchanged, biology can be considered as a discourse that is able to appreciate these processes in theoretical terms (Maturana, 1978).

Although there may be overlap, the discourses of 'psychology' and 'sociology' refer analytically to two different systems of reference: individuals and the coordination mechanisms among individuals, respectively. Because of differentiation within the social system, the reflexive study of this system—sociology—can be expected to proliferate its discourses endogenously (Leydesdorff, 1997a). An action-theoretical perspective in sociology, for example, takes an angle for reflection that differs from a systems-theoretical one. From a general systems perspective, one may be inclined to consider the different orders as superimposed layers. However, there is no given order or priority in the organization of theoretical reconstructions. They provide us with windows on the complex dynamics under study which compete for explanation. The more the perspectives are orthogonal, the more complexity can be processed by these subsystems of communication.

The substantive interpretations require metaphors for the appreciation of the complex dynamics under study. These metaphors can be thought of as geometrical stabilizations that are useful in the codification of a specific type of scholarly communication (Hesse, 1980). They provide analysts with a structure that can sometimes be stabilized (into a scientific discourse) and perhaps even globalized (into a paradigm). As substantively specific, the use of metaphors enables us to handle the algorithmic complexity in the data without becoming continuously confused by the ongoing processes of change at various levels. For example, the concepts of 'variation' and 'selection' can themselves be considered as two geometrical perspectives on the algorithmic operation of generating probabilistic entropy. The system of reference for the variation is different from that for the selection. In classical evolution theory, for example, variation was defined at the species level, while selection was attributed to nature as a super-system.

The notion of geometrical metaphors which are functional for communication brings language into play (Hesse, 1988). The perspectives can be considered as codified at the supra-individual level, that is, by using one selection or another for the stabilization of the complex dynamics under study into a discursive (that is, geometrical) representation. This representation can contain an instantiation of the system under study at one moment of time or entail the development of a trajectory over time. The synchronic representation of an instantiation highlights the complexity, whereas the diachronic representation of a trajectory focuses on the dynamics. The complex dynamics, however, develops beyond these representations in terms of fluxes. An information *calculus* would be required for the specification of the probabilistic operation at interfaces (Bar-Hillel, 1955). The global level of communication can be accessed in terms of expectations on the basis of the codified knowledge contained in the representations, for example, with the help of an algorithmic simulation model. In the algorithmic model, the discursive representations are represented as subroutines, that is, as equations spanning the modelled system.

2.11   The incursion of knowledge-based expectations

Human language first enables us to codify the relationship between uncertainty and the meaning of a message. As meaning is generated interactively through the use of language, it can be considered as a reflexive function of language at the level of the social system (Pask, 1975). I have deviated here from Luhmann's social systems theory by considering language as the 'first-order' or naturally operating system of society. Languages emerge spontaneously among human beings as 'natural' languages (Pinker, 1994; Maturana, 1978). However, languages can also be cultivated using higher-order codifications, for example, as in scientific discourses (Searle, 1998).

Luhmann proposed that 'meaning' would itself be the operator of social systems. 'Meaning' was therefore considered as a kind of transcendental (or given) precondition of both reflection and language, but not as a consequence of the linguistic operation itself (Luhmann, 1971). Luhmann (1986a) generalized the idea of meaning generation and processing, but he had not yet reflected upon the idea of meaning from the perspective of a mathematical theory of communication. The focus on using historical examples implied that the globalization of meaning was considered a virtual operation that could only be discussed with reference to Husserl's *transcendental* phenomenology. However, the social construction of meaning has been analyzed as thoroughly contingent by scholars working in the pragmatist tradition and symbolic interactionism (Blumer, 1969; Mead, 1934).

The exchange of meaning provides communication with a second layer that reflects and interacts with the first layer of uncertain exchanges in the social system. I have suggested above that language can be considered as the evolutionary achievement that facilitates communication by using these two channels simultaneously. This duality enables us to capture the complexity of the algorithmic operation, a problem having two sides: an *a priori* expectation and an *a posteriori* update value. Meaning draws in the present upon exchanged information when it 'incurs' upon the information as uncertainty. It is also continuously generated as a recursive (i.e., historical) update of previous meaning(s). The difference between these two operations can be observed in social systems, since meaning can be codified at different levels of the same system, and to variable extents.

The organization of scientific knowledge production, for example, has led to the differentiation between the context of justification and the context of discovery within the sciences (Popper, 1935). Knowledge produced in the context of discovery can first be considered as a knowledge claim when submitted to a journal for further communication. The editor of the journal can send the draft to referees for review. The knowledge claims can thus be validated. The two contexts provide different meanings to the same knowledge and, accordingly, distinctions in the epistemological status of this knowledge can be observed (Gilbert and Mulkay, 1984; Leydesdorff, 1995a, 1996b).

Thus, the incursive subroutine doubles the historical authenticity of the social system by providing it with a co-evolutionary layer that is future-oriented in the present. The complex social system as the subject of cultural evolution is continuously reconstructing its history from different perspectives, while operating reflexively and in a distributed mode. Because of this distributed mode, the reconstruction cannot be completed without further selection. A previous codification may provisionally be stabilized through translation (at an interface by a receiving discourse), since the meaning may have been rewritten as historically specific.

In other words, the system can be doubled in its representation because the linguistic operation is itself layered. The appreciation of incursion *within* the recursive routines enables us to reconstruct the historical dimension of these processes through the use of a reflexive discourse. Beyond the doubling in language, a knowledge-based system can entertain more than two representations. What was first considered as two hierarchical levels can be considered as orthogonal dimensions of codification along different axes. Over time, however, the operation is neither exclusively historical nor completely reconstructive: it always contains uncertainty, also in the time dimension, because information processing is involved. Cultural evolution, once unleashed as an interaction among these degrees of freedom drives the communicative competencies of the carriers at an increasing speed, since the social system provides us with ranges of options for realization at each reflexive turn.

While reflection is often associated with a turn of 180 degrees, the addition of another dimension to the social system assumes a turn of only ninety degrees. Interaction terms among the perpendicular dynamics of reflection can lead to non-linear recombinations of meaning. However, the number of possible combinations—and therefore the selection pressure—increases exponentially with the number of relevant dimensions. As awareness of these dimensions is absorbed, the carriers can experience this pressure as globalization of the social system. Insofar as the dimensions can be specified as hypotheses, they can be made the subject of discursive reasoning. The analytical specification of these systems of reference can thus be expected to become crucial for the further development of knowledge-based communication systems. The degree of codification determines the complexity that can be processed.

Chapter 3

The Processing of Meaning in Anticipatory Systems

In the previous chapter, I discussed how meaning is provided to observations and how meaning can be communicated in addition to—and on top of—the underlying processes of the information exchanges. Meaning is provided to observations from the perspective of hindsight, while information processing follows the time axis. In this chapter, I shall demonstrate how simulations of anticipatory systems enable us to show how an observer can be generated within an information process, and how expectations can also be exchanged. Cellular automata will be used for the visualization of these effects. The exchange of observations among observers generates (1) uncertainty about the delineations of the observed system(s) at each moment, and (2) uncertainty about the dynamics of the interaction over time.

3.1   Simulations and the second-order perspective

In their seminal study of the simulation of social systems, Epstein and Axtell (1996) used the metaphor of 'growing artificial societies' on 'sugarscapes.' Human beings are then considered in terms of their observable behavior. In general, multi-agent models begin with the specification of activities at the nodes. Relations among the agents are modeled using a (potentially complex) function. The results of these simulations can be appreciated in terms of the quality of modeling the phenomena. The epistemological assumption of this approach, however, has remained meta-biological: even if reflexivity is declared in the model, the exchange among agents is considered as a means to the ends of improving the performance of agents in terms of 'survival' rates (e.g., Axelrod 1997; Dittrich *et al.* 2003).

Arrangements of communicating agents exhibit the capacity to learn. This has been addressed in neural network models (e.g., Hutchins and Hazlehurst, 1995; Parisi *et al.*, 1995). In a neural network model, the network dynamics themselves are black-boxed. Second-order social systems theory, however, focuses on the dynamics of networks in terms of the links. What do first-order exchanges of information *mean* for the evolving network systems? The links represent interactions and can be considered as the units of operation of the network. These operations of the links stand analytically orthogonal to the agents operating at the nodes. The nodes and links are structurally coupled in the co-variation like the woof and warp of a textile or, using a more formal metaphor, like the rows and the columns of a matrix. Given the perpendicularity of the reflexive angles, however, one can expect the perspectives of first-order and second-order systems theory to be very different.

Interactions at the level of social systems provide meaning to actions. From this perspective, human agency can be considered as the distributed and reflexive operator of the coordination mechanisms among people. The coordination mechanisms (e.g., economic exchange relations, command and control structures in organizations, the symbolic mediation of meaning in scientific communication) thus generate a second layer of communication. This layer can develop its own dynamics when it adds value to the exchanges. The communication of meaning is not a biological, but a cultural (that is, socially constructed) phenomenon (Luhmann, 1986b).[15]

For example, commodities can be exchanged using money. Prices are set in terms of supply and demand, but the circulation of money may influence prices, as in the case of inflation. Prices can be considered as expectations of the values of the commodities; prices are defined at the level of the social system. The resulting attribution of value is no longer a biological, but a cultural phenomenon. Human language is first required for this communication. The next-order exchanges can be further codified into knowledge-intensive exchanges because some meanings can be more meaningful than others. For example, stock exchanges are no longer driven only by supply and demand, but also by expectations about future price developments.

In this chapter, I shall show that simulation studies enable us to address the horizon of meaningful expectations as a phase space that can be distinguished from a landscape of observable events (Husserl, 1929; Luhmann, 2002). While the observable events develop by information processing along historical trajectories, the processing of anticipations by and among human beings can be considered as a selection mechanism that operates from the perspective of hindsight. These

---

[15] Using Luhmann's definitions, there can be no meaningless information in meaning-processing systems. Information is defined by Luhmann (1984, at pp. 102f.) as a selection by the system—that is, as observed information—and not as uncertainty or expected information (Shannon, 1948). Luhmann (1984) defines the system itself as an operation at an interface with an environment. Consequently, the uncertainty in the environment can no longer be specified as an expectation of the system; the focus is on observations and observed information (see Chapter Two above for the elaboration of this point).

reflexive expectations import representations of future states into the present, that is, as a feedback mechanism against the arrow of time. In the next chapter (Chapter Four), I shall turn to the question of codification of meaning and examine how different codifications can be expected to operate upon each other under conditions of functional differentiation among the codes.

Systems which entertain models of their future states in the present can be considered as anticipatory systems (Rosen 1985). First, I shall abstract the anticipatory model from its biological basis by using Dubois's (1998) mathematical formalization of 'incursion.' Second, a system which is both socially distributed and anticipatory will be decomposed into an observing system and a system under observation. In a third step, the quality of the observation is varied. The concept of anticipation is elaborated for a multi-agent system in terms of aggregation of and interaction among observations (Dubois and Sabatier 1998; Leydesdorff and Dubois 2004). The interaction among *observers* can then be distinguished from the interaction among *observations*. Interactions among observers may lead to structure in aggregates of observations. Interactions among observations can be considered as providing a second-order mechanism in addition to interactions among observers. This latter point will further be elaborated in the next chapter.

3.2   Anticipatory systems

In 1985 the mathematical biologist Robert Rosen introduced the concept of anticipatory systems, which he defined as systems that contain a representation of the system itself (Rosen 1985; Dubois 2000). The internal representations can be used by the system for the anticipation, because the system's parameters can be varied and recombined within the system by the system itself. A biological system can use this degree of freedom for anticipatory adaptation, that is, by making a selection in the present from among its possible representations in a next (phenotypical) exhibition. The other possible representations remain internal to the system, 'theoretical,' and in this sense 'genotypical' (Langton, 1989, at pp. 22f.).

In an anticipatory system the clock in the model runs faster than the clock in the system that is modeled. Because the model system is part of the modeled system, such systems can be considered from two perspectives at each moment of time, and thus a paradox is generated (Kauffman, 2001). One can understand the system both from the perspective of the model within the system and from a perspective external to the system including the model. Changing from the one to the other perspective requires a *Gestaltswitch*. The different perspectives can be entertained with potentially different frequencies. One then generates 'a movie' or an animation with changing perspectives.

By thus having the option to play with the time axis as a degree of freedom, the anticipatory system increases its capacity to process complexity. While the alternative perspectives in a *Gestaltswitch* stabilize different geometrical representations (pictures), the algorithmic approach of the historically evolving system encompasses the various perspectives as in a movie. The system can vary the camera positions, for example, by oscillating between two or more perspectives.

In electrical engineering, anticipatory models have been used to simulate the future behavior of systems that contain delays in their operation (Dubois, 2002). However, in order to make these models relevant for social systems theory, one has to specify how the communication among anticipatory agents can result in an anticipatory feedback at the systems level on the information processing among the agents. Let us perform this analysis step by step. I shall first specify the anticipatory model and then combine this mechanism with multi-agent modeling (that is, information processing) in a next step. Using a cellular automaton, the generation of an observer will be made visible as a possible result of the interaction between the two mechanisms of anticipation and networking. After the specification of possible differences among observers in terms of their perspectives, I turn in the final parts of this chapter to the exchange of observations as a next-order level of the communication. The interaction among observers can be distinguished from the interaction among observations or, more precisely, observational reports (Pask, 1975; De Zeeuw, 1993).

3.2.1 *Derivation of the anticipatory model*

The study of anticipatory systems requires a model of the system that is complex enough to accommodate the different representations of the system within the system under study, in addition to, and as analytically different from, the representations in the model of the analyst. Anticipatory systems no longer model an external world, but instead entertain internal representations of their relevant environments in terms of the ranges of possible further developments. The external analyst of such systems can be considered as a super-observer who is able to use a language different from that of the observers generated within the system (Maturana, 1978). In other words, the potential for anticipation *within* systems can be considered as a consequence of the complexity of the analytical model which the analyst uses to study these systems: are we reflexively able to distinguish between the system's models and our own models? Independently of the question of whether the systems under study really 'exist,' one can only study systems which contain models if the analyst's model can consider the systems under study as potentially entertaining a model. Thus, the black box of the system has to be opened and the anticipatory mechanism has to be specified.

How can our model allow for a model within the system under study? This additional complexity is made available by recognizing the time dimension as another degree of freedom available for providing historical events with interpretations that differ from ours as analysts. When the clocks at the respective levels (external and internal to the system) tick at different frequencies, different representations can be generated from the perspective of hindsight. Within the system this degree of freedom allows for proactive adaptation in reaction to changes in the environment. This anticipation is accomplished within the system by inverting the arrow of time locally. The modeling subroutine informs the system about possible events in an anticipatory mode because the clock in the model runs faster than that of the system as a whole. Analysts function as super-observers who can reconstruct the anticipatory mechanism using their own discourse as another frequency for the reflection.

How can this degree of freedom in the time dimension be incorporated into the simulations? When one simulates a process in discrete time steps, it is possible to evaluate the behavior of a system over time using a forward or a backward appreciation of the differential equation. When these different formulations are provided with other (alternative) appreciations, an anticipatory model can be generated analytically. In general, the differential equation $dx/dt = f(x_t)$ can be written as a difference equation (in discrete time) either as follows:

$$x_{t+\Delta t} = x_t + \Delta t\, f(x_t) \tag{1a}$$

or equivalently backwards as:

$$x_{t-\Delta t} = x_t - \Delta t\, f(x_t) \tag{1b}$$

It follows from a reorganization of Equation 1b that:

$$x_t = x_{t-\Delta t} + \Delta t\, f(x_t) \tag{1c}$$

This latter function allows for the following rewrite after one time-step Δt:

$$x_{t+\Delta t} = x_t + \Delta t\, f(x_{t+\Delta t}) \tag{1d}$$

Equation (1d) is different from Equation (1a) in terms of the time subscripts, so that different classes of solutions can be expected. In Equation (1d) the state of a system at time $(t + \Delta t)$ depends on the state at the present time t, but also at the next moment in time $(t + \Delta t)$. The prediction 'includes' (or 'implies') its own next state. Dubois (1998) proposed that this evaluation be labeled *incursion*.

The behavior of incursive models can be very different from recursive ones, even when the two models are based on the same differential equations. As will be shown below, the anticipatory (incursive) subroutine may balance the historical (or recursive) one and thus counteract instabilities (e.g., emerging bifurcations) in an evolving system. These effects of anticipations are highly relevant for understanding social systems because social systems are driven both historically and by the expectations available and exchanged within them.

The economics of technological innovation provide an excellent example of the dual role that recursive and incursive operations can be expected to play within a system. The price of a commodity can be considered as its expected value on the market. The price is based both on an intrinsic value and on feedback from the market system. The intrinsic value stems from historical production with given factor prices, while the feedback of the market originates in the present and is based on the current dynamics of supply and demand. This economic system of expectations can be modeled using the anticipatory version of the logistic or Pearl-Verhulst equation for the growth of biological systems (Pearl 1924; Verhulst 1847; Wolfram 2002, at p. 198).

The widespread use of the traditional (that is, only recursive) format of this model is inadequate in the case of a cultural system, since the two subdynamics of production and diffusion are then not sufficiently distinguished in terms of the differences in their dynamics. Production proceeds historically along the time axis, and the progression of production technology changes prices along this axis. Diffusion on the market takes place under competitive conditions in the present. The selection mechanism—in this case, the market—can be considered as an evolutionary feedback term on historical development (Nelson and Winter, 1982).[16] I shall now focus on the Pearl-Verhulst equation in order to show how the

---

[16] In Chapter Five we shall specify that the two different subdynamics in production and diffusion processes can under certain conditions co-evolve, while they can be expected to bifurcate at other values of the parameters.

anticipatory formulation of this model can be used for the simulation. In the next chapter, I shall generalize the model and prove that the anticipatory formulation of the Pearl-Verhulst equation can be used for modeling *social* systems (Leydesdorff and Dubois, 2004).

3.2.2 *Historical developments and evolutionary feedback*

The following model is known as the Pearl-Verhulst equation or the logistic map (Devaney 2003, at pp. 33 ff.):

$$x_t = a\, x_{t-1}\, (1 - x_{t-1}) \tag{2}$$

This equation can be used to model the growth of a population. The feedback term $(1 - x_t)$ inhibits the further growth of the system as the value of x_t increases over time. This so-called 'saturation factor' generates the bending of the sigmoid growth curves of systems for relatively small values of the parameter $(1 < a < 3)$. For larger values of a, the model bifurcates (at $a >= 3.0$) or increasingly generates chaos $(3.57 < a < 4)$.

An anticipatory equivalent of the logistic equation can be formulated as follows (Dubois, 1998):

$$x_t = a\, x_{t-1}\, (1 - x_t) \tag{3}$$

In this model, the selection pressure prevailing in the present is analytically independent of the previous state of the system that produced the variation. The recursion on x_{t-1} can be considered as the historical subdynamic of the system. As noted, technological systems which develop historically within an economy experience interaction with the market at each moment of time. In other words, the horizontal diffusion in the market stands in orthogonal relation to the historical development of the technology over time. In terms of the production function approach—following Schumpeter—this orthogonality was modeled above (Figure 1.2) as shifts along the production function versus shifts of this function towards the origin.

The results of the interactions among the subdynamics are continuously input to a next cycle that builds both recursively on the previous state and incursively experiences another feedback of the market at a next moment. However, the incursive subdynamic can be expected to have properties that differ from those of the recursive one (from which it was derived). For example, the anticipatory model based on the logistic equation does not exhibit bifurcation or chaos for larger values of the parameter *a*.

Let us first specify the model analytically and then—in a next section—demonstrate and discuss the behavioral differences between recursive and incursive systems by using cellular automata to visualize their effects. The analytical reformulation of the Equation 3 proceeds as follows:

$$x_t = a \, x_{t-1} \, (1 - x_t) \tag{3}$$
$$x_t = a \, x_{t-1} - a \, x_{t-1} \cdot x_t$$
$$x_t + a \, x_{t-1} \cdot x_t = a \, x_{t-1}$$
$$x_t \, (1 + a \, x_{t-1}) = a \, x_{t-1}$$
$$x_t = a \, x_{t-1} \, / \, (1 + a \, x_{t-1}) \tag{4}$$

Equation 4 specifies x_t as a function of x_{t-1}, but it is analytically equivalent to a model for incursion embedded in historical recursions as specified in Equation 3. In the case of pure incursion (that is, only environmental determination in the present, as represented by the second term of Equation 3), one would no longer be able to produce a simulation because one would lose the historical axis of the system in the model. Thus, there would be no historical instantiations. In other words, the anticipatory model containing both recursive and incursive factors imports the global or system's perspective into systems which are developing historically. The incursive term enriches the historically developing system with an orientation towards the future.

3.3   The simulation of an anticipatory system

Cellular automata enable us to display the dynamics of distributed (multi-agent) systems in terms of colors on the screen.[17] Each point on the screen can be considered as an agent. Each agent is positioned by a horizontal and a vertical coordinate, that is, x and y. Different colors can be used to indicate the state of the various agents over time. However, the state of each agent (and consequently its color on the screen) can be determined by the algorithms running at the level of the system and/or in local networks. In order to handle this mathematically, the value

---

[17] When agents are defined in terms of 'consciousness' (Luhmann, 1986), the states of the agents does not have to be identified with behavior. The colors can also indicate different states of mind.

of each pixel (representing an agent) will be mapped in an array(x, y) with the size of the screen. In the simulations below, I use these two-dimensional array values and input them into the equations in a distributed mode, that is, at the randomly chosen place where change is generated.[18] The screen colors are consequently updated.

For example, the logistic model reads in the two dimensions of the screen coordinates as follows:

$$[x, y]_t = a\,[x, y]_{t-1}\,(1 - [x, y]_{t-1}) \tag{2a}$$

This equation is used, for example, in line 130 of the computer program exhibited in Table 1.

```
10   SCREEN 7: WINDOW (0, 0)-(320, 200): CLS
20   RANDOMIZE TIMER: a = 2.1
30   ' $DYNAMIC
40   DIM scrn(321, 201) AS SINGLE
50   FOR x = 0 TO 320            ' array and screen are filled in
60      FOR y = 0 TO 200
70         scrn(x, y) = .1: PSET (x, y), (10 * scrn(x, y))
80      NEXT y
90   NEXT x

100 DO
110    x = INT(RND * 320)          ' an array element is randomly
120    y = INT(RND * 200)          ' selected
130    scrn(x, y) = a * scrn(x, y) * (1 - scrn(x, y))
140    PSET (x, y), (10 * scrn(x, y))
150 LOOP WHILE INKEY$ = ""
160 END
```

Table 3.1: Model for the logistic curve in BASIC (*a* = 2.1)

In order to enhance the transparency, I formulate the simulation models in standard BASIC.[19] For example, the array from Equation 2a is defined in line 40 of Table 1 so that it can contain a representation of the screen in CGA-mode (200 x 320 pixels). The CGA-mode (line 10) was chosen in order to take full advantage of the visibility of the effects on the screen. A pixel—representing an agent—is selected randomly in lines 110 and 120. The results of the logistic evaluation of the

[18] The extension to more than two dimensions is straightforward (Leydesdorff, 2001a).
[19] I used Microsoft's QBasic, but the programs can easily be adapted for higher or commercial versions of Basic, and for other languages. In Visual Basic the programs formulated in this paper can be imported as subroutines.

corresponding array value (line 130) are brought to the screen in line 140: the pixel affected by the routine is thereafter repainted.

Both the array and the screen are initially filled with a constant value in line 70; the screen is painted monochromatically. In the next loop (lines 100-150), a pixel is accessed randomly (lines 110-120), evaluated (line 130), and repainted accordingly (line 140). This transformation is performed continuously.

Figure 3.1: Resulting screen of Table 1 with bifurcation for $a = 3.1$.

For the value $a = 2.1$ (line 20), the color of the screen changes gradually because the distributed system exhibited on the screen goes through a transition.[20] For $a = 3.1$, however, bifurcation is expected. This results in two colors randomly distributed across the screen (Figure 3.1): when an agent is activated (lines 110-120), the color on the screen changes into the alternative one at this place. Thus, the bifurcation leads to an oscillation between the two colors on the screen. For higher values of the parameter a, the system exhibits increasingly chaotic patterns of change.

---

[20] In the compiled simulations, the values of the colors were augmented with five in order to use the brighter colors in the palette of QBasic.

Let us now turn to the anticipatory formulation of the logistic curve as specified in Equation 4 above. Table 2 provides the source code using a format similar to that of Table 1. However, following upon line 130 the screen is now split into two halves. The upper half of the screen (y > 100) is modeled using the *incursive* equation (Equation 4) in line 140, while the lower half remains recursive (Equation 2 in line 150 for y ≤ 100). The additional code in the first line enables the user to choose the parameter value interactively.[21]

```
1    CLS : LOCATE 10, 10: INPUT 'Parameter value'; a
2    IF a > 4 THEN a = 4                      ' prevention of overflow

10   SCREEN 7: WINDOW (0, 0)-(320, 200): CLS
20   RANDOMIZE TIMER
30   ' $DYNAMIC
40   DIM scrn(321, 201) AS SINGLE
50   FOR x = 0 TO 320
60     FOR y = 0 TO 200
70       scrn(x, y) = .1: PSET (x, y), (10 * scrn(x, y))
80     NEXT y
90   NEXT x

100 DO
110    x = INT(RND * 320)
120    y = INT(RND * 200)
130    IF y > 100 GOTO 140 ELSE GOTO 150      ' split of screens
140        scrn(x, y) = a * scrn(x, y) / (1 + a * scrn(x, y)): GOTO 160
150        scrn(x, y) = a * scrn(x, y) * (1 - scrn(x, y))
160    PSET (x, y), (10 * scrn(x, y))
170    LOOP WHILE INKEY$ = ""
180 END
```

Table 3.2: Incursion and recursion in the case of the logistic curve

Figure 2 shows that the incursive simulation leads to a transition, while the representation of the recursive system in the lower half of the screen exhibits the same bifurcation illustrated in Figure 1. The incursive model converges to a stable state (in this case, exhibited as white) because the incursive version of the logistic model $\{ax / (1+ax)\}$ grows towards unity with increasing values of x. In a mathematical formulation: $\text{Lim}_{x \to \infty} \{ax /(1+ax)\} = 1$. A fixed point is reached independently of the starting value.

---

[21] In order to prevent overflow while running this model, values of the parameter *a* larger than 4 are reset to *a* = 4 (in line 2).

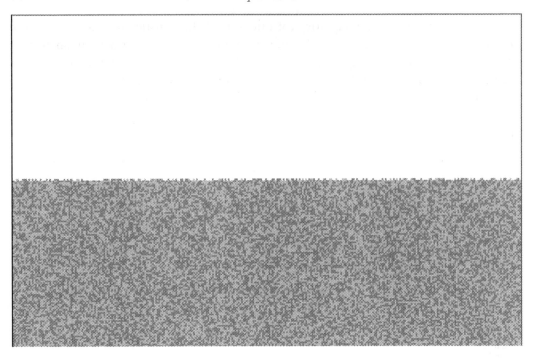

Figure 3.2: Upper half of the screen incursive, lower half recursive; *a* = 3.1

One can also combine the two subdynamics of incursion and recursion into a single screen by making the choice between the two models within the same system. The necessary changes in the codes are provided in Table 3. In this model the loops for the incursive or recursive routines are randomly assigned in line 130.

```
[...]
100 DO
110    x = INT(RND * 320)
120    y = INT(RND * 200)
130    IF RND > .5 GOTO 140 ELSE GOTO 150
140       scrn(x, y) = a * scrn(x, y) / (1 + a* scrn(x, y)) : GOTO 160
150       scrn(x, y) = a * scrn(x, y) * (1 - scrn(x, y))
160    PSET (x, y), (10 * scrn(x, y))
170 LOOP WHILE INKEY$ = ""
180 END
```

Table 3.3: Incursion and recursion alternating randomly, but using the same data set

When the incursive model operates within a recursive system of which it is also a part, the incursive routine reduces the uncertainty produced by the recursive one. The recursive sub-dynamic produces probabilistic entropy, but incursion drives steadily towards a transition in the longer run. From an (historical) actor perspective, this incursive selection mechanism appears as a latent attractor in the structure of communications among the agents; the structure filters the variation.

The longer-term prevalence of incursion over recursion demonstrates the importance of accounting for expectations in models of cultural evolution, since both subdynamics can be expected to occur in a social system. The emerging layers of social coordination can be expected to provide additional stabilities because of their selective capacity. Stabilization is a result of selections over time operating on (structural) selections at each moment of time. In other words, instantaneous selections on disturbances can be selected recursively for stabilization over time and thereby structure (e.g., in the anticipations) can be retained. When a difference can be processed recursively, this may generate a reflexive stabilization.

By using incursion and therefore time as another degree of freedom, some stabilizations can further be selected for meta-stabilization or globalization (Mackenzie, 2001). However, before moving to these next-order systems of communication, let us keep to the strategy of taking single steps and first simulate the emergence of an observer using an anticipatory model.[22]

3.4   The generation of an observer

Can the result of the interacting dynamics of a complex system that contains both incursive and recursive subroutines also be decomposed into an observing and an observed sub-system? In the model described in Table 4 and exhibited (below) in Figure 3, the two routines of 'observed' and 'observing' are decomposed and thus an observer is generated.[23] The upper half of the screen is reserved for the results of the incursive observations of the lower half of the screen, while the lower half exhibits the historical development of the observed system.

---

[22] As argued in Chapter Two, an observation can also be considered as the stabilization of a representation or, in other words, the specification of an expectation.

[23] The subsystem entertaining the model of the system in the present state can be considered as an endogenous observer of the system's history. 'Endogenous' means here that this observer remains a result of the network in which the observer effect is generated (Maturana 1978). One can consider this observer as an incursive subroutine of the complex system. Note that the metaphor is biological because this observer is not positioned refexively in a (next-order) communication among observers. The observer remains completely embedded and follows developments in the observed system reflexively.

```
   1   a = 3.3

  10   SCREEN 7: WINDOW (0, 0)-(320, 200): CLS
  20   RANDOMIZE TIMER

  30   ' $DYNAMIC
  40   DIM scrn(321, 201) AS INTEGER
  50   FOR x = 0 TO 320
  60       FOR y = 0 TO 200
  70           scrn(x, y) = INT(RND * 16)      ' change to 16 colors
  80           PSET (x, y), scrn(x, y)
  90       NEXT y
 100   NEXT x

 110   DO
 120     y = INT(RND * 200)
 130     x = INT(RND * 320)
 140     IF (x = 0 OR y = 0) GOTO 220          ' prevention of network errors
 150     IF y > 100 GOTO 160 ELSE GOTO 180
 160         scrn(x, y) = a * scrn(x, y-100) / (1 + a* (scrn(x, y-100) / 16))
 170         GOTO 210                          ' paint upper screen
 180         scrn(x, y) = a * (scrn(x, y) * (1 - (scrn(x, y)) / 16))
                  ' spread new value in the Von Neumann environment
 190             scrn(x + 1, y) = scrn(x, y): scrn(x - 1, y) = scrn(x, y)
 200             scrn(x, y + 1) = scrn(x, y): scrn(x, y - 1) = scrn(x, y)
 210         PSET (x, y), ABS(scrn(x, y))
 220   LOOP WHILE INKEY$ = ""
 230   END
```

Table 3.4: The generation of an observer by using incursion

In order to generate an observable structure (because one cannot recognize patterns in the random observation of randomness), a small network effect was first added to the observed system (in lines 190-200 of Table 4). This network effect spreads the update in the lower-level screen in the local (Von Neumann) neighborhood of the randomly affected cell. (The Von Neumann environment is defined as the cells above, below, to the right, and to the left of the effect.) Note that the network effect structures the system at each moment of time and locally, whereas incursion and recursion are defined over the time axis of the system.

The network effect enables us to appreciate on the screen the development of both the observed system and the relative quality of the observation depicted in the upper half of the screen. In order to exhibit more details on the screen, I will henceforth use the full range of 16 colors available in BASIC. This is achieved by changing the decimal base of the above simulations to the hexadecimal basis of 16 (line 70 of Table 4). Whenever necessary normalizations in the formulas for incursion and recursion are added (by dividing again by 16; for example, in lines 160 and 180).

A random attribution (line 120) determines (in line 150) whether the recursive or the incursive routine is entered. The incursive routine (line 160) operates on the value of the corresponding array element in the lower half of the screen by evaluating scrn[x, y-100]. The result of this evaluation is attributed to the upper half of the screen and to the corresponding array value of scrn[x, y]. The effect is that an observer is generated, as shown in Figure 3.

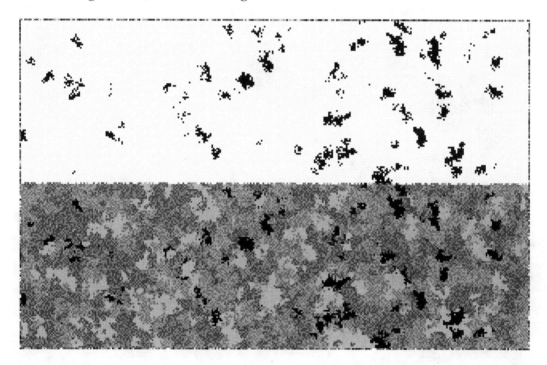

Figure 3.3: Incursion generates an observer in the top-level screen ($a = 3.3$)

In Figure 3, the parameter a is set at the value of $a = 3.3$ so that four colors are continuously produced by the logistic map operating in the lower half of the screen. The network effect in the Von Neumann neighborhood (lines 190-200) adds observable structure to each bifurcation into two colors. The incursive top-half screen filters the black areas as an element of the observable structure. Under these conditions, however, the observer (that is, the modeling subsystem) can distinguish only in black and white.

3.5   The generation of blind spots by different observers

The previous simulation has shown that a reflexive observer observes selectively, for example, only in black and white. By changing the parameter of the incursion, one can change the window of an observer. Figure 4, for example, shows a similar simulation, but with the incursive parameter b set at half the value of the parameter for the recursion a ($a = 3.2$ and $b = 1.6$, respectively). The observer in this case observes detail in the structure in the lower half of the screen and different colors. However, the observer's reflections remain considerably less detailed than the representation of the observed system as exhibited on the lower half of the screen.[24]

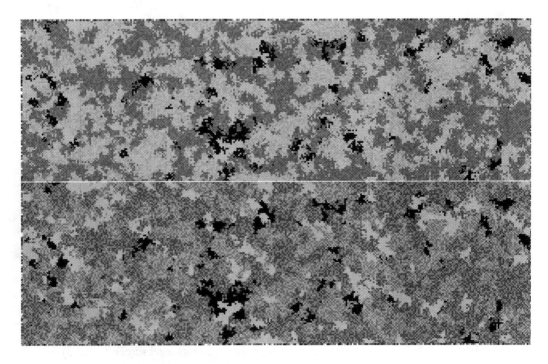

Figure 3.4: Incursion and recursion with different parameter values produce observers with potentially different positions and corresponding blind spots ($a = 3.2$ and $b = 1.6$).

---

[24] In the program in Table 5, the two parameters (a for the recursion and b for incursion, respectively) can be chosen by the user in the lines 2 and 3 of the routine. In Visual Basic the more sophisticated user interface would require the programming of an additional subroutine.

```
  1  CLS
  2  LOCATE 10, 10: INPUT 'Parameter value for recursion (a) '; a
  3  LOCATE 11, 10: INPUT 'Parameter value for incursion (b) '; b
  4  IF a > 4 THEN a = 4

 10  SCREEN 7: WINDOW (0, 0)-(320, 200): CLS
 20  RANDOMIZE TIMER

 30  ' $dynamic
 40  DIM virtual scrn(321, 201) AS INTEGER
 50  FOR x = 0 TO 320
 60     FOR y = 0 TO 200
 70         scrn(x, y) = INT(RND * 16)
 80         PSET (x, y), scrn(x, y)
 90     NEXT y
100  NEXT x

110  DO
120    y = INT(RND * 201)
130    x = INT(RND * 321)
140    IF (x = 0 OR y = 0) GOTO 230        ' prevention of errors by
150    IF (x = 320 or y =, 200) GOTO 230   ' effects at the margins
160    IF y > 100 GOTO 170 ELSE GOTO 190
170        scrn(x, y) = b*scrn(x,(y-100))/(1 + b*(scrn(x,(y-100))/16))
180        GOTO 220
190        scrn(x, y) = a * scrn(x, y) * ((1 - (scrn(x, y)) / 16))
200        scrn(x + 1, y) = scrn(x, y): scrn(x - 1, y) = scrn(x, y)
210        scrn(x, y + 1) = scrn(x, y): scrn(x, y - 1) = scrn(x, y)
220        PSET (x, y), ABS(scrn(x, y))
230  LOOP WHILE INKEY$ = ""
240  END
```

Table 3.5: Incursion and recursion with potentially different parameters

By playing with the parameters, it becomes evident that an observer perceives more detail when the parameter for the incursive routine is lower than for the recursive one. High values for the incursion parameter (b) drive the observing system into a more homogeneous state (because of the above noted limit transition in the formula), while higher values of the recursive parameter (a) drive the historically developing system towards more chaotic bifurcations.

3.6   Interactions among observers and observations

The possibility of generating observers with the different qualities of their respective observations raises the question of the possibility of interaction among the observers. What would happen if the observers were also able to observe one another's observations? This would require the observations to be made available for communication in observational reports. In this chapter, I limit the interactions among observers to the simple interaction among and aggregation of observations. Human observers interact additionally by using more sophisticated mechanisms like human language or symbolically generalized media for the communication (Luhmann 1982 and 1997a; Parsons 1963a and 1963b). However, the elaboration of the case of differentiation of the system using different codes of communication is the subject of the next chapter (Chapter Four).

In the model of Table 6, two observers are defined differently in terms of the values of their respective parameters for the incursive routine. For the purpose of the presentation, the upper half of the screen is divided between them into a left and right half. Furthermore, one of the observers (the left hand one) is embedded in the recursive system under observation (as in the program of Table 3 above). The other observer remains external to the system under observation. Additionally, the two observers can differ in terms of the qualities of their observations by providing them with different parameters (*b* and *c*, respectively).

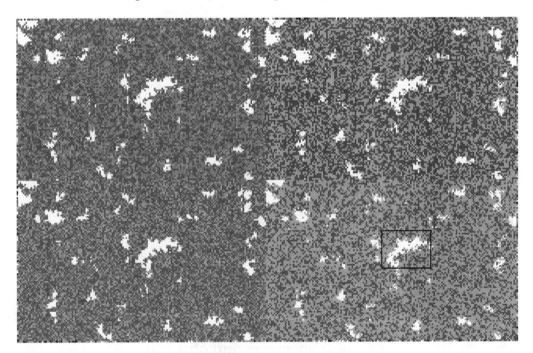

Figure 3.5: Two observers observing a single screen and each other (lower right screen). (Colors optimized in black and white by using the negative of the picture for the visualization.)

```
  1 a = 3.2: b = 1.6: c = 1.9
 10 SCREEN 7: WINDOW (0, 0)-(320, 200): CLS
 20 RANDOMIZE TIMER
 30 ' $DYNAMIC
 40 DIM scrn(321, 201) AS INTEGER
 50 FOR x = 0 TO 320
 60    FOR y = 0 TO 200
 70        scrn(x, y) = INT(RND * 16)
 80        PSET (x, y), scrn(x, y)
 90    NEXT y
100 NEXT x
110 DO
120   y = INT(RND * 201)
130   x = INT(RND * 321)
140   IF (x = 0 OR y = 0) GOTO 390         ' prevention of errors
150   IF (x = 320 OR y =, 200) GOTO 390    ' at the margins
160   IF x < 160 AND y >= 100 THEN N = 1   ' definition of four
170   IF x >= 160 AND y >= 100 THEN N = 2  ' subscreens
180   IF x < 160 AND y < 100 THEN N = 3
190   IF x >= 160 AND y < 100 THEN N = 4
200   SELECT CASE N
210      CASE IS = 1                       ' upper left screen
220         scrn(x,y) = b*scrn(x,(y-100))/(1+b*(scrn(x,(y-100))/ 16))
230         PSET (x, y), ABS(scrn(x, y))
240      CASE IS = 2                       ' upper right screen
250         scrn(x, y) = c * scrn((x-160),(y-100))/ _
               (1+c*(scrn((x- 160),(y-100))/ 16))
260         PSET (x, y), ABS(scrn(x, y))
270      CASE IS = 3                       ' lower left screen
280         IF RND > .5 GOTO 290 ELSE GOTO 300
290         scrn(x, y) = b * scrn(x, y) / (1 +  b* (scrn(x, y)) / 16):_
               GOTO 330
300         scrn(x, y) = a * scrn(x, y) * ((1 - (scrn(x, y)) / 16))
310         scrn(x + 1, y) = scrn(x, y): scrn(x - 1, y) = scrn(x, y)
320         scrn(x, y + 1) = scrn(x, y): scrn(x, y - 1) = scrn(x, y)
330         PSET (x, y), ABS(scrn(x, y))
340      CASE IS = 4                             ' lower right screen
350         scrn(x, y) = c * scrn((x-160),(y+100))/(1 + _
               c*(scrn((x-160),(y+100))/ 16))
360         scrn(x,y) = (scrn(x,y)/2) + (b * scrn(x,(y+100)) / _
               (1 + b*(scrn(x,(y+100))/16))) / 2
370         PSET (x, y), ABS(scrn(x, y))
380   END SELECT
390 LOOP WHILE INKEY$ = ""
400 END
```

Table 3.6: Two observers (incursion with $b = 1.6$ and $c = 1.9$) observe the same screen (recursion with $a = 3.2$) and each other. The left-side observer is additionally embedded (line 290).

The observed system is represented in the lower left quadrant. The lower right quadrant is reserved for the averaged result of the observers observing each other's observations. The observers use their respective parameters for observing both the observed system and each other's observations.

Figure 5 shows that the different values of the parameters for the observation lead to differently colored perceptions of the system under observation. The embeddedness of the left-side observer makes no apparent difference from the representation in the upper-right quadrant upon visual inspection of these screens. The color differences are generated only by the parameters of the observing systems. In this model, the observations of the observations are aggregated, and the average of these two observations is exhibited in the lower right quadrant.

Both upper half screens provide less detail than the observed system (in the left bottom quadrant). The combination of the two observations is even poorer, but the boundaries of the (inverted) black spots exhibit an additional color. In order to show this in black and white (printing), I added Figure 6 which amplifies the area indicated in Figure 5 by a factor of ten. The two observations differ somewhat and therefore the boundaries become uncertain when the observations of the observations are aggregated and averaged. (This is indicated with an additional shade of grey in Figure 6.)

Figure 3.6: Part of Figure 3.5 enlarged ten times.

In the next model (Figure 7), aggregation is replaced with interaction between the two observations. Whereas aggregation and the averaging of observations is based on interactions among *observers*, interactions among *observations* can be appreciated as meaning processing, since this exchange is taking place in a next-order layer. Note that the interaction and potentially meaningful coordination among observations remains structurally coupled to the underlying layer of first-order observers (Luhmann 1999). However, let us first study analytically the effects of introducing this interaction term.

```
[...]
340       CASE IS = 4                          ' lower right screen
350         scrn(x, y) = c * scrn((x-160),(y+100))/_
                          (1 +c*(scrn((x-160),(y+100))/ 16))
360         scrn(x, y) = (scrn(x, y)) * (b * scrn(x,(y+100)) /_
                          (1 + b*(scrn(x,(y+100))/16)))
370         scrn(x, y) = d * scrn(x, y)        ' interaction parameter d
380         PSET (x, y), ABS(scrn(x, y))
490     END SELECT
400 LOOP WHILE INKEY$ = ""
410 END
```

Table 3.7: The effect of interaction among the two observations

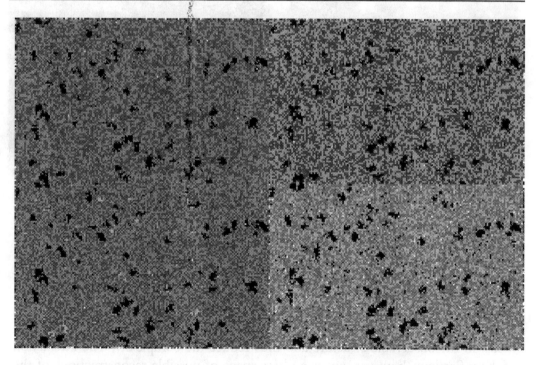

Figure 3.7: Interaction effects among the two observations with *d* = 0.2.

In order to see the pure effect of interaction—that is, without aggregation—I changed the plus sign in line 360 of Table 6 into a multiplication sign in Table 7. By adding a parameter d for the interaction (in line 151), one can then produce representations that are as rich in colors as the originally observed system ($d = 0.2$ exhibited in Figure 8) or as poor as an observer who observes only in black and white ($d = 1.0$).

Figure 8 combines the two subdynamics of interaction and aggregation by assigning 40% of the visual effect to the interaction and 60% to the aggregation.

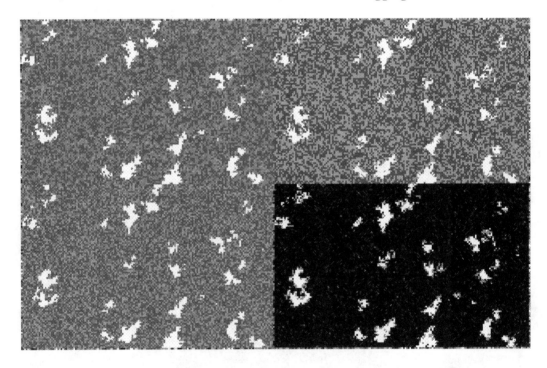

Figure 3.8: Interaction and aggregation of observations combined

My analytical point is that interaction is a non-linear operation which enables us to reconstruct the dynamics in and the various shades of the observed system by fine-tuning the interaction parameter. The two incursive observers first operate at random frequencies, but with different parameters. Consequently, an interaction among their observations contains a dynamic uncertainty that represents elements of the originally observed system that are lost in the individual reflections. The latter focus on the observable structure and thus reduce the complexity. The interaction of the reflections, however, opens a phase space of possible reconstructions of the observed system. This phase space can be appreciated at the social level if a cumulation of interactions were to be stabilized recursively as another axis of the system.[25]

Given these parameters, all four (sub)screens visible in Figure 7 continue to reflect the network structure generated by the network effect in the observed system in the lower-left quadrant. The two observers, however, mainly observe structure. They tend to lose sight of the different colors of the arriving pixels generating the dynamics of change in the underlying screen (bottom left). The picture based on the interaction (in the lower-right quadrant) represents the ongoing dynamics of the system under observation by showing individual pixels that exist temporarily in colors other than the ones that reflect the network structure. These pixels are generated by dynamic frictions between the two observations which are out of phase because of (a) random differences in the update frequencies and (b) structural differences in the incursive parameters.

The resulting picture (in the lower right quadrant) shows the two effects described above: (a) the aggregation makes the observations uncertain in terms of the boundaries, and (b) the interaction shows the dynamics of the system under observation as pixels that temporarily light up on the screen. Because the two observers operate at random frequencies and with different parameters for the incursion, they are out of sync and entertain different representations. The latter effect provides a static uncertainty and the former a dynamic one.

In a next round of simulations the observers could be enabled to appreciate the effects of the aggregation and interaction of their observations. The next-order system of interacting observations can be further developed, for example, along emerging axes that stabilize new perspectives for the observation.[26] In this chapter, however, I wished to show first that the simulation of social systems that exchange expectations is possible.

---

[25] This phase space can only be appreciated at the social level if the cumulation of interactions was previously stabilized as another dimension of the social system. The emergence of such a new dimension can, for example, be modeled as the effect of an unintended 'lock-in' (Arthur, 1989, 1994). I elaborate on this further development of the social system in the next chapter.

[26] From a perspective along the time axis, these stabilizations can be considered as a consequence of potential resonance (Smolensky, 1986; Leydesdorff, 1995b).

3.7   Conclusion

Luhmann (1984, at pp. 240f.) defined social systems as consisting of communications and *their* attribution as actions. The system of communication reproduces itself by linking communications to one another over time, while the attribution of these events as actions serves the observability of the system in historical time. The communications are operations which cannot be observed directly, but one can make inferences about them by testing hypotheses against the observable interactions among the agents (Luhmann, 1984, at p. 226). The communications and agents are structurally coupled and therefore the states of the agents can be used as *indicators* of the evolving communication processes among them.

Simulation models are needed for showing visually what can be reasoned analytically, but the modeling requires the analyst to specify assumptions with mathematical clarity. By taking the steps of anticipation, observation, aggregation, and interaction one by one, the construction of a social system of expectations could be made transparent. The dynamics of a social system, however, can be expected to remain complex and non-trivial because a social system contains a variety of different and interacting subdynamics.

The operation of second-order systems that process expectations cannot be observed directly. An observer is able to observe only the fingerprints that such operations leave behind. In a meaning-processing system the parameters of the observation are set by the system. An analyst first needs an interpretative frame for the observation of reflexive exchange processes (Luhmann, 1984, at p. 226; Leydesdorff, 2003b, at p. 269). The exchange of meaning in relation to underlying information exchanges can be studied as a process of changing expectations by using simulation models. The simulations enable us to demonstrate the relevance of theoretical specifications about the dynamics of systems of expectations. For example, the differently expected effects of aggregation and interaction can be made visible.

One is able to distinguish analytically between anticipation by the system and the information exchanges with its environments which provide the variation. The latent structure of social systems (Lazarsfeld and Henry 1968) can be expected to contain an internal subdynamic. Giddens (1979) used the word 'virtual' for this operation at the network level of what he called 'the duality of structure.' The operation over time can feedback on the structure at each moment of time.

For example, the intellectual organization of a scientific specialty provides us with a level of expectations that does not coincide with the social organization of the field in terms of observable institutions like university departments (Whitley 1984). This other level of distributed control emerges within the social structure, and its structure can be conjectured reflexively by the scholars trained in the specialty. But once in place, the intellectual organization may further develop, stagnate, or go into crisis without the departments being necessarily dissolved in the short term. The observable exchange relations process information historically, but the processing of meaning opens a global perspective on top of these 'instantiations' (Giddens 1984).

The instantiations of a social system can only indicate the existence of a system of expectations at a certain moment of time if this system was first hypothesized. For example, the institutions can indicate continuity in history as a retention mechanism for the puzzles that the social systems have solved hitherto. When expectations can operate upon one another, solutions at interfaces can be selected and sometimes stabilized. However, an analyst can only recognize the instantiations and institutions as sustaining a second-order dynamics of expectations if the anticipatory mechanisms of meaning exchange have first been specified as relevant hypotheses. The observable variation can then be considered as provided with meaning by the agents, and this process can also be reconstructed.

Empirically observable phenomena inform us about cases that have occurred historically, but not about what could have occurred. The historical observables themselves cannot provide sufficient control for the quality of theorizing about meaning. In other words, one is not able to specify the uncertainty in the expectation on the basis of historical variations because the distribution of other possibilities is not 'given' in reality. However, some expectations about how observable reality can be reconstructed by reflexive observers may yet be more 'realistic' than others, that is, with reference to the reflected system. Simulations of social systems at the second-order level of expectations enable us to hypothesize selection mechanisms operating at the social level on theoretical grounds and to study the effects of these assumptions. Simulation studies can be considered as addressing a phase space of possible events which is different from the landscape of observable events. Thus, simulation studies can contribute to sociological theorizing in a way that is very different from empirical observations (Hanneman, 1988).

Whereas empirical data enables the researcher to specify theoretical expectations, the simulations of incursive systems of expectations have to remain on the analytical side. The simulations enable us to improve the specificity of our analytical expectations. In the above simulations, for example, relatively simple worlds containing both structural (network) elements and various subdynamics of change were generated. The system under observation could then be observed from different perspectives, and the implications for understanding the social character of observations could be specified.

The observers could first be distinguished in terms of the quality of their observations. One can focus on the communality in their observations. For example, the communality can be appreciated by comparing the observations. However, this comparison can also be made by the observers themselves using their incursive routines with the respective parameters for the observation. When these incursive routines were applied by the observers not only to the system under observation, but also recursively to each other's observations, two further perspectives could be made visible. First, an uncertainty in the delineations was induced at the margins of the structures visible on the screen. The two observers perceive somewhat differently, and therefore, the aggregate of their observations can be expected to contain an uncertainty. In other words, structures and delineations cannot be sharp in second-order exchanges. For example, the uncertainty among observations can lead reflexively to discussions about the quality of the observations (given that a code or language would be available for guiding this exchange).

Second, the dynamics of the observed system were brought back on stage by appreciating an interaction term among the observations. While the individual observers perceive the dynamics in the observed system, their focus remains on the structural network effects. However, the asynchronicity of the observations makes it possible to perceive dynamics in the interaction. In the lower right quadrant of Figure 9, this was visible as the single points that are generated with a different color. In the two upper quadrants (representing first-order observers) these changes were perceived as ongoing changes within the range of the prevailing colors.

Among the two observers a fourth position is analytically possible, namely one which inverts the time axis in the interaction among the observations by using another incursive loop. In the simulations of Figure 8, the lower right screen exhibited change and stability over time, but this process was followed along the historical arrow of time. The reflection of this emerging order in relation to 'adjacent possibilities' (Kauffman, 2000) assumes the exchange of meaning at the level of the social system. Such a system of meaning processing would require a symbolic layer like a code of the communication. A range of possible worlds might then be specifiable. This next-order loop can 'globalize' the historically stabilized systems of second-order expectations under specifiable conditions. Luhmann (2002a) in this context made reference to Husserl's (1929) phenomenology to indicate the notion of meaning as occurring always within a horizon of possible meanings. In other words, the simulations studies of anticipatory systems provide us with a program for further research into the dynamics of second-order social systems.

Chapter 4

Codification and Differentiation of Meaning in Social Systems

While weakly anticipatory systems contain a model of themselves as a prediction, a strongly anticipatory system can construct its next stage and overwrite its past. In this chapter, I argue that the social system can function as a strongly anticipatory system since it can develop two anticipatory mechanisms: (1) meaning is provided with hindsight, i.e., by a time-step difference from the reflected operation; and (2) the differentiation in the social system generates an asynchronicity (Δt) between the operations of its subsystems. The communications in terms of different codes of communication provide the different subsystems with representations of each other at each moment of time. When the two anticipatory mechanisms are left free to operate on each other, a strongly anticipatory system can be shaped as a resonance between these two subdynamics.

In general, the possibility of anticipation is based on using time as a degree of freedom. The clock time of the modeling system runs faster than the clock of the system itself. Therefore, the model can anticipate a future state of the reflected system. The time axis is locally inverted by this operation; the system lags on its representation in the model and is therefore differentiated over time. Once this differentiation by using different clocks is successfully stabilized, a hierarchical control system can first be developed within the system. The representation then provides the system with a prediction of its next stage. This anticipatory property can have evolutionary advantages in terms of survival value, because an anticipating system has a degree of freedom to adapt its phenotype proactively, that is, before changes in the environment actually occur.

Mental models, for example, function in this mode of *weak* anticipation. As a strongly anticipatory system, however, the social system is able endogenously to generate mechanisms for its renewal at interfaces between its subsystems. A prime example of this is the techno-economic evolution at the interface between technological and economic developments. As Marx (1848) predicted in *The Communist Manifesto*, 'all that is solid will melt into air' because of the ongoing processes of modernization and innovation (Berman, 1982). While Marx considered this as a meta-historical process (towards communism), we are able to consider this as an interplay between historical and evolutionary mechanisms with potentially very different outcomes (Hanneman and Collins, 1986).

The historical dimension anchors the system, while the coordination mechanisms of society are continuously reconstructed. After a technological revolution, for example, the systems of reference may have to be redefined. When the selection of meaning is reproduced recursively, and this configuration is additionally retained (that is, stabilized) in a knowledge infrastructure, a knowledge base can increasingly be developed as a hypercycle of expectations on top of the knowledge-producing institutions. Unlike the relatively stable forms of organization, one can expect a knowledge base of the system and its subsystems (e.g., the economy) to remain organized as a system of expectations. Expectations can be meta-stable or global, that is, they may reach beyond the previously stabilized organizations in a self-organizing mode.

4.1 The sociological perspective in systems theory

Both 'actions' and 'interactions' can be considered as micro-operations that can be aggregated from a systemic perspective. Actions can be aggregated, for example, into 'institutional agency,' whereas interactions may become increasingly complex by operating upon one another in a non-linear mode. Because action is performative, it can be considered as an operation integrating social systems historically (Parsons, 1937; Habermas, 1981). Interactions, however, enable the actors both to integrate different perspectives by taking action and to reproduce the differentiation at the network level. Differentiation and integration can thus be considered as two sides of the same operation.

In sociological discourse, 'systems theory' has often been opposed to 'action theory' (Habermas and Luhmann, 1971; Habermas, 1981; Münch, 1982; Giddens, 1984). 'Action theory' may seem less alienating than 'systems theory' because actions can be intentional. The analytical distinction between theories that are based on 'action' or 'interaction' as micro-operations of social systems, however, is more fundamental than the one between action and systems theory (Knorr-Cetina and Cicourel, 1981). Luhmann's sociology can be considered as different from previous systems-theoretical approaches because it assumes communication as the basic operation of social systems. Luhmann (1975b; 1982b) added that at next-order levels one can expect stabilizations of interaction patterns into organizations, [27] and the globalization of communication at the level of society in a self-organizing mode.

The two micro-operations of action and interaction lead to different research designs (Goffman, 1959; Glaser and Strauss, 1967; Glaser, 1992). For example, the constructivist Latour (1987) proposed as a methodology to 'follow the actors' in terms of their actions. Actions are then used as a historical *explanans* of the observable phenomena. Evolutionary economists have equally considered entrepreneurial behavior—that is, action—as an *explanans* for evolutionary success in the 'survival of the fittest.' For example, the emergence of trajectories and regimes was mainly explained in terms of entrepreneurial decisions about trade-offs in production and diffusion processes (Nelson and Winter, 1982). As discussed in Chapter One, Andersen (1994, at pp. 144 ff.) proposed as an alternative program to focus on 'strategies of interaction.' However, these strategies were analyzed in terms of actor-categories. In other words, the actions of agents remained the *explanans* of the interactions.

The epistemological difference between the approaches dominant in evolutionary economics and in constructivism is thus not found in the distinction between assuming action or interaction as the *explanans,* because both these theories focus on action as performative integration and therefore stabilization. However, the two theories are different in terms of how one declares the time axis (Blauwhof, 1994). The evolutionary model explains success from the perspective of hindsight, whereas the constructivists wish to account symmetrically for success and failure by following actors along the time axis (Pinch and Bijker, 1984; Bijker *et al.*, 1987). The evolutionary model assumes asymmetry *ex post* because of the ongoing selection processes, while the constructivist explanation assumes symmetry *ex ante* as a methodological postulate (Bloor, 1976).

The focus on 'interaction' generates a reflexive perspective. Like actions, interactions occur in history, but the system of reference for interaction is by definition an interhuman construct. Because interaction is reflexive, this operation is no longer additive. A non-linearity is implied. The observation of an interaction necessarily assumes a perspective, i.e., a reduction of the complexity in a model. Given a perspective on the interactions, one can reconstruct the observable events—and among them, actions—as meaningful (Weber, 1904). Furthermore, one can take another perspective reflexively. By improving the model, one may also

[27] I follow Luhmann below and use 'organization' as a systems category, while institutions are considered as historical. Institutions therefore can also exhibit (institutional) agency.

improve the attribution of actions to agents. In summary, the two operations of 'action' and 'interaction' cannot be reduced to each other because of this difference in their epistemological status (Mead, 1934).

From an interactive or network perspective, one can attribute an action to an actor, but this attribution can be reconsidered with hindsight. Interactions potentially rewrite the past, for example, from the perspective of the present. 'Interaction' thus provides us with an evolutionary category which operates at the network level, whereas actions remain to be attributed to the historical development of agency in terms of individuals or groups who carry the evolution of systems of social interaction. While actions can be expected to vary, interactions can be expected to evolve into systems of mutual expectations. These systems of expectations can be organized in institutional arrangements, but they can be expected to develop in the present and with a dynamic that is different from that of previous arrangements.

By considering communication as the unit of operation of social systems, Luhmann's sociology shares with symbolic interactionism this focus on reflexivity (Gibson, 2000). The proposal to consider 'meaning' as the crucial category in the study of social systems has been a central assumption in symbolic interactionism: inter-human interactions generate meaning in social situations (Blumer, 1969; Glaser and Strauss, 1967; Lindesmith *et al.*, 1975; cf. Luhmann, 1997a, at pp. 205 ff.). In this elaboration of the American pragmatist tradition, and with equal reference to Weber as in the systems-theoretical tradition, 'meaning' has always been considered as the constitutive operator which distinguishes the domains of the social sciences from the natural and life sciences (Glaser, 1992; Lazarsfeld, 1995). While the latter define their objects naturalistically, in sociology objects of study are approached reflexively (Weber, 1904, 1917; Schutz, 1932).

Whereas symbolic interactionism focused on interactions and their so-called 'concatenations' (that is, aggregation) into networks (Blumer, 1969),[28] Luhmann (1975b) recognized that communications can be organized non-linearly into systems, and that systems of communication are self-organizing (Grant, 2003). Three levels of systems differentiation were distinguished: interaction, the organization of

---

[28] 'The concatenation of such actions taking place at the different points constitutes the organization of the given molar unit of large-scale area. (…) Instead of accounting for the activity of the organization and its parts in terms of organizational principles or system principles, it seeks explanation in the way the participants define, interpret, and meet the situation at their respective points. The linking together of this knowledge of concatenated actions yields a picture of the organized complex.' (Blumer, 1969, at p. 58.)

interactions in a setting, and self-organization in the fluxes of communication at the global level. Luhmann's (1984) thesis of the functional differentiation of society was developed with reference to this global level. Science, for example, can be considered as a functional subsystem of society with a code of communication that is different from those of economy or religion. In scientific institutions, however, different types of communication (e.g., economic transactions and management decisions) have to be recombined with scientific communication in a specific organizational format.

4.2   The functional differentiation of communication

A third tradition which resounds in social systems theory is the quantitative one where theorizing is based in operations research and simulation studies. The issues here are control and communication (Wiener, 1948; Shannon, 1948). At several places Luhmann made reference to modeling efforts in systems research. For example, when discussing the relative autonomy of science as a subsystem of communication within society, he argued that the closure of communication in scientific paradigms can be understood from an epistemological perspective as a condition for scientific progress.

The epistemological perspective does not exhaust the advantages of the systems-theoretical description. Additionally, one can study scientific communications from a sociological perspective: what is the specific function of scientific communication for the reproduction of society? Luhmann (1990a) formulated this as follows:

> In addition to the philosophical reconstructions, the theme of relative autonomy based on functional differentiation provides options for the further development of the theory. The differentiation of science in society also changes the social system in which it occurs, and this can again be made the subject of scientific theorizing.
>
> Developing this perspective, however, is only possible if an accordingly complex systems-theoretical arrangement is specified. It remains the case that science can only communicate what it communicates; science observes according to its own procedures. This is also the case when considering questions about the social system that encompasses the science system. However, if the social system is analyzed as a differentiated system, science can also be considered reflexively as one of its subsystems. From this external perspective the sociologist can

study the sciences scientifically and compare their development with other subsystems of society.[29] (Luhmann, 1990a, at p. 340)

How can such 'an accordingly complex systems-theoretical arrangement' be constructed? How can one move from these theoretical reflections to a model specified in terms of systems operations? Would the specification of a model of a complex system enable us also to run simulations? (Kron, 2002). Although Luhmann often disclaimed standard methodologies of the social sciences like statistical testing, he saw a key role for methodological formalization, but he never specified in other than theoretical terms what he meant by the intervention of methodological programs into theoretical ones. For example, he formulated:

> In order to validate the binary code that distinguishes true from false, one needs programs of a different type. Let us call these programs *methods*.
>
> Programmatically, methods provide the perspective that the system has lost when it was codified in binary terms. The methods force the specification of the observation in terms of levels and therefore the specification of second-order observations, that is, observations of previous observations by the same system. [...] The methodology enables us to formulate programs for a historical machine. (Luhmann (1990a, at pp. 413f.) [30]

---

[29] 'Damit sind jedoch die Aspekte, die man dem Thema der Ausdifferenzierung von Wissenschaft abgewinnen kann, bei weitem noch nicht erschöpft. Die Ausdifferenzierung verändert auch das System der Gesellschaft, in dem sie stattfindet, und auch dies kann wiederum Thema der Wissenschaft werden.

Das allerdings ist nur möglich, wenn man ein entsprechend komplexes systemtheoretisches Arrangement zugrundelegt. Es bleibt dabei: die Wissenschaft kommuniziert nur das, was sie kommuniziert; sie beobachtet nur das, was sie beobachtet, und nur so, wie sie beobachtet. Das gilt auch, wenn sie Fragen des sie umfassenden Gesellschaftssystems behandelt. Behandelt sie die Gesellschaft als differenziertes System, kann sie aber zugleich sich selbst behandeln—sich selbst als ein Subsystemn dieses Systems. Sie kann sich, mit diesen ihren eigenen Vorgaben, so betrachten, als ob sie van außen wäre, und sich auf diese Weise mit anderen Subsystemen des Gesellschaftssystems vergleichen.'

[30] 'Um den binären Code, die Unterscheidung von wahr und unwahr, zur Geltung zu bringen, benötigt man daher Programme eines anderen Typs. Wir nennen sie *Methoden*.

Methoden lösen auf der Ebene der Programme das ein, was dem System durch binäre Codierung aufgegeben ist. Sie erzwingen eine Verlagerung des Beobachtens auf die Ebene einer Selbstbeobachtung zweiter Ordnung, auf die Ebene des Beobachtens eigener Beobachtungen. [...] Die Methodologie formuliert Programme für eine historische Maschine.'

Such a methodological program would require the specification of problems in a language more formal than the language of theory. In other words, theories and methods have first to be distinguished and then to be recombined in an analytically controlled manner (*ibid.*, at p. 428).

There are many differences between substantive theories and formal methodologies. In this context, however, it is mainly relevant that theories provide us with geometrical metaphors for the representation of the world, while algorithmic approaches enable us to consider different representations as specific selections which reduce the complexity from a given perspective. These perspectives can be sequenced over time. Using discursive knowledge, one can try to stabilize a picture, but in a simulation the position of the camera can also be changed. What is true from one perspective is no longer necessarily the case from another, particularly if the codes of the communication are different, as in the case of incommensurable paradigms.

Different perspectives can be recombined by using the time axis as a degree of freedom. Luhmann formulated this as follows:

> If one follows this notion of a radical temporalization of what it means to observe (…) then knowledge loses the attribution of a property that one can 'posses' and 'keep.' Instead of such representations of states, one has to address the question of under which conditions and by whom states can be actualized. Consequently, the question 'what is?' is replaced with the question 'how is this representation selected?' (Luhmann, 1990a, at p. 107).[31]

A system is able to select a representation from a set of possible representations only if it entertains a model of the represented system. In the case of self-organization, the representation is selected by a system from the possible manifestations of the same system. A system which entertains a model of itself can be expected to develop anticipatory properties (Rosen, 1985).

---

[31] 'Folgt man dieser Vorstellung einer radikalen Verzeitlichung dessen, was Beobachten ist und tut, dann müssen nicht nur alle Objektkonstanzen und all Aufzeichnungen daraufhin relativiert werden, dann verliert auch Wissen die Eigenschaft von etwas, das man "haben" und "behalten" kann, und an die Stelle solcher Bestandsvorstellungen tritt die Frage, wer was wann und unter welchen Bedingungen aktualisiert. Und damit tritt and die Stelle der Frage "was ist?" die Frage "wie wird selegiert?"'

4.3 The formalization of functional differentiation

Among Luhmann's students, Dirk Baecker (1993, 2002, 2005) has been most rigorous in attempts to use George Spencer Brown's (1969) *Logic of Forms* for the formalization of this social systems theory.[32] Following Von Foerster, Pask, and other systems theoreticians (cf. Glanville, 1996), Baecker (2002) distinguished between two types of models. First-order models aim to improve the quality of theoretical statements about observations; second-order models consider the first-order descriptions as operating within the systems under observation.

For example, scientists report on their observations in the scientific literature, and these reports (e.g., articles) can again be observed. These second-order observations can be studied systematically, for example, in science studies. Because the second-order observations can also interact informally with the first-order ones, one can attribute uncertainty to two sources of error: the first-order observations and/or the reflections on these observations. Because the sources of error can no longer be distinguished, the causality can be expected to become 'undetermined' in reflexive systems, and these systems can consequently be considered as non-trivial machineries.

In general, a dually-layered system—processing both information and meaning—can be expected to produce an output on the basis of two operations in parallel. Furthermore, the two parallel operations can interact with each other. Thus, a whole range of outputs becomes possible on the basis of a single input. The output is no longer dependent on the input only, but also on the path of the processing of the signals through the complex system. Furthermore, the processing of meaning on top of the information exchange generates meaningful (that is, new) information that can be communicated recursively within the system and then again be provided with meaning. The system under study develops an internal dynamics in addition to its observable behavior in terms of transforming inputs into outputs (Goguen and Varela, 1979).

One can study such a complex system from an external perspective in terms of inputs and outputs, but one can also open the black box and study the internal development of this system. The two perspectives—the behavioral and the recursive one—can be considered as orthogonal ones. One looks along the time axis, the other at each moment of time. The recombination of these two

---

[32] For another elaboration of Spencer Brown's logic see also Goguen and Varela (1979).

perspectives requires an algorithmic approach. A complex dynamic is always composed of different (in this case, two) subdynamics. The task of the methodological program which Luhmann envisaged, would thus be to provide us with the algorithmic tools to distinguish between the two (or more) operative subdynamics, and their interaction effects, and thus to clarify the operation of a second-order system by developing the 'accordingly complex systems-theoretical arrangement.'

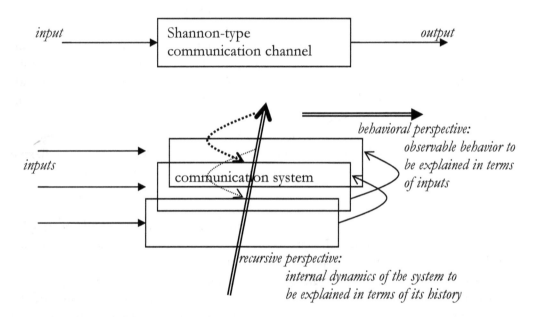

Figure 4.1: The behavior and the internal dynamics of a system provide a behavioral and a recursive perspective, respectively. These two perspectives can be considered orthogonal (Goguen and Varela, 1979, at p. 34).

This task is urgent because the 'undetermined determinateness'—as Baecker called this non-trivial machinery—leads to what is sometimes called a 'paradox of observation' that lames the empirical analysis. Luhmann (1993a), for example, formulated this paradox as follows:

> The second-order observer, mind you, is a first-order observer as well, for he must distinguish and designate the observer he intends to observe. Second-order observation thus does not rid us of the problem. It only confirms that we are dealing here with a universal problem, one with which every observation is confronted. (Luhmann, 1993a, at p. 20).

Under the pressure of such 'universal' problems, the discourse tends to shift to the epistemological level (Baecker, 1999; Kauffman, 2001). Gumbrecht (2003), for example, argued in a critical appraisal of Luhmann's legacy that the focus on the epistemological paradox of observation has led increasingly during the 1990s to discussions which have added no new insights to the already well-known problem of the hermeneutic circle in the philosophy of language.

It will be argued here that these paradoxes of observation are generated by using geometrical perspectives and logically structured frames on systems in which both the values of the variables and the variables themselves are changing. The paradoxes can be solved by changing the perspective from a time-independent logic with its consequently geometrical representation to the time-dependent approach of a calculus and simulation studies (Bar-Hillel, 1955; Varela, 1975; Varela and Goguen, 1978). [33] By using simulations, one can consider the phase space of possible combinations of the various subdynamics. The geometrical perspectives can then be appreciated as discursive windows on the systems under study, but from different (and potentially orthogonal) angles and/or at different moments in time.

An algorithmic reformulation enables us to solve the puzzles posed by the paradoxes because the incommensurabilities among the perspectives can be considered as a consequence of the geometrical metaphors that have to be used in the narratives (Shinn, 1987). Weber (1904) already noted that social science research requires the specification of a perspective or, in his words, 'ideal types' for historical explanation (Watkins, 1952). However, computer code enables us to process more complexity than using the sumtotal of reflexive discourses based on specific perspectives. The interaction terms can also be specified.

---

[33] In a much later discussion, Spencer Brown (1994, at p. 51) added the possibility of an evolutionary process to the *Logic of Forms* (1969), but he formulated this mathematically as only an oscillation between the states: "Similarly, when we get eventually to the creation of time, time is what there would be if there could be an oscillation between states." The conditional is used by the author because one needs the additional assumption of, for example, evolution theory that an oscillation between two subsystems can be expected over time. The recursive operation (i.e., the clock of the system), however, is created on grounds external to the mathematics in the *Logic of Forms*, notably on the basis of substantive theorizing (Varela, 1975, at p. 20; Leydesdorff, 2006b).

4.4   Specification of the differentiated system

Let me follow Baecker (2002) for the initial formalization of Luhmann's theory. The author proceeded by focusing on Luhmann's core notion of a system as an operation that distinguishes the system itself from its environment. With reference to Spencer-Brown (1969), an observation is defined by Luhmann (1984, 1997a) as a distinction and a designation.[34] First, a system is distinguished from its environment, and by the designation the system is identified. Following Von Foerster (1963a and b), this dual operation of identification and distinction is formalized by Baecker (2002, at p. 86) in two steps. First, the system (S) is specified as a distinction between itself and its environment (E) in a functional relationship:

$$S = f\,(S, E) \tag{1}$$

In the second step, the system is operationally closed by attributing the functionality of the distinction to the system itself. This attribution produces an 'identification' as follows:

$$S = S\,(S, E) \tag{2}$$

In other words, given this paradox the social system no longer contains a 'self' which can be identified unambiguously. Under the condition of functional differentiation, however, the identification can even be codified in more than two, potentially orthogonal dimensions (Figure 3). Several elements thus have to be added to the formalization. First, because the identification cannot be resolved for the different referents at the same time—either a tautology or a paradox is generated—time subscripts must be attributed to the different factors in the equation. Secondly, the differentiation of the social coordination into subsystems has to be appreciated in the formalization. For example, the environment

Figure 4.2: The Rubin vase induces a *Gestaltswitch* between system and environment for an observer

---

[34] Spencer Brown (1969, at p. 76) used the word 'identification,' but many systems theoreticians prefer the word 'designation' to characterize this operation.

for a subsystem can be another subsystem. Thus, one has to specify the various (sub)systems of reference. This further complicates the analysis.

Let us first write the time subscripts into Equation 2, as follows:

$$S_t = S\ (S_{t-1}, E_{t-1}) \qquad (3)$$

This system at a next moment in time S_t is a result of its own operation S on a distinction between its previous state S_{t-1} and its environment E_{t-1}. (The operator S is not provided with a time subscript because the recursive function is codified, and therefore one may expect it to be

Figure 4.3: Hofstadter's (1979) Triplet Gödel-Escher-Bach

more stable over time than the substantive communications on which it operates.) At each time step, the operator synchronizes the past operation of the system with its past environment into the currently emerging state.

Let us now add to the formalization that the social system is also differentiated into a set of subsystems $s_1, s_2, \ldots, s_n$. (I shall use the lower case s for the subsystemic level and the italic *s* more specifically for the operational codification.) Luhmann, in my opinion, has wished to argue that under the condition of functional differentiation, the operation of the social system can increasingly be considered as a result of the interactions among social *sub*systems. The subsystems use different codes for the communication. For example, in the science system statements are investigated and selected in terms of whether or not they are true. In economic communications, however, the codes of the communication are very different from those of scientific communications.

Each subsystem processes the same formula at its level when distinguishing between itself and its environment using its specific code *c*. However, when the formula is specified at the subsystemic level, the environment of each subsystem has to be replaced with the other subsystems. The autopoietic system is operationally closed. In the historical configuration of functional differentiation among the codes, the environment remains only an external referent to disturbances (ε) in the interactions among the subsystems. One can therefore formalize this configuration as follows:

$$s_t = s_c \, (s_{t-1}, E_{t-1}) \tag{4}$$

$$S_t = S \, (s_1, s_2, \ldots, s_n, \varepsilon) \tag{5}$$

The subscript c in the function s_c refers to the specifically coded operation of the subsystem in a given case. The subsystems develop in terms of variation along their own axes using their historically developed codifications as selection mechanisms. As noted, one can expect the operator (s_c) to be less time-dependent than the development of the subsystem itself because it represents a condensation of previous recursions. The environment E of the previous equations is reduced in Equation 5 to a disturbance term ε because the subsystems provide environments for each other.

If the environment is thus no longer considered external to the social system, but as one or more other subsystems of the system, this has consequences also for the time subscripts in the equations. In the previous chapter I used the example of a new technology entering the market. Let me elaborate on this example of two subdynamics with different functions. On the one hand, the newness of the technology can only be defined with reference to its previous state (*t-1*); the market, on the other hand, operates as selection pressure on this technology in the present (*t*). A price is set on the market in terms of *current* supply and demand, and—in more sophisticated cases—expectations about further technological developments. The code of the market is different from the one internal to the historical development of the technology. Thus, the economy operates at each moment in time, that is, in the present, by using a representation of the historical development of the technology over time when making, for example, a price/performance comparison in economic terms.

The two subdynamics are different in terms of their operations, but the two operations can be coupled in the case of innovation.[35] The relations between the subsystems are formally symmetrical, but the *ex ante* symmetry in their relations is broken in such an event because the selecting codes are substantively different. The subsystems have a window upon one another, but develop according to their own dynamics in parallel, and therefore asymmetrically. For example, a (de-)selected

---

[35] In Chapter One (Figure 1.2) the two functions were defined in terms of the production function as market clearing by substitution versus the potential shift of the production function towards the origin because of technological progress. These two mechanisms can be considered as analytically independent and therefore orthogonal in the representation.

technology may be further developed while taking market perspectives into consideration, but these anticipations on possible markets are introduced into engineering practice only as external referents, that is, in terms of representations using the code of the technological production system itself (Lancaster, 1979; Saviotti, 1995; Frenken, 2001).

In general, a representation can be considered as a model of the represented system. The model is constructed and entertained by the representing system. The representations are coded in the code of the representing (sub)system. The model thereupon enables the representing (sub)system to reduce the complexity of the represented (sub)system. This selection mechanism operates in the present, while each (sub)system itself operates over time using its own code with reference to its previous state. However, when the representing system and the represented system are the same system, we obtain the type of diachronic anticipation which was discussed in the previous chapter. When the representing and the represented systems are different subsystems of the same system, these subsystems can anticipate on one another's operations alongside each other.

For example, the market operates as a selection mechanism on the variations among the commodities and the technologies provided on the supply side. The price mechanism appreciates the alternatives available in the present, independently of their historical origins. *Vice versa*, the market develops historically, but not in relation to the potentially asynchronous development of the various technologies, which develop along their own respective trajectories (Dosi, 1982; Nelson and Winter, 1982; Leydesdorff and Van den Besselaar, 1998a).

In terms of the model system the replacement of the relation between a system S_t and an environment E_{t-1} with a subsystem s_t that relates to other subsystems in its environment thus implies that the time subscripts can be formulated as follows:

$$s^i_t = f^i_c (s^i_{t-1}, s^j_t, \ldots s^n_t, \varepsilon) \tag{6}$$

Each subsystem *i* develops according to its own subdynamics using its specific code f^i_c, but the distinction between this recursive development and the development of other subsystems is made not with reference to the other subsystem's history, but in terms of a representation of the other subsystems at the present moment *t*. Note that this formula contains a paradox very different from the one discussed by Luhmann and Baecker (Baecker, 1993). While the previously specified paradox was of an epistemological nature, the paradox in this model can be investigated algorithmically for potential solutions. For example, under specifiable conditions two subsystems may begin to co-evolve along a trajectory as in a techno-economic system. One can consider this co-evolution as a relative equilibrium or a resonance between different subdynamics (Aoki, 2001).

In summary, the functionally differentiated system develops in terms of models of both the histories and the present states of different subsystems. Thus—using the definitions provided in Chapter Three (Rosen, 1985; Dubois, 1998)—another anticipation is implied. The anticipatory character of the above model can be made more explicit by moving the model one time step ahead using the following rewrite (of Equation 6):

$$s_t^i = f_c^i (s_{t-1}^i, s_t^j, \ldots s_t^n, \varepsilon) \tag{6}$$

$$s_{t+1}^i = f_c^i (s_t^i, s_{t+1}^j, \ldots s_{t+1}^n, \varepsilon) \tag{7}$$

In other words, the next stage of the subsystem is dependent not only on its current state, but also on the expected state of the subsystems in its environment. Each subsystem contains a representation of the other subsystems only as an expectation. In other words, the subsystems reproduce themselves by solving the puzzles generated by the paradoxes: They provide the incoming information with meaning using their own codes. The puzzles can be solved because of this orientation on other subsystems in an anticipatory mode.

Note that the respective solutions of the paradoxes in the different subsystems remain a consequence of the functional differentiation because this evolutionary assumption went into the derivation of Equation 7. We did not yet declare here the incursive function of providing meaning at the systems level over the time axis as in Chapter Three. Let us first investigate some conditions under which the anticipatory equations can be solved in the social dimension before recombining this structural mechanism with the previous one of providing meaning over the time axis.

4.5   Paradoxes and their algorithmic resolutions

In the previous chapter, I discussed the solution of the paradox generated in an anticipatory system because of the different clocks entertained by the system itself and by the model of the system which was also part of the same system (Dubois, 1998). When the modeling system is part of the modeled system, this leads to an infinite regress and therefore to a paradox in the imagination (Dubois, 2000; Kauffman, 2001). A paradox is generated because the model of the system contains another model of the system, etc. In the previous chapter, I showed how this paradox can be resolved when time is considered as a degree of freedom. I shall now proceed by showing how this paradox can be solved for the differentiated system in a manner that differs from the solution in the undifferentiated case (that is, with one single time axis). The undifferentiated case had only one paradox to solve, namely, the one over the time dimension. The differentiated case contains different representations of the system at each moment of time.

While a hierarchically organized system can only provide weak anticipation in terms of codifying the meaning of information, a functionally differentiated one has also a horizontal degree of freedom: In addition to generating meaning over time, the functionally differentiated subsystems can be expected to contain other anticipatory mechanisms. These can be considered as a structural dimension which causes asynchronicity. The interaction between anticipation over time with this structural anticipation in the differentiation provides us with a strongly anticipatory system if the two anticipatory mechanisms happen to reinforce each other. Unlike a weakly anticipatory system, a strongly anticipatory one not only makes a prediction of its own environment, but is able to reconstruct its own configuration and consequently to redefine its relevant environments (Dubois, 2000). Thus, the operation can be closed at the systems level. However, the frictions among subsystems operating in parallel provided this other degree of freedom in the synchronization. The frictions have also to be reproduced, and therefore the strongly anticipatory system can no longer come to rest. A strongly anticipatory system can be expected to remain in transition (Etzkowitz and Leydesdorff, 1998).

Each weak anticipation provides the system with meaning. When two mechanisms for weak anticipations can operate within the same system, some meanings can be selected as more meaningful than others and a knowledge base is increasingly generated. In other words, some meanings are increasingly codified while others are not. The knowledge base allows for a rewrite if the modeled system can also be stabilized in the representation, that is, if the momentary representations can be stabilized over time. This requires an additional reinforcement of the two weak anticipations operating upon each other, or the generation of another (third) dimension for their co-evolution. Let us postpone this extension to three dimensions to later chapters and focus first on deriving the relevant algorithms for the social system at each moment of time as an addition to the insights into the development of anticipation over time that were provided in Chapter Three.

In Chapter Three, I applied the anticipatory formulation of the logistic equations and this formalization enabled me to show the emergence of an observer as a reflection of the system under study. The argument for using this equation was based on Rosen's (1985) theory of anticipatory systems and Dubois's (1998) mathematical extension of this theory. These theories were used as heuristics for the generation of different representations of the same system. I shall now proceed by providing first the formal proof that differentiation in the social system can also be modeled using this equation (Leydesdorff and Dubois, 2004).[36] It will be shown that the sole assumption of variability in social relatedness provides a sufficient basis for deriving the anticipatory formulation of the logistic map as a model of anticipation both in the interaction term and in the aggregation among subgroups. The argument is valid for any social system as a system of different actors.

In other words, it will be shown that the mechanism of anticipation in the social dimension (across boundaries among any subsystems) is similar to the mechanism of anticipation along the time axis of the system, that is, the application that provided us with an observer and thereafter different observers in the previous chapter. Both mechanisms—the synchronic and the diachronic one—can be modeled with the anticipatory formulation of the logistic equation. Although one would expect different parameter values along the two respective axes (because the dimensions represent substantively different mechanisms), the mechanisms involved are formally equivalent.

For example, the observer(s) specified in Chapter Three can equally be interpreted as providing representations of the system under observation. Representations provide meaning to the represented systems. The synchronic and the diachronic mechanisms are formally the same, but the two mechanisms of anticipation operate in (analytically) orthogonal dimensions. Their interaction will provide us in a next step with a co-variation that over time can be developed into a co-evolution. My argument will be that this co-evolution provides a necessary (but not a sufficient) condition for generating the knowledge base of social systems because it entails the operation of two types of meaning processing as devices that select upon each other.

The organization of knowledge in terms of an institutional knowledge infrastructure requires a resolution of the tension between the different anticipations in a historical organization. In a further extension (Chapter Five), I will also invert this historical axis into an emerging dimension by changing it from a recursive into an incursive subdynamic. The possibility of self-organization and globalization of the knowledge base can then be explained.

---

[36] Needless to say, I am indebted to my coauthor Daniel M. Dubois for the mathematical proof.

4.6   The social system as an algorithmic operation

Let us first consider two groups x and y in a social system. The behavior of these groups can be described by the following equations:

$$dy/dt = -axy + bx \qquad\qquad (8a)$$
$$dx/dt = +axy - bx \qquad\qquad (8b)$$

The sociological interpretation of this system of equations is as follows: the two groups x_t and y_t interact with an interaction given by the product of the two populations $x_t y_t$ at the rate a. The group y_t represents isolated persons, and the group x_t persons already entertaining relations with each other at that moment. When there is interaction, Equation 8a specifies that the number of isolates decreases with the interaction term $(-axy)$, while the chance of interaction increases with the number of persons already pertaining relations $(+bx)$. In Equation 8b, similarly, the number of related persons increases because of the interaction $(+axy)$, but the chance of further relating decreases (with $-bx$) when a larger part of the population is already related.[37]

The interaction between the two groups x and y can be considered as the sociability factor of the population. The parameter a models this probability of the interaction. Let us assume that x + y = Constant = C; for example, C = 1. For $a = 0$, x can become zero and the whole population would be constituted of isolated persons;[38] y is in this case equal to C because x + y = C. The parameter a can thus be considered as a measure of the sociability of the population (Dubois and Sabatier, 1998).

---

[37] The model is known in the literature as the SIS model of Bailey (1957) which simplifies on the classical SIRS model of infectious diseases by Kermack and McKendrick (1927).

[38] For $a = 0$, Equation 8b becomes:

$$dx/dt = -bx$$
$$x = -\tfrac{1}{2}bx^2$$
$$bx^2 + 2x = 0$$
$$x * (bx + 2) = 0$$

The one root of this equation is x = 0. For the case of $b = 1$, the other root of the equation is that x = –2. Since x + y = 1, y = 3 in this case. This solution does not have an obvious interpretation.

4.6.1   Derivation of the logistic equation

The parameter b can be taken as $b = 1$, without losing any generality. Assuming $b = 1$ in Equations 8a and 8b, the corresponding discrete system can be formulated as follows:

$$(y_{t+1} - y_t) = - ax_t y_t + x_t \tag{9a}$$
$$(x_{t+1} - x_t) = + ax_t y_t - x_t \tag{9b}$$

Equation 9b can be written as:

$$x_{t+1} = ax_t y_t \tag{9b'}$$

Because additionally:

$$y_{t+1} + x_{t+1} = y_t + x_t = \text{Constant} = 1 \tag{10a}$$
$$y_t = 1 - x_t \tag{10b}$$

It follows (by replacing Equation 10b into Equation 9b') that:

$$x_{t+1} = ax_t (1 - x_t) \tag{11}$$

This is the well-known logistic map that generates chaotic behavior for $a = 4$.

4.6.2   Derivation of the anticipatory version

One can consider two anticipatory versions of the above model in the case of a social system. First (A), one may expect the grouping process to contain anticipation. For example, isolated individuals may consider reflexively whether it is to their advantage to enter into relations. Second (B), one can assume that the interaction term between the two groups (xy) contains an anticipation. It will now be shown that both assumptions lead to the anticipatory formulation of the logistic map.

A. Proof for the case of anticipation at the individual level (y)

Let us rewrite Equation 9a with anticipation in y:

$$(y_{t+1} - y_t) = -ax_{t+1}y_{t+1} + x_{t+1} \tag{12a}$$
$$y_{t+1} = y_t - ax_{t+1}y_{t+1} + x_{t+1} \tag{12b}$$

Equation 12b shows that y is the operator in Equation 12a. In Equation 12b, y—that is, the grouping of isolated persons—operates upon both its previous and its present state at the same time. Without a further assumption of anticipation in the interaction term xy (to be discussed in the next section B), the development of x_t would therefore remain unchanged (i.e., as in Equation 9b):

$$(x_{t+1} - x_t) = +ax_ty_t - x_t \tag{9b}$$
$$x_{t+1} = ax_ty_t \tag{9b'}$$

Because of the anticipation in y, however, y_t in the model of Equation 12b relates y_{t+1} not to x_t, but to the next state of x_{t+1}, and therefore:

$$y_t + x_{t+1} = \text{Constant} = 1$$
$$y_t = 1 - x_{t+1} \tag{13}$$

By putting Equation 13 into 12b, one obtains:

$$x_{t+1} = ax_t (1 - x_{t+1}) \tag{14}$$

Q.e.d.

B. Proof for anticipation in the interaction between x and y

Let us now assume, alternatively, that the interaction term between x and y contains the source of anticipation. In this case, anticipation affects both equations 9a and 9b as follows:

$$y_{t+1} = y_t - ax_ty_{t+1} + x_t \tag{15a}$$
$$x_{t+1} = x_t + ax_ty_{t+1} - x_t = ax_ty_{t+1} \tag{15b}$$

For analytical reasons, one can also write the interaction term itself as a difference equation in relation to its previous state, as follows:

$$x_ty_{t+1} = x_ty_t + x_t (y_{t+1} - y_t) \tag{16}$$

Or after division on both sides by x_t:

$$y_{t+1} = y_t + (y_{t+1} - y_t) \tag{17}$$

In other words, the anticipatory interaction depends exclusively on a supplementary factor given by the derivative of y.[39] However, x was already implied in the anticipation specified in Equation 15b. While in the previous model only y was implied in the anticipation, in this model both terms are implied and therefore:

$$y_{t+1} + x_{t+1} = \text{Constant} = 1$$

and therefore:

$$y_{t+1} = 1 - x_{t+1} \tag{18}$$

By replacing Equation 18 into Equation 15b, one obtains again:

$$x_{t+1} = ax_t (1 - x_{t+1}) \tag{19}$$

Q.e.d.

4.6.3 *Summary and conclusion*

The introduction of anticipation into a basic model of the social system can be shown to lead to the anticipatory formulation of the logistic equation. The model was derived from assumptions about the two possible contingencies between subpopulations, namely aggregative grouping and interaction (Parsons, 1968). In both situations the growth of a system of expectations is not constrained by a feedback from the past, but by an expectation that feeds back as a constraint in the present $(1 - x_{t+1})$, while it develops historically in relation to its previous state.

---

[39] The third option of adding also anticipation in terms of the x of the interaction would lead to the following equivalent of equation 15b:

$$x_{t+1} = ax_{t+1}y_{t+1} \text{ and therefore } y = 1/a$$

Since $x + y = 1$, then also $x = (a-1)/a$. This system cannot evolve because the values of x and y are constant. A possible interpretation is that anticipation on the interaction in the already related group (x) closes this group, and the social system consequently would become segmented.

The substantive example provided above was that one would expect a market to feedback on the growth of a technology in the present. Thus, this anticipation at each moment in time is not only derived on mathematical grounds, but was also appreciated as a meaningful operation of the social system. This intuitive appreciation can be formalized. In other words, the theoretical *and* methodological 'programs' can be recombined into the inference that the social system operates in terms of representations which can be modeled using the anticipatory formulation of the logistic equation.

4.7 Differentiation at each moment and different clocks

The appreciation of anticipation at the *sub*systemic level is further improved by using the anticipatory formulation of the logistic model because the feedback term is then no longer defined in terms of the other subsystems (s^j ..... s^n) as in Equation 7 above, but the anticipated representation of the selecting subsystem operates *within* each subsystem. The subsystems develop substantively—that is, in terms of whatever they communicate specifically—in relation to their previous states (x_t), but this development is reflected in a second process that contains a future-oriented representation of the options and constraints of the respective subsystem in the next stage ($1 - x_{t+1}$). The subsystem is provided with a representation of these selection environments (that is, other subsystems) by using its own code. This internal representation feeds back as a selection mechanism on the variation generated historically.

Although Rosen's model was originally developed for understanding control in hierarchically organized systems (Luhmann, 1997a, at p. 206n.), it can thus be provided with another interpretation if the system S is differentiated into subsystems (s_i, ..., s_n). Functionally differentiated systems are not synchronized *ex ante*, but *ex post*, that is, by their interaction. Thus, the subsystems potentially can differ with a Δt, and this time difference can be used by the system as a structural form of anticipation. Additionally, the processing of meaning can be considered as an anticipation over time.

Note that meaning processing as discussed in Chapter Three did not yet require functional differentiation. Meaning processing can be defined at the level of general systems theory in terms of the update of systems (Chapter Two). For example, a single mind can also be expected to exhibit anticipation, albeit 'weak' anticipation. However, a social system is able to use *two* forms of anticipation. When these two forms of anticipation can be brought into resonance, an eigendynamic or self-organization can be developed in an anticipatory layer of the system or, in other words, a knowledge base can be generated endogenously.

So long as the social system is *not yet* differentiated, the feedback at the system-environment distinction can come only from the environment of the system. However, the system would have no access to its environment other than in terms of its previous, that is, historical, experiences. This coupling of a system with its environment can be considered as the evolutionary mechanism of *structural coupling* (Maturana, 1978). In a differentiated system, however, subsystems already belong structurally to the same system. The system gains one degree of freedom when developing from the stage of being organized as a hierarchy towards self-organization in terms of subsystems that are juxtaposed to each other. Maturana (1978, at p. 49) expressed this emergence of a new degree of freedom when he formulated that 'an observer is operationally generated' when 'the relations become perturbations and component for further consensual behavior.'

In other words, the subsystems operate in parallel and synchronize in terms of their interactions (*ex post*). This *coupling* can be made functional to the reproduction.[40] Since all subsystems are expected to update periodically by using their specific codes, one can expect cycles with different frequencies to emerge from these couplings. (A stronger codification can be expected to lead to a longer cycle.) Without anticipation over the time axis, such a system would tend towards chaos when more than two subdynamics are involved (Schumpeter, [1939] 1964, at pp. 174f; Li and Yorke, 1975). Anticipation, however, functions as a filter on the chaos or, equivalently, as another selection mechanism.

---

[40] Schmitt (2002, at p. 34) has argued that different systems cannot be operationally coupled because then they would not be able to distinguish themselves in terms of their operations. In accordance with Luhmann's theory, he maintains that systems can be coupled structurally, but they remain operationally closed. However, it follows from the reasoning above that the relation system/environment changes when the system of reference is functionally differentiated into subsystems. Functionally differentiated subsystems are both operationally closed and dependent upon one another, for example, with reference to the reproduction of the next-order system. The operational closure in this case can be considered as a tendency that allows for the processing of more complexity at the systems level. However, the subsystems also communicate in terms of providing functions for each other (Luhmann, 1990, at pp. 635 ff.). According to Equation 7, a subsystem relates to itself and to other subsystems of the same system as its relevant environments. Thus, this form of coupling is (one order) more complex than in the case of structural coupling. Elsewhere (Leydesdorff, 1994a, 2001b), I have distinguished among structural, operational, and loose coupling in terms of the number of interfaces involved.

4.8 The social system as a strongly anticipatory system

When an anticipatory and a historical subdynamics (that is, a modeling system and a system to be modeled) co-evolve as in a process of mutual shaping, this may imply relational hierarchization. Thus, a control system is first shaped on the basis of meaning-processing as in a process of mutual shaping between the represented and the representing system. However, if the represented system is differentiated, more than two subdynamics can interact and this changes the evolutionary dynamics. In addition to mutual relations, the three subdynamics can be expected to develop positions in their relations among one another (Burt, 1982). When three subdynamics are involved, the mutual information in three dimensions (that is, the probabilistic entropy generated in the relations) can under certain conditions become negative (McGill, 1954; Abramson, 1963, at pp. 129f). In the empirical chapters of this study (that is, Chapters 7-10), I return to the development of this negative entropy as an indicator of self-organization and emerging order in knowledge-based systems.

Emerging order is based on synchronization among the subdynamics at specific moments in time *and* on reflexive anticipation along the time axis within each of the subsystems. The reflexive operation over the time axis precedes the functional differentiation (because it is already present in a hierarchically organized system), but the anticipation is modified when the system is increasingly differentiated. However, the functionally differentiated system would tend to disintegrate without the reflexive operation along the time axis. Therefore, the reflexive anticipation precedes the synchronization among differently coded subsystems. Functionally differentiated subsystems not only communicate horizontally in terms of functions (Luhmann, 1990a, at pp. 635 ff.), but always also along the time axis in terms of the frequencies of the updates. Thus, a multivariate model of the complex system is never sufficient for the modeling. One needs a calculus which allows for a variety of system clocks that disturb one another along the time dimension (Leydesdorff, 1994c).

The formulas derived above were originally developed in studies of the spread of infectious diseases in populations (Dubois and Sabatier, 1998). How does the processing of meaning as a reflexive dimension of the exchange add to these meta-biological models? Changes in belief systems (e.g., paradigms) have previously been modeled in terms of epidemics (e.g., Sterman, 1985, 1999), but a meta-biological model would not yet sufficiently appreciate the complexity caused by the reflexivity in inter-human communication (Leydesdorff, 2000d; Luhmann, 1997a, at p. 206n.). I shall now proceed by specifying how the reflexive operation of inter-human communication systems along the time axis adds analytically to the structural anticipatory mechanism which is a consequence of the functional differentiation of the social system.

The two anticipatory mechanisms—that is, the one based on functional differentiation at each moment of time and the other based on reflexivity along the time axis—can be expected to co-evolve at the level of the social system. After an initial phase (of segmentation), some selections can be made for the stabilization of a culture in meaning processing, as distinct from the natural processing of information (with the time axis). The stratified high culture that then emerges cannot yet exploit the anticipatory mechanism of functional differentiation. Both functional differentiation and reflexivity are preconditions for the development of a strongly anticipatory system.

The recombination of the two mechanisms can make the anticipation so strong that a knowledge base is further developed. If this knowledge base is not only stabilized but also globalized, the social system can increasingly be reconstructed in terms of a techno-economic evolution (Leydesdorff, 2002b). Without any reflexive recombination, however, disorder would be expected to prevail in an increasingly differentiated system. The transition from an organized and integrated high culture to a self-organizing regime that recombines both spatially and over the time dimension in an evolutionary mode can be expected to develop on the edge of chaos. The knowledge-based innovations counteract the crises which remain pending (Freeman and Perez, 1988).

The functional differentiation provided us with a time-difference because of the asynchronicity prevailing between subsystems operating in parallel at each moment in time. Meaning, however, is provided with hindsight, that is, over the time axis, in *all* systems and subsystems that process meaning. When meaning is generated in a differentiated mode (that is, under the condition of functional differentiation), it operates in all these subsystems by using a time axis orthogonally to the structural differences in codification between and among the subsystems. Meaning processing in the social system is affected by the differentiation, because meaning is codified differently in the various subsystems. The clocks tick with a spectrum of different frequencies. While the processes in the different subsystems are formally analogous because the generation and processing of meaning are systems operations,[41] the

---

[41] Meaning can be specified at the level of general systems theory; information can be defined mathematically, that is, without reference to a system (see Chapter Two).

differentiations break the symmetries and the synchronicity. This generates another degree of freedom.

For example, in the empirical studies (Chapters 7-10) I shall distinguish between the bilateral relations between systems and the trilateral relations among more than two systems when using the Triple Helix model. While bilateral relations can co-evolve along a trajectory, three (sub)systems can be expected to generate a complex relationship including a next-order (hypercyclic) development. The interaction between the two anticipatory mechanisms (the structural one and the temporal one) can transform the system from a weakly anticipatory system into a strongly anticipatory one operating historically, that is, along a trajectory. When the substantive dimension is added as a constraint, one can distinguish between stabilization meta-stabilization, and globalization, and a knowledge-based regime can also be induced.

4.9 Expectations as the substance of social systems

Social systems reconstruct reality in terms of meaning that is provided to the system (Bhaskar, 1997, 1998). While information is processed historically, that is, following the time axis, meaning is provided to the information exchange from the perspective of hindsight (*a posteriori*). The interaction between these two layers can be expected to produce meaningful information: not all information is meaningful, and not all meaning is communicated. However, the two processes are structurally coupled when meaningful information is generated (Figures 4 and 5).

Meaning processing adds an evolutionary feedback mechanism to the system that inverts the time axis locally. This structural coupling produces a co-variation at each moment of time and potentially a co-evolution over time. [42] The historical configurations of social systems change in a forward mode in terms of processing both uncertainty and meaningful information (Georgescu-Roegen, 1971; Theil, 1972). [43] However, information processing (including the exchange of meaningful information) is subject to reflections *ex post* within these systems and among them.

---

[42] In information-theoretical terms one can consider the covariation also as the mutual information between the two subdynamics. The shaping of a co-evolution can be assessed using the so-called Markov property as a test (Leydesdorff, 1995a).

[43] It can be shown mathematically that the Second Law is equally valid for probabilistic entropy (Theil, 1972, at pp. 59f.).

Meaning processing reduces the uncertainty contained in the distributions of first-order networks locally.

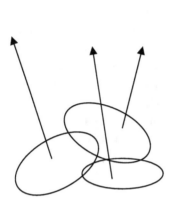
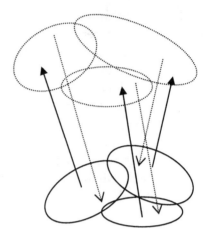

Figure 4.4: Information processing differentiates with the axis of time

Figure 4.5: Meaning processing incurs on information processing locally, i.e., system-specific

The operation of generating meaning is not dependent on the systems *level*: incursion can take place with reference to all levels and across subsystems. Meaning generation only assumes the historical stability of an axis along which the incoming (Shannon-type) information can be appreciated. This axis can be stabilized either at the systems level, as a hierarchical control mechanism, or at the level of differentiated subsystems, as specific codes that control the respective subdynamics. In other words: whether or not a codification is differentiated does not yet affect the mechanism of meaning production *per se*. A hierarchically organized system processes meaning for its integration. In the differentiated case, however, the anticipatory mechanism contained in meaning production over time may begin to interact with the anticipatory mechanism contained in the differentiation at each moment of time.

When different anticipatory mechanisms interact, meaning is not only generated but also positioned among subsystems. This positioning is specified in Luhmann's theory as codification according to the function of the subsystem. Meaning processing over time enables us additionally to reposition the information across interfaces. As noted, these interfaces can be expected to contain another time difference. The continuous interaction among the anticipations potentially globalizes meaning processing beyond the stabilizations that could provisionally be shaped locally as borderlines between (sub)systems and environments. Hence, the previously stabilized borderlines can be expected to develop into interfaces which function for the next-order or globalized systems of expectations. The borderlines themselves can then be changed within the system because of the reflexive character of expectations (and their interaction terms).

Providing information with meaning can be considered as a selective operation because the noise is discarded. Thus, meaning processing structures information processing. Meaning processing continuously reflects on the systems of information processing under observation, but in an evolutionary (that is, with hindsight) mode. The two processes of meaning and information processing can be considered 'structurally coupled' within the social system: at the level of the social system, the anticipatory processes cannot operate without the historical one which anchors these processes in information processing. At the interface, meaningful information is generated as part of the information processing on the historical side. This probabilistic entropy generates an axis of time and drives the system in a forward mode.[44]

Meaning can be further refined into knowledge on the side of meaning processing because meaning processing uses and generates codes in the communication. The higher-order codifications can be expected to feed back on the lower-order ones. Whereas *biological* systems can provide meaning to information, they cannot exchange the meanings thus generated among themselves because they cannot be expected to develop meaning into codified meaning or discursive knowledge that can be exchanged. Thus, they are able to retain (that is, to reproduce) a first-order codification in the hardware, but not to process a second-order one of providing meaning with specified (that is, knowledge-based) meaning. Maturana (1978), for example, carefully distinguished between the generation of observers within the networks and super-observers who are able to use the language of biology as a science for studying biological processes.

The *psychological* system is expected not only to process meaning, but also to generate identity. Thus, the anticipation is towards control at a center. Unlike the social system—which remains distributed by definition—the dynamics at the level of the individual identity can under certain conditions become historically fixed. Only the

---

[44] The linear definition of time can be contrasted with the Greek definition of time as cyclical (Heidegger, 1962). In the modern perspective, the cycles are considered as contained within a forward movement of time.

social system—Luhmann sometimes used the word 'dividuum' as against 'individuum'—can entertain all these degrees of freedom at the same time. Globalization of meaning can be realized historically when the processing of meaning is not only variable but also differentiated in terms of the codes of the communication.

The next-order knowledge base in a social system enables us to distinguish the various meanings analytically, but the different meanings remain interactive at the same time. The social system is both hyper-reflexive and infra-reflexive (Ashmore, 1989; Latour, 1988). At the level of the social system, next-order operations cannot be completely uncoupled from lower-order ones because the system and its subsystems remain historical expectations. They occur in interactions among people. However, partial uncouplings from the regime in trajectories can be tolerated for relatively long periods of time because of the decentralization at the global level. Thus, these knowledge-based systems operate by including and excluding lower-level carriers of the communication (Luhmann, 1997b; Leydesdorff, 1997b).

In other words, reflections at the level of the social system provide us not only with mirror images, but the angles and foci are also developing dynamically. Under the condition of functional differentiation, one would expect variously codified perspectives. The more orthogonal the discursive perspectives are, the more complexity can be processed. When the various reflections can again be communicated, they can be built recursively into the historical (that is, forward) development of the social system in terms of interaction terms. The advantages can then be retained and the system can become structurally more knowledge-intensive. By operating upon each other, some meanings can be privileged as 'knowledge' at the subsystems level. Knowledge can be considered as a meaning that makes a difference.

For example, within the science system one would expect the development of discursive knowledge with a dynamics different from idea generation and knowledge-based intuitions at the actor level. However, subsystems other than science can also be expected to contain second-order codifications (albeit in orthogonal directions). For example, the economy can develop price/performance comparisons as a codification more complex than the price mechanism. Performance comparisons can be considered as an economic assessment of the technological state of the market in terms other than prices.

Markets of commodities can further be developed into capital markets and then also stock exchanges. These markets build on these symbolic generalizations by codifying the exchange media in the lower-order markets. For example, one needs the relative stabilization of currencies for capital market and the further development of credit for stock exchanges. All these media can be interfaced recursively, but the globalizing system fails to be integrated. It remains fragile, and subject to internal pressures for change.

4.10 The algorithmic turn

In the next chapter I will specify how the various couplings and possible uncouplings lead to Luhmann's theoretical model of systems differentiation in three layers—interaction, organization, and society—under the condition of functional differentiation into subsystems which contain different codes. The level of organization is crucial for the understanding of how the institutional and the functional subdynamics couple (Luhmann, 1997a, 2000; Baecker, 2003).

'Organization' in institutional domains means something different from organization in the dimension of the communication, because these two (sub)systems of reference are different. While an institutional shape can be considered a manifest form of organization, the organization of communication remains a latent expectation of structure. In some sociological theorizing, this duality of organization has already been reflected by distinguishing the field level from the group level. For example, Whitley's (1984) sociology of science was entitled *The Intellectual and the Social Organization of the Sciences*. While the social organization can be observed in terms of institutions like professional organizations and departments, the intellectual dimension is organized at a next-order level in terms of scientific expectations (Gilbert and Mulkay, 1984; Leydesdorff, 1995a).

The operation of (temporal) codification on the structural differentiation—it does not really matter for the formal model which dimension is first—can be considered as knowledge generation within the system because it is based on using standards for the selection of meaning from among possible meanings. Thus, a higher-order dynamics of self-organization can be shaped increasingly within a system of previously stabilized meaning processing. Meaning processing at the individual level provides the resources from which this system 'lives,' but—as Luhmann (1986a) noted—the social system is not alive. Both the aggregate of the individual contributions (e.g., knowledge claims) and the interaction terms are important for its further development towards a system of knowledge-based expectations.

The continuous filtering of noise both between the subsystems and over time provides us with a cultural level of anticipation as a strong—and even hyperselective (Bruckner *et al.*, 1994)—filter on chaotic developments because the system reconstructs itself not in an adaptive mode, but in an anticipatory mode. Thus, social order can be constructed as an expectation and is no longer a subject only of engineering the relevant institutions (Callon and Latour, 1981; cf. Hobbes, 1651). The knowledge-based filters, however, remain fragile and fragmented, since socially constructed.[45] The reconstruction of the system, for example, in terms of new technologies, can be expected to remain failure-prone. Technologies break down in an unorganized way.

The meanings provided in the relevant discourses can be further informed when new knowledge becomes available. One expects periodical reconstructions of the various meanings and their codifications.[46] Discursive theories provide us with codifications of the meanings operating in the systems under study, but the reflected systems are expected to develop further at the same time as the reflecting ones. Under the condition of functional differentiation, the generation and processing of meaning in scientific discourses have thus proliferated exponentially (Price, 1961). Because of the recursions and incursions implied, the dissipation of these meanings can be expected to transform society and its subsystems at an increasing speed.

The study of second-order communications, which develop as fluxes at the network level on top of the instantiations that have developed historically, requires an algorithmic turn. The patterns of communications can be observed, but not their further development. This algorithmic turn can add reflexivity to the substantiveness of sociological theorizing. When the system processes both self-fulfilling and self-denying expectations, the counter-intuitive results enable us also to improve the knowledge base, but this process cannot be controlled as by an

---

[45] All derivatives from 'esse' (to be; e.g., ontology) should perhaps be replaced with derivatives from 'frangere' (that is, 'to break;' cf. Leydesdorff, 1997b; Stewart and Cohen, 1997).

[46] From an historical perspective (that is, with the arrow of time) one would consider this instability as a destabilization, but from an evolutionary perspective (that is, with hindsight) it can be considered as a meta-stabilization because a degree of freedom is gained in the bifurcation. Initially, the bifurcation is fixed as an oscillation, but when the frequency interacts with other bifurcations in a complex system, a more complex dynamics (including the generation of negative entropy in the mutual relations in three or more dimensions) can be expected. Thus, the degree of freedom in the meta-stabilization can be used by a system for its globalization.

individual at the top of a hierarchy (Beck, 1992a; Fukuyama, 2002). The knowledge base of social systems is therefore increasingly self-organizing, that is, beyond the control of any of the subsystems (Leydesdorff, 2001b; Beck *et al.*, 2003). The fluxes of the events are carried by structures which were shaped historically. However, the fluxes contain anticipations as also different from historical manifestations.

Luhmann's program of social systems theory can also be considered as an expression of this algorithmic experience in systems research. For example, as he formulated it in an essay entitled 'The Modernity of Science':

> Knowledge serves—as does, in a different way, art—to render the world invisible as the "unmarked state," a state that forms can only violate, not represent. Any other attempt must be content with paradoxical or tautological descriptions (which is meaningful as well).
> [...] The soundness of this reflection, however, arises—and this can still be ascertained by this reflection—from a form of social differentiation that no longer allows for any binding, authorative representation of the world in the world or of society within society. (Luhmann, 2002b, at pp. 74f.)

Sociological categories refer to expectations and not to facts with an ontological status. Provisional stabilizations by discursive theorizing, however, remain necessary because they reduce an otherwise overwhelming uncertainty. They are based on reducing the algorithmic complexity to the stability of a geometry that can be represented using language instead of computer code (Luhmann, 1997a, at pp. 205 ff). However, the meaning processing from different perspectives can further be codified in terms of potentially incommensurable paradigms (Kuhn, 1962; Leydesdorff, 1994b, 2001b). From an algorithmic perspective, the various forms of discursive theorizing reduce the uncertainty only as different heuristics along the time axis. While the geometric metaphors reduce the complex dynamics under study by one degree of freedom, each of these selections makes it possible to formulate a perspective and then also a research design.

The corresponding reduction of complexity can be reflected in the simulation model as the proposal for one or more equations. Without these equations the phase space of the simulation cannot be specified. The equations provide us with the relevant dimensions—potentially different in the various equations—and their relations, and therefore they enable us to hypothesize that certain states and transitions are more likely than others. When nevertheless these unlikely events happen to occur within a subsequent run of the simulation, then one's theoretical assumptions may have to be revised. The distinction between true/false has thus been put to the test. However, a single test is no longer decisive; it only generates a puzzle.

Given the constructed nature of the setting in a sociological discourse, the results can always be appreciated from different perspectives. One can change either the interpretation or the codification. Human languages provide us with interpretative flexibilities in providing meaning to information (Hesse, 1984; Leydesdorff, 1997c). One can try to improve the estimates of the parameters in simulations on the basis of the assumption that the underlying theories are not in need of revision, or one can specify empirical research for improving the substantive theories. Both are needed, and both can be guided by previous theorizing, but the various perspectives stand orthogonal and hence one can claim no epistemological priority among these research perspectives. They stand orthogonally since the perspective of the simulation abstracts from the substantive variations, while the latter are the subject of positive theories.

This methodological perspective of the algorithmic approach enables us to move beyond Luhmann in terms of the philosophy of science. While Luhmann insisted on the binary character of the code (e.g., true/false), the methodologist also entertains notions like 'unlikely' or 'less probably true.' The distinction true/false can be considered as epistemological because the movement from 'less' to 'more true' statements in research efforts presumes this distinction as a next-order standard. From an algorithmic perspective, one can use such observations for the specification of an expectation, but one can no longer warrant an unambiguous identification. All inferences remain statistical (that is, uncertain) and identification requires substantive theorizing. The system of representations loops through the next order of testing before anything can be identified as an outcome. The two programs of theorizing and developing methodologies distinguished above are both needed for the specification of knowledge-based systems.[47] The knowledge base itself, however, can be expected to remain an order of expectations.

---

[47] For example, when designing an airplane, one has to tinker endlessly with degrees of freedom in possible designs (Frenken, 2000; Frenken and Leydesdorff, 2000). The computer model appreciates the current state as only one among a variety of possible states. But one is not able to jump from one to another attractor without historically developing the trajectory for the transition.

Chapter 5

The Transformation of Organization and Agency

In the previous chapters I have argued that an evolutionary mechanism of change can be distinguished from a historical one because of the inversion of the time axis in the modeling within and by an anticipatory system. However, my argument has hitherto been analytical and not yet elaborated in terms of the observable consequences. In this chapter, some observable consequences of distinguishing between the two subdynamics of historical recursion and evolutionary incursion will be specified. I shall argue that the evolution of a knowledge-based system cannot be understood without paying attention to its incursive dynamics.

As systems become increasingly knowledge-based, the balance between the incursive and the recursive subdynamics can be expected to change. A bifurcation in the mode of operation within the system can be a consequence. Because the dynamics change after such a transition, organization and action have functions in a knowledge-based system that are different from the previous stage of development. While in the recursive system organization and action can be considered as integrating mechanisms, the incursive dynamics brings the function of reproducing the differentiation to the fore. Action and organization can thus be provided with a different meaning.

From the evolutionary perspective, the historical dynamics provides the variation. Evolution restructures history because selection operates from the perspective of hindsight. The evolutionary mechanism can be considered as a feedback on the historical mechanism. Reflexive systems are additionally able to entertain different representations of their histories and sometimes to make selections among these reflections. When the selection mechanisms are also at variance, the selections can be optimized under given environmental constraints. Thus, the anticipatory system is endogenously informed about its conditions by entertaining a model of itself in which different selection environments are distinguished.

This reflexive mechanism is further reinforced when the meaning of a representation can also be communicated within the system. In a strongly anticipatory system the model, no longer only anticipates on the conditions but has this additional degree of freedom available for the representation of its conditions. At this level, the meaning can be varied and some meanings can further be codified into knowledge. Codified knowledge can again be communicated as discursive knowledge. The knowledge base of the social system thus increasingly provides discursive (that is, scientific) knowledge as a resource at the supra-individual level for restructuring the system in a techno-economic co-evolution.

Because the representations are entertained and interfaced *within* the history of the system, these communications and the reconstructions based upon them become part of the history of the system at a next moment of time. Thus, the social order is gradually transformed, but only the footprints of these changes can be traced historically. The communication of meaning adds continuously meaningful information to the information layer upon which the system rests. Meaningful information can be stabilized recursively, for example, in organization and institutions. The two layers—of expectations and institutions—are both organized, but in different terms. While the institutions provide local (quasi-)equilibria, the expectations induce a non-equilibrium dynamics by using these historical equilibria as footholds.

In a first approximation, one can consider the organization of the social system by using the metaphors available for studying biological organization. The social system is then externalized as a subject under study. One observes agents solving the puzzles of their lifecycles within it by organizing their preferences in social relations. Such agents following their 'natural preferences' have been the subject of most economic theorizing. As preferences are further informed, however, they can evolve into decisions and become organized knowledge. The layer of expectations is organized by the codification of meaning on top of the organization of information by agents and in institutions; the institutions and agents are entrained in a cultural evolution. The expectations provide an evolutionary feedback on the carriers that restructures them in the longer run because more efficient equilibria (puzzle solutions) can be invented. This invention of new solutions can be reinforced by organizing knowledge. The communicative competencies of agents and organizations, that is, their learning capacities, can be expected to change with the evolution of these social coordination mechanisms (Leydesdorff, 1997b; 2000d).

The tension between the institutional arrangements in the knowledge infrastructure and the overlay of expectations or knowledge base has been central to the theoretical specification in the first two chapters of this study. In Chapter Three, the formal model of anticipation was specified. In the previous chapter, social differentiation was further elaborated as another domain for puzzle-solving and therefore potential anticipation. In this chapter, the focus is on the interaction between the two differentiations, that is, the horizontal one between differently codified systems and the vertical one between different layers. I shall argue that organizations provide the interfaces between the layers and the functions.

Luhmann (1964, 1978b, 2000) conjectured that organizations function specifically on the basis of decisions. I shall first show mathematically that the strongly anticipatory system needs choices and decisions in order to move the system forward historically along a trajectory. The trajectory is historically specific in a phase space of other possible organizations of expectations. When expectations can operate upon differently codified operations—because of functional differentiation among the various expectations—too many options are available for historical processing. The system tends then to lose its grounding without *organization* as a third context. The communicative competencies of organizations—that is, the quality of decisions by actors and institutional agents—become rate-limiting to the capacity of the system to process complexity. In the next chapter, I return to the historical appreciation of these dynamics, but first I focus on the specification of the evolutionary dynamics in formal terms because this specification forces me to be parsimonious. The program of studies, however, is still to combine the mathematical reasoning and the theoretical interpretation in order to specify the dynamics of the knowledge base of social systems.

5.1   Hyper-incursion and the requirement of decisions

How can one model the operation of a meaning (x_1) upon a differently codified meaning (x_2) at an interface? In Chapter Four, I argued that the operation of two differently codified incursions upon each other may lead to lock-in and the consequent stabilization along a trajectory. Let us try to formalize this. This formalization will enable me to distinguish between stabilization in a co-evolution between two subdynamics and the possibility of globalization in the case of three subdynamics.

In the case of the logistic equation (Chapter Three), selection is represented by the feedback term, that is, by $(1 - x)$. For populations which compete, one can generalize the logistic equation to the so-called Lotka-Volterra equation in which competition coefficients (α) are added to the selection mechanisms (May, 1973; May and Leonard, 1975; Sonis, 1992, 2000; Reggiani and Nijkamp, 1994, at p. 98). In both the logistic equation and the Lotka-Volterra equation, selection is represented by the feedback term ($k - \alpha x$, in the case of Lotka-Volterra) or assuming unity of the parameters and without loss of generality: $(1 - x)$. Two selections operating on a technological variation v (v is modeled in the logistic equation as the other factor in the equation: αx_i) result in a quadratic expression for the resulting selection environment of the following form:

$$x_{t+1} \quad = v (1 - x_t)(1 - x_t)$$
$$= v (x_t^2 - 2 x_t + 1) \tag{1}$$

This selection environment no longer operates as a homogeneous field. The function can be represented as in Figure 1a (on the left side): a system with two selections can be stabilized at the minimum of the quadratic curve. When this minimum is extended along the time dimension, a valley is shaped in which the system develops along a trajectory (Sahal, 1985; Waddington, 1957).

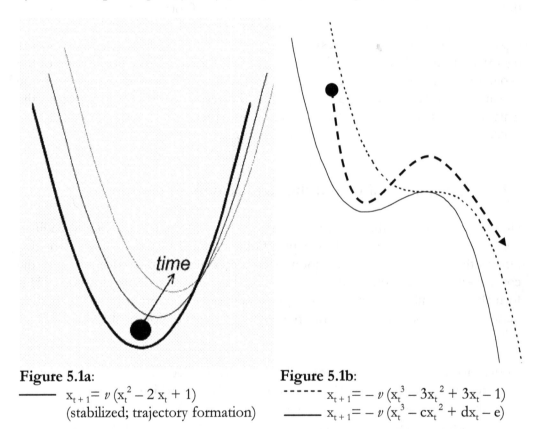

Figure 5.1a:
——— $x_{t+1} = v (x_t^2 - 2 x_t + 1)$
(stabilized; trajectory formation)

Figure 5.1b:
- - - - $x_{t+1} = -v (x_t^3 - 3x_t^2 + 3x_t - 1)$
——— $x_{t+1} = -v (x_t^3 - cx_t^2 + dx_t - e)$

Adding one more selection term leads analogously to the following equation:

$$x_{t+1} \quad = v (1 - x_t)(1 - x_t)(1 - x_t)$$
$$= -v (x_t^3 - 3 x_t^2 + 3 x_t - 1) \tag{2}$$

This latter function is represented as the dotted line in Figure 1b. As long as the different selection mechanisms operate synchronously on a single variation with the same parameters (a; α), the global and the stable points of inflection coincide in a so-called "saddle point." The historically stabilized system can then be identical with the global one. In Nelson and Winter's evolutionary theory of economics, such a meta-selection mechanisms upon previous stabilizations can be considered as a "natural trajectory" (Nelson & Winter, 1997, at p. 57; 1982, at pp. 258f.; Leydesdorff, 2006d). In a later section, I shall consider such a harmonized system more generally as the model of a sustainable identity.

Figure 1b shows as the drawn line the configuration resulting when stabilization and globalization are no longer selecting with the same parameter values. In this (more general) case one expects the curve to show both a minimum and a maximum. At the minimum the system is stabilized, but at the maximum it can be considered as meta-stable. A bifurcation is induced because the system can either go backward (to the stabilization along a trajectory) or forward (to globalization into a regime). As long as the system remains stable (that is, at the minimum), it can develop along a trajectory. However, the flux attracts the system towards the other basin.

Beyond the meta-stable point a global regime prevails. Stabilization can thus be considered as a result of integration by organization, while global differentiation among the self-organizing fluxes prevails at the systems level. However, the distinction between these two subdynamics remains analytical; in the social system they can be expected to concur at potentially different rates. The interactions between these subdynamics make the system complex and result in the expectation of continuous transitions between provisional (that is, local) stabilizations and globalizations at the systems level.

While the above mechanism explains how a regime can be formed from a trajectory, that is, by losing a fixed synchronization mechanism among subdynamics over time, it does not yet show how such a system would be able to return temporarily to a trajectory when in the regime phase. This mechanism would have to reduce the uncertainty (against the arrow of time) and thus to self-organize the system endogenously, that is, by using another subdynamic. In order to invert the time axis, an anticipatory model is required. In Chapter Four, I showed that differentiation can add this other degree of freedom so that a *strongly* anticipatory system is able to operate by organizing its self-organization. This corresponds with the quadrant in the bottom right of Table 5.1.

A differentiated system can be expected to contain more than a single subdynamic, so that the system can be both globalizing and stabilizing at the same time. It was proven above (in Chapter Four) that both incursive subdynamics are to be modeled at the level of the social system using the anticipatory formulation of the logistic equation: $x_t = a x_{t-1} (1 - x_t)$. An incursive subdynamic contains a reference to its previous state of the respective system x_{t-1} and a reference to its selection in the present state. The reference to the previous state anchors the system in its history.

two subdynamics A and B operating upon each other	*A recursive*	*A incursive*
B recursive	Co-evolution between A and B; stabilization by mutual shaping; emerging organization (e.g., firms)	Organization A (e.g., the economy) provides the basis for Self-Organization
B incursive	Organization B (e.g., science) provides the basis for Self-Organization	Self-Organization provides the basis for Organization (globalization)

Table 5.1: Two functionally differentiated subdynamics of the social system (A and B) can operate upon each other both with the axis of time and against the time axis.

When two anticipatory mechanisms operate upon each other, these subdynamics can first be expected to alternate in terms of generating variation and providing a selection mechanism for each other over time. Both options (recursive and incursive routines) are continuously available. Thus, a recursive subdynamic can become an incursive one at a next moment in time, and *vice versa*. The interaction among the subsystems of the social system can be sustained because these subdynamics remain part of the same system. In the fourth box this generates the option of an interaction between the two anticipatory subdynamics in which one anticipation operates upon the anticipation in the other without needing to refer to a historical configuration at each pass. Such a system would become hyper-incursive (Dubois and Resconi, 1992). Using the same logistic equation, hyper-incursivity can be modeled as follows:

$$x_t = a x_{t+1} (1 - x_{t+1}) \tag{3}$$

This system no longer contains a historical reference to its previous state x_{t-1} (at $t = t$), but the emerging state is a function of different expectations about the future operating upon each other in the present.[48] It may seem difficult at first to provide

---

[48] There are two additional formulas which merit investigation:

$$x_t = a x_t (1 - x_{t+1}) \tag{3a}$$
$$x_t = a x_{t+1} (1 - x_t) \tag{3b}$$

continued >

this non-historical configuration with a sociological interpretation. However, it is not uncommon to specify different expectations into a scenario or a strategic plan without an immediate reference to the historical situation. For example, a national government may combine expectations about the development of the economy with political expectations about desirable outcomes and thus shape an economic policy. In strategic management, technological options are interfaced with market opportunities. The two types of expectations are differently codified, but can be recombined by making decisions. The decisions reduce the uncertainty in a historical configuration. They add a third subdynamic to the emerging interface which, without this elaboration, would remain only a representation.

In the case of interfacing two incursive dynamics, the historical moment for making a decision follows operationally after the specification of the expectations at a strategic level (Chandler, 1962; Galbraith and Nathanson, 1978). Let me show how this same conclusion was derived formally by Dubois (2003).

Equation 3 can be rewritten as follows:

$$x_t = ax_{t+1}(1 - x_{t+1}) \tag{3}$$
$$x_t = ax_{t+1} - ax_{t+1}^2$$
$$ax_{t+1}^2 - ax_{t+1} + x_t = 0$$
$$x_{t+1}^2 - x_{t+1} + (x_t/a) = 0 \tag{4}$$

For $a = 4$, x_{t+1} is defined as a function of x_t as follows:

$$x_{t+1} = \frac{1}{2} \pm \frac{1}{2}\sqrt{(1 - x_t)} \tag{5}$$

Depending on the plus or the minus sign in the equation, two future states are thus generated at each time step. Since this formula is iterative, the number of future

---

• Equation 3a evolves into $x = (a - 1)/a =$ Constant. I submit that this evolution towards a constant through anticipation can be considered in modeling the self-reference of an (individual) identity.
• Equation 3b evolves into $x_{t+1} = (1/a)\{x_t / (1 - x_t)\}$ Since the latter term approaches -1 as its limit value and the former term is a constant $(1/a)$, this representation can alternate between itself and its mirror image. This subdynamic thus formalizes the reflexive operation.

Both these dynamics (that is, Equations 3a and 3b) can be expected to play a role in social systems. I return to these formulas in the final chapter (Chapter Eleven).

states doubles with each next time step. After N time steps, 2^N future states would be possible. For $N = 10$, the number of options is larger than one thousand. Dubois (2003, at pp. 114f.) specified the consequences of this uncertainty as follows:

> This system is unpredictable in the sense that it is not possible to compute its future states in knowing the initial conditions. It is necessary to define successive final conditions at each time step. As the system can only take one value at each time step, something new must be added for resolving the problem. Thus, the following decision function u(t) can be added for making a choice at each time step:
>
> $$u(t) = 2\,d(t) - 1 \hspace{6cm} (8)^{49}$$
>
> where u = +1 for the decision d = 1 (true) and u = –1 for the decision d = 0 (false). [...] It is important to point out that the decisions d(t) do not influence the dynamics of x(t) but only guide the system which creates itself the potential futures.

For d = 0 or d = 1, the uncertainty would vanish completely.[50] In a social system, however, more options than only true or false are possible. Social systems operate in a distributed mode and therefore one expects a probability distribution of preferences. A distribution contains an uncertainty. However, decisions can be organized and codified in decision rules that are more complex than the above (binary) rule.[51]

In other words, decisions specify instantiations among the available options when anticipations act upon one another. The organization of decisions along a historical axis potentially stabilizes a trajectory within the phase space of expectations. Thus, social order is made contingent by coupling global expectations about other

---

[49] The numbering of the equation in the quotation follows the original text.

[50] The uncertainty can be formalized as $H = - \sum_i p_i \log p_i$ (Shannon, 1948). For the binary case ($p_1 = 0$, $p_2 = 1$), the uncertainty vanishes because: $H = -\,0 \log 0 - 1 \log 1 = 0 - 0 = 0$.

[51] Luhmann at many places insisted on the binary character of codes. However, he did not distinguish sufficiently between the epistemological distinction (e.g., between true and false) and the methodological operationalization. In the case of social systems, one has to appreciate the (social) distributedness at each moment in time *and* the historical contingency as sources of uncertainty. The binary case is too abstract for sociological analysis. Codes are embedded and elaborated in textures. For example, the sciences are able to operate with grey shades between the extreme values of true and false. Unlike religious truths, scientific truths are uncertain and provisional. Information theory enable us to specify these uncertainties in a model (Theil, 1972; Leydesdorff, 1995a).

possible expectations with the historical reality of observable actions and institutions.

5.2   Decisions and organization

Decisions provide the social system with a mechanism for being organized as a system of expectations. The reflection into a historical organization by decision-making enhances formal organization *in addition to* informal organization. The latter (informal organization) can also be the result of 'natural' (that is, not yet reflected) patterns of interactions. Interactions are non-linear and hence may lead to pattern formation for stochastic reasons. (I shall elaborate on this stochastic process below for the case of the lock-in.) Formal organization, however, presumes a reflexive turn and decision-making (Luhmann, 1964, 1978b, 2000).

By taking a decision, one reduces complexity by a degree of freedom. For example, an individual or an organization has more options before a decision is made than thereafter. The specific role and function of organization in social systems is to reduce the complexity in the self-organization of the fluxes of expectations with different codifications by establishing a (provisional) boundary between what is currently relevant and what is not. Thus, uncertainty is not reduced as far as in the case of an individual, but the dimensionality of the uncertainty is nevertheless reduced. The organization creates a focus or—in other words—a geometrical representation that can be stabilized, while the algorithmic fluxes of expectations in the relevant environments remain volatile.

When challenged by a complex dynamics, this reduction of the complexity—by maintaining a perspective diachronically or an organization at each moment of time—generates stability and order. In sociological discourse, for example, one needs a model for accessing the complexity, since otherwise the complexity of the (non-trivial) machinery under study would be overwhelming. The chaos would be insufficiently organized without choosing a perspective. However, order is constructed piecemeal by specifying the *relations* among the events. Each specification can be considered reflexively as a decision. The consequent order is by definition hierarchical. The perspective has a focus and therefore a center of the representation.

From the perspective of hindsight, each perspective can be recognized as implying a specific *position* among other possible ones. When an order can be maintained over time, it can also be institutionalized, for example, in a corporation or a state apparatus. Note that the natural sequencing of decisions with the historical flow of time already reduces the self-organization of the system so that it can develop along a historical trajectory. Historical development precedes the reflection. The reflection makes it possible to formalize the organization as a series of reflexive actions.

At the individual level, one can thus consider action as a first ('primitive') reduction of complexity (Luhmann, 1984, at p. 419; 1995, at pp. 308f). Without reflection, action is based on 'natural' preferences (as in economic theorizing). When action is elaborated into institutional agency (Turner, 1990) or principal agency (Guston, 2000; Van der Meulen, 1998), organization can be expected to play an increasing role in sustaining the performative functions of taking action. At the supra-individual level, the reflexive coordination of actions induces organization by taking decisions. Although organizations can contain a diversified structure, they reduce the complexity by providing a focus to action.

From a functional perspective, organization can also be considered as a subdynamic that is needed for the maintenance and reproduction of a complex system of communications. Luhmann formulated this as follows:

> Organizations generate possibilities for decisions which otherwise would not have been provided. They use decisions as contexts for decisions. [...] As a result, an autopoietic system is shaped that distinguishes itself because of its specific form of operation: it generates decisions on the basis of decisions. Behavior can then be considered as a decision. [...] The past is uncoupled by the construction of alternatives. (Luhmann, 1997a, at pp. 830f.)[52]

In biological models, decisions are considered as taken under the pressure of 'natural' selection. The agents have to act for their 'survival.' This model is dominant in computer simulations. In the sociological model, however, decisions internalize the options reflexively within the deciding system. This can be an individual, but social systems can also make decisions when organized. For example, decisions can be the outcome of a process of negotiations or can be made by voting (that is, by using a decision rule). When different selection environments for making

---

[52] 'Organisationen erzeugen Entscheidungsmöglichkeiten, die es anderenfalls nicht gäbe. Sie setzen Entscheidungen als Kontexte für Entscheidungen ein. [...] Im Ergebnis kommt auf diese Weise ein autopoietisches System zustande, das sich durch eine besondere Form von Operationen auszeichnet: Es erzeugt Entscheidungen durch Entscheidungen. Verhalten wird als Entscheidung kommuniziert. [...] Die Vergangenheit wird durch die Konstruktion von Alternativen abgehängt.'

decisions are distinguished reflexively, however, the epistemological status of the selection also changes. Selection can no longer be considered as 'natural' when a variety of selection mechanisms can be specified on theoretical grounds. The reflexive specification of a selection environment provides the latter with the status of a hypothesis. At the level of the social system, furthermore, this specification can be done by an analyst and/or by the subjects under study.

In an economic model, the subjects pursue individual interests by following their preferences (e.g., Epstein and Axtell, 1996; Axelrod, 1997), but in the sociological design one has to account for reflexive decisions of the analysts and the human beings under study. Furthermore, each participant-observer is able to alternate between these roles by using a double hermeneutics (Giddens, 1978; Latour, 1988).[53] The layer of informal communication can be expected to remain available for transgressing formal boundaries among systems 'infra-reflexively' (Habermas, 1981; Leydesdorff, 2000d). Thus, the dynamics are complex since they develop at different levels at the same time. However, the organizations construct a historical order that provides bench marks for further development.

5.3   The historical contingency of organizations

While most evolutionary models are based on agents taking performative actions for their survival, interactions among human beings are by definition reflexive (Parsons, 1968; Blumer, 1969; Habermas, 1981; Luhmann, 1984). Interaction among human beings can, therefore, be considered as the basic operation of the social system. A social system cannot operate without interaction because this generates the double contingency in which *Ego* can imagine that the *Alter* entertains expectations (Elmer, 1995). In Chapter Four, it became clear that the sole assumption of interaction

---

[53] Latour (1988) distinguished between infra-reflexivity and reflexivity. One can also add hyper-reflexivity (Ashmore, 1989). However, Latour attributed various forms of reflexivity to non-human 'actants' (cf. Callon and Latour, 1981; Latour, 1987). From the perspective of this social systems theory (see also Chapter Two; Leydesdorff, 2001b), the non-human environment is only infra-reflexive—it communicates information—but never hyper-reflexive. The non-human environment participates in the social process insofar as it is mediated to the social system by reflexive human agency (cf. Knorr-Cetina, 1997). The social system feeds back on the non-human environment by reconstructing the latter by means of technological innovations at the supra-individual level, that is, hyper-reflexively. This hyper-reflexive operation can again be reflected by agents, in interactions, and by organizations, and be made the subject of further decisions.

containing anticipation is sufficient for understanding grouping. Grouping can be more or less organized. In general, organization remains a historically contingent result of grouping and interaction.

Because of this historical contingency of organizations, one cannot specify organizations without specifying the relevant environments or system(s) of reference about which decisions are made (Lawrence and Lorsch, 1967). Which environments are relevant to a specific organization? What are the relevant selection environments? For example, enterprises have to survive in a market environment, while governments have to account for how they shape and reconstruct markets in a political context. Furthermore, institutions are organized differently from codifications in the communication (e.g., regulation and legislation). Organizations thus provide an intermediary layer between interactions and the social system as a whole: both expectations are organized, and insofar as the organization is institutionalized, another mechanism is added. Thus, organizations provide a contingency between the layers of the social system; they are both shaped recursively in institutions and can be developed incursively by becoming increasingly knowledge-based.

While Luhmann's focus was on general theorizing, he first distinguished organization theory only negatively—as contingent:

> [...] in all social relations, under all circumstances a difference between society and interaction is unavoidable, but not all societies are acquainted with organized social systems. We therefore exclude organizations, but only from treatment on the level of a general theory of social systems. On the next level, that is, of concretizing the theory, one would perhaps need to distinguish between societal systems, organizational systems, and interaction systems and develop separate theories for each type because these three separate ways of forming systems (i.e., dealing with doubling contingency) cannot be reduced to one another. (Luhmann, 1984, at p. 551n. [1995, at p. 600n])

Organization theory indeed provides this concretization. From the perspective of systems and evolution theory, a positive heuristics about how the organization of systems evolves can first be specified by using the biological metaphor. In general, the evolutionary sequence in systems formation along the time axis proceeds from segmentation to stratification, and then differentiation. For example, the cells of an embryo first window upon each other as equal segments. In this first stage (*morula*), cell cleavage is synchronized by direct contact. After a number of cleavages, a head and a tale are induced which provide the hierarchical order (*blastula*). Thereafter, the organism folds (*gastrula*), and an inside and outside are functionally differentiated as different cell types (Leydesdorff, 1994a).

These evolutionary metaphors have been used for studying social formations since the very beginning of sociology (e.g., Comte, [1838], 1864; Parsons and Dupree, 1976; Spencer, 1897). As long as interactions are not formally organized, the social system can be expected to remain segmented in groups which operate in parallel (e.g., tribes). When the system is organized hierarchically as in a high culture, leadership is expected at the center, for example, in the person of an anointed King or an Emperor (Innis, 1950). In this configuration, action at the top of the hierarchy is sacrosanct and legitimated by a priesthood (the so-called 'Second Estate'). However, organization can further be developed historically.

Organization allows for modes of decision-making other than by taking individual action at a centralized top and represented by a single individuum. For example, a variety of divisions of labour can historically be invented (Durkheim, 1930; Simon, 1973; Habermas, 1981). The processing of communication in functionally different dimensions provides the social system with more options for processing complexity. When the coding in various dimensions can also be organized, the interactions between the coded expectations can be generalized symbolically—for example, in terms of decision rules. Decision rules codify the communications. However, one would expect the decision rules to be different, for example, in science and on the market. The reflexive organization of the social system in subsystems can thus increasingly become a function among the other functions. The organization of the codes into an arrangement allows for their reproduction. Accordingly, one can improve reflexively on organizations by reconstructing the interfaces among the functions which are organized. At each moment of time, however, organizations provide boundaries which include and exclude agents in terms of their access to the relevant communications.

Organization first plays a historical role in stabilizing stratified systems as in high cultures. Under the condition of modernity, social organizations can be made flexible by reconsidering decisions about boundaries from a functional and reflexive perspective, that is, by developing intersubjective criteria. In other words, one can distinguish analytically between organization as a functional subdynamic among other subdynamics, and organization as a layer which stabilizes the social system. This latter function is older than the functional differentiation among the codes of communication. The functionality of differentiation in later stages of evolutionary development adds reflexivity to the code of communicating decisions.

How does this relate to Lumann's model? Luhmann's (1997a) model of the social system was developed along these two axes: (1) *social differentiation* in terms of codes functional to the communication (e.g., science, economy, religion, etc.), and (2) *systems differentiation* at the three levels of interaction, organization, and society.

In my model, the organizational dimension provides the historical link between the two analytically distinguished axes of differentiation: systems differentiation and social differentiation. What is organized, however, is different from both these perspectives. In addition to serving the reproduction of social order in general, organization can also be considered as a specific function, but only when functional differentiation prevails at the level of society (and therefore functions play a role in organizing the social coordination). In a system which is not (yet) functionally differentiated, organization provides only a horizontal layer supporting the top of the hierarchy. This system is stabilized against organizational change.

	Science	*Economy*	....	*Religion*
Interaction	mediated exchange relations			
Organization	research groups; corporations; associations; etc.			
Society	symbolically generalized media of communication			

Table 5.2: Systems differentiation and functional differentiation cross-tabled.

Functional differentiation reorganizes codes of communication along increasingly orthogonal dimensions. Organization can then be considered as the specific function that reorganizes functions by integrating them. Thus, the subsystems can remain interactive and contained within a historical system. Organizations organize interfaces and thereby reproduce the system in the previous mode of hierarchical integration, that is, by reducing its complexity. The complex system can thus be expected to remain in transition between its historical manifestations (organization) and its next-order layer of expectations (self-organization). The mechanisms for going back and forth between these two modes of operation were specified above in section 5.1.

In other words, the function of organizations is to organize the complexity of self-organizing (sub)systems of expectations so that the complex system can perform historically, that is, by providing and retaining wealth. Without organization as an integrating mechanism, differentiation could easily prevail to such an extent that the system would disintegrate in the longer run. An unorganized system might not have sufficient resilience against disturbances and thus perish. The tendency of the self-organization towards crisis is countered by reflexive attempts to (re)organize the communications.

Let me add that the operation of an organization has been considered in terms of sequences of decisions by previous authors in organization theory (e.g., March and Simon, 1958; Lawrence and Lorsch, 1967; March and Olsen, 1976). These authors focused on historical organizations. However, I use another theoretical framework here because our system of reference includes the social system of expectations. Decisions can then be taken either recursively, that is, following the axis of time using an intuitive mode (yes/no), or incursively, that is, based on reflexive considerations (in the present) and using symbolically generalized media of communication. In the historical dimension, observable actions denote underlying decisions, but reflexively one can also decide not to act (Bachratz and Baratz, 1963). Reflexive decisions are incursive and therefore not always observable.[54] Both decisions and non-decisions leave historical traces which further organize the systems of communication about which the decisions were taken.

One level below organizations—following Luhmann and using the scheme of Table 5.2 above—interactions are increasingly under pressure to become functionalized when functional differentiation among the codes of communication becomes the dominant format for social coordination. For example, relations among colleagues, intimate relations, etc., are transformed (Giddens, 1992). In a strongly anticipatory system which continuously rewrites its conditions on the basis of the functional differentiation of the organizational function (among other subdynamics), all interfaces function increasingly as selection mechanisms that restructure the communication. Observable actions can be considered as 'natural' indicators of decisions taken under survival pressure. In interactions and organization, however, ranges of possible actions function as reflexive integrators of preferences and decisions (Leydesdorff, 2003c).

The two forms (natural preferences and reflexive decisions) are intertwined and remain structurally coupled at the level of the individual. However, at the level of an organization this coupling does not mean that all actions are reflexive decisions, nor that all decisions include all actors. The reflexive layer is available and continuously informed because of interactions. The social system as a complex system is both organized and self-organizing. The different levels and functions disturb one

---

[54] As Napoleon's diplomat Talleyrand (1754-1838) is alleged to have said: 'God has given us language so that we can hide our thoughts.'

another. Decisions and non-decisions may therefore have counter-intuitive effects in this non-trivial machinery. For example, a lock-in can be an irreversible consequence of a series of previous decisions. Not the individual decisions and actions, but the sequencing and distributions of decisions are crucial for changing the social system.

5.4   Decisions, lock-ins, and trajectory formation

The mechanism of the lock-in into a dominant technology provides us with an example of the unintended consequences of the non-linear dynamics of decision-making. Lock-ins are generated when decisions relate recursively to previous decisions. This can be expected when decisions are structured in organizations according to (sometimes implicit) decision rules. As Arthur (1988, 1989) showed, when adopters arriving on a market with natural preferences take the number of previous adopters of a specific technology into account, a lock-in can be expected. The lock-in follows 'naturally' at the systems level, that is, without incursive reflections at the individual level. The lock-in is considered 'natural' because it follows necessarily and with the arrow of time, given the specification of an organizational mechanism of increasing returns at the systems level.

The specification of this mechanism will enable me to show how the system can lose a degree of freedom. For example, the trajectory of a technological development is irreversibly changed after the lock-in. One can also consider this as the generation of a path-dependency within the system (David, 2000). In this and the next section I discuss the conditions for both the emergence and the dissolution of this path dependency, respectively. The conclusion will be that the trajectory functions as a pathway—that is, an organization over time—which can bring the system from one (suboptimal) regime or basin of attraction into another (Dosi, 1982; Bruckner *et al.*, 1994).

Sub-optimalization of a technology in a dominant design because of a lock-in has been a well-known phenomenon in technological developments. For example, the QWERTY keyboard was invented in order to prevent jamming of the keys in the case of mechanical typewriting. For various reasons (e.g., network externalities and learning curves) the consequent lock-in could no longer be reversed after the conditions for the technological fix had disappeared. Although the use of the

QWERTY keyboard in the case of an electronic computer is sub-optimal, attempts to reverse the prevailing lock-in have failed hitherto (David, 1985).[55]

The focus in studies of the lock-in has been on the consumer side rather than on the production system, but the mechanism can be generalized as an interaction between any two subdynamics. In general, the lock-in as a mechanism provides us with a model of the relations between two functionally differentiated subsystems—in this case, markets and technologies—that can be coupled in a number of different ways. Under the neo-classical assumption of free competition and open markets, two subdynamics are distinguished as analytically independent: market clearing and technological innovation. In Chapter One, for example, I distinguished shifts along the production function due to changing factor prices from changes of the production function due to technological progress (Schumpeter, [1939] 1964; Sahal, 1981b; see Figure 1.2). Coupling between the subdynamics may generate non-linear interaction terms; emerging rigidities can then increasingly structure the system (Leydesdorff and Van den Besselaar, 1998a). While both subsystems can operate at the global level of the system (e.g., free markets versus universally applicable technologies), the lock-in shows how localized decision-making structures (e.g., network externalities) generate interaction terms that can change the system structurally in the longer run. As we shall see in a next section, the unlocking of a lock-in thereafter requires another context to be specified additionally as a relevant environment.

Unlike the neo-classical framework, the perspective of evolutionary economics initially assumed the two subdynamics of trajectory formation and selection environments as the subjects of theorizing (Nelson and Winter, 1977; 1982). The feedback terms were recognized by Nelson and Winter, but provisionally black-boxed (1977, at p. 49). In this model, trajectory formation—specific organization over time—is induced by the recursive coupling of relevant environments and resources in entrepreneurial practices (e.g., routines). Entrepreneurial practices were considered as the 'natural' operators of the economic system. More recently, however, the focus in these studies has shifted to explaining the mechanisms of how trajectories are formed in terms of dominant designs (e.g., Abernathy and Utterback, 1978, Anderson and Tushman, 1990; Klepper, 1997; Nelson, 1994). The

---

[55] David's thesis of an irrational 'lock-in' of a dominant technology has been opposed by Leibowitz and Margolis (1999), who defend the notion of market equilibrium as a basic premise of economic theorizing. Learning curves can be steep, however (Arrow, 1962), and competition under increasing returns tends to amplify small historical events that favor one technological option over another (David, 1999).

mechanism of the lock-in provides us with a formal model to the emergence of such a dominant design.

5.4.1 Arthur's (1988) simulation model for the lock-in

Arthur (1988, 1989) specified the mechanism for the lock-in in the case of two competing technologies with randomly arriving adopters following their natural preferences under the condition of a market with marginally increasing returns. This means that each adopter reinforces the situation for adopters thereafter. For example, it can be more attractive to buy a brand that is common in the market-place than one that is rare. Thus, the market is structured and in this sense organized at the systems level.

Using the theory of random walks, it can be shown that the gradual aggregation of the 'network externalities' leads necessarily to a lock-in in the long run. Arthur used the example of VCR technologies: if a standard (e.g., VHS versus Betamax) is increasingly accepted, one passes a point of 'no return' and soon video-stores will only have the dominant type of tape on their shelves. (Since the VHS tape was recently replaced by the DVD, this example will provide us with a model for a break-out from lock-in in a later section.)

Let me recapitulate the formalization of Arthur's (1988) model: two competing technologies are labeled A and B. These are cross-tabled with two types of agents, R and S, with different 'natural inclinations' towards the respective technologies. In Table 3, a_R represents the natural preference of R-type agents towards technology A, and b_R their (in this case, lower) inclination towards B. Analogously, one can attribute parameters a_S and b_S to S-type agents ($b_S > a_S$). The network effects of adoption (r and s) are modeled as coefficients to the number of previous adopters of the respective technologies (n_A and n_B).

	Technology A	Technology B
R-Agent	$a_R + rn_A$	$b_R + rn_B$
S-Agent	$a_S + sn_A$	$b_S + sn_B$

Table 5.3: Return values for R- and S-type agents to adopting technology A or B, given n_A and n_B previous adopters of A and B. (The model assumes that $a_R > b_R$ and that $b_S > a_S$. Both r and s are positive.)

The values of the cells in Table 3 indicate the return that an agent receives for adoption of the respective technology. In addition to the satisfaction of obtaining the technology of one's choice—that is, following a natural inclination—the global appeal of a technology is increased by previous adopters with a term r for each R-type agent, and s for S-type agents. If R-type and S-type agents arrive on the market randomly, the theory of random walks predicts that the competition will eventually lock-in on either side (A or B) in the case of positive network effects.

For example, an agent of the S-type would naturally prefer to buy Technology B (since $b_S > a_S$), but when the total return for buying Technology A ($a_S + sn_A$) is larger than the return for buying Technology B ($b_S + sn_B$), this agent will buy Technology A. In formula format, one can specify the condition for this lock-in as follows:

$$a_S + sn_A > b_S + sn_B \qquad (6)$$

Similarly, the condition for the lock-in into the other technology can be specified.

```
10    INPUT N
20    SCREEN 11: WINDOW (-2, 0)-(N, 100): CLS
30    FOR J = 1 TO 25
40        LINE (-2, 50)-(N, 50)
50        Ar =.8: Br =.2: sA =.2: Bs =.8: NA =1: NB =1: s =.01: r =.01
60        RANDOMIZE TIMER
70        FOR I = 1 TO N
80            IF RND < .5 THEN
90                RETURNA = Ar + r * NA: RETURNB = Br + r * NB
100           ELSE
110               RETURNA = sA + s * NA: RETURNB = Bs + s * NB
120           ENDIF
130           IF RETURNA > RETURNB THEN NA = NA + 1 ELSE NB = NB + 1
140           Y = NA + NB: Z = 100 * NA / Y
150           PSET (Y, Z)
160       NEXT I
170   NEXT J
180   END
```

Table 5.4: Code for the simulation of Arthur's (1988) model. (Source: Leydesdorff and Van den Besselaar, 1998b).[56]

Arthur's model can be programmed as a computer simulation (Leydesdorff and Van den Besselaar, 1998b). Table 4 provides the code for the simulation in BASIC. By

---

[56] 'sA' is used as the variable name for declaring the natural inclination 'a' for an S-type agent, a_S, since 'AS' is a reserved term in BASIC.

varying the parameters (a_R, b_R, a_S, b_S, r, and s) one can test different scenarios. Figure 2 provides the resulting representations of lock-ins on a computer screen.

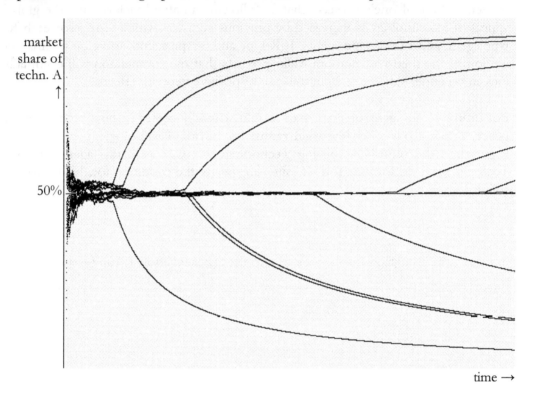

Figure 5.2: Arthur's model as specified in Table 3, after ten simulation runs (10,000 adopters)

Table 5 provides the same code for running this model using a cellular automaton (like the ones used in Chapter Three). The use of a cellular automaton enables us to visualize the effects of the lock-in in interaction with local network effects. In the case of a lock-in, the screen will sooner or later be turned into a single color. Given the parameter values in lines 20 and 30 of this simulation, a lock-in is unavoidable.

```
1     REM Arthur model with spatial representation on the screen
10    SCREEN 1: WINDOW (0, 0)-(320, 240): CLS
20    AR = .8: BR = .2: SA = .2: BS = .8
30    NA = 1: NB = 1: S = .01: R = .01
40    RANDOMIZE TIMER

50    DO
60       y = INT(RND * 240)                ' draw random case
70       x = INT(RND * 320)
80       IF RND < .5 THEN                   ' evaluation
90          RETURNA = AR + R * NA: RETURNB = BR + R * NB
100      ELSE
110         RETURNA = SA + S * NA: RETURNB = BS + S * NB
120      ENDIF
130      IF RETURNA > RETURNB THEN          ' consequences
140         NA = NA + 1: PSET (x, y), 1
150      ELSE
160         NB = NB + 1: PSET (x, y), 2
170      ENDIF
180   LOOP WHILE INKEY$ = ""
190   END
```

Table 5.5: Arthur (1988 and 1989) model with representation in colors on the screen

Using these simulations, it can be shown that lock-ins are robust against changes in parameter values by orders of magnitude. A technological breakthrough affecting natural inclinations cannot lead to a break-out, return to equilibrium, or replacement with a lock-in into the new technology. Strong reduction of the network effect for the winning technology (e.g., r) or, alternatively, enhancement of the network effect of the losing technology (in this case, s), even by orders of magnitude, is not likely to change the configuration (Leydesdorff and Van den Besselaar, 1998b).

If one forces a break-out by further increasing (or decreasing) parameter values by orders of magnitude, the replacement pattern reverts to the curve for lock-in of the *other* technology. Figure 3 illustrates this reversal of the lock-in. Although highly unlikely in the case of increasing returns, substitution will be fast and ordered if successful. These rapid, but ordered substitution processes have been noted by Fisher and Pry (1971) in seventeen cases of technological substitution. Their finding was that the rate of a substitution in all the cases, once begun, did not change throughout its history, but was to be considered as a systems property. Thus, the rate is not proportional to historical advancements in the technology, but is determined by an evolutionary mechanism underlying substitution. In other words, the dynamics are no longer a result of aggregates of actions, but an interaction effect among network dynamics at the systems level.

The dissolution of one lock-in or another, given a choice between competing technologies, is not determined by the emergence of a new and superior technology, but by the *balance* between the interlocking networks (David and Foray, 1994). Evolutionary networks can be considered as hyper-networks that are able to suppress relevant subdynamics (Bruckner *et al.*, 1994). If one repression is lifted, another subdynamic can become dominant. For example, the simulation results of Figure 5.3 show that substitution processes are expected to follow the lock-in line of the substituting technology.

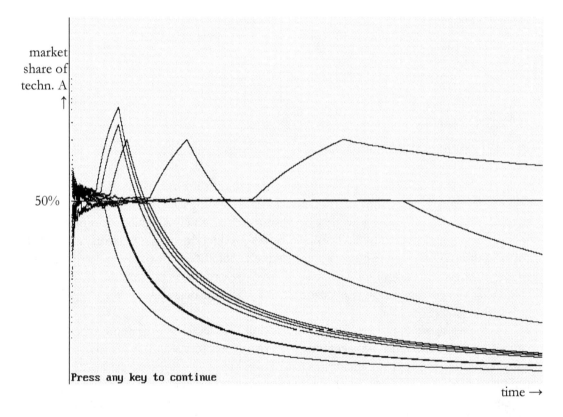

Figure 5.3: Forcing technological break-out from a lock-in and possible return to equilibrium (20,000 adopters)

Note that there is also a window for return to equilibriua if the market is sufficiently large. This can, for example, be observed in case of the rightmost curve in Figure 5.3. Equilibrium remains available as a meta-stable state of this system.

In the following sections I will show that the lock-in at the systems level cannot be prevented by *local* networking, that is, spatial dependence, given these parameter values (Leydesdorff, 2001a). The lock-in is an effect at the level of the system and is therefore next-order or *global* from the perspective of the agents involved (as long as these agents are not reflexive on the system, but only following their natural preferences). Changes in the parameter values can sometimes cause a return to equilibrium or an avalanche towards lock-in into the competing technology, but the conditions for these break-outs are *counter-intuitive*.

5.4.2 The network effects of local neighborhoods

In the next simulation, a local network effect is added to the dynamic of the lock-in. A network effect can be considered as a specific selection mechanism operating on the variation in local neighborhoods. For example, in the program exhibited in Table 5, each point, when (randomly) selected, first evaluates its local ('Von Neumann'-)environment, that is, its four immediate neighbors in terms of their color.[57] If the majority of the neighbors has one color, then the selected cell (in the center) is given this color (line 110).[58] Otherwise (line 120), the cell will be given a color using the random procedure described in the previous case. The value of the colors are stored in an array with the same size as the screen (320 x 200). For convenience the values are set at plus one for one color and minus one for the other (lines 200 and 220, respectively).

In Table 6, lines 140-230 are equivalent to the lock-in as exhibited by the program in Table 4. If the (Von Neumann) network environment remains indecisive with respect to a choice between the two technologies (colors), the selection is made according to the routine of increasing returns at the global level (i.e., the 'GOTO 140' in line 120).

---

[57] I used the Von Neumann neighborhood for reasons of parsimony. The Von Neumann neighborhood is simpler than the Moore neighborhood, whereas the effects of the two neighborhoods were rather similar in the case elaborated above. The extension from a Von Neumann environment to a Moore-environment, which includes the four corner cells as well, can be achieved, for example, by inserting one line in Table 6 (after line 110) of the following format:

$$111 \quad z = z + scrn(x-1,y-1) + scrn(x-1,y+1) + scrn(x+1,y-1) + scrn(x+1,y+1)$$

[58] The model described here is equivalent to the cellular automata majority rule, and it behaves exactly as one would expect from such a cellular automaton (Gilbert and Troitzsch, 1999, at pp. 130 ff.; cf. Toffoli and Margolus, 1987).

```
1    REM original model of W. Brian Arthur (1988)
2    REM with network effect of the Von Neumann environment added
3    REM (in lines 110-130)

20   SCREEN 1: WINDOW (0, 0)-(320, 240): CLS
30   AR = .8: BR = .2: SA = .2: BS = .8: NA = 1: NB = 1: s = .01: r = .01
40   ' $DYNAMIC
50   DIM scrn(321, 241) AS INTEGER
60   RANDOMIZE TIMER

70   DO
80      y = INT(RND * 240)
90      x = INT(RND * 320)

        REM first evaluate the network environment
100  IF (x = 0 OR y = 0) GOTO 140      ' prevention of errors
110     z = scrn(x- 1, y)+ scrn(x+ 1, y)+ scrn(x, y- 1)+ scrn(x, y+ 1)
120     IF z = 0 GOTO 140              ' go to routine for the lock-in
130     IF z > 0 THEN GOTO 240 ELSE GOTO 250
131
        REM if not decisive proceed with the lock-in model (Table 4)
140     IF RND < .5 THEN
150        RETURNA = AR + r * NA: RETURNB = BR + r * NB
160     ELSE
170        RETURNA = SA + s * NA: RETURNB = BS + s * NB
180     END IF
190     IF RETURNA > RETURNB THEN
200        NA = NA + 1: PSET (x, y), 1: scrn(x, y) = 1
210     ELSE
220        NB = NB + 1: PSET (x, y), 2: scrn(x, y) = -1
230     END IF
240  LOOP WHILE INKEY$ = ""
250  END
```

Table 5.6: Code for the combination of a local network effect with the global lock-in effect

Figure 4 shows that the network effect leads in this case to islands of a different color in a sea of the already locked-in and therefore dominant technology. (The black dots indicate potential adopters who have not yet been drawn by the random process, for example, after 250,000 adopters.) The islands are not stable over time; at the edges of the islands newly arriving adopters tend to buy the dominant technology, and eventually (for example, after 500,000 adopters) a one-sided lock-in will prevail. The network effect is local and operates as a selection environment at each moment of time, but the network externality induces lock-in at the global systems level over time. The temporarily stabilized islands are likely to disappear on the screen even before all the black dots have been accessed by adopters arriving randomly.

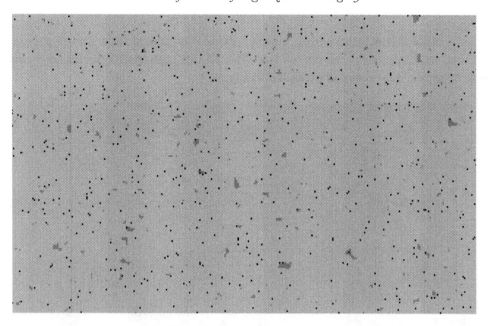

Figure 5.4: Temporary network effects with a prevailing lock-in after 250,000 adopters

5.4.3 An additional routine for the simulation of 'learning'

In order to achieve stability against the phenomenon of lock-in, one has to add a temporal (sub)dynamics to the network effect. I shall use 'learning' by the previous adopters as this additional dynamics. Let us assume that 'learning' occurs whenever one adopts. Thus, the value of the array element can further be augmented if one returns to the network a second time. This is modeled in Table 7 by increasing and decreasing the value of the corresponding array element by one unit count upon each local adoption (see the boldfaced additions to lines 200 and 220 in the code). This means that an adopter who buys the same technology for the second time will now be attributed a value of (plus or minus) two in the corresponding array element, etc. The network thus becomes more stable over time.

```
[...]
190    IF RETURNA > RETURNB THEN
200       NA = NA + 1: PSET (x, y), 1: scrn(x, y) = scrn(x, y) + 1
210    ELSE
220       NB = NB + 1: PSET (x, y), 2: scrn(x, y) = scrn(x, y) - 1
230    END IF
240 LOOP WHILE INKEY$ = ""
250 END
```

Table 5.7: Code for the extension of a network effect with local learning

If this routine is combined with both the Arthur-routine and the network routine, as specified in Table 6, the islands of the ('locked-out') alternative technology indeed become stable. This result is exhibited in Figure 5.

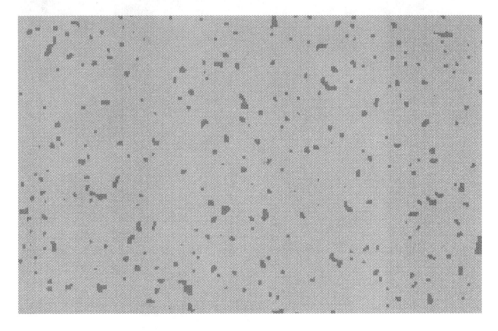

Figure 5.5: Stable network effects based upon learning with prevailing lock-in after 500,000 adopters

The resulting configuration can also be considered as a *deadlock* between the dominant technology and the niches in which the alternative technology is able to survive. Some actors will increasingly augment the value of their array element and thus tip the balance for the new adopters arriving at the borders in favor of the alternative technology. Thus, the configuration is not completely 'frozen.' However, the 'hills' and the 'valleys' of this 'landscape' have become 'rugged' (Kauffman, 1993). The transitions at the borders are steep when compared with the previous case, so that this segmentation of the market may no longer be reversible within this model.

The configuration depicted in Figure 5 can also be appreciated as a model of social stratification, when, for example, the minority (red) represents an elite and the majority (blue) represents a larger class. While in the previous configuration (Figure 4), local networking led first to a relatively stable pattern that was then dissolved by the global dynamics of the Arthur routine over the time dimension, the new configuration can be considered as *hyper*-stabilized over time. Learning reinforces the already available stabilization. However, the additional routine does not have to reinforce the stabilization. We shall see below that by adding reflexivity to the actors, one can prevent the occurrence of a lock-in. Reflexivity operates against the arrow of time, and therefore changes the dynamics of the network system.

Analytically, the reinforcement into this hyper-stabilized configuration is a consequence of the decision rule that adds (or substracts) one unity at either side with each time step (lines 200 and 220 in Table 5). This decision rule generates a third dynamic in the system, in addition to the dynamics of the lock-in over the time dimension and the dynamics of local selection in the neighborhood. Two subdynamics can be expected to co-evolve into a lock-in and then shape a trajectory as in a process of mutual shaping. A third subdynamic, however, is needed to organize the trajectory into a hyper-stable or meta-stable, and then also potentially globalized configuration.

5.4.4　*Conditions for the 'break-out' from a 'lock-in'*

In order to understand the possibility of a return to equilibrium, let us return to the analytical conditions for the lock-in specified in Equation 6 above. Lock-in into technology A, for example, occurs when it becomes more attractive for S-type agents to buy this technology despite their natural preference for technology B. From Table 3, we derived Equation 6 which specifies that a lock-in is possible if:

$$a_S + sn_A > b_S + sn_B \tag{6}$$

Thus:

$$sn_A - sn_B > b_S - a_S$$
$$(n_A - n_B) > (b_S - a_S)/s \tag{7}$$

From this result, two further conclusions follow with respect to the possibility of preventing lock-in and the possibility of a break-out, respectively:

1. Given a parameter set, lock-in is only a consequence of the difference in the number of previous adopters. This difference is $(n_A - n_B)$ if technology A is the leading technology, and $(n_B - n_A)$ in the other case (line 80 in Table 8). With increasing diffusion, this difference becomes smaller as a percentage of the total number of adopters $(n_A + n_B)$. Consequently, the difference in market share

becomes more difficult to assess by new arrivals who therefore tend to decide on the basis of their natural preferences and thus to prolong equilibrium.

```
10    INPUT N
20    SCREEN 11: WINDOW (-2, 0)-(N, 100): CLS
30    FOR J = 1 TO 25
40        LINE (-2, 50)-(N, 50)
50        RA =.8: RB =.2: SA =.2: SB =.8: NA =1: NB =1: s =.01: r =.01
60        RANDOMIZE TIMER
70        FOR I = 1 TO N
80            IF (NA - NB) > 0 THEN M = (NA - NB) ELSE M = (NA - NB)
90            IF RND < .5 THEN
100               IF M < 0.05 * (NA + NB) THEN
110                   NA = NA + 1: GOTO 230
120               ELSE
130                   RETURNA = RA + r * NA: RETURNB = RB + r * NB
140               ENDIF
150           ELSE
160               IF M < 0.05 * (NA + NB) THEN
170                   NB = NB + 1: GOTO 230
180               ELSE
190                   RETURNA = SA + s * NA: RETURNB = SB + s * NB
200               ENDIF
210           ENDIF
220           IF RETURNA > RETURNB THEN NA = NA + 1 ELSE NB = NB + 1
230           Y = NA + NB: Z = 100 * NA / Y
240           PSET (Y, Z)
250       NEXT I
260   NEXT J
270   END
```

Table 5.8: Code for the simulation of Arthur's (1988) model with an uncertainty of 5% in the market shares. Sentences added to Table 5.4 are boldfaced. (Source: Leydesdorff and Van den Besselaar, 1998b).

If one assumes reflexivity on the side of consumers, for example, as expressed by uncertainty about the relative market shares they represent, a window is created for prolonged periods of equilibrium. In the simulation routine provided in Table 5.8 and leading to Figure 5.6, for example, adopters select according to their natural preferences when the difference in market shares (M) is less than five percent (lines 100 and 160). The lock-in effect disappears with the exception of the case when it happens (for stochastic reasons) in a very early phase of the development.

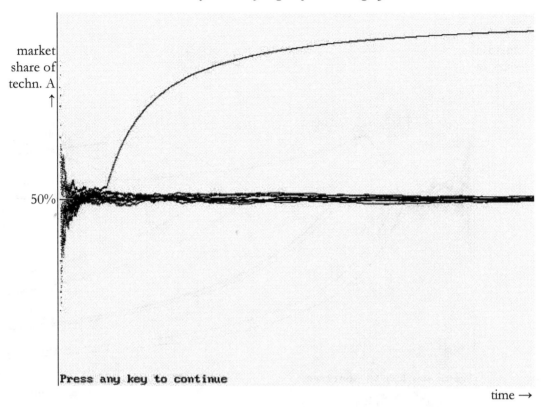

market
share of
techn. A
↑

50%

Press any key to continue

time →

Figure 5.6: Uncertainty about a difference in market shares smaller than 5% of the market leads to suppression of lock-in in nine out of ten cases

2. Another important consequence can be derived from the right-hand side of Equation 7. If the network parameter of the losing technology (e.g., technology *B* as the preference of *S*-type agents) is reduced to zero, the locked-in system reverts to equilibrium since the network-parameter *s* is part of the denominator in the equation. The system is then necessarily 'locked-out.' The condition of *s* = 0 sets the *S*-type agents free from the constraints of any previous lock-in, and thereby enables them to return to their natural preference (b_S) for Technology B. In Figure 7 the parameter *s* is set to zero whenever technology *A* captures more than two-thirds of the market. Note that the system then always returns to equilibrium.

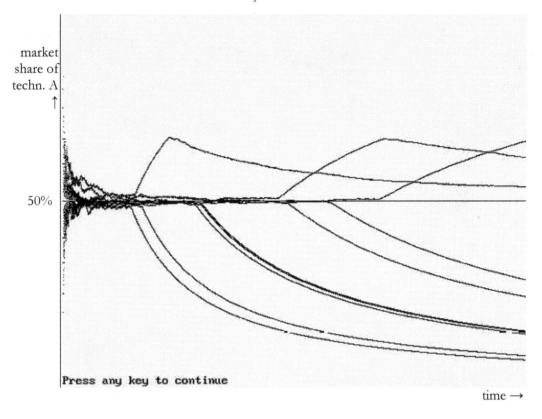

market
share of
techn. A

↑

50%

Press any key to continue

time →

Figure 5.7: S-type agents no longer profit from the network externalities (s = 0). Thus, the lock-in of the prevailing technology (A) is broken.

The normative implication of this model is counter-intuitive: in the case of a technology *B* that had to give way to the lock-in of a competing technology *A*, a return to the market is not likely to be based on competition in terms of the existing conditions. Dissolution of the network effects may imply a radical innovation that sets the technology free from those contextual factors that were advantageous to the further development of the technology during the previous generation. Thus, the technological regime has changed.

Paradoxically, a technology which has lost the competition should not be improved in terms of the current competition, since that was already lost. For example, the network externalities of video-stores offering the VHS system as a technology for VCR can be expected to disappear when video movies can be downloaded directly from the Internet. Customers could then use storage media other than a single brand of magnetic tape. Moreover, with personal computers it is easier to store movies on DVDs than on VHS tapes.

Changes in the relevant contexts of the technology are conditional for the lock-out. These changes can be induced by new technologies that are more pervasive in their effects on the economy than only videotapes. Thus, the system of reference is changed. DVDs, for example, can be considered as a systems innovation when compared with VCRs (Sahal, 1985). DVDs can be used for both video recording and data storage (like CD-Roms previously for audio recording). Two technologies were recombined, and the new technology serves a market much larger than the old one.

In summary, Arthur (1988) noted that equilibrium is enhanced if lock-ins can be postponed. As shown above, this is dependent on the relation of the absolute difference between market shares $|n_A - n_B|$ and the total number of adopters ($n_A + n_B$). For example, if a government wishes to keep a system in equilibrium, it needs to make the assessment of relative market shares difficult for adopters, for example, by keeping alternative technologies in the race until markets are well established. As soon as there is an obvious winner, competitors can be expected to jump on the bandwagon, even to the extent of destroying previous competences (Frenken and Leydesdorff, 2000). When a lock-in has occurred, the only other option is radical innovation affecting and involving the structural conditions of the technology.

Radical innovation implies that one has to break out of one's trajectory at the price of 'creative destruction' of in-house competencies and network externalities. In a corporate world, such a shift of trajectory may require a different set of institutional alliances (Frenken, 2000). Since the technological restructuring is radical, it is based on a reconstruction and not on existing practices. One then abstracts from the current situation and invokes a knowledge base for making decisions. The decisions are informed differently from those taken in the past.

5.5 Reaction-diffusion dynamics: bifurcation and morphogenesis

In the case of two sources of noise operating selectively upon each other at an interface, the formation of a trajectory is possible because of a lock-in, while in the case of three a complex regime can be generated. In general, the recombination of three subdynamics enables us to generate the various species of chaotic behavior (Poincaré, 1905; Li and Yorke, 1975). However, the complex dynamics of three sources of historical variation can be expected also to contain lock-ins between two sources as relative stabilities. The third dynamic induces a life-cycle into these more organized densities. This configuration is consistent with the prediction of local and global optima using Kauffman's (1993) NK-model (Kauffman, 1993; Frenken, 2000, 2001), and was further elaborated in this other context (Leydesdorff, 2002a).

In the above models, the option of return to equilibrium was generated by historical events such as the advent of new technologies on the market. Historical events are exogenous to the evolutionary model; but my claim about the life-cycle induced by a third selection environment implies that return to equilibrium can also be considered as endogenous to the evolutionary model. May "break-out" from "lock-in" or, more generally, a co-evolution also be endogenous to the evolutionary model?

I turn to reaction-diffusion dynamics to understand this process. While the lock-in provides us with a mechanism to lose a degree of freedom in the system, the reaction-diffusion mechanism enables us to understand how a degree of freedom can be gained by a system endogenously. In Chapter One, I discussed this mechanism in intuitive terms, for example, with the example of a coupled process of co-evolution between production and marketing in a small enterprise (or in an industrial district). If the smaller production unit is in a next stage absorbed by a multinational corporation or otherwise internationalized, the tight coupling between production and marketing at the local level may become a constraint on its further development. Under the pressure of the global diffusion dynamics, one may then have to take reallocation decisions about the production system. Thus, while originally the linear sequence of production and then marketing prevailed, in a later stage the feedback of the market may increasingly reshape the production process from the perspective of hindsight.

Reaction-diffusion dynamics have been elaborated in the natural sciences (Rashevsky, 1940; Turing, 1952; Rosen, 1985, at pp. 182 ff.). However, these insights have hitherto not influenced the context of economics or other social sciences (Bruckner *et al.*, 1994). If two systems are tightly coupled (as in a co-evolution; see Figure 8), the simplest coupling mechanism can be specified by the following differential equations:

$$dx_1/dt = - ax_1 + D(x_1 - x_2) + S \qquad\qquad (8a)$$
$$dx_2/dt = - ax_2 + D(x_2 - x_1) + S \qquad\qquad (8b)$$

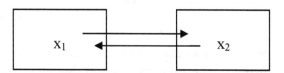

Figure 5.8: Two coupled processes. (Source: Rosen, 1985, at p. 183.)

Let us assume that x is produced in both compartments at a constant and equal rate *S*. The parameter *a* represents the decay of x; *D* is the diffusion constant across the membrane. (For the sake of simplicity, these parameters are assumed to be equal on both sides.) The diffusion is asymmetrical depending on the concentrations of x_1 and x_2 in the two compartments.

This system of equations provides a value for the steady state at:

$$x_1^* = x_2^* = S/a \tag{9}$$

The concentrations of x in the two cells are then equal: the system is homogeneous. The operational stability of the system, however, is determined in general by the eigenvalues of the matrix of the coefficients of x_1 and x_2 in Equations 8a and 8b. This matrix is:

$$\begin{vmatrix} D-a & -D \\ -D & D-a \end{vmatrix}$$

The two eigenvalues of this system are (Rosen, 1985, at p. 184):

$$\lambda_1 = -a; \qquad \lambda_2 = 2D - a \tag{10}$$

While the first eigenvalue is always negative ($\lambda_1 = -a$), the second can become positive if $D > a/2$. Thus, if diffusion of the material x to the other system becomes more important than the flux in the production process (divided by 2), a positive and a negative eigenvalue coexist. The system then becomes unstable because a so-called *saddle point* (see Figure 5.1 above) is generated in the phase diagram.

The consequence is that in this case any deviation from homogeneity will be amplified, and the system can go through a phase transition. A phase transition changes the dynamics of the system irreversibly. In the case of two previously coupled dynamics, the bifurcation leads to a polarization, that is, a situation in which all the materials are either in the one cell or the other. Which subdynamic will prevail depends on the initial (and potentially random) deviation from homogeneity.

Note that this mechanism can also explain the lock-in into either Technology A or Technology B as discussed in the previous section, but then the understanding is generalized. When the equilibrium is disturbed as a specific coupling mechanism between two communication systems, the system can be expected to lock-in on either side. However, the example of reaction-diffusion dynamics enables us also to understand how the resulting lock-in between a single technology and the market can be dissolved in a later stage, for example, when the context has changed. The previous co-evolution along a single trajectory can then be 'unlocked.'

Mutual shaping between production and market dynamics can be reinforced by local conditions, but the lock-in was defined by Arthur (1988, 1989) in terms of a competition between technologies at the level of the global market. However, when a third dimension becomes relevant to any locked-in system, the new configuration may begin to tilt this system as soon as diffusion at the new interface becomes more important than half of the rate along the trajectory of the system. Because an economic production system is attracted by market opportunities, it will tend to exploit a trajectory to gain market share. Thus, the diffusion rate can be expected to increase for the technology that was locked-in. The lock-in can thus be expected to erode the condition for its existence in the longer term. The globalization of the technology triggers another subdynamic to emerge, because later alternatives can build on the lock-in as a historical given and develop that situation further.

For example, given the locked-in situation of the VHS as the dominant technology for VCR in the 1990s, the DVD became increasingly relevant as an alternative, but this did not mean that the lock-in was immediately broken. The system is also resilient (Frenken and Leydesdorff, 2000). After a while, however, when the DVD-share grows independently for other reasons (e.g., data storage), the system can be tilted and the substitution process can then be expected to generate an avalanche. As shown in Figure 3, the expectation is that the newly emerging lock-in will follow the curve of the alternative technology. The alternative technology is in this case a new technology (Nooteboom, 1999).

In other words, the techno-economic system dwells in one regime or another along a trajectory. Each regime can be considered as a suboptimum, but the system may be locked into a given suboptimum because the fitness landscape is rugged (Kauffman, 1993; Frenken, 2001). While the system has also materiality and a history in which it leaves traces, some traces may become more important than others, and a preferential pathway may be locked-in along a trajectory. Along this trajectory the techno-economic system under study is thereafter relatively stabilized against disturbances. However, the trajectory leads the system increasingly into another context. Within this other context, reaction-diffusion dynamics may open the lock-in, but the dimensionalization of the result will be substantively different from the dimensions which went previously into the lock-in because a new environment has been shaped in the meantime. This new context may have been made available to the system because of the lock-in. Using a trajectory as a path-dependency, the system has thus been moved from one regime into another.

5.6 Adding reflexivity to the non-linear dynamics

The formulas used above for the lock-in cannot be made into anticipatory models because Arthur's (1988) model evaluates the function $x = a_r + rN_A$. In this formula, the dependent variable x is not developed recursively over time, but evaluated at each moment in time. (The time axis was considered by Arthur as naturally given.) However, we can add reflexivity to the adopters who make the evaluation. If they were reflexive, one would expect them to be more inclined to stay with their natural preferences than if they were driven only by market forces. This can be modeled, for example, by adding a 5% cost to switching to a technology other than the one naturally preferred. (The additions are again boldfaced in Table 5.9 below.)

```
10   INPUT N
20   SCREEN 11: WINDOW (-2, 0)-(N, 100): CLS
30   FOR J = 1 TO 25
40      LINE (-2, 50)-(N, 50)
50      AR =.8: BR =.2: SA =.2: BS =.8: NA =1: NB =1: s =.01: r =.01
60      RANDOMIZE TIMER
70      FOR I = 1 TO N
80         IF RND < .5 THEN
90            RETURNA = AR + r * NA: RETURNB = BR + r * NB
100           IF RETURNA > 0.95 *RETURNB THEN NA = NA+1 ELSE NB =NB+1
110        ELSE
120           RETURNA = SA + s * NA: RETURNB = BS + s * NB
130           IF RETURNB > 0.95 *RETURNA THEN NB = NB+1 ELSE NA =NA+1
140        ENDIF
150        Y = NA + NB: Z = 100 * NA / Y
160        PSET (Y, Z)
170     NEXT I
180  NEXT J
190  END
```

Table 5.9: Adopters keep to their original inclinations when the expected profit is smaller than 5%

The results are the same as in the case of adding 5% uncertainty about the market shares of the two technologies (Figure 6). The global lock-in occurs incidentally as a consequence of swings in market shares before equilibrium is achieved. Both in the case of uncertainty in the market perceived by the agents, and in the case of adding reflexivity to each of the agents, the reflexive dynamic tends to keep the system in equilibrium.

Similarly, one can envisage what reflexivity would mean in the case of the reaction-diffusion mechanism. Reflexivity means in a minimal definition that the system has developed an axis on which the interactions and disturbances can be provided with a reflection. In this case, the two coupled systems in Equations 8a and 8b would not only be decaying and diffusing, but would also have developed a process within the two compartments x_1 and x_2.

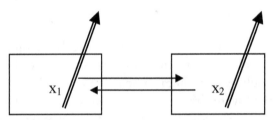

Figure 5.9: Two coupled processes with internal axes added

The processing along the internal axes can be expected to counteract the diffusion since *ceteris paribus*—that is, if the decay rates a and production rates S are kept constant—less substance is available for diffusion across the membrane. Reflexivity can thus be considered as generating a buffer of internal processing within each system (Figure 9). D declines relatively (because less material is available for diffusion), and the condition $D > 2/a$ is less easily met. Consequently, the system is more stable than before.

In summary, adding reflexivity to a system reinforces stabilization in the present. This insight accords with the results of our simulations of systems containing reflexivity in the previous chapters. In Chapter Three, for example, the modeling (sub)systems *filtered* the uncertainty in the observed (sub)systems reflexively. Reflexivity can be considered as adding another (stabilizing) selection mechanism over the time axis, whereas selection on the variation takes place structurally, that is, at each moment in time (Leydesdorff, 1995b).

The stability in the system can be used by anticipatory systems to stabilize the prediction of the system that is modeled. A control (sub)system is then added to the internal mechanism, and thus the system is stabilized endogenously. When the incursion is thus modeled as two (sub)systems in a hierarchical relation (of control) to each other, the modeling system can also be considered as a slave following the master system reflexively (that is, by observing it). If the master system changes historically, but with a delay τ in the manifestation of this change, the slave system is able to synchronize the modeling with this delay in the master system. This incursive synchronization enables the slave to predict the behavior of the master (Dubois, 2001, 2002).

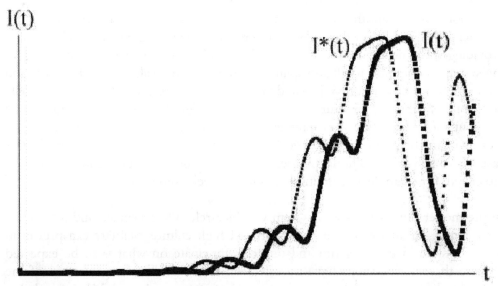

Figure 5.10: Anticipatory synchronization of I*(t) and I(t) with delay $\tau = 50$ (Source: Dubois, 2001, at p. 15).

Dubois (2001) discussed the example of the spread of an infectious disease in a social system. The manifestation of the disease can be delayed because of its incubation time. Incubation times are specific for diseases, and thus an anticipatory monitor is able to predict the further development of an epidemic.[59] The condition, however, remains that a hierarchy between the conroled and the controlling system is constructed by the engineer of naturally given. Thus, the prediction remains a

---

[59] Dubois (2003) showed that anticipatory systems can improve on (so-called) Model Predictive Control in engineering (Camacho and Bordons, 1999).

form of weak anticipation. I have argued that the social system can be considered a strongly anticipatory one under the condition of functional differentiation among the codes of communication. When the hierarchical structure breaks down, the systems dynamics can no longer be predicted, and self-organization can be expected to prevail increasingly. In the next chapter, I shall focus on the dynamics of this transition in the social system.

5.7   Summary and conclusion

A strongly anticipatory system contains one degree of freedom more than a weakly anticipatory one. The subdynamics have become heterarchical, that is, they process predictions of one another's development in anticipation of their own updates. In Chapter Four, I distinguished this transversal mechanism from the mechanism of providing meaning to the information. The subdynamic of providing meaning to the system is common to all anticipatory systems (both weak and strong ones) and therefore historically prior to the subdynamic of transversal updates which can only be stabilized (that is, structurally reproduced) under the condition of functional differentiation. Functional differentiation transforms meaning-processing, since meaning can then be provided in a differentiated mode. The social system in this case has to solve an additional puzzle, namely how the different rationalities can be integrated, for example, in a political system of checks and balances.

In pre-modern times the social system was hierarchically organized and integrated, for example, in an Empire or other form of high culture. Stability can prevail in such a system in the long run and one can anticipate on what is to be expected because these anticipations have no effect on the hierarchical organization of the system itself. In terms of the inflection points of Figures 5.1a and 5.1b (provided at the beginning of this chapter), the stable and the global resolution were still harmonized in this stage of development. High cultures, for example, have remained firmly rooted in territories as natural constraints.

Using the model of reaction-diffusion mechanism, I submit—and I shall elaborate this in the next chapters—that one can understand *why* the invention of new means of communication like the printing press (1455) could gradually lead to a phase transition in the social system (Eisenstein, 1979; 1983; Kaufer and Carley, 1993; McLuhan, 1962). Innis (1950) already argued that transitions in the medium of communication (e.g., clay tablets, papyrus, etc.) have shaped the specific organization of empires. Even more fundamentally, one can point to the transition from oral to text-based civilizations (McLuhan, 1964; Meyerowitz, 1994).

Reflexively, we can position ourselves currently in the middle of a comparable ICT-revolution. As McLuhan (1962) noted, the digital medium is less confined to the visual dimension than print communication. In other words, transitions in the communication regime have occurred more often in history. Why and how, then, did the printing press induce this phase transition?

Eisenstein (1983) pointed to the enormous momentum that this new technology provided to the diffusion process. While previously the diffusion of manuscripts was rate-limited by the production of manuscript, and therefore the two processes of production and diffusion were firmly coupled in a co-evolution, the diffusion parameter went through orders of scale when the printing press became available. For example, Luther's thirty publications presumably sold over 300,000 copies between 1517 and 1520. Previous revolts against Rome (e.g., Jan Hus's translation of the Bible into the Czech language in the early 15th century; Henry VIII's schism of the Anglican church in 1508) had remained within territorial confines, but the printing press redefined the relevant environments beyond strata (priesthood) and geography. Not incidentally, Luther advocated reading the Bible itself, that is, without Catholic control.

The diffusion tilted the balance in favor of an instability, that is, a bifurcation. However, in terms of the reaction-diffusion mechanism, one would expect that the system would then evolve either to the one side or the other. Thus, one would expect Protestantism or Catholicism to have prevailed in the long run. However, this is not what has happened historically in the longer run. After hundred years of religious wars in Europe, a decision rule was developed and then locked-in into the system by the peace treaties of Westphalia (1648), namely *cujus regio, eius religio* ('whoever reigns imposes his religion in his realm'). This principle would hold for most of continental Europe. France was initially the one exception given the Edict of Nantes (1604), which proclaimed freedom of religion. This charter was reinvoked in 1685, and France again became uniformly catholic. However, the system had become more complex, so that it did not bifurcate to the one extreme or the other (as predicted by the reaction-diffusion mechanism).

This tolerance of the system for processing more complexity was based on the increased reflexivity which had become available in communication at the systems level. Human agents, of course, have always been reflexive. The crucial point is that the mechanical reproduction of communication on a massive scale had induced another dynamic, namely an incursive one at the level of the social system. One had to learn to live with this new system and to discover its advantages. The new possibilities had to be developed by being reflected semantically.

First, the printing press generated in the second half of the 15th century an incursive routine in the reproduction of the Bible and other manuscripts[60] which drove the system towards a bifurcation. At the level of the social system, however, these incursive routines could gradually be developed into hyper-incursive routines between expectations. For example, from the 18th century onward one could also print banknotes as a mechanism of monetary organization that was much more abstract than precious metal coins. Although selection pressure increases with increasing complexity within the system, the social system can be expected to exhibit crises and catastrophes (that is, temporary unbalances). However, the stabilization and globalization of a more complex networked system, that is, one potentially bifurcating into a next-order hypercycle, had become possible.

The mediation required the stabilization of a decision rule. *Cujus regio, ejus religio* first provided this decision rule historically. On this basis, geographical units could increasingly be organized in Europe next to one another and on the basis of different (e.g., national) solutions for how to integrate the further differentiating social systems. In the next chapters I shall argue that the distinction (in Chapter One) of the geographical, the economic, and the knowledge-based dimensions of the social system enable us more recently to dissolve this stabilization in favor of its globalization. The transition between modernity and post-modernity can then become a structural feature of the social system (Bernstein, 1995).

My thesis in the following chapters will be that cultural evolution can increasingly be considered as including a hypercycle of the social system. Chapter Six first explains the concept of a hypercycle and then discusses some fundamental objections against using a functionalist explanation and the biological metaphor. I shall argue that the objections presume a historical model and not an evolutionary one which includes incursion and hyper-incursion. Incursion appreciates reflexivity. Reflexivity can be organized at the level of the social system and then have a function. When incursion is further developed at this hypercyclic level—as a processing of meaning in addition to information—the transition to a globalizing knowledge-based economy can be expected because of the recursivity of the incursion.

---

[60] For the first two centuries more than ninety per cent of all books printed were of medieval origin (McLuhan, 1962, at p. 184; Febvre and Martin, 1950)

Chapter 6

Reflexive Globalization and
the Emergence of a Knowledge-Based Order

Sociologists, historians, and economists have been fascinated with the transition from mediaeval high culture to the modern social system. What has happened to the social system in evolutionary terms? How might this transition be explained? Marx explained the advent of modernity in terms of changing class relations; Weber emphasized the function of Protestant values in the emerging social relations of modern capitalism. In science studies, the latter thesis was elaborated by Merton (1938) when discussing the social origins of the scientific revolution in 17th-century England, while Zilsel (1942/1976) analyzed the emergence of the modern sciences in terms of the development of new scientific practices and rearrangements in the division of labour (Shapin and Shaffer, 1985). Others have pointed to tensions internal to the mediaeval system like the struggle over investiture (Luhmann, e.g., 1989, at pp. 262 ff.) or the revolution in communication brought about by the discovery of printing (Eisenstein, 1979, 1983; Kaufer and Carley, 1993; McLuhan, 1962).

These different explanations have in common that one assumes that a transition at the systems level is to be analyzed in terms of causes *ex ante* from a historical perspective. From an evolutionary perspective, however, the new order is dependent on the specificity of *ex post* selections and is therefore an emergent property of the system. The historical generation of relevant variation is then considered as a necessary, but not a sufficient condition for shaping structure. Selection optimizes in terms of functions which feedback on the historically prior arrangements. When the functions are given (like in biology), this leads to adaptation. In the sociological model, however, the functions are not given, but constructed and then reflected by agency. The agents have thus limited capacity to change the structures, but not as individuals. The dynamics at the network level are structural.

In other words, links at the network level can be expected to operate with dynamics different from those of the agents at the nodes. The variations leading to a transition are less important than the selection mechanisms for understanding the dynamics of the emerging system (Rosenberg, 1994). I shall first discuss this in terms of the *biological* model. Thereafter, I proceed to the sociological specification of the selection mechanisms, and in the next two chapters I will provide empirical operationalizations. I shall argue in this chapter that during the last few centuries the social system has developed an incursive hypercycle on top of the recursive one(s). National systems can be considered as recursive stabilizations (like niches in an ecology), while the incursive hypercycle of the social system can be identified as the knowledge base of a society. The addition of this hypercycle can be indicated, for example, in terms of university-industry-government relations by using the Triple Helix model (Chapter Seven). The measurement technique to be developed in Chapter Seven will be generalized in Chapter Eight and then applied to measurement of the knowledge base in the economies of the Netherlands and Germany as examples.

6.1   The emergence of a global level

Let me first summarize the argument hitherto. Variation can initially be considered as only a perturbation, but different sources of variation can reinforce each other selectively. In other words, the relevant distributions can become skewed for stochastic reasons, and then develop structural properties given historical conditions. This dynamic was discussed in the previous chapter as a recursive development, for example, in terms of the lock-in (Arthur, 1988).

In the case of a lock-in, the emerging structure feeds back on the variation. This further selection can, for example, lead to the stabilization of a dominant design. In the biological or economic model, it is sufficient to understand selection as this recursive operation: some selections can be selected for (provisional) stabilization; some stabilizations can be selected for globalization. Thus, an emerging system self-organizes its complexity by selecting recursively upon selections. Each next-order selection mechanism adds a new dimension.

Although this general model can be used for understanding the social process (Epstein and Axtell, 1996), the major difference is that human beings are also enrolled as *reflexive* agents in the evolutionary development of the social (that is, supra-individual) system. From the perspective of the participating agents, evolutionary mechanisms like selection, the emergence of new structure, and functionality remain surprising since these are effects of communicative interactions among these agents. The emerging structures cannot be explained or predicted by them in terms of the structures available *ex ante*. One has to take a reflexive turn. For reflexive agents, however, an emerging dimension can only be hypothesized as a hitherto latent dimension. One can tell one story or another about the development, but each hypothesis remains in need of corroboration.

Although the reflexive agents are able to infer subjectively on the basis of observations that variation was selected, the inferred selection mechanisms remain uncertain and may also be at variance. Thus, the selection mechanisms of the social system should be considered as expectations with the epistemological status of hypotheses. Hypotheses, however, can be theoretically informed. Sociological discourse has been reflexive with respect to this epistemological status of the reflection. Weber (1904, 1917) argued that one needs to specify a perspective in the social sciences. Giddens (1976) distinguished between the perspective of the participant-observer and the external observer. He introduced the idea of a 'double hermeneutics' as a rule of sociological method. The two roles span other domains and roles for observers, but they can inform each other. The distinction between the two roles is thus analytical. In inter-human communication, this degree of freedom can also be handled informally, for example, by using language. Latour (1988) has called this latter operation 'infrareflexivity.' The formalization, however, will require us to distinguish more carefully between infrareflexivity, reflexivity, and hyper-reflexivity (Ashmore, 1989; Leydesdorff, 2000d).

The assumption of reflexivity in the social system and the distinction between various kinds of possible reflection have been expressed differently in various sociological traditions. For example, in anthropology the 'emic' perspective has been distinguished from the 'etic' perspective in anthropology (Geertz, 1973). Whatever its precise expression, the codification of this reflexivity in methodological terms spans the domain of sociological discourse (Giddens, 1979, 1984; Habermas, 1987). Events have meanings for participants that are potentially different from their meanings for external observers. Under what conditions and precisely how can an analyst add knowledge to the knowledge of the participants? Can this knowledge be codified in a discourse that is different from and/or reflexive to the discourse of the subjects under study? Strydom (1999) argues that a 'triple contingency' is thus generated. In addition to the double contingency of the interacting *Alter* and *Ego,* communication systems generate the external perspective of the public. Under the condition of functional differentiation, however, different publics can no longer be harmonized *ex ante*, and a set of different axes becomes available for reflexive codification in discourses which attempt to explain the communications under study.

Because the selection mechanisms of the social system remain hypotheses, it matters which theories one uses for the formulation of these hypotheses. For example, a model can focus on selection mechanisms at each moment in time (e.g., on the market) or on the selection mechanisms involved over time (as in the case of studying processes of change and stabilization in engineering). The two perspectives stand orthogonal: variation and selection operate at each moment in time, while change and stabilization operate over the time axis. The conclusions from these two perspectives may eventually be largely incommensurate.

Analogously to differentiation at each moment in time, one can entertain structurally different perspectives along the time axis. In addition to a focus on different time horizons (e.g., daily practices or longer-term developments), one can use different perspectives for studying developments along the time axis. Two of these perspectives have been discussed above as recursive and incursive ones, respectively. It could be shown that the anticipatory formulation of the logistic equation (against the time axis) provides us with a model that is very different from the recursive formulation. Furthermore, these various subdynamics can also interact, and then a range of temporal dynamics can be generated. Some of these subdynamics may resonate, and then a specific frequency can be stabilized as a differentiation functional to the stabilization of a (sub)system over time. The functional subsystems of communication can thus be expected to tick with different frequencies.

While 'natural selection' was defined with reference to the forward arrow of time and an idealized notion of time (Prigogine and Stengers, 1988), sociological selection mechanisms can operate with a variety of clock frequencies (Leydesdorff, 1994c; Nowotny, 1989/1994). Functions can be defined only with reference to an identifiable system, but in the sociological context the system is no longer given. Therefore, the functionality of a differentiation can no longer be taken for granted. When the next-order system is not given but constructed and complex, the selecting instances can only be specified as hypotheses, i.e., on the basis of theorizing about the emerging systems. What is functional and what contextual depends on the perspective adopted in the reconstructing discourse. Sociological discourse knows itself reflexively to be contingent among other possible perspectives. Each discourse runs in its own cycles, but since the external reference is to a system under study, the discourses also disturb one another with their 'empirical evidence.' Hypotheses and reconstructions compete for the explanation.

There is no single Archimedean point or focus from which one can claim to have a complete overview other than in terms of generalities. Each universalistic claim can be deconstructed by changing the perspective. However, the research programs in each of the scholarly traditions require specification. Functional differentiation develops not only historically, as in the biological case, but can also be changed incursively because of the further development of meaning processing into a knowledge base within the social system. Thus, a cultural evolution is induced with dynamics different from those of biological evolution. In the previous chapters, I showed how the combination of weak anticipation in providing meaning and functional differentiation can make the social system a 'strongly anticipatory' one, that is, a system containing the capacity to restructure itself on the basis of providing new meanings to meanings, that is, of generating knowledge endogenously. Such restructuring may have consequences for the definition of functions within the system, but the systems are thoroughly buffered. Thus, the functions are no longer 'fixed' or 'naturally given' at each moment in time, but may increasingly become knowledge-based. With hindsight, the biological model itself can also be reconsidered from this perspective as the results of a specific (biological) discourse. However, in most biological research one does not need this reflexivity because the externally given reality provides a warrant for empirical evidence.

In the biological model, for example, functions can be expected to change over time along a life-cycle, but in the sociological model, this assumption about a biological necessity has to be suspended. A social system with fixed functions at specific moments in time (e.g., birth and death), would function as a hierarchically integrated system. The social system, however, was not born and there is no life-expectancy for its age. The dynamics of its historical organization can be considered as one among many subdynamics of the more complex self-organization of the fluxes of communication. Each perspective, however, adds the possibility of reflexive globalization of its specific window. Each discourse can claim universality for its claims, but each discourse organizes the complexity necessarily from its own specific perspective.

The various discourses compete in terms of their explanatory and therefore potentially restructuring power. This competition among discourses carries the knowledge base and drives its further development, but the cultural evolution which it generates, is beyond the control of the carrying discourses. The latter organize the complexity by providing a window on it. The knowledge base can then be considered as a hypercycle among the disciplines and specialties, but this self-organization takes place in the domain of a cultural evolution which is taking place both historically and reflexively. When this hypercycle comes to fruition in a hyper-reflexive turn, the harvest can only be a wealth of ever further specified expectations (Beck, 1992b; Beck *et al.*, 2003).

As a system of expectations, this hypercycle of cultural evolution cannot be completed. Completion would lead to a hierarchical integration and thus temporarily block further development because of a return to a previous (that is, hierarchical) mode. The hyper-reflexive perspective knows itself reflexively to contain a reduction of the complexity, namely, by using the meta-biological metaphor (Habermas, 1987; Leydesdorff, 2000d). Unlike meta-physics, the meta-biological perspective can remain reflexive on its own status and is thus able to improve on its metaphor, for example, by specifying how the social system is different from the biological one.

The proof of the pudding remains in the eating! In the case of a theoretical argument, 'the eating' is equivalent to the empirical testing. I turn to the measurement of the knowledge base of systems in the next chapters, but let me first specify the meta-biological metaphor in relation to its biological precursor. The specification of a hypercyclic perspective in sociological theory has recently become possible as a new semantics because electronic communication makes us increasingly aware of the volatility of communication, and of the limitations and functions of organization in electronic communication. I return to this historical condition in a later section and will provide empirical evidence using Internet data to substantiate my claim. However, the abstract mechanism of a hypercycle can only be understood by using a biological metaphor: the modeling of natural phenomena provides us with a metaphor which we generalize thereafter for studying the processing of meaning.

6.2   Hypercycle theory

Dictyostelium discoideum has functioned as an exemplary model for explaining a hypercycle in developmental biology (Prigogine and Stengers, 1984, at pp. 158 ff.). Under the condition of starvation individual cells of this slime mold enter into a biological hypercycle on top of the biochemical exchange processes among them. First, the cells are able to notice one another's presence by the secretion of so-called chemo-attractants. Subsequently, the individual cells aggregate, form a multicellular organism (a mushroom), and start a well-defined developmental cycle, resulting in two differentiated cell types in a specific spatial arrangement (Gerisch, 1968; Berstein *et al.*, 1981).[61]

---

[61] A detailed analysis of the literature in this specialty based on Bernstein *et al.* (1981) provided the core of my empirical argument for using entropy statistics in *The Challenge of Scientometrics* (Leydesdorff, 1995a; cf. Amsterdamska and Leydesdorff, 1989; Leydesdorff and Amsterdamska, 1990).

How do the individual cells manage to send and receive these mutual signals in a controlled manner in order to coordinate biological action at a next-order systems level? Prigogine and Stengers (1984) argued that one has to consider the time dimension in understanding this cyclic event. Interaction along the time dimension using chemical clocks provides a new medium of communication among the cells (*ibid*, at p. 159). Under certain conditions the system becomes 'critical' and then a phase transition is possible. These dynamics were illustrated by these authors using the diagram provided in Figure 1.

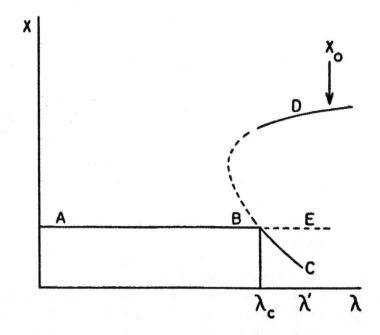

Figure 6.1: Bifurcation diagram as a model for the development cycle of *Dictyostelium discoideum*. (Source: Prigogine and Stengers, 1984, at p. 160.)

The figure shows the steady state (line AB) as a function of the bifurcation parameter λ . The dashed part of the line (on the right side) represents unstable states. If two conditions are fulfilled ($\lambda > \lambda_c$ with the concentration of X_0 considerably greater than the value corresponding to the stable part of the E-branch of AB) the system becomes meta-stable. Any stochastic disturbance is then sufficient to cause a switch to the D-branch. While the concentration of X may have increased gradually, the transition can happen suddenly as in a catastrophe (Thom, 1972; Zeeman, 1976) or an avalanche (Bak and Chen, 1991). Such a transition can be considered as a phase transition.

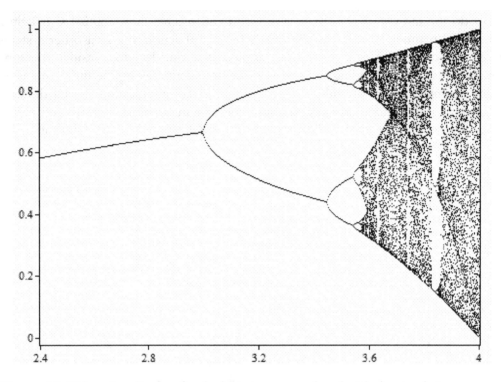

Figure 6.2: Bifurcation diagram for the logistic map produced with the simulation program *E&F Chaos* (at http://remote.science.uva.nl/~remco/EFChaos.html; 12 May 2006.)

The drawing of this type of bifurcation diagrams for a parameter like λ is nowadays included in standard software for simulation studies. The bifurcation diagram for the logistic map (Figure 2), for example, shows an initial bifurcation at the value of *a* = 3.1, and the subsequent development of chaotic behavior with increasing values of *a*. We have used this effect in the simulations of Chapter Three. In Chapter Five, furthermore, bifurcation was discussed as the specific mechanism causing the more complex system to emerge. In other words, the complexity emerges because a symmetry is broken by the bifurcation.

These various diagrams are analytical and the biological phenomena (in the case of *Dictyostelium discoideum*) can be replicated. This replicability indicates that a deterministic structure is operating in these systems despite the phenotypically chaotic phenomena. What appears as chaotic can be understood as order if one takes a reflexive turn. The reflexive turn adds one more degree of freedom to the model. The new dimension allows for hypothesizing another subdynamics (e.g., an incursive one) with a potentially different frequency. However, the bifurcation diagrams shown above assume an external observer as in the natural sciences.

Although Prigogine and Stengers (1988) reflected on the time axis of these systems, they assumed that all clocks are eventually integrated into a physical time horizon. Therefore, these models remained objective.

For an observer within the system—like a human observer participating in a social system—the symmetry in the time dimension is broken when the various cycles operate with different frequencies. Where one is positioned then makes a difference for how one perceives the dynamics. By using a reflexive discourse, the chaotic pattern can be decomposed into a variety of underlying regularities. The symmetry in the time dimension is broken because each context can select from the other discourses from the perspective of hindsight. The relation between prior and posterior thus becomes ambiguous in the reconstruction.

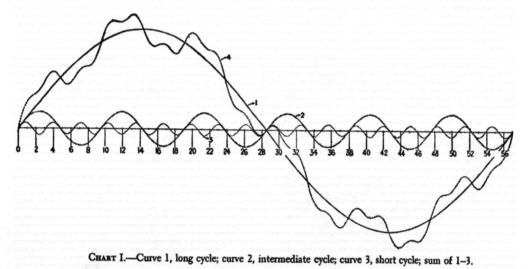

CHART I.—Curve 1, long cycle; curve 2, intermediate cycle; curve 3, short cycle; sum of 1–3.

Figure 6.3: The interaction among three regular cycles can lead to a chaotic pattern. Source: Schumpeter (1939, at p. 175).

Using Figure 3 as an illustration, Schumpeter ([1939] 1964) argued in his study of business cycles that the simple sum of three regular cycles may generate an apparently chaotic pattern: "For the stranger to statistical technique the fact alone that extreme regularity of but three components may result in so very irregular-looking a composite should be instructive" (p. 174). Mathematical techniques like Fourier-analysis enable us to analyze the resulting graph in terms of its constituent frequencies. In principle, one can also test whether a new frequency has emerged from the patterns of interaction in the time dimension (Smolensky, 1986).

After a symmetry-break in the time dimension—operationalized as the addition of another frequency—the system undergoes a phase transition. A next-order cycle is added to the cycles which generated this 'overtone' historically as an interaction effect among the subdynamics of the system. In the terminology of the previous chapter, a hypercycle can be considered as a diffusion process that is bifurcated from the reaction mechanisms in the underlying dimensions. This diffusion can then be reinforced so strongly that a phase transition becomes unavoidable. Furthermore, the concept of a hypercycle model enables us to understand why the interactions among a number of cycles can lead to an operationally closed system. The bifurcation is then made catalytic within a more complex arrangement. It provides the system with another degree of freedom and therefore with new options. This enhances the diffusion, and the preceding bifurcation is thus reinforced and made irreversible. The newly emerging system contains the (n + 1) composing cycles as its subdynamics.

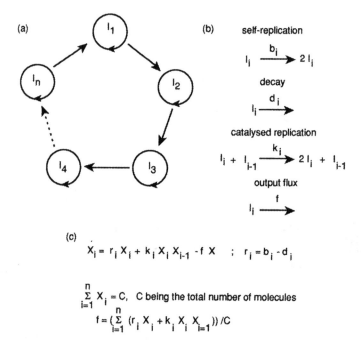

Figure 6.4: (a) Schematic diagram of a hypercycle. (b) Kinetic steps. (c) Differential equations. Source: Boerstijn and Hogeweg (1992, at p. 272). After Eigen (1979).

Eigen and Schuster (1979) first developed the theory of hypercycles at the molecular level. When a bifurcation happens to close a cycle of reactions, a hypercycle can begin to act on top of the underlying reactions (Figure 4). The various cycles are then auto-catalytically regulated by each other. Given sufficient complexity in an environment, hypercycles can be induced as next-order resonances among cycles. In a related paper, Maynard-Smith (1979) argued that one can explain the origins of life as a formation of such hypercycles.

The selection at the level of the hypercycle can be expected to counteract upon the selections at the level of the substantive dynamics that feed *ex ante* (forward) into the hypercycle. Using cellular automata, Boerlijst and Hogeweg (1992) showed that hypercyclic configurations can produce mutants—by searching randomly for resonances—that are able to accelerate the communication among cycles. The auto-catalysis of the complex system is then changed because the cycles are coupled in a different configuration. This mechanism is illustrated in Figure 5.

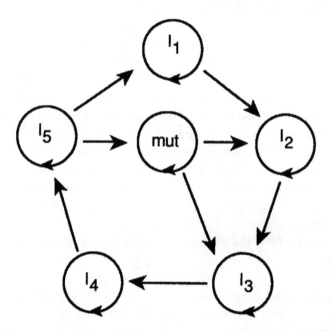

Figure 6.5: A mutant enables a hypercycle with four members. Source: Boerlijst and Hogeweg (1992, at p. 267).

If we apply these insights to the social system, we are able to hypothesize the following conclusion: Social and cultural systems that operate incursively can be expected to develop a hypercycle when the decision rule needed for solving the hyper-incursive equation at their interface (derived in Chapter Five as Equation 4, that is, $x_{t+1} = \frac{1}{2} \pm \frac{1}{2} \sqrt{(1 - x_t)}$) is no longer solved only at each instance, but further developed along a trajectory shaped by the hypercycle operating in terms of the two anticipatory mechanisms that are interfaced by this third mechanism. The interface can thus be developed into another subsystem with the specific function of providing organization to the hypercyclic development. This newly emerging subsystem can also be considered as the third helix of a Triple Helix model. The historical format for taking decisions enables the system both to maintain the specific differentiation at interfaces between incursively developing subsystems and to integrate them locally. Because the localization can be varied, this mechanism can function increasingly as a dynamic solution to a puzzle. In other words, one can improve on the solution. The tension between different expectations can be resolved by compromises and trade-offs in the historical manifestations. A differentiated social order can thus be maintained.

6.3   The hypercycle of cultural evolution

Decisions by human agents have always been taken in a reflexive and therefore anticipatory mode. However, the invention of printing in the second half of the 15th century allowed for the first time for communication to be organized in an *incursive* mode that could increasingly be stabilized at the level of the social system. Previous forms of organization had been hierarchical: although the social system could allow for variation, decisions had *eventually* to be taken or sanctified at the top. In a functionally differentiated system, decisions can be processed in a distributed mode and handled to a large extent at the level of the subsystems. Order is then no longer given *ex ante*, but emerges operationally, that is, *ex post*, and the historical process of change can affect the structure of the society because a rewrite becomes possible. However, the new dimensions emerge within the historical system. The degree of transition depends on how the *sequences* of decisions are organized in terms of their incursive or recursive components.

During a relatively short period, the number of books in Europe increased from approximately thirty thousand to nine million (Strydon, 1999, at p. 2). Protestant churches no longer needed a Pope as Vicar of Christ to provide the Catholic interpretation of the Gospel, because they had direct access to authenticated versions of the Bible. One text (e.g., the New Testament) can contradict another (the Old Testament),[62] but reading both of them is instructive. The intertextuality provides surplus value (Kristeva, 1980). The Bible was increasingly translated into the vernacular and mass-produced. Subsequent versions of the Bible could be

---

[62] The New Testament reflected the personal meaning of substantive communication in the Old Testament. Christianity, however, initially adapted to the Roman system, which spanned the whole world (κατ' ὁλην γην or Catholic) in the form of a stable Empire.

improved with reference to the original by comparing Latin translations with Greek and Hebrew texts (Eisenstein, 1979).

While the effects of printing on the historical system were almost immediate—for example, in disseminating Luther's writings—the transformation that became evolutionarily possible because of this new mechanism of social coordination had to be understood, organized, and gradually provided with meaning by the carrying agents. New meanings had to be communicated and stabilized. The process of exploiting the advantages of this new scale of communication would take centuries and developed in reflexive stages.

Until recently, for example, authors in political philosophy have defended the position of a 'priority of the political system' despite their recognition of a 'structural transformation of the public sphere' (e.g., Habermas, 1974; Rorty, 1988). A model with a fundamental priority in the order among its functional systems is still hierarchical (Bernstein, 1995). The hierarchical model uses a biological metaphor of levels of integration to describe and explain social phenomena. For example, the higher functions of the brain require the integrated activity of several brain areas. The biological model of levels of integration is deeply rooted in the semantics of our common language about social organization. In German (as in Dutch), for example, one uses the word 'Obrigkeit' ('aboveness') for the public authority of the state. If the system contains one more degree of freedom, different centers of control may begin to compete for this priority.

Functions in the communication develop heterarchically, that is, juxtaposed to one another. Functional differentiation of the communication is based on different codifications in the communication. The previous hierarchies are eroded by the incursive organization of the communication because the emerging hypercycle can be more efficient for the dissemination. In the heterarchical system which emerges thereafter, the axes of codification can be expected to develop increasingly in orthogonal directions like the eigenvectors of a network. Reflection of one dimension into another is thus no longer to be considered as a mirroring among levels (using 180 degrees), but as a projection on a different axis (using 90 degrees). The reflected substance can be considered from different (and potentially orthogonal) angles. The relations between different reflections require translations because each reflection uses a different code. The biological metaphor obscures this more complex operation of translation in the social system.

While in the biological model the manifest phenomena are the *explanandum*, in the sociological model the manifestations are only instantiations of the dynamics of communication (Giddens, 1984). The functions in the communication can no longer be considered as functions of a given system. The eigenvectors that indicate these functions may also change with the further development of the network. These codes of the communication are not only different as functions at each moment in time, but differentiated like structures that last over some time. Because they operate as expectations (while they are not given), these structures are potentially incursive: they span eigendynamics along orthogonal axes in an expanding universe of possible communications. For example, one can be deeply religious and yet entertain scientific theories as truths, that is, with a status other than religious truth.

6.4   Smbolically generalized media of communication

When the organization of society could no longer be contained within a single hierarchy (at the end of the Middle Ages), another format for the organization of communication was gradually invented in the social system, namely, that of functional differentiation. This new form was shaped in the fifteenth century, for example, in the Low Countries when the House of Burgundy ruled over these regions.

The Dukes of Burgundy were neither Emperors (of Germany) nor Kings (of France), and therefore, they suffered from a lack of religious legitimation for claiming sovereignty. Given the social and power relations of the time, monetary unification was invented as a means to bind together their 'Empire of the Middle' (between France and Germany) on the basis of the increased wealth in the cities. Philip the Good unified the monetary systems of Flanders, Brabant, Holland, and Hainault in 1433. In 1489, the silver 'stuiver' (or 'sous') was legally standardized as one twentieth of a golden guilder (florin) in all the Burgundian Netherlands (Groustra, 1995). This monetary union lasted until 1556. The coordination eroded because of the inflationary import of silver from the Spanish colonies during the 1540s and the Protestant uprisings in the Netherlands in the 1550s.

Monetary union was at first an institutional means to a political end. With the further extension and globalization of the Habsburg empire in the first half of the sixteenth century, the relation between gold and silver coins became related to their global value.[63] When the Dutch revolt gained momentum in the 1570s and 1580s,

---

[63] Gresham's law states that "bad money drives out good money," which means that once silver is more cheaply available than gold, people will tend to bring the cheaper coins into

continued >

the northern provinces also decided that they no longer needed a King 'by the Grace of God,' but that they could organize the political system as a Republic. The Dutch guilder became the symbol of the new Republic. The sciences and the arts, once set free from religious control, could then begin to flourish. The principle of functional differentiation entails that various symbolically mediated communication systems can operate to solve problems in society in a heterarchical mode, that is, alongside each other. Over time, these parallel systems can be expected to develop functionality for one another. Functionality, however, is developed along orthogonal dimensions. Thus, one can expect that it would take time to develop from the stage of a horizontally stratified hierarchy into differentiation with functions along orthogonal axes as another mode of social organization.

The different function systems use specific codes to provide meaning to communications. Whereas the hierarchical (Catholic) system had eventually a single center of control—based on a holy text and its sole interpretation by the Vatican— economic exchange relations, for example, can be handled by making payments in a decentralized mode. One needs more abstract mechanisms to sustain such a mode of social coordination. The symbolically generalized medium of money makes it no longer necessary to communicate by negotiating prices verbally or imposing them by force. The specification of a price as an expected market value speeds up the economic transaction processes by organizing the communication in a specific (that is, functionally codified) format.

While these processes can be interfaced successfully in local niches—that is, organizations which reduce the complexity given geographical constraints—one would expect ongoing instability at the systems level when the mode of organization is increasingly differentiated. Although the semantics of the reformation with its claim of religious freedom made it possible to solve these interface problems locally, for example, in bourgeois cities, the mechanical reproduction of communication on a massive scale induced another dynamic, namely bifurcation at the level of the social system. First, in the latter half of the fifteenth and the sixteenth century the printing press generated an incursive routine in the reproduction of the Bible and other books. The bifurcation induced historical instability. At the level of the differentiated system, however, the potentially incursive routines could gradually be developed into a hyper-incursive routine between expectations as it enabled some regions to stabilize their independence. The selection pressure is then so increased that the system can be expected to exhibit crises and catastrophes. As explained in

---

circulation and save the gold ones. In 1551 Sir Thomas Gresham managed to make extremely large profits based on this principle.

Chapter Five, their mediation requires a decision rule. Constitutions have provided these decision rules at the level of emerging national systems, but it would take centuries to invent them.

Let me specify the qualitative difference of the incursive routine implied in the invention of the printing press. When manuscripts have to be transcribed, the communication system operates recursively: each next version is a copy of a previous one. The new version can be expected to have lost signal from the original because of transcription errors and an increasing time difference. Thus, this system becomes highly reliant on its archival function (Eisenstein, 1979; 1983). This order in the reproduction of communication changed after the introduction of the printing press. For example, each new version of a scientific textbook is expected to improve on the previous ones. In addition to adding new insights, previous errors and typos can be corrected with hindsight. The editing of texts becomes increasingly an incursive mechanism. One can operate with hindsight and reflexively improve on previous versions. These improvements are informed, for example, by making comparisons with other Bible translations. Thus, another dynamics is introduced into the reproduction of communication and a space is carved out for another type of evolution at the level of the social system.[64] Thereafter, knowledge-based communication could increasingly be organized during the 17th and 18th centuries (Foucault, 1972). Because of the focus of this study, let me shortly return to the symbolic mediation of communication in science.

---

[64] In 1981 Luhmann formulated the consequences of the printing press as a main driver in shaping the conditions for scientific progress:

> The consequences of the introduction of the printing press have not yet been elaborated theoretically. For our purposes it is most important that the space for communication was greatly enlarged, the learning process was accelerated, the reaction time shortened, and that taking responsibility for one's position became a public practice. Furthermore, a new book is now better than an old one, new knowledge better than old knowledge, while previously the distance from sources and transcriptions provided sources of error. In any case, technology and technique now for the first time became the subjects of a special literature (Luhmann, 1987 [1981], at pp. 51f.; my translation, L.)

Texts can be coded differently for different purposes and audiences, and thus differentiation is further induced. The historian Eisenstein (1983) also mentioned this change in the dynamics of reproducing a text, but she did not elaborate it from a sociological perspective.

The differentiation of the communication is well known for the distinction between scientific and religious truth as this played a key role in Galilei's trial before the Inquisition. While forced to reinvoke his thesis in the *Dialogo* of 1632—by stating that the Copernican model could be considered as another hypothesis—Galilei was able to publish the *Discorsi* in 1638 in the Netherlands. The protestant environment could more easily accept a difference between religious Truth and the provisional truth claims of science (Leydesdorff, 1994c, 2001b).[65]

When dimensions of the communication are differentiated in terms of the meaning that they provide to communication, these different structures can operate upon each using hyper-incursive routines. The decision rules needed, can be further developed into interfaces, but these decisions can be expected to mean different things

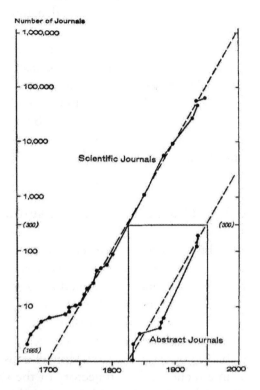

Figure 6.6: Total number of scientific and abstract journals founded, as a function of date. From: Price (1961).

for the two systems of expectations. The symmetry is broken and a dimension added to the complexity of the system. A system which systematically stores its previous decisions by using the newly invented printing press can then develop also institutional momentum.

Along the knowledge-based axis of organizing scientific communication, one would historically locate the bifurcation between local knowledge production and global

---

[65] The differentiation first—during the 15th century—took place in the distinction between political and religious texts. For example, in the Dutch declaration of independence, *Plakkaat van de Verlaetinge* (1581), the Estates General of the United Netherlands declared the King of Spain 'to be from his authority and sovereignty of these Netherlands, and forbid to use his name and seal in these countries' because he has abused his religious prerogative by exerting political tyranny.

control in the invention of scientific journals (Figure 6). After 1665 the historical recursion of this incursive dynamics within the social system would grow exponentially. The *intellectual* (e.g., disciplinary) organization of the sciences, as different from its social organization in local institutions, was organized increasingly on the basis of mechanisms like peer review of journal submissions at the global level (Bazerman, 1983; Biagioli and Galison, 2003; Leydesdorff, 2001b). This knowledge-based organization provides a model that is able to handle more complexity than a local organization, and therefore exerts evolutionary pressure on all the subsystems which operate at lower levels in parallel and in interaction with one another.

6.5   The experience and semantics of hyper-incursivity

The differentiated system can be expected to couple at some places more than at others. At the level of the social system, therefore, incursion and recursion are no longer unambiguously coupled at each moment in time as they are (structurally) at the level of an individual or in a social system which is still integrated as an identity. The retention mechanism of the networked systems, however, remains historical. The instantaneous advantages of a specific recombination of codes have yet to be stabilized over the time axis. Initially this leads to a local reduction of the complexity as in a niche, but the trajectory of the subsystem may carry over into changing the next-order regime after a bifurcation.

The historical stabilization in an organization is thus a necessary but not a sufficient condition for the globalization of the innovative dynamic of a knowledge base. The series of decisions implied is constructed historically, but only if this subdynamic of making decisions is further codified in a (set of) decision rule(s) can it begin to operate at the supra-individual level with reference to the future instead of the past. A knowledge-based organization emerges from this uncoupling of analytical decision-making from historical routines (Nonaka and Takeuchi, 1995).

The focus on decision rules and organizing planning cycles has long been accepted in knowledge-intensive organizations like diversified and multinational corporations (e.g., Chandler, 1962; Galbraith and Nathanson, 1978; Newman and Logan, 1981). Interfaces between marketing and R&D have to be carefully constructed and maintained in cycles of strategic and operational planning because the expectations on both sides remain highly uncertain. The need to organize knowledge-intensive processes *in the public domain* of government was felt only recently in the late 1970s (after of the global oil crises) and articulated most pronouncedly by the OECD (e.g.,

OECD, 1980; Rothwell and Zegveld, 1981; Freeman, 1982). Knowledge intensity, however, opens the system of decisions to future perspectives and thus generates uncertainty in public policy-making. The technocratic arguments for proceeding in this direction were reflected intellectually in debates about the risk society (Beck, 1992a).

In the political domain it is extremely difficult to take responsibility for a system that evolves in terms of uncertainties and expectations (Beck *et al.*, 2003; Leydesdorff, 1993c; Luhmann, 1986b).[66] The political domain was stabilized, for example, in terms of constitutions so that uncertainties could be balanced in an institutional setting like the nation-states. The history of European integration in terms of supra-national policies and the role of knowledge-based innovations can be rewritten from the perspective of how knowledge-based ideas interact with the need for normative integration (Frenken and Leydesdorff, 2004). Future-oriented incursions disturb the historically formed systems continuously. However, let me develop the argument here in terms of how the communication system itself operates.

The development of the personal computer during the 1980s and the development of ICT (the Internet) during the 1990s has made the experience of a system of communications that operates incursively accessible from the perspective of our everyday life. More than print communication in previous centuries, electronic communication reinforces the incursive subroutines of communication with another loop and therefore potentially with another dimension. The incursivity of the communicative operation is reinforced at the Internet because of the volatility of the medium. Consequently, the concepts of incursivity and hyper-incursivity can nowadays be provided with a semantics that is much less abstract than heretofore.

For example, search engines like AltaVista and Google operate not only incursively, but also with a hyper-incursive subroutine. The engines are able to overwrite and therefore gradually lose their histories. Without further provisions (for example, by saving historical records for research purposes), the historical reconstruction can become impossible because the index is being continuously updated. The historical trajectory of the generation of this system is no longer important for the functions of the system at a next moment in time (Mackenzie, 2001).

---

[66] Normative expectations operate differently from cognitive ones. The failure of cognitive expectations can be expected to generate a breakdown of trust in a relation, while the failure of normative orientations generates anxiety (Luhmann, 1993b; Herrmann, 2001).

The search engines use 'spiders' which 'crawl' the Internet. When an Internet-page that was previously listed as from 2001 is visited by the spider again, a recent update (e.g., in 2003) is used to update the index of the search engine accordingly. Thus, the previous reference to a date in 2001 is overwritten with a reference to the updated page with the new time stamp of 2003. The more recent information provides a representation of the past that is more functional for information retrieval in the present than the previous representation.

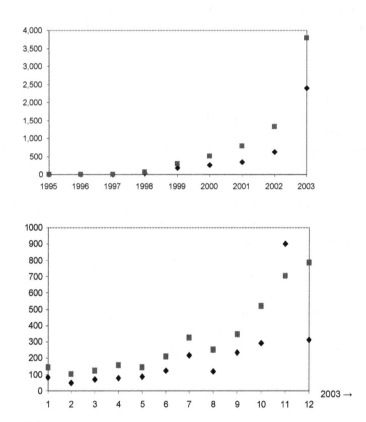

Figure 6.7a and 6.7b: Search results using 'Frankenfood*' as search terms in *Google* on 21 January (■) and 20 February 2004 (♦), respectively. Source: Hellsten *et al.*, forthcoming.

Figure 7 shows the results of using Google for precisely the same search with a time interval of only one month. All searches were done on 21 January and 20 February 2004, respectively. The left-hand picture can be considered as a representation of the long-term memory of this search engine, and the right-hand one of its short-term memory function. The latter searches used the 12 months in 2003 as the domains. With the exception of one point (November 2003), both graphs are systematically lower for the later searches because the system loses its history in accordance with the expectation specified above.

Over longer periods of time the effect of the incursive subroutine—operating in the present—is dampened by the historical continuity of the search engines. In general, the search engines are engineered, and engineered systems are not expected to change their mode of operation on the fly. However, in the most recent periods the intervention of a social system of communication using an incursive dynamics disturbs the recursively constructed stability. In other words, social systems operate differently from engineered systems. They also change their mode of operation over time. This is reflected in the historical records, but the changes cannot be explained in terms of engineering. The effect is a consequence of the incursive dynamics which determines what is meaningful and what not. The incursive routine operates in the present by reconstructing the past, but this restructuring does not always have to reach into deep layers of the past.

Information retrieval systems are designed specifically so that the user can optimize the information for its functions in the present. The search engines use an incursive routine for the update of their functionality in the present without having to bother about how this functionality was achieved historically. The availability of this subroutine in everyday life and its common use as a technology makes it increasingly possible to provide incursion with substantive meaning. The very abstract concept of incursion has been quasi-materialized in the virtual domain. Because of this historical realization, the concept can be provided with a substantive (and not only a formal) semantics (Hollak, 1963). Unlike engineered systems, the stability in social systems is not engineered *ex ante*, but continuously reconstructed and therefore self-generated *ex post*. The search results provide us with a fingerprint of these moving systems.

The institutional layer of the social system can be considered analogously as a retention mechanism for the solutions of puzzles at the interfaces that have been achieved hitherto by the differentiated subsystems of communication. The functionally differentiated system is no longer integrated in a center, but coordinated by communications in cycles and hypercycles which operate both incursively and recursively. The communications can be codified differently —for example, in terms of markets or in terms of policies—and the communication is also always doubled in terms of historical information processing and organization versus the processing of meaning and its evolutionary codification. At each interface innovative restructuring is possible, in principle, because communications, their network structures, their frequencies, and their potential globalizations remain cultural constructions.

6.6   Layers of selectivity in the social system

Functional differentiation among codes of communication was constructed as a viable form of social organization in Europe on the basis of a century of (primarily religious) wars between 1550 and 1650. Institutional differentiation became possible when this social order of modernity became fully established during the 18th century. In the Triple Helix model, the institutional differentiation is considered as a retention mechanism of functional differentiation. The surplus value of this model for understanding the systematic absorption of knowledge-based innovations at the interfaces will be elaborated in a next section. But let me first provide a short rewrite of the macro history of the social system from this perspective.

Historically, the crucial differentiations have been those of geographical autonomy, economic liberalization, and the freedom of thought from religious control. Since Galileo, for example, scientists have had a particular need to differentiate scientific communication structurally from the code of communication prevailing in belief systems. In science, one needs room for provisional interpretations that can be adjusted with hindsight. Unlike belief systems, the sciences can be considered as systems of rationalized expectations. The expectations remain grounded in the beliefs of individuals and communities, but the dynamics of the interactive layer of scholarly communications provides the operation of the system. While beliefs are attributes of actors or communities of actors, rational expectations belong to a discourse.[67]

A focus on agents and their belief structures obscures the dynamics of the communication in science. Beliefs tend to be integrated normatively, but the sciences can in the longer run allow for normative control only over the conditions of a communication (e.g., the resource allocations). When normative control is

---

[67] The so-called 'Durkheimian program' in the sociology of science has programmatically proposed to analyze the sciences as belief systems (Bloor, 1976; Douglas, 1982). This provides a different heuristics from the one proposed in this study, namely the research program of social constructivism. In social constructivism the system is constructed socially, but with the axis of time. The reconstruction 'follows the actors' (Latour, 1987). In the research program of this study, however, the social dimension is considered as constructed (and continuously reconstructed) by the reflection and differentiation of the communication (Leydesdorff, 2002c).

temporarily extended to the incursive core of the discourse, the scientific discourse can easily degenerate. For example, the Lysenko-affair in the Soviet Union is a case in point (Graham, 1974; Lecourt, 1976).

Functional *differentiation* requires first the longer-term stabilization of two levels of communication: scientific communication, for example, has both a substantive value in itself and a function for the emerging next-order system of 'universal' theorizing. In principle, substantive novelty (the 'context of discovery') and methodological warrant (the 'context of justification') can then be distinguished analytically (Popper, 1935). The construction of the scholarly communication as a layered system was central to the Scientific Revolution of the 17th century (Biagioli and Galison, 2002; Cohen, 1994; Price, 1961). In science, the knowledge claims of individual authors are evaluated for inclusion in the communication at a next-order (that is, relatively globalized) level.[68]

Marx's distinction between 'exchange value' on the market and 'use value' in concrete production can be considered analogously as references to two subdynamics that operate asymmetrically. Under the condition of functional differentiation, the market can be expected to operate using an abstract code like the price mechanism, while production and consumption have to be organized locally. Market forces can be expected to incur on the local conditions. Marx labeled this 'alienation.' Alienation, however, is still defined with reference to human beings who can be identified. The alienating forces themselves cannot be objectified; they remain hypotheses, that is, codified expectations which are constructed in scholarly discourse (e.g., in terms of Marx's critique of political economy). However, the codification of these expectations generates an incursive feedback on the dynamics of social life. With hindsight, Marx overestimated the revolutionary power of this reconstructive subroutine. Incursion and subsequent reconstructions tend to dampen the expected crises in historically observable systems because uncertainty is removed from the system by these selection mechanisms (Hanneman and Collins, 1986).

---

[68] Gilbert and Mulkay (1984) showed empirically that this differentiation works asymmetrically on the *ex post* evaluation of knowledge claims. When knowledge claims are accepted, a rationalist repertoire tends to dominate the reconstruction by participants. Claims that are not validated in later stages and experimental error, however, are with hindsight discussed in terms of empirical contingencies. Thus, the history of the claims is reconstructed from the perspective of the results of historically later selection processes.

The adjustment of historical organizations to constructed functions under the selection pressure of a next-order regime can be considered as a process of adaptation to the expectations. Adaptation is a gradual process taking place through selection from among possible formations, and therefore institutional change can be expected to lag behind processes of codification and functional differentiation in the communication. The new subsystem emerges within the old system and only then can the restructuring feedback on the layer from which it emerged. In institutional terms this transformation meant the change of territorial integration from the model of a high culture into a model of nation-states.

During the 18th century—perhaps with the exception of the United Kingdom— national state formation lagged:[69] the organization of society had remained in some places entrenched in the mediaeval differentiation of nobility (France, Austria, Spain, and Italy), while in other places regional differences opposed centralization into a nation-state (Germany, The Netherlands). At the end of the eighteenth century, however, the American and French revolutions established two nation-states based on the semantics of a differentiation between civic society ('the pursuit of happiness') and the national state (Montesquieu, 1748).

Although Napoleon tried to export the new ideas about political codification as 'universal,' developments during the period 1815-1870 (German unification) can be characterized as the social elaboration of this differentiation between civic society and the various national states (Gouldner, 1976). The institutional development of the modern state went side by side with the transition from mercantile capitalism (universally oriented) to industrial capitalism (locally organized). Marx noted this transition on the occasion of the revolutions of 1848. When he published *Capital I* in 1867, the new institutional setting was nearing completion. After the American Civil War (1865), the Meji Restoration in Japan (1868), the Commune de Paris in 1870, and the subsequent German and Italian unifications, the major nation systems were in place with their respective (capitalist) economies.

Thus, a dually differentiated system was established: the nation-states contain institutional mechanisms which (like niches) are able to reinforce specific selections from the functional differentiations, for example by maintaining national boundaries. While in a functionally differentiated system the control mechanism is based on specific codes using symbolically generalized media for the communication, a

---

[69] After the English Civil Wars (1640-1660) and the Glorious Revolution (1688/1689), the Act of Union between England and Scotland (1707) centralized Great Britain as a single nation-state.

dually-layered system can periodically shift control between the functional codes and the institutionally stabilized organization (e.g., the bureaucracy). In this oscillation, control tends to become 'trans-epistemic' (Knorr, 1982; Gibbons *et al.*, 1994). The system can also alternate between phases of contraction and expansive modernization (Freeman and Perez, 1988). The two subdynamics of historical continuity and incursive renewal can also be expected to operate concurrently.

When the organization of society becomes so complex that two mechanisms are available for reproduction, ranges of interactions become possible. At specific sites the functional and the institutional layer may begin to reinforce each other, as in a resonance. However, at most places two selections can be expected to extinguish a signal. A lock-in between an institutional dynamic and a functional dynamic can therefore be expected to occur locally and discretely, and if stabilized, the resulting patterns can be expected to follow relatively independent trajectories. When a distribution of stabilizations has been shaped, some stabilizations can be selected for globalization, and then the trajectory can evolve into a regime (Schumpeter, [1911] 1949).

In addition to the two layers, the differentiated system also contains horizontal interfaces. A lock-in between two functional dynamics can be expected to follow from hyper-incursive interactions among function systems because of trajectory formation in the decisions. The decision trajectory can then be locked-in into an organization (Chapter Five). The prevailing format for this organization of interfacing the various functions has been the nation-state during the period 1870-1940, but gradually the multi-national corporation has developed another format for these interfaces (Galbraith, 1967). The institutional solutions can be considered as generating equilibria conditions (Aoki, 2001). They buffer the system in an institutional layer against the disturbances generated by the fluxes. As the organization itself becomes more knowledge-intensive, it can be restructured for reasons of functional optimization or for institutional reasons. Thus, the organizational level is itself transformed into a function of the organization and self-organization of communications. The globalization of this format into a next-order network configuration can then increasingly be explained by using the Triple Helix model of university-industry-government relations.

6.7   The Triple Helix overlay

The Triple Helix model takes the traditional forms of institutional differentiation among universities, industries, and governments as the starting point for developing the metaphor. The evolutionary perspective adds to this historical configuration the notion that human carriers are able to reshape these institutions reflexively. The model thus takes account of the expanding role of the knowledge sector in relation to the political and economic infrastructure of the larger society. From this evolutionary perspective, the institutions can be considered as the fingerprints of the communication patterns that have been functional for the reproduction of the system(s) hitherto. The functionality of differentiation leads to longer-term institutionalization. When the various cycles resonate, this hypercycle can increasingly be closed (e.g., first within a national system).

Historically, the organized interaction between markets and sciences has been traced back to the second half of the 19th century (Braverman, 1974; Noble, 1977). As noted, institutional differentiation between the nation-state and the economy preceded this period. In other words, the Triple Helix can be considered as a result of an interaction between functional and institutional dynamics in society. This interaction became possible when the two dynamics were fully established, that is, after approximately 1870.

Functions *Institutions*	**Science**	**Economy**
Public	**Academia; University**	Patent legislation; Science, Technology, and Innovation Policies
Private	Industrial R&D labs; Industrially owned universities	**Trade and Industry**

Table 6.1: The interaction between functional and institutional differentiation in university-industry-government relations

In Table 1, the functional differentiation between the sciences and the market, and the institutional differentiation between private control by entrepreneurs (civic society) and public control by the state are cross-tabled. Over time this cross-tabulation leads to a model of technological developments in terms of interactions in university-industry-government relations. As argued in Chapter One, three functional subdynamics are involved: wealth generation, novelty production, and control by decisions at interfaces. As I have shown above, three dynamics are sufficiently complex to generate a hypercycle as a next-order system. Specific solutions at one interface can then be reinforced (or eroded!) by the third subdynamic.

Three subdynamics generate a configuration, while two subdynamics can be resolved in a co-evolution. A configuration no longer necessarily has a single center of (hierarchical) control. A functionally differentiated configuration can be expected to emerge because functional differentiation has the evolutionary advantage of enabling the system to process more complexity. Functions provide the subsystems with models of each other, and thus a hypercycle can be maintained. As long as the hypercycle is still integrated in a quasi-equilibrium like a nation-state, the recursive dynamic prevails. However, the incursive dynamics invert the time axis within the complex system. Consequently, the integration tends to shift to the next-order (network) level, but whether this flexibility can be allowed depends on the communicative competencies of the carriers. The operation of the links tends to take over control from the nodes, but the agents at the nodes can be expected to resist this evolution. Thus, the system can be expected to remain in transition.

I shall model this configuration in the next part of this study in terms of the Triple Helix, using the plus or the minus sign of mutual information in three dimensions as an indicator of the advancement of this development. Let me first describe the historical development of the knowledge-based economy in the period since World War Two.

Chapter 7

The Historical Evolution of the Triple Helix

As organizational control mechanisms in state apparatuses and in knowledge-intensive industries become increasingly anticipatory, a knowledge-based economy emerges as an interaction effect among institutions and functions. The role of the state can in this case be expected to change. Historically, however, these processes take time because they take place at the supra-individual and the supra-institutional level. The infrastructures maintain their (quasi-)equilibria and tend to resist change. Thus, the system can be expected to alternate between periods of change and stability.

After the Second World War, the instruments of science, technology, and innovation policies had first to be developed (1950-1970). Funding agencies and ministries for science and technology policy had to be put in place. The oil crises of the 1970s made it possible to formulate new policies at the supra-national level of, for example, the Organization of Economic Cooperation and Development (OECD) and the—at that time emerging—European Union. Unlike national policies, the policies of the European Commission cannot be focused on the institutional level because the European dimension is supposed to add surplus value by combining existing capacities. The focus has therefore been on newly emerging 'platform sciences' like ICT, biotechnology, and new materials in the so-called 'pre-competitive stage' of their development (Langford and Langford, 2001; Leydesdorff and Gauthier, 1996). The focus on the 'pre-competitive' stage has legitimated the construction of a new set of university-industry-government relations.

During the Cold War the liberal mode of organizing society and the political economy—grounded in nationally shaped institutions—stood in sharp contrast to the planned economies of the Soviet Union and its allies. In a knowledge-based economy, however, the role of the state begins to change because the dynamics of developing scientific knowledge is different from the economic dynamics of the market or the institutional dynamics of state apparatuses. One can follow this development in terms of science policy instruments over time. For example, the so-called Framework Programs of the European Commission have increasingly formulated an incursive program of political intervention in the development of science, technology, and innovation. The work program for Targeted Socio-Economic Research of the European Commission formulated this focus in its Fifth Framework Program as follows:

The capacity of economies to develop, innovate and generate employment also depends heavily on the structure of its public and private institutions, both formal and informal, and on the effect of their formal or informal codes of practice. Institutional inertia and outdated practice act as a brake on progress and the adoption of new technologies and best practice: alternatively, the institutional conditions may provide support for innovation. The introduction of change needs an appreciation of the cultural/gender and historical factors which shape institutions and practices, a reassessment of the relationship between the public and private sector and a thorough understanding of the impacts on innovation and employment. (European Commission, 1997, at pp. 14f.)

A similar emphasis on intervention in order to strengthen knowledge-based innovation can be found in other world regions. Etzkowitz (1994), for example, called attention for the increasingly interventionist character of the U.S. government in matters of science, technology, and innovation policies. The legitimation of government support for knowledge-based innovation programs in the post-Cold War era, however, can be 'by no means assured given the strength of *laissez faire* ideology' in the U.S.A. (Etkzowitz, 1996, at p. 22).

The demise of the Soviet Union in 1991 is an interesting case at the other end of the political spectrum. The crisis of the communist system had been foreseen during the Prague Spring of 1968 by the Czechoslovak Communist Party. The institutionally shaped bureaucracies of the Soviet economies would be unable to absorb the emerging knowledge-based dynamics sufficiently (Löbl, 1967; Richta *et al.*, 1968). The program of the Communist Party of Czechoslovakia of 5 April 1968 formulated this as follows in a document which has become historical because of the events thereafter:

[…] it will be necessary to prepare the country for joining the scientific-technical revolution in the world, which calls for especially intensive cooperation of workers and agricultural workers with the technical and specialized intelligentsia, and which will place high demands upon the knowledge and qualifications of people, on the application of science (ČSSR, 1968, at p. 3).

In 1968 this argument could not be substantiated with convincing support from economic theorizing. (Note that the 'scientific-technical revolution' was not specified in terms of the economic system, but in terms of its consequences for labor.) After the demise of the Soviet Union, however, the 14th National Congress of the Chinese Communist Party (1992) decided promptly to introduce "the market

system" structurally and "to rejuvenate the country through science and education."
A neo-evolutionary model for managing human resources in niches and for
restructuring institutional relations among universities, industry, and government
was increasingly elaborated (Tong, 1996; Li and Guoping, 1999). The expansion and
commercialization of the Internet after 1995 boosted China's modernization
process. Universities and their spin-offs play an increasingly important role in the
transformation of Chinese society towards a knowledge-based economy
(Leydesdorff and Guoping, 2001; Zhou and Leydesdorff, 2006).

These examples are meant to demonstrate the urgency of understanding the
knowledge base of an economy in the current reorganization of society. In this
chapter I specify the history of science and technology policy from this perspective.
The understanding of the knowledge base in terms of a Triple Helix overlay—or, in
the words of the previous chapter, a hypercycle—will be developed into a
methodology for measurement in the next chapters. The epistemological critique of
the functionalist assumptions of the Triple Helix model is discussed in this chapter,
as is the sociological critique of importing a biological model. I return to the
philosophical implications of the neo-functionalist model in the final chapter with
the conclusions.

In general, two types of critique have been voiced against using a neo-functionalist
model in a sociological explanation: one from the side of biologists who argue that a
functionalist model is no longer valid if functions cannot be specified
unambiguously (because they are networked), and another from the side of
sociologists who argue that because of this uncertainty one should abandon the
effort to model society in evolutionary terms. I shall argue that these critiques are
valid if the biological model were used for social systems theory without reflection.
However, the communication turn in social systems theory makes the functions
uncertain, while they remain measurable as uncertainties by elaborating on the
mathematical theory of communication. Therefore, in my opinion, the project of
measuring the knowledge base of an economy is feasible. This will be the focus of
Chapters Eight to Ten.

In summary, I accept the critique of biologists that communications cannot be
observed unambiguously. However, the resulting uncertainties can be measured. I
also accept the critique of sociologists that human communications cannot be
modeled without paying attention to reflexivity as the *differentia specifica* of social
systems. Unlike the problem of the ambiguity of the functions at each moment in
time, the question of reflexivity first addresses the uncertainty in the dynamics along
the time axis. Information theory enables us to measure these two uncertainties (at
each moment and over time) in a single design (Bar-Hillel, 1962; Theil, 1972;

Leydesdorff, 1995a). The knowledge base will in the following chapters be identified as the possible reduction of the probabilistic entropy (that is, against the increase of entropy along the axis of time) *within* a Triple Helix because of the possibility of specific configurations among the sources of uncertainty.

7.1   Science and technology policies

The military impact of science and technology through knowledge-based development and mission-oriented research during World War II (e.g., the Manhattan project) made it necessary in 1945 to formulate a new science and technology policy under peacetime conditions. Vannevar Bush's (1945) report to the U.S. President entitled *The Endless Frontier* has been considered a landmark for the emergence of this new science policy. The report contained a plea for a return to a liberal organization of science. Quality control should be left to the scientific elite, for example, through the peer review system.

This 'pure science' model of the U.S. National Science Foundation (1947)[70] was quickly followed by other Western countries. For example, the Netherlands created its foundation for Fundamental Scientific Research (ZWO) in 1950. With hindsight, one can consider this period as the institutional phase of science policies. The main policy instrument at that time was the support of science with institutions to control the funding (Brookman, 1983).

The launching of Sputnik by the Soviet Union in 1957 turned the tables for the emerging science policies. The Soviets—who had used a non-liberal model (Graham, 1974)—had unexpectedly become more successful than the West in mission-oriented research.[71] A far-reaching reorganization of the American research

---

[70] The first N.S.F. act of 1947 was vetoed by President Truman so that the creation of the N.S.F. was postponed until 1950. The later and more detailed "Steelman Report," *Science and Public Policy*, published in 1947, set in motion the eventual role the federal government would play in supporting fundamental research at universities (NSF, 2000).

[71] President Eisenhower felt the pressure of the alliance between the scientific elite and the military to enlarge the funding of the science system after the Sputnik shock. In addition to his warning (in his farewell speech) against the pressure of a 'military-industrial complex,' he formulated as a less known 'second warning:'

> Yet in holding scientific research and discovery in respect, as we should, we must also be alert to the equal and opposite danger that public policy could itself become the captive of a scientific-technological elite. (York, 1970, at p. 9).

system was one of the consequences. The National Aeronautics and Space Administration (NASA) and the Advanced Research Projects Agency (ARPA), in particular, were created in response to the launch of Sputnik and the perception of military threat (Edwards, 1996). The situation was ready for this change because during the second half the 1950s, it had become clear that the continuing growth rates of Western economies could no longer be explained in terms of traditional economic factors such as land, labor, and capital. The 'residue' which remained after this traditional explanation of economic growth had to be attributed to the development of knowledge in the economy (Abramowitz, 1956; OECD, 1964; Rosenberg 1976a). In 1961, the *Organization for Economic Co-operation and Development (OECD)* was created in order to organize and to coordinate science and technology policies among its member states.[72] The study and coordination of science and technology as a factor of production was thus placed on the agenda.

In 1963, the OECD published the *Frascati Manual* in which parameters were defined for the statistical monitoring of science and technology on a comparative basis (OECD, 1963). Comparisons among nation-states, however, make it possible to raise questions with respect to strengths and weaknesses in their respective portfolios. During the 1960s national S&T policies thus began to emerge in the OECD member states. For example, the statistics showed that physics had been very successful after World War II in organizing its interests both within the various nation-states and at the level of international collaborations (e.g., CERN). Other scientific communities (e.g., molecular biology) claimed more budgetary room given new developments and the increases in overall science budgets. During the period 1965-1975, the preferred instrument for dealing with these issues at the national level was a differentiation in the increase rates of budgets at the disciplinary level. In summary, the focus remained on (financial) input-indicators, while the system relied on peer review for more fine-grained decision-making (Mulkay, 1976).

Since the late 1970s, in the light of proposals for reindustrialization after the oil crises typically involving the reorganization of connections between the state and industry, and academia and industry (e.g., OECD, 1980), a more proactive science, technology, and innovation policy has been developed. Scientific and technological development and knowledge-based innovation first required the recursive stability of *national* coordination between industrial policies and science and technology policies. Geographical proximity stimulates the solution of puzzles by local agents.

---

[72] The OECD was based on the OEEC, the Organization for European Economic Cooperation, that is, the organization which had served for the distribution of the U.S. and Canadian aid under the Marshall Plan during the postwar period.

More recently, however, innovation policies across institutional spheres have taken hold in Western countries that had achieved a high degree of separation between institutional spheres in the period after the Second World War.

7.2 The European Union and research evaluation

The *Single Act* of the European Community in 1986 and the *Maastricht Treaty* of the European Union in 1991 have marked a gradual transition within Europe to a supra-national technology and innovation policy. Policies at the European level have continuously referred to science and technology, because these have been considered as the strongholds of the common heritage of the EU-member states (Vavakova, 2000). However, the 'subsidiarity' principle prescribes that the European Commission should not intervene in matters that can be left to the nation-states. Therefore, a 'federal' science policy of the EU could not be developed without taking the detour of a focus on *innovation* as a science-based practice (Narin and Noma, 1985; Frenken and Leydesdorff, 2004).

The so-called *Research, Technology, and Development (RTD) Networks* of the European Union have promoted transnational and transsectoral collaboration by rewarding the participation of research groups that capitalize on *complementarities* among national origins and institutional spheres. Thus, the operation of 'a Triple Helix of university-industry-government relations' has been reinforced by the European level of policy making. First, the institutional domains with different functions (industry and academia) and with different national backgrounds were facilitated by these networks. More importantly, however, the resulting 'consortia' of industries, universities, and public sector laboratories had to show complementarity by defining themselves functionally with reference to the programmatic objectives of the European programs. A system of negotiations and translations among expectations thus added a dynamic overlay to the nationally institutionalized systems (Etzkowitz and Leydesdorff, 2000).

Interactions and complementarities can be optimized *ex post* with objectives other than the institutional rationales of the interacting agents *ex ante*. When repeated over time, the reflexive dynamics at the network level may increasingly feedback on the historical drivers. From this perspective, the institutional layer can be considered as the retention mechanism for a network that is developing at another level in terms of its functions. The European Union has provided this type of feedback by stabilizing the next-order level in a bureaucracy with an agenda different from those of the national research systems. This overlay system with its own dynamics can be conceptualized as a network mode—named 'Mode 2' by Gibbons *et al.* (1994)—or as 'transnational' when compared with the 'national systems of innovation' previously studied by evolutionary economists (e.g., Lundvall, 1992; Nelson, 1993). Note that the institutional interests are the drivers in the initial phase, but may lock-in into a hypercycle at the network level for stochastic reasons. The resulting system may evolve into a carrier of more specific functions in a later stage when the various layers have been differentiated as dimensions of the new system.

The Triple Helix combines the two perspectives (of institutions and functions) by distinguishing both layers in a model: the institutional one and the communicative overlay on top of it. The two layers function as feedback mechanisms on each other, but they have different functions and are of a different nature. In terms of the analytical model, they no longer interact with each other as layers on top of each other, but as dimensions, that is, as axes that stand orthogonally (see Chapter One, Figure 1.4). The system of reference at the overlay level can be considered as a hypercycle in which interaction terms are communicated differently from the substances that are communicated in the institutional dimensions of the system (that is, academia, industry, government).

This differentiation resounds with tensions between functions and missions in each of the carrying systems. When the environment is differentiated, each subsystem can be expected to internalize the differentiation by using its interface mechanisms for the mediation. For example, the intellectual dynamics of science is not determined by the institutional dynamics in a national context, but by the possibility to advance the understanding in a discourse at the global level. While political decision-making focuses on institutional means and resource allocations to achieve its goals, it needs a political discourse which discusses these investments functionally in terms of priorities. National systems have elaborated a relative equilibrium (of 'checks and balances') among these very unequal dimensions, and thus the interfaces within the subsystems are already available. The new configurations change the evolutionary functions of existing subsystems.

The emerging European system has been successful insofar as it was able to exploit advantages of *recombining* these different dimensions within its arrangements. The recombination provides a dimension potentially tangential to the previously stabilized systems in the member states. The analytical distinctions among the subdynamics enable us to understand each organization as a specific solution. The subdynamics of the market, for example, are different from those of knowledge production. However, these analytically different subdynamics can be expected to interact in the case of innovation. Additionally, within each of the systems, more than a single subdynamic can be appreciated. Thus, the model becomes holographic:

all subsystems need reproduction and therefore organization. Organization constructs a relative equilibrium or a steady state among the fluxes of different communications at their respective levels of organization. The next-order systems build on the relative stabilities of the lower-order ones at each level, but control can shift from one level to another both within (sub)systems and among them. Although historically constructed as levels, the next-order systems can also be considered as orthogonal dimensions. The dimensions are analytical, and the resulting phenomena are based on the interactions among them.

More than in the case of the national systems which emerged historically (in the 19th century) with an emphasis on institutionalization, understanding organization and control at the level of the European Union requires us to make these analytical distinctions. The reconstruction enables us to appreciate the potential for surplus value of the European constructs. For example, one can understand the so-called subsidiarity principle—which states that the European level should not assume functions which can be addressed sufficiently by the individual member states—as a functional requirement and not only as an institutional one which regulates relations between authorities.

The institutions may initially be next-level copies of national formats. For example, the European Commission may have a kind of minister of foreign affairs or a central bank, but these institutions have to be constructed carefully in terms of their functions. In some case (as in the case of monetary integration in the Eurozone) one may adopt a federalist model. In other cases, an intergovernmental model can be expected to prevail, since one cannot assume that a federal model will work in each dimension. For example, the democratic deficit of the European Union can be considered as a structural problem because the European Parliament cannot function as a replica or a sum-total of the national parliaments.[73]

If policies in a knowledge-intensive context do not sufficiently distinguish among the different subdynamics, political interventions can easily generate confusions and misfits (Dits and Berkhout, 1999). For example, national governments have often been dramatically unsuccessful in developing transdisciplinary programs (Van den Daele *et al.*, 1977; Studer and Chubin, 1982). The institutional means of policy makers can be expected to affect the self-organization of the sciences only marginally (Krohn *et al.*, 1990; Leydesdorff and Van der Schaar, 1987; Leydesdorff *et*

---

[73] The one exception is the European Central Bank in Frankfurt a.M. This institution has replaced the need for national central banks in the countries participating in the Euro (Leydesdorff and Oomes, 1999).

al., 1994). The construction of Europe, however, legitimated recombining the various dimensions in order to solve puzzles at the institutional level.

The point remains that the newly constructed mode affects not only the inputs but also the outputs of the systems which are (re-)engineered. This may require a redefinition of the output. For example, the main objective of the European RTD-Programs has shifted during the 1990s from scientific output in terms of publications in the traditional format (e.g., in the ESPRIT program; Van den Besselaar and Leydesdorff, 1993) towards technological achievements and so-called 'deliverables.' The quality control of these deliverables is relatively unhindered by the evaluation schemes of national research councils and scientific communities. Therefore, they can become carriers for next rounds of policy formation in a new mode of research evaluation. From this perspective, the scientific literature is expected to lag behind the shifting research agendas in the European Framework programs (Lewison and Cunningham, 1991). The bureaucratic discourses reinforce the evaluation of change because changing patterns can be considered as the results of successful implementations of previous policies. Thus, a next and even larger Framework Program can be legitimated.

Research groups are sorted by the trans-national evaluation scheme in terms of their reliability in providing deliverables to the bureaucracy, and therefore in terms of their competencies to serve these audiences. In 'Mode 2' research not only the social, but also the intellectual organization of projects and programs is increasingly functionalized in terms of serving relevant audiences. Kobayashi (2000) compared the performances of these 'research consortia' with theatre or ballet. It should be noted that the shift does not necessarily imply a commercialization of science, since the mechanisms remain mainly institutional and non-market (Nowotny *et al.*, 2001). However, the interface with the environment is endogenized within the system as crucial to its reproduction. The interface itself thus becomes an institutionalized system of knowledge-based innovation and change.

Innovations by definition take place at interfaces. Therefore, they may affect both the innovating and the innovated systems. The emergence of new interfaces also changes the systems. The delineation of a knowledge-based innovation system itself, therefore, begs the question. Innovation systems are not given, but constructed, and their epistemological status consequently remains uncertain. In other words, innovation systems can be hypothesized for heuristic reasons, but should not be reified. 'Innovation' can be considered as the analytical unit of operation of 'innovation systems' that by innovating incorporate knowledge-based developments (Foray, 2004; Leydesdorff and Etzkowitz, 1998). Since innovations take place at interfaces they are interactive and they can build upon one another. Thus, a non-linear dynamics is induced. The rules of systems formation themselves remain operational and therefore contingent on the historical trajectories of the innovating systems.

Evolutionary economists have emphasized the national and institutionalized character of innovation systems in order to comprehend this system, that is, for heuristic reasons in research practices (Lundvall, 1992; Nelson, 1993). National systems, for example, can easily be compared among one another. However, the focus on technological developments has suggested the sectoral level as the most relevant system of reference (Pavitt, 1984; Freeman, 2002). Others (e.g., Carlsson, 2002) have argued in favor of new technosciences like biotechnology as the frameworks of knowledge integration into the economic process. These various subsystems of innovation overlap and crisscross in the organization of society. They can be expected to drive (or to inhibit) one another at the next-order level as in a hypercycle. The hypothesis of this study is that this overlay can be considered as the knowledge base of an economy. Because more than a single system can be expected to feed into the hypercycle, the specification of the systems of reference for the evaluation of innovation systems has itself increasingly become a research question (Carlsson, 2006).

7.3   The internet

The emergence of the Internet during the 1990s has turned the tables again. Globalization takes place at a supra-institutional and supra-national level that is beyond the control of individuals or institutional agents. The new communication media reinforce direct relations between science, technology, and the market as different communication mechanisms. From this perspective, the institutional organizations (e.g., at the national levels or in transnational corporations) can be considered as providing niches of communication that develop (or stagnate) as relative equilibria by drawing on available resources and earning credit in their dynamic environments (Leydesdorff and Curran, 2000; Park *et al.*, 2005).

Although the carrying organizations continue to provide the original materials (variation) for their representation at the level of the communication networks, the representations at the level of the Internet can circulate as 'actants' in the networked relations independently of their originators (Callon and Latour, 1981). When the interactions among the representations resonate at the network level, the actors behind these representations may become increasingly invisible as the originators of the communication. The dynamics of the 'actants' can thus become relatively independent from and even incursive on the actors. The dynamics at the different levels are not synchronized *ex ante*; they update each other *ex post*. Thus, the dynamics of the represented systems may become increasingly dependent on their representations at the network level, and in a next round these carrying systems can become reflexively aware of this operation of being continuously reflected in communication (Wouters, 1999).

Under these conditions, research evaluation can only position itself reflexively with reference to the representations being evaluated. The systems of reference have to be constructed reflexively. Without further specification it becomes unclear what is precisely being reflected and represented (Rip, 1997). The reflection is available as a result as an indicator or map of the system under study. However, the reflected systems contain interaction effects which may allow for reflections from other perspectives. The different audiences can be served by different discourses using different data, or from various perspectives on the same data. The representations are evaluated in terms fulfilling their functions at interfaces. All texts are embedded in *con*texts, and the latter provide the former with (potentially new) meanings. In terms of the philosophy of science, one could say that not only is the context of discovery to be distinguished from the context of justification of new knowledge claims (Popper, 1935), but the contexts of justification are increasingly at variance (e.g., between colleagues and clients). These differentiations can be expected to change over time and to vary among societal domains.

For example, an innovation like the introduction of a new drug onto the market has a meaning for the pharmaceutical corporation introducing it which differs from its meaning for patients suffering from a disease or for the scientists and pharmacists who developed the drug. The latter can use *Chemical Abstracts* as their system of reference, or perhaps *Medline* for searching and reference. The generic name of the drug used in scientific communications may not be familiar to most of its users, who latter know the same substance only by its trade-name. The evaluation schemes of these different audiences can be expected to vary, for example, even between molecular biologists and medical scientists involved in the clinical testing (Leydesdorff, 2001c). Thus, the differentiation in the reflecting discourses becomes increasingly fine-grained. The agencies carrying these different discourses have only limited capacities and time available to interface with relevant discourses in their environments ('contexts'). This structuration of the discourses, however, enables them to focus on the quality of their own communications at certain interfaces.

The social organization of the exchange of knowledge-based expectations, in addition to the institutional mechanisms of political economy, gradually transforms the national economies into a knowledge-based economy. The new regime entrains the old ones among its subdynamics (Kampmann *et al.*, 1994). The hypercycles remain incomplete because further development is structurally coupled to the historical dimension. The latter provides the retention mechanism that in turn generates the second-order variation for the next selections by resisting and/or adapting.

7.4   The functionalist assumptions in the model

As Maddox (2002) noted in a biological context, a Triple Helix is by its very nature unstable (Ramachandran and Kharta, 1955; Lewontin, 2000). One implication of the Triple Helix model is the analysis of the mutually binding forces among different, yet interacting subdynamics. Can the institutional networks change the differences in the communications that are continuously reproduced for functional reasons? Which are these hypothesized functions at the systems level, and how can they continue to select when the system from which they select no longer has a stable center of control or even an identifiable existence?

I have argued in Chapter Three that this uncertainty can be reduced by an incursive operation. Let us hypothesize that functions operate as an incursive mechanism at the overlay level. The incursive dynamics counteracts the increasing disorganization at the interfaces among systems in a network by removing noise. The incursive *model* entertained by the system removes noise within the system—at the cost of adding probabilistic entropy globally—because a model is (by definition) simpler than the system it represents. Thus, incursivity provides us with a condition for sustaining a system which dwells in meta-stable configurations for longer periods of time.

In the case of a strongly anticipatory system, the model is expected partially to overwrite the system that is modeled. This means that additional entropy can be externalized as the differentiation of the construct from its environment.[74] Thus, the constructed system develops orthogonality in relation to its environment and estranges itself increasingly from developments along its tangents (Casti, 1989). Under the condition of functional differentiation, the social system is enabled to operate in this hyper-incursive mode (Chapter Four). First, cultural evolution in a high culture incurs on historical dynamics which would tend to become chaotic

---

[74] It can be shown that the Second Law of Thermodynamics holds equally true for probabilistic entropy (Theil, 1962, at pp. 59f.; cf. Georgescu-Roegen, 1971). In other words, the second law is a consequence of the formalism.

without central control. Thereafter—that is, without central control—the hyper-incursive dynamics reconstruct the social system evolutionarily, but with the effect that the cultural system becomes increasingly orthogonal to the natural one. The latter is transformed in a techno-economic evolution at the hypercyclic level. 'Natural' selection is replaced with a variety of selections within the reflecting systems, and the resulting dynamics overwrite the historically primitive ones.

Can the selection mechanisms still be specified if one can no longer assume that selection is taking place 'naturally'? Since the social systems of communication do not exist other than as orders of expectations, the notion of functional differentiation—introduced by Parsons and inherited in Luhmann's social systems theory—can no longer be specified without further reflection about the status of these biological concepts. The uncertainty in the expectation leads to uncertainty in the functionality. If this next-order system does not 'exist' other than as an expectation within the system, how can one then determine the functionality of phenomena (events, actions) other than by rationalizing them *ex post?*

This problem of operationalization is generated by defining the social system no longer as an identifiable action system, as in Parsons's (1937, 1951) social systems theory, but as a configuration that remains under continuous reconstruction. As long as the social system was considered as performatively *integrated* in action, a general schema (like Parsons's four-function paradigm AGIL)[75] could be used for analytical purposes. The units of integration would 'compete' for 'survival' albeit in a variety of (hierarchically organized) environments. Evolutionary theorizing did not yet need to be reconsidered (Nelson, 1995). However, if the system under study is considered as *differentiated* mainly in terms of asynchronous communications that are heterogeneous, the directions that are functional to the communication become uncertain. The axes of communication may change over time, and new dimensions can also be developed. From this perspective one can no longer specify the functions to be expected (Luhmann, 1980; Jensen and Nauman, 1980; Künzler, 1989), and consequently the evolutionary framework has to be reconsidered.

Herbert Simon (1973) once suggested that any complex system can be expected to work with an alphabet of components. But how could one know or even conjecture the nature and number of these components if the systems under study are defined as uncertain and therefore 'in transition'? Can the components be specified as analytically different (micro)operations? In a strongly worded critique of the Triple

---

[75] AGIL (or LIGA) stands for the four functions of Adaptation, Goal-attainment, Integration, and Latency (Parsons, 1953, at pp. 61f).

Helix model, O'Malley, McOuat, and Doolittle (forthcoming)[76] pointed to this problem both in Luhmann's models and in my elaboration of this theory into the Triple Helix model. Reasoning from their background in biological evolution theory, these authors claim that:

> In the Triple Helix of scientific innovation, although the focus on three institutional spheres is sensible and the importance of interactions undeniable, the way in which they have been modeled in no way approaches the precision of the biological model.

This critique highlights that the functionalist assumptions of a sociological theory of communication cannot be operationalized in the biological model because the functions could no longer be specified unambiguously. For authors who wish to adhere to biological assumptions, consequently, claims based on the Triple Helix model are invalid. Using this model, one would not be able to reproduce measurement results since the operationalizations become context-dependent and therefore inherently uncertain.

This critique of functionalism at the level of the social system was voiced previously within sociology as an argument against using functionalism for explanation: the functions of social systems cannot be specified without inherent ambiguity (Turner and Maryanski, 1979; Maryanski and Turner, 1992). Using their biological perspective as a benchmark, O'Malley *et al.*, however, consider the definition of functions in terms of (uncertain) expectations as an 'abnegation of naturalistic research' that they deem 'very damaging' (*ibid.*, p. 10). This last step seems to me an epistemological generalization of their essentially methodological critique that measurements become unreliable when functions are hypothesized with uncertainty. While I agree that the methodological problem of a functionalist explanation relates to the epistemological stance of the analyst, the sociological argument, in my opinion, needs to take a step in the opposite direction because of the reflexive positions of the analysts, the subjects of study, and their potential relations. The levels of participant-observers and external observers can no longer be clearly distinguished as in biological explanations (Maturana, 1978).

In other words, I agree with the epistemological consequences of this critique, but I decline the methodological problem because the sociological design is different from the biological one. The epistemological shift finds its origin in considering the

---

[76] A draft version of this paper was presented by Maureen O'Malley at the Fourth Triple Helix Conference in Copenhagen, November 2002.

social system no longer as a naturalistically given one—like a body or a population—but as an order of expectations. When the expectations are further exchanged, an uncertainty is generated which can be distinguished analytically from the uncertainty in the systems that are being modeled. Keeping the levels apart and specifying their interactions are the methodological tasks of a reflexive research design in the social sciences. The uncertainty in the modeled system is reduced by the expectations in the modeling system, and the analyst has to model both the systems under study and the model of it, and to control for their potential interactions. Since the processing of meaning in a modern society is differentiated (that is, uses different codes) the dually layered mechanism (of modeling and modeled) can further be developed into a three-dimensional (or *n*-dimensional) contingency table when innovations at interfaces are also modeled. As noted, three subdynamics suffice to generate complexity.

The research design adds a control system to the system under study and the reflection of this system. The quality of the reflection is the subject of this discourse. However, this control system can only be stabilized provisionally; it provides a heuristics. The system is inherently in transition, as is its reflection. This non-trivial configuration has been reflected in the social sciences, for example, in terms of self-fulfilling prophecies (Merton, 1948). From this perspective, sociological reflection is itself dynamic and reflexively embedded in ·discourse. Unlike the biological reflection, the appeal to an external given (e.g., gender differences) is itself recognizably discursive and therefore potentially rhetorical (Foucault, 1966 and 1972; Haraway, 1988).

In summary, O'Malley *et al.*'s epistemological critique accords with my thesis that the social system is not to be considered naturalistically without missing the point about how meaning-processing systems operate in terms of uncertainties differently from information-processing systems. At the level of social systems it is no longer the facts which matter, but what they mean. Meaning is not given naturalistically, but constructed socially and continuously reconstructed. The systems of reference are potentially redefined when provided with meaning, and this redefinition of the system of reference changes the relevant probability distributions (that is, the 'facts'). In terms of operationalizations and methods, however, one is able to measure the uncertainties probabilistically in terms of the expected information value of a distribution. Although communications cannot be observed directly—one can observe only the communicators and their communication channels—communications can be measured when the media of communication are properly specified.

For example, one can specify the market or the economy as functions of the social system. How an economy is defined, however, depends on the discourse. If one specifies the economy in terms of economic transactions, one can measure transactions both at each moment of time and over time. At each moment, this network of relations can be modeled as a transaction matrix. If one adds the time dimension, a three-dimensional array of information is generated. This type of data can be modeled and evaluated using information theory in dimensionalities also higher than three (Leydesdorff, 1995a). The theoretical significance of the results is not given, as with biological findings, but has to be evaluated carefully in terms of the relevant theorizing and by developing instruments for the explanation of significance.

Previous attempts to analyze cultural evolution naturalistically (like Parsons's social systems theory) have failed precisely because one has attempted to compromise between the biological model and the very different character of social systems. Social systems have an epistemological status that differs from that of biological systems. When one fails to consider this difference in methodology, sociological discourse can easily be reduced to a meta-biological or social-philosophical one about 'the' evolution of the social system or one of its subsystems. O'Malley and her colleagues, for example, point to the work of the philosopher David Hull (2001), who applied Darwinian evolution theory to the growth of (populations of) ideas in science. Such a philosophical approach idealizes the growth of science as distinct from the development of its social relations, and thus ignores empirical questions about the possible interactions among these analytically different dimensions.

I do not propose to analyze the growth of science exclusively as the development of social relations and regimes as in the social-constructivist tradition (e.g., Bloor, 1972; Barnes and Edge, 2002). My proposal is to consider the different dimensions as analytically orthogonal. For example, in science the dynamics of social networks are coupled to the dynamics of intellectual organization to variable extents, and this is reflected in the organization of textual archives (e.g., journal literature) along a third axis (Leydesdorff, 1995a). The functionalist approach is able to appreciate the results of philosophical analysis as the study of one perspective, namely, the one with a focus on the intellectual organization. However, one can consider the various subdynamics as analytically orthogonal and also interacting in the phenomena. From this perspective, cognitive development remains a subdynamic that is analytically different from the institutional one. Each subdynamic is expected to interact with other subdynamics, for example, in the competition for resources (that is, the economic subdynamic). Two subdynamics can temporarily co-evolve, but the conditions for bifurcations can also be specified (see Chapter Five).

Let me add the following in order to prevent a possible misunderstanding. When my critics argue in favor of a 'naturalistic approach,' they do not mean observable facts in the strictly positivist sense. The Darwinian model is always theoretically guided: expectations are specified. Otherwise, biologists would, for example, have been unable to specify the search for 'a missing link.' Since the missing link was not yet observed, it had first the status of a hypothesis to be corroborated. The difference from the model proposed in this study is the importation of biological evolution theory into the study of social systems theory and the philosophy of science without a sociological reflection about the status of the observables. The selection mechanism is not considered as a differentiated set of various selection mechanisms operating as subdynamics within a complex system. In the sociological design one needs careful specification of these different expectations on the basis of historical analysis, and from this perspective the 'facts' remain also constructs.

7.5   The sociological critique

Theorizing about social systems has become more complex than the biological metaphor can carry. No 'natural selection' has remained in cultural systems (otherwise than as an ideology of free competition and the 'survival of the fittest'; e.g., Fukuyama, 2002). If the historical dynamics are nevertheless considered as a 'naturalistic' subject of social studies, one invokes irreflexively a selection by a next-order system (e.g., 'nature'). However, this system of expectations cannot exist in the physical or biological sense of the word (Bhaskar, 1975, 1997). It is argued in this study that 'culture' operates incursively on 'nature' and that functions have therefore to be specified at this systems level, that is, in terms of expectations.

With a fine sense for the theoretical problems of sociology, Giddens formulated his critique of a (meta-)biological position repeatedly and emphatically:

> According to the ideas I have tried to formulate above, 'social reproduction' is not an explanatory term: it always has itself to be explained in terms of the structurally bounded and contingently applied knowledgeability of social actors. It is worth emphasizing this, not merely in respect to criticizing orthdox functionalism, but also in regard to the not infrequent tendency of Marxist authors to suppose that 'social reproduction' has magical explanatory properties—as if merely to invoke the term is to explain something. (Giddens, 1981, at pp. 172f.)

In *The Constitution of Society* (1984, at p. xxxvii), Giddens added that he 'repudiates' for this reason endeavors 'to develop Parsons's work in novel ways, particularly Luhmann and Habermas.' Giddens formulated that these ideas include 'the tendency to assume that societies are easily distinguishable unities, as biological organisms are; and a fondness for evolutionary-style theories' might obscure the uncertainty in 'the more mundane, practical aspects of social activity.'

In my opinion, it is too easy to discard Luhmann's and Habermas's contributions with these generalizations, but the issue of the biological metaphor has to be taken seriously. Habermas (1987), for example, opposed the biological metaphors used by Luhmann with arguments very similar to those of Giddens. Despite their differences in philosophical positions, both Luhmann and Habermas struggled intensively with this problem (Habermas and Luhmann, 1973). Particularly in a German context, one cannot simply return to biological models like social-darwinism.

Habermas (1981) inherited from Parsons the focus on a theory of action. However, he added that *communicative* action implies a horizon of meaning. Whereas Husserl ([1929], 1973) had attempted to ground intersubjectivity in a transcendental phenomenology, Habermas (1981 (2), at pp. 196 ff.; 1987, at pp. 378f.) considered this philosophical attempt as failed from the sociological perspective.[77] Note that Habermas and Luhmann agree that the problem of defining 'intersubjectivity' should be solved *sociologically*.

According to Habermas, intersubjectivity cannot sufficiently be appreciated as providing meaning to the events at the supra-individual level when the sociological model is defined only in terms of social systems theory. The human subject and the social system are then coupled only in an objectified interaction among these systems. Both Luhmann and Parsons would thus have reduced 'intersubjectivity' to interpenetration as a systems operation without sufficient appreciation of the normative and affective components that bind people together at the communal

---

[77] The sociological argument against Husserl's transcendental philosophy of 'intersubjectivity' was first developed and elaborated by Schutz (1952, at p. 105). Habermas (1981 (1), at pp. 178f.) notes that Schutz's sociological elaboration of Husserl's phenomenology is based on a methodological decision of the researcher to give priority to the analytical values of the research design over those of the subjects under study. Both the latter and the former remain constructs, but according to Schutz (1932/1967) the sociological analysis provides the constructs with their basis in the meaningful construction of the social world. See Chapter Eleven for a further elaboration of these issues.

level.[78] Thus, the intentionality in human interactions would not be appreciated sufficiently. (Habermas himself proposed everyday language as the operator that enables us to be both included in the social system of communication and reflexively enrolled at the level of the life world.)

In my opinion, Habermas (1987) is right that Luhmann (1984, 1997a) did not pay sufficient attention to the tension between the dynamics of the social system and the problems of social life. However, these problems can be solved within social systems theory by introducing incursive routines into the model. Incursive routines require *reflexive* agency. This extension enables us to model the operation of providing meaning to the information and the construction of 'intersubjectivity' as a result of incursive operations (which in turn operate recursively). The hyper-incursive operation at the systems level challenges the intentionality of the reflexive agents because the system tends to become hyper-reflexive—that is, it contains more than one possibility for the reflection. The generation and processing of meaning is thus no longer reduced to the individual level, but this process is hypothesized as a reflexive operation at the level of the social system.[79]

The social system does not contain a single anticipatory mechanism, but two analytically orthogonal ones (Chapters Four and Five). This double incursion can be expected to organize the intersubjectivity along a trajectory into different functions at the level of the next-order regime. Habermas stated that ordinary language is to be considered as the operator that generates meaning, but the differentiation of meaning into symbolically generalized media of communication cannot be explained without Luhmann's systems-theoretical apparatus of different codes operating along the time axis independently of each other and in potentially different directions. The independence of the functionality in the expectations remains analytical, however, and should not be reified. The problem with Luhmann's text is that the author sometimes slips into a reifying language even though he states that his program is to

---

[78] Wenn man die Situation des handelnden Subjekts als Umwelt des Persönlichkeitssystems deutet, lassen sich die Ergebnisse der phänomenologischen Lebensweltanalyse bruchlos in eine Systemtheorie Luhmannscher Observanz einholen. Das hat sogar den Vorzug, daß man jenes Problem, an dem Husserl in den Cartesianischen Meditationen gescheitert ist, unbeachtet lassen kann, ich meine die monadologische Erzeugung der Intersubjektivität der Lebenswelt. Dieses Problem tritt gar nicht mehr auf, wenn die Subjekt-Objekt-Beziehungen durch diejenigen zwischen System und Umwelt ersetzt werden. (Habermas, 1981, Vol. II, at p. 197.)

[79] This reflection can again be reflected and potentially internalized by individuals (Leydesdorff, 2000d).

'de-ontologize' the status of social systems (e.g., Luhmann, 1984, at p. 243; 1995, at p. 177). The focus on observation generated 'paradoxes' in Luhmann's theory which could no longer be solved without an algorithmic turn. One cannot analyze further using language when studying phenomena which include and exclude linguistic expressions differently at various moments of time.

Codes are generated as codifications of meaning, but they no longer necessarily require the use of language at later stages in each operation. From this perspective, ordinary language can be considered as an informal medium of communication, that is, a medium without a privileged status. For example, one can buy something and pay with money without saying anything. While the symbolically generalized mediation is historically more recent, the more abstract media of symbolically generalized communication can be expected to assume control in later stages of the development (Weinstein and Platt, 1973). Thus, the systems-theoretical apparatus is richer than the language-theoretical.

Habermas agreed with this richness of Luhmann's descriptions:

> As Luhmann's astonishing job of translation demonstrates, this language can be so flexibly adapted and expanded that it yields novel, not merely objectivating but objectivistic descriptions even of subtle phenomena of the lifeworld. [...] (T)o the extent that systems theory penetrates into the lifeworld, introducing into it a metabiological perspective from which it then learns to understand itself as a system in an environment-with-other-systems-in-an-environment—as if the world process took place through nothing but system-environment differences—to that extent there is an objectifying effect. (Habermas, 1987, at p. 385).

The reverse arrow (from the lifeworld towards the system), however, was not an object of theorizing by Luhmann because for programmatic reasons he abstracted from the uncertainty in the variation at each moment of time. The focus is on meaning-processing and not on the (Shannon-type) information processing. The latter is considered as the variation on which the meaning-processing reflects and thus shapes the social system. Meaning-processing systems remove noise by identifying and reproducing meaningful signals. With a similar appeal to Husserl's notion of a horizon of meanings, however, Luhmann (e.g., 1995a, 2002a) acknowledged uncertainty *over time* as fundamental to his perspective:

> It could be that this style of thinking, in comparison with Husserl's, presupposes a radically different relation to time. Husserl had located the intentions of transcendental consciousness in time, a time that

consciousness also observes, so to speak, out of the corner of the eye. And he has correspondingly located the crisis of the modern sciences in the historical time of the occidental history of reason. In all this, time was conceived as a river, a movement, a process. The theory of rediscription, by contrast, has to engage in a very different relation to time, for it envisions the described descriptions as its past and the prospect of further new descriptions of its own concepts as a future. (Luhmann [1995a], 2002a, at p. 60)

Thus, Luhmann was sensitive to uncertainty along the time dimension, but he objectified the operation of social systems at each moment of time. Systems, in his opinion, are 'not of "purely analytical relevance" for systems theory.' Systems theory would have 'the responsibility of testing its statements against reality' (Luhmann, 1995a, at p. 12). This 'de-ontologization' affects only the communications as elements within these objectified systems (*ibid.*, p. 177).[80] Thus, the biological metaphor is rejected for studying operations over the time axis (with reference to Husserl), but it is used in the same narrative when studying the system as naturally given at each moment of time. The design thus becomes inconsistent, and with repetitive references to Spencer Brown (1969), Luhmann used the notion of the paradox as an excuse for hiding these inconsistencies.

If the time axis contains uncertainty, more than a single representation is possible at each moment in time and the 'reality' can no longer be considered as an unambiguous test bed. The selection mechanisms needed for the construction of social 'reality' have first to be specified. In various contexts, different meanings are provided for the expectations. In other words, the subsystems are expected to tick at different frequencies, and thus a spectrum of frequencies is generated. Updates and resonances are possible. These resonances may generate temporary solutions, but they remain to be explained.

7.6   The priority of the perspective

Luhmann was not familiar with the elaboration of the mathematical theory of communication provided by Theil (1972) which allows for the measurement of communication in more than a single dimension and over time (Leydesdorff,

---

[80] At pp. 30 and 243 of the German edition (Luhmann, 1984), respectively.

1995a).[81] The elaboration of Rosen's (1985) theory of anticipatory systems into an algorithmic approach became available only during the second half of the 1990s (Dubois, 1998 and 2000). While he was aware of Rosen's theory, Luhmann at the time considered it only as a contribution to mathematical biology (Luhmann, 1997a, at p. 206, note 25). The concept of a society as a strongly anticipatory system that constructs its own future states in a cultural evolution of expectations with a different dynamics could therefore not be distinguished sufficiently from the biological model.

Despite this confusion, Luhmann's crucial proposal remains very fruitful. The 'inter' of Husserl's concept of 'intersubjectivity' can be considered as the subject of social systems theory (Luhmann, 1995b, at pp. 177f.). Without the concept of inversion of the time dimension by the reflexive operation, however, the perspective of social systems theory generates a paradox in the representation (Chapter Four). The social system as a 'second-order observer' can in this case make observations only as a first-order (historical) observer. The two perspectives can no longer be clearly distinguished.

For example, the incursive systems operation and the historical subject of the observer were further identified by Luhmann when he noted that '(t)he second-order observer, mind you, is a first-order observer as well, for he must distinguish and designate the observer he intends to observe' ([1993] 2000, at p. 20). However, this focus on an observer ('he'?), unlike the concept of an observation among other possible observations, leads us back to the biological metaphor. The 'observer' is no longer conceptualized as a (social) distribution of observations containing an uncertainty, but as a single point of reflection. An 'observer' has a specific position, and thus the metaphor of social systems theory is *a priori* anthropomorphized.[82]

The systems-theoretical perspective allows for an algorithmic approach. The discourses provide only the specification of subdynamics (e.g., lines in the code). In

---

[81] Luhmann's definition of communication as a unity of three operations (information, utterance, and understanding) would imply that each communication consists of two communications in the mathematical theory of communication, namely one between the sender and the network and one between the network and the receiver. For the elaboration of this tension between a sociological and a mathematical definition of communication, see Chapters Three and Four of Leydesdorff (2001b).

[82] Fuchs (2004) discussed this anthropomorphization of 'the observer' as a consequence of the limitations of human language. Indeed, languages operate with geometrical metaphors because one stabilizes a perspective.

an algorithmic approach the perspectives can be changed or provided with different weights. The changes of perspectives can be visualized, for example, as animations. Epistemologically, one should keep firmly in mind that a communication system is uncertain both at each moment in time (because the social system is distributed by its very nature) and over the time-dimension.

From this perspective of entertaining knowledge-based reconstructions, observable ('life-world') events are considered as the phenotypical results of interacting subdynamics. The subdynamics are analytical. The specifications serve us as 'genotypes' which provide analytical perspectives (Langton, 1989, at p. 22). The 'phenotypes' can be provided with meaning using one or another of these perspectives. They can then no longer be considered as 'natural.' Although some of the codes may manage rhetorically to label their perspectives as 'natural,' each label rests necessarily on theoretical assumptions. In other words, the 'natural' is based on a 'naturalistic' perspective. The cultural incursion changes the system on which it incurs as a feedback mechanism that overwrites the previous ('natural') states. For example, biological categories have precise meaning only within a biological discourse. An observer, for example, can be considered as a relatively unproblematic category in biological discourse (Edelman, 1989), but a social system cannot observe or be observed like a human being. It remains a distribution of observations that contains an uncertain expectation about the subjects of observation. The discourses process observational reports, while individual observers are able to process observations.

The expectations generated in exchanges can be expressed in language or they can be communicated in terms of symbolically generalized media of communication (like money, love, or truth). Human language provides us with the initial format of the complexity of communication because each statement can be expected to contain information and can be provided with meaning. Meaning incurs on the information in the message, and this incursion can be made reflexive. Knowledge is shaped when the meaning of certain meanings can be distinguished from common sense. Counter-intuitive knowledge, however, can by definition only be produced as discursive knowledge. The strongly anticipatory system thus generated potentially reshapes us intimately by imposing its improved definitions, but this reshaping can only be produced in a differentiated mode because it is an operation of the social system. Thus, the social system does not work like a personal God who 'converts' human subjects, but it conditionalizes expectations. One of the consequences of this model is that the carriers integrate meaning by reflexively *organizing* the differentiation at their specific levels of organization. One may wish to label this their 'life-worlds' because it includes the pleasures and worries of their physical existence as individualized meaning-processing systems.

The mind of an individual occupies a mediating position between the biological and the sociological levels. By having perceptions, it provides us with a window on the body as a natural system, and as a psychology it provides us with a window on communication as a cultural process. Thus, it can be considered as a specific form of (relatively integrated) organization which imports observations about the environment into the social system. The social system, however, has a dynamics very different from our bodies or our minds. When the self-organization of communication is differentiated—that is, when communication operates using a variety of codes—the control of the development of the system may shift evolutionarily from the institutional domain of (hierarchical) organization to more abstract mechanisms of coordination like the market and the sciences.

These symbolically mediated mechanisms cannot be observed like living or institutionalized systems, but they can be measured accurately given a research design. For example, one can measure the latent structure at the network level using methods from social network analysis, or one can measure prices and quantities of commodities or stocks. Stock exchanges or scientific paradigms can no longer be provided with a naturalistic interpretation. However, they can be studied as orders of expectation using information theory. For example, scientific knowledge claims are organized by the operation of paradigms in disciplines and specialties, but to a variable degree. As argued in the previous chapters, one needs an algorithmic approach (that is, using a calculus) for the study of these multi-layered communication structures. Information theory provides us with such a calculus (Bar-Hillel, 1955). I shall turn to the empirical operationalization of the Triple Helix in these terms in the chapters below.

In summary, let me repeat my argument about the changing status of functions under these conditions of uncertainty by providing an example of why the biological model and the focus on observable events does not suffice for the sociological explanation. In Parsons's (1937) social systems theory, action was considered as the observable unit of operation. This approach can still be made compatible with the (meta-)biological model. Action can be assigned with functions for the competitive 'survival' of the actor. 'Survival,' however, has to be considered as a metaphor under cultural conditions. For example, human actors can also make sacrifices. Sacrifices can be studied from the perspective of symbolic interactionism and ethnography as instances of providing specific meaning to events (Lynch, 1988), but the dynamics of these reflections cannot be understood from the perspective of Darwinian evolution theory.

The function of providing meaning to sacrifices itself evolves historically, but with a dynamics different from those of its historical manifestations. For example, when mediaeval knights went on a crusade and risked death somewhere along the road, they were supposed to do so—and probably they firmly believed this—for the salvation of their soul and in the name of the Christian faith. When soldiers died in the First World War, they did so mainly for nationalistic reasons—invoking the fatherland—while in World War II ideological principles like 'the defense of democracy' colored these nationalistic backgrounds differently. Whether a soldier dies in Turkey or in Flanders may phenotypically ('in reality') not make much of a difference. It would be disrespectful to describe these sacrifices in terms of the survival of the fittest. The symbolic value of the sacrifice has to be taken into account. Inter-human communication is codified and the codes are invoked, reproduced, and reconstructed by being communicated. In this case, the meaning of the sacrifice is more important than the facts. The sacrifice meant something very different in the various contexts and in these other periods.

7.7   Translations and translation systems

Sustained interaction is expected to change the interacting codifications because an organization may be added to the trajectory of the decisions developing over time. This third context conditions *and* interacts with the interfacing systems. At the level of the social system, the organization of a set of interfaces first became institutionalized at the level of national systems. Constitutions, for example, codified the relations between the functional systems by providing the organizational format of a nation-state. When national systems were increasingly in place as institutional formats (from about 1870 onwards), the so-called 'scientific-technical revolution' took place at the industrially organized interfaces between science and the economy.[83] The new institutions (e.g. corporate laboratories) provided the basis for an institutionalized interaction among codifications. Eventually, this development led to the emergence of corporate capitalism with its typical industrial R&D facilities and 'technostructure' (Galbraith, 1967; Schumpeter, [1911] 1949).

---

[83] Braverman (1974) identified the 'scientific-technical revolution' at the level of social structure because, as he put it: 'the key innovation is not to be found in chemistry, electronics, automatic machinery, aeronautics, atomic physics, or any of the products of these science-technologies, but rather in the transformation of science itself into capital' (*ibid.*, at pp. 167f.). He placed this development historically for Germany after unification in 1870. For the United States, Noble (1977, at p. 6) mentions the period 1880-1920, that is, including World War I.

The absorption of science by capital has also transformed the latter: the productive forces are no longer necessarily linked to managerial decisions and the instrumental actions of concrete people engaged in a labor process (Habermas, 1968). Economic selections can be discussed increasingly in terms of knowledge-based representations, e.g., utility functions. I have explained in Chapter One how abstraction from 'natural preferences' leads to the option of micro-foundations in economic theorizing beyond the neo-classical assumptions. Given innovative dynamics over time, scientific and technical selections could no longer be considered as exogenous to the economic system (Schumpeter, [1939] 1964; Nelson and Winter, 1982).

The analytically independent subdynamics of wealth generation and retention versus innovation provide each other with resources and feedback on the basis of their organization within an evolving framework. Unlike a constitution which is intended to provide stability to the state, a corporation can be expected to change its organization and to update its decision rules when market conditions or technological options change. Thus, the institutional organization between the two functional codifications allows for the organization of a third helix which can be developed at local interfaces. Public control by government and private control by firms participate in developing this third interface of making decisions.

A co-evolution among two interacting subsystems may lead to a lock-in in a process of mutual shaping. But the consequent trajectory can later be bifurcated in terms of reaction-diffusion dynamics (Chapter Five). Thus, translations which was first organized along a trajectory can become part of a regime. The next order of the regime can be expected as a codified system of translations that operates incursively. The various translations are no longer synchronized *ex ante* or controlled at a center, but they can be integrated in a fragmented way at the level of a virtual hypercycle. This subsystem operates in terms of distributions of decisions based on expectations. A *system of translations* emerges when translations are organized within a corporation and—since the Second World War—at the level of the state, and when these levels begin to interact and to anticipate on each other about knowledge-based expectations. The translations then become uncertain, and knowledge-based information can be used to improve them, but not unambiguously. In translation systems, the selecting instances can flip-flop between codes of meaning which co-evolve while selecting upon each other. These discursive systems no longer follow a single logic, but next-order translations that recursively contain the various logics which operate within them as their 'genotypes.'

For example, increasingly in a system of translations scientific communications are no longer selected only in terms of their 'truth'-value as their intrinsic codification, but also in terms of their utility as another (e.g., economic) codification. Analogously, a production system can be stabilized against (short-term) market pressures when innovations are selected from a perspective of longer-term (e.g., technological) potentials. The trade-offs at each moment of time are traded off against the trade-offs along the envisaged time dimension. A decision structure has to be organized for this purpose and periodically to be restructured.

The epistemological and social consequences of such a transition are almost beyond imagination. While the previous *episteme* was based on the geometrical metaphor of an internally consistent panopticum (Foucault, 1972), the new one is based on a multitude of perspectives. Therefore, it requires algorithmic modeling and dynamic representations (e.g., animations and video-clips). The future possibilities of emerging systems of translations extend beyond the possibilities that can be imagined at any given moment because the human imagination and its discourse try to focus on geometrical representations (McLuhan, 1962).

Systems of translation are intuitively familiar from problems of interpretation when using foreign languages. The same word may have different meanings in different languages; various translations are sometimes possible. A system of translations can be understood as a system in which the interpreters continuously communicate among themselves about possible translations. This meta-communication potentially improves the quality of the communication, but one can easily be confused. Interpreters among natural language users, however, may try to settle their disputes by appealing to codifications like dictionaries. In a system of translations among codes, the dispute between different perspectives is provisionally institutionalized. The translations on top of functional domains, however, may change the relevant dictionaries on functional grounds, that is, when this allows for the processing of more complexity in an organized way.

If the translators had completely different backgrounds in terms of languages, their communication would cease, as in the case of the Tower of Babel. But since communication is noisy and selective, the institutionalization of a translation system can lead to highly specific second-order communications. A translation system can be codified as a *trans-episteme*. This complex and flexible code of communication reinforces mutual understanding, and thus self-understanding at lower levels of interaction. The communicators increasingly know that their communications only contain expectations. Trans-epistemic knowledge enables the carrying agents to distinguish reflexively between what may function as a signal at a next-higher level and what can be discarded as noise.

In a communication system under the previous *episteme,* each human being was universally presumed to have access to the communication. The transcendental assumption of a panopticum has to be suspended when discussing translation systems (Knorr, 1982; Elzinga, 1985). Translation systems are based on reflexive selections among communications on the basis of the functionality of a communication for the translation. The subdynamics (e.g., languages) are reproduced at the supra-individual level and in a distributed mode. The carriers of the original communications are selected by systems of translation in terms of the quality of their communications, for example, in professional practices (Leydesdorff, 2003c). In other words, translation operates on representations by making them more knowledge-based.

Chapter 8

Measurement of the Knowledge Base

In 1953, Linus Pauling and Robert B. Corey proposed that DNA was made up of three chains, twisted around each other in ropelike helices (Pauling and Corey, 1953). A few months later, James Watson and Francis Crick proposed the double helix, which was then quickly accepted as the correct structure of DNA (Watson and Crick, 1953). This discovery led to a Nobel Prize (Watson, 1970). Double helices can under certain circumstances stabilize in a co-evolution, but triple helices may contain all kinds of chaotic behavior (Poincaré, 1905). However, Triple Helix models continue to be useful in studying transition processes, for example, in crystallography and molecular biology.

More recently, Richard Lewontin (2000) used the metaphor of a Triple Helix for modeling the relations between genes, organisms, and environments. In a different context, Henry Etzkowitz and I introduced the Triple Helix model for studying university-industry-government relations (Etzkowitz and Leydesdorff, 1995). University-industry-government relations provide a networked infrastructure for knowledge-based innovation systems. The infrastructure organizes the dynamic fluxes. However, the knowledge base remains emergent given these conditions. Whereas the relations between institutions can be measured as variables, the interacting fluxes generate a probabilistic entropy. The mutual information among the three institutional dimensions provides us with an indicator of this entropy.

When this probabilistic entropy is negative, the development is self-organizing because the operation of the links reduces the uncertainty in the configuration. This negative entropy cannot be attributed to any of the nodes, since it is a consequence of the configuration. However, the self-organizing dynamic of interacting expectations can be volatile or it may be stabilized in an overlay of communications which functions as a hypercycle among the carrying agencies. This second question will require further testing. The dynamics of Triple Helix relations at the global and national levels in various databases and in different regions of the world will be analyzed in this chapter by applying and developing the indicator using scientometric and webometric data.

8.1   Triple Helix dynamics

How can the values of variables at each moment in time be related to the dynamic operation of variables over time? One needs a calculus for this. Using a calculus one can study the value of a variable (x = a) in relation to changes in the variable (dx/dt). Two problems can then be studied within a single design: (1) the system is complex at different levels at each moment of time (the aggregation problem, which can be studied using multi-variate analysis); and (2) the various subdynamics can be recombined algorithmically (the interaction problem, which requires time-series analysis). Following a suggestion of Bar-Hillel (1955), I used information calculus for the purpose of studying scientific communications in such an integrated design (Leydesdorff, 1995a). In this chapter, I elaborate this calculus for the dynamics of the Triple Helix. However, let me first explain the concept of mutual information in three dimensions using a series of graphical representations.

In 1979, Goguen and Varela proposed a representation of a complex and self-organizing system using a holographic model of three interacting dynamics:

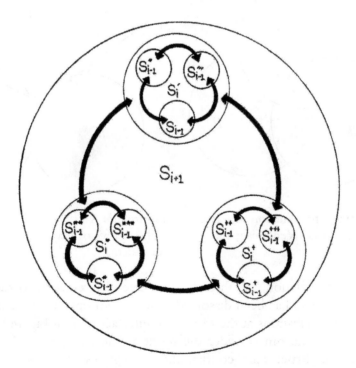

Figure 8.1: A schematic depiction of a complex system by Goguen and Varela (1979)

At each step (i-1, i, i+1), the emerging system is composed of interaction effects among the previous stages of the three participating systems. In addition, however, to the recursion of the *interaction* among the helices, a model of university-industry-government relations should encompass the dynamics *within* each of the helices along their respective time axes. The differences in these subdynamics (of aggregation and interaction, respectively) may break the symmetries which are suggested by the visualization in Figure 8.1.

How can a Triple Helix model be both interactive and recursive at the same time? First, consider three helices as sets that overlap in the intersections, as depicted in terms of Venn diagrams in Figure 8.2. In this configuration, the three helices share a common ground or origin in the overlap area indicated in the figure as *i*. Under certain conditions, however, this overlap can also become negative. This configuration is depicted in Figure 8.3: the center not only fails, but it has become a hole.

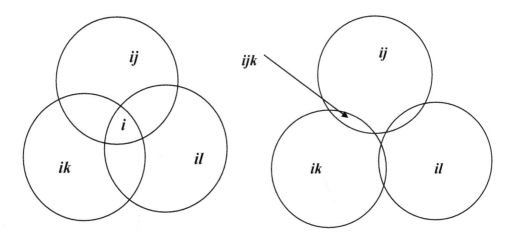

Figure 8.2: Static representation of a Triple Helix configuration as a Venn diagram.

Figure 8.3: A Triple Helix configuration with negative overlap among the subsystems.

In the latter representation, the three helices have differentiated to such an extent that the commonality *i* has been dissolved. This system operates over time in terms of different communications at the respective interfaces (*ijk* in Figure 8.3). If all the interfaces operate, one can consider the result as the emergence of a 'hypercycle' (Figure 8.4). The hypercyclic configuration integrates the three systems in a distributed mode. It fails to integrate completely, or one could also say that the integration remains subsymbolic.

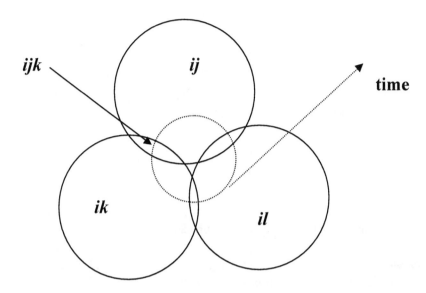

Figure 8.4: *Ex post* integration in an emerging hypercycle by recombining different interactions

This configuration can be expected to exhibit self-organizing properties because the various transmissions are no longer integrated at a single place. A common domain of instantaneous integration is lacking, and therefore each integration leads at the same time to a re-differentiation. Integration fails in this configuration at each moment in time, but it can take place over the time dimension.

Unlike integration in the previous model, this hypercyclic mode of integration is no longer controlled hierarchically by a position at the center. First, the center is now void, or one might even say negative. Only an expectation of a center has remained. But more importantly, the circles in the plan and the hypercycle on top close in this configuration around a failing center. In a next section, we will indicate this cavity as negative entropy within the system.

The four cycles can be considered as four corners of a tetrahedron as depicted in Figure 5. However, a tetrahedron can be tumbled, and thus each of the corners can become the top from the perspective of the other three cycles. The hypercycle and the various cycles stand in heterarchical relation to one another.

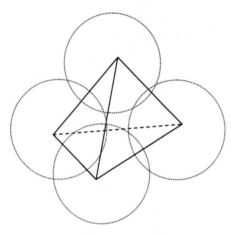

Figure 8.5: The hypercyclic closure of communication.

In other words, the historical structuring in terms of relations and the functional organization in terms of positions—relative to the axes of the system—operate as different subdynamics in this complex system. A system can be considered as complex when it can be decomposed into more than two subdynamics. Two subdynamics can still be modeled by extending the Darwinian model into a co-evolution model (Cook and Campbell, 1979). Three subdynamics may have a common zone and then be integrated in a hierarchical mode given a center of control, but they can also be developed into this heterarchical configuration. The hypercyclic model assumes one degree of freedom more than the configuration on which it rests (Chapter Six). This additional degree of freedom can be used for knowledge-based anticipation at the network level.

8.2   Methodology

When more than a single function is assumed, and when the functions can change positions in relation to one another, the operationalization may become ambiguous. In Chapter Seven, this was discussed as a major argument against a functionalist approach in sociological research designs (Turner and Maryanski, 1979; Maryanski and Turner, 1992). Using an evolutionary model, O'Malley *et al.* (2004) argued for evaluating the Triple Helix model only in institutional terms. The operationalization would then be unambiguous. It has been argued in the previous chapter that the functions are discursively constructed and therefore contain an uncertainty. I shall now proceed by formalizing this neo-functionalist model for Triple Helix dynamics.

How can the conceptualization of functions in terms of fluxes of communication be related to the measurement? Triple Helix relations can first be measured in terms of relevant variables (e.g., budgets, collaborations, citations). From this perspective, the historical description of a specific configuration can be considered as a first-order measurement. In detailed ('thick') descriptions, one is already able to evaluate whether something (defined analytically) was the case or not. However, one can often specify the intensity of the relationship at a more aggregated level using measurement scales more refined than nominal descriptions.

For example, when comparing science parks, one may be able to count instances in which government agencies were involved in these academic-industry relations, and show the extent to which this was the case. In other cases, one may be able to measure more precisely, for example, along a scale. The measurement can be based on various scales, but the networks can eventually be compared as relative frequency distributions. Independently of the question of how network relations are operationalized and measured, the observations of Triple Helix configurations can thereafter be organized in a three-dimensional array using the format visualized in Figure 8.6:

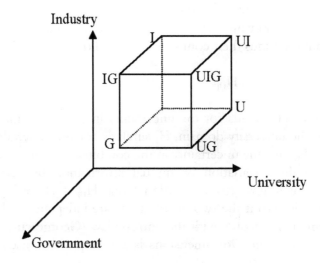

Figure 8.6: The three dimensions of measurement in a Triple Helix configuration and their combinations

The different variables can also be measured in more than one of the three institutional dimensions. Thus, one can measure the co-variation or mutual information between the dimensions. However complicated the empirical data gathering itself may be, this complexity does not affect the methods for *analyzing*

Triple Helix data in terms of the three dimensions indicated in Figure 8.6. In other words, methodological questions about data collection and the measurement itself can thus be distinguished from methodological questions about data analysis. This study focuses on the development of an indicator that can be used after and relatively independently of how the data was collected. In the following chapters, I shall apply the same indicator to a different type of (econometric) data.[84]

In general, network data can be considered as relative frequency distributions. A relative frequency distribution can be written as a probability distribution. The description of network data in terms of probability distributions enables us to use Shannon's (1948) mathematical theory of communication. A probability distribution contains an uncertainty. The expected information content of the message that events have happened with an observed frequency distribution can be expressed in terms of bits of information using the Shannon formulas (Abramson, 1963; Theil, 1972; Leydesdorff, 1995a).[85]

We are interested here not only in the information content of each of the observed distributions, but also in the information contained in their relations at the network level. The mutual information between two dimensions of the probability distribution (for example, in university-industry (UI) relations) is also called the *transmission T*. The transmission is defined as the difference between the sum of the two uncertainties minus their combination, as follows:

$$T_{UI} = H_U + H_I - H_{UI} \tag{1}$$

In this formula H_U stands for the uncertainty in the distribution of the variable(s) measured in the university domain, H_I similarly for the uncertainty in the industrial domain, and H_{UI} for the uncertainty in the combined system. This last uncertainty is reduced with the covariation or mutual information between the two relating systems, since it follows from Equation 1 that $H_{UI} = H_U + H_I - T_{UI}$. The mutual information T is zero if the two distributions are independent, but otherwise it is a positive term. This accords with the entropy law (Georgescu-Roegen, 1971): Since mutual information in two dimensions is always positive, a co-evolution between

---

[84] A similar (three-dimensional) scheme was proposed in Leydesdorff (1995a, at p. 3) for studying communication in science with the argument that authors, texts, and cognitions are related, but cannot be reduced to one another.

[85] A probability distribution $\sum_i p_i$ can be expected to contain an information $H = -\sum_i p_i \log p_i$. If two is used as the basis for the logarithm, the information is measured in bits of information.

two systems generates a probabilistic entropy. Thus, a double helix is observable and can be measured directly.

It can be shown (McGill, 1954; Abramson 1963, at p. 129) that mutual information in three dimensions can become negative in the case that was described above in the hypercyclic configuration. Mutual information in three dimensions is defined as follows:

$$T_{UIG} = H_U + H_I + H_G - H_{UI} - H_{IG} - H_{UG} + H_{UIG} \tag{2}$$

This T_{UIG} can be positive or negative depending on the terms of the equation. The uncertainty of the variables measured in each of the interacting systems (H_U, H_I, and H_G) is reduced at the systems level by the relations at the interfaces between them (H_{UI}, etc.), but the three-dimensional uncertainty (H_{UI}) adds positively to the uncertainty that prevails. Each next-order relation counteracts the uncertainty in the previous order like a selection mechanism. The sign of the contributions therefore alternates in the net result.

Because of this alteration of the signs, it remains an *empirical* question whether the three-dimensional transmission will be positive, negative or zero. A reduction of the uncertainty by the negative transmission is a result of a network configuration of bi-lateral relations that develops without central coordination (Figure 8.4). This subdynamic is counteracted if there is a common zone of overlap that contributes positively to the probabilistic entropy generated by the underlying agency. Thus, the measure provides us with an instrument to distinguish between configurations in which the decentralized network dynamics prevail against a hierarchically controlled organization of communication.

How can negative entropy produced at the network level reduce the uncertainty within a complex system? In Chapter Two, I gave the intuitive example of a child entertaining relations with both its parents. In addition to these two components of the expected information content of this family system and its common component in the configuration (when the three are together, for example, at dinner time), the relation between the two parents can reduce the uncertainty for the child beyond its control. This model can now be generalized for any system with three (or more) dimensions.[86]

---

[86] I elaborate on the three-dimensional model as the parsimonious case, but the extension to more than three dimensions is straightforward.

In other words, the latent structure of relations can sometimes reduce the uncertainty locally as a feedback mechanism on historically unfolding events. From the perspective of each interface, the third dimension remains latent as a structural given in the background. This third subdynamic may entertain interfaces with each of the other two, but not directly (or much less so) with the interaction term between these two. The structural function of the third system thus remains (at that moment) beyond the control of either of the two relating systems. However, this latent structure in the network may reduce the uncertainty that prevails when the first two systems interact. For example, it makes a difference for a government whether university-industry relations in a region or nation are flourishing or hardly developed. In the latter case, the government may wish to develop proactive policies, while one can be more reactive in the former.

The latent dimension operates over time as a virtual structure. If the systems are not independent but interacting, the configuration conditions the interactions *ex ante,* and it positions the relationships *ex post.* Thus, the virtual dimension can be considered as another subdynamic which interacts with the local subdynamics, but partly beyond their control. The 'global' mechanism operates at the systems level as a feedback potentially dampening or regulating the progressions in the other relations. This structural differentiation provides the system with an anticipatory mechanism if it contains this triple contingency (Chapter Five). (I return to the issue of the meaning of this third-party perspective in Chapter Eleven.)

It has been my argument throughout this study that the time dimension can provide us with a degree of freedom for making an assessment about the integration of a system. When the Triple Helix model is applied to university-industry-government relations, the hypercyclic integration can be identified as an overlay of negotiations and exchange relations among the institutional carriers of the Triple Helix dynamics. The overlay of expectations may restructure the underlying arrangements, but to a variable extent. Mutual information in three dimensions can be used as an indicator of this operation because it is a measure of the probabilistic entropy generated in mutual *relations.* Insofar as the hypercycle operates, it functions as a virtual feedback that operates with another information content on the network of relations among the institutional agents at each moment in time. Thus, the model provides us with an empirical operationalization of an anticipatory system in operation.

For example, the network relations include interaction terms at various levels in addition to the aggregation of each sector along its own axis. These interaction terms are non-linear and may thus generate dynamics other than those intended by the interacting agents. Conceptually, the generation of negative entropy within a network system corresponds with the idea of complexity that is contained or 'self-organized' in a network of relations that lacks central coordination. The network system may then be able to propel itself in an evolutionary mode by alternating and recombining the various subdynamics. As shown above (Equation 2), the reduction of the uncertainty is a result of bi-lateral relations operating upon each other. However, the network contains more uncertainty-reducing structure than is visible for the interacting agents at their respective interfaces. This additional dimension is grounded in the interaction and spans the social (that is, supra-individual) dimension of the system. The negative entropy is generated because the flux is *constrained* by the existing structure of relations. This existing structure can be characterized as a triple contingency which over time evolves as a Triple Helix. The negative entropy in turn *enables* the system to take a reflexive turn on its historical conditions hitherto because the time axis is locally and momentarily—that is, presently—inverted.

8.3 Results

In order to show the usefulness of this indicator, I first apply it to relatively straightforward data like search results with the terms 'university,' 'industry,' 'government,' and their combinations with Boolean AND operators in various databases. As noted, the measurement problems in data collection are backgrounded in this study in favor of the methodology for data analysis. The data collection was based on search strategies that result in approximate figures, but which serve us here mainly as an illustration of the argument.

The question behind the searches is whether or not and to what extent relations among the retrieval terms (i.e., co-occurrences) enable us to reveal a Triple Helix dynamics in operation. At what level can a self-propelling dynamic of network relations be observed, and to what extent? I first turn to the Internet to retrieve the relevant time-series data at the global level. In the next sections, I use also the *Science Citation Index* (SCI) and the database of the *U.S. Patent and Trade Office* (USPTO) to measure these relations at national and international levels.

8.3.1 Triple Helix relations at the Internet

University-industry-government relations can be measured at the Internet, for example, in terms of occurrences and co-occurrences of the words 'university,' 'industry,' and 'government' (Leydesdorff and Curran, 2000). Replicating these searches with various search engines, Bar-Ilan (2001) showed, among other things, how sensitive the Internet is to measurements at different moments in time (Rousseau, 1999). Two search engines—*Google* and *AltaVista*—enable the analyst to combine the various search options with specific time frames (e.g., years) so that time series of data in various dimensions can be generated conveniently (Leydesdorff, 2001c). [87] At the time of this research *AltaVista's Advanced Search Engine* seemed to be more stable than before its restructuring in 1999 (Thelwall, 2001) and somewhat surprisingly also more stable than Google (Hellsten *et al.*, 2006).[88]

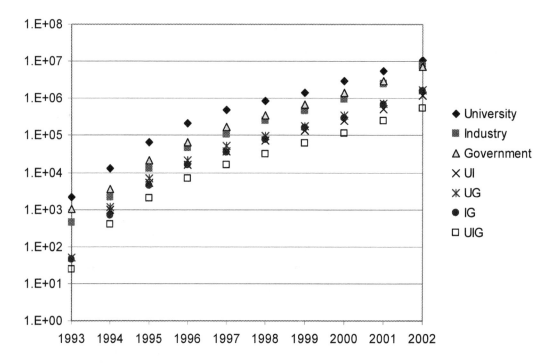

Figure 8.7: Results of searches using the *AltaVista Advanced Search Engine* on May 15, 2003

The search terms 'university,' 'industry,' 'government,' and their combinations with Boolean AND-operators were used in the AltaVista domain for the years 1993-2002.

---

[87] *Google* offers an API-service that allows for programming searches in this domain, including the Julian calendar date (Sylvan J. Katz, *personal communication*). The time searches can also be done on-line by using the meta-search facilities at http://www.faganfinder.com/google.html .

[88] In April 2004—that is, after the period of the research reported here—the AltaVista Search Engine was taken over by Yahoo!, but advanced search capacities using Boolean operators are still available only in AltaVista.

The first round of searches was performed on March 24, 2002. During the data collection the stability of the *Altavista Advanced Search Engine* was checked at least once an hour. All searches were repeated on May 15, 2003.

Figure 7 first shows that the Internet continues to expand rapidly even after the dot-com crisis. The two series of these results (collected in 2002 and 2003, respectively) are very comparable, but again the results in the later year are lower than in the previous year (because of the ongoing updating as was discussed in Chapter Six).

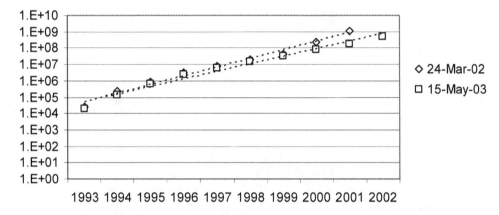

Figure 8.8: The exponential growth curve of the *AltaVista* domain during the period 1993-2002

In Figure 8 the continuous growth of the number of all documents in the AltaVista domain is shown using a logarithmic scale. One can observe the relatively lower retrieval for the number of websites in recent years when measured at the later moment. (Both trend lines, however, fit an exponential curve with $r^2 \geq 0.98$.) The reader should keep in mind that AltaVista provides us only with a specific representation of the data available at the Internet (Butler, 2000; Leydesdorff, 2001c).

When the data is organized in a three-dimensional array, the transmission in three dimensions T_{UIG} can be calculated for each year using the formula provided in Equation 2 above.[89] This leads to Figure 9.

---

[89] For the computation of the mutual information among the three dimensions, one has to assume that the search for 'university' provides us with the (margin) total for this search term. The results of the searches 'university AND industry', etc., have then to be subtracted from the total number of hits in order to find the relevant number for single occurrences of

continued >

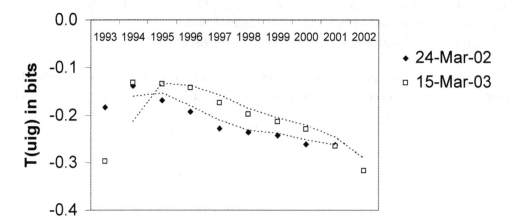

Figure 8.9: Mutual information in three dimensions ('university,' 'industry,' 'government') as measured using the *AltaVista Advanced Search Engine* in 2002 and 2003, respectively. The two-year moving averages are added as trendlines.

Figure 9 shows that the values for T_{UIG} are always negative. The curves decrease linearly during the period 1995-2000. This period witnessed the booming and the potential self-organization of the so-called new economy.[90] The decrease in the value of the transmission in three dimensions is steady during this period ($r^2 = 0.95$). In the results collected in 2002, the curve seemed to flatten, but in 2003 the self-organizing dynamic in these relations was resumed at an increasing speed. Thus, the process of endogenous expansion of the Internet was interrupted temporarily as e-business entered a recession. Note that these changes in the dynamics were not noticeable upon visual inspection of the growth data in Figures 7 and 8.

8.3.2 *Testing for systemness in Triple Helix relations*

What can the effect of increasingly negative values for T_{UIG} teach us when compared to the descriptive statistics provided by the above figures? Does it

---

the word 'university'. The subtraction assumes Boolean consistency in the search engine, but in the case of search engines at the Internet, this condition is only statistically true. For the purposes of this study the relatively small error terms in data gathering were neglected. As noted, the focus here is on developing the indicator for data analysis and not on improving techniques for retrieval and data collection.

[90] Before 1995, military and university websites were more prevalent on the Internet than commercial sites (Leydesdorff, 2000e).

indicate the self-organization of a virtual dimension in the overlay of relations generated by the co-occurrences? Can this, indeed, be considered a sign of the increasing self-organization of the system of relations? Is the underlying data in each of the helices also reorganized by the emerging system at the overlay level?

Emerging systemness in data sets can be tested against the alternative of the historical development of elements of the system along the time axis (Leydesdorff, 1995a). While the overlay in the Triple Helix model may exhibit systemness, the carrying institutions continue to develop historically. However, the overlay system can be considered as another selection environment at the global level, that is, in a (historically changing) present. The negative entropy indicates that the overlay system is providing the carrying systems with information relevant to reduce the uncertainty in the present. The present, however, remains a specific moment in time. In Figure 9, this was extended by using two measurement points, but in the case of comparing two states the research design is only 'comparatively static.' Can we also trace the relevance of the emerging subdynamics for the further development of the system? Has the interactive feedback that we signalled at these two moments in time also become stabilized?

In the case of emerging systemness, one can expect a data set increasingly to display the Markov property. The Markov property states that the current state of a system is the best prediction of its next stage.[91] If systemness is *not* achieved, however, the (normalized sum of the) longitudinal predictions for the various elements provide us with the best prediction for a next state. These two hypotheses (of systemic development versus independent development of the elements, respectively) can be tested against each other in predicting next year's data. When the predicted values are subsequently observed, the quality of the two predictions can be evaluated (e.g., Leydesdorff, 2000a; Leydesdorff and Oomes, 1999; Riba-Vilanova and Leydesdorff, 2001).[92]

This test was applied using the two time series data (retrieved on 24 March 2002 and 15 May 2003, respectively). In the first case, the data 1993-2000 was used for the prediction of 2001 data, and in the second, the time series data 1993-2001 for

---

[91] Complex systems can also exhibit non-Markovian features when they have a memory. Such systems can be modeled as Markov processes with memory (Ebeling *et al.*, 1995).

[92] Since the historical prediction is dependent on the year taken as the first year for the longitudinal analysis, the predictions for all possible starting years are routinely calculated and the prediction with the best fit is selected in order to maximize the possibility of rejection of the hypothesis of systemness in the data under study.

the prediction of 2002. Comparison with the observed data for 2001 and 2002, respectively, leads to the following results:

prediction of the value in *2001* and 2002, respectively	seven categories (U, I, G, UI, UG, IG, UIG)	four categories (UI, UG, IG, UIG)	three categories (UI, UG, IG)
on the basis of the univariate time series	*2.06*	*5.93*	*5.06*
	9.24	0.33	0.36
on the basis of the previous year (Markov property)	*2.83*	*5.54*	*4.15*
	26.60	0.15	0.06
hypothesis of systemness	*− 0.77*	*0.39*	*0.91*
	− 17.36	0.19	0.30
	(rejected)		

Table 8.1: Testing the hypothesis of systemness in the Triple Helix overlay of University-Industry-Government Relations for data in 2002 (italic) and 2003, respectively. (All values are in millibits of information.)

A better prediction leads to a more precise match between the expected and the observed values and therefore to a lower value of the probabilistic entropy generated. The results thus show that the predictions of the 2001 and the 2002 data on the basis of the same data for the previous years (Markov property assumed) are at both moments inferior to the prediction on the basis of the time series of the various categories in the case of considering the whole system of seven search categories (second column of Table 1). Thus, the hypothesis that this representation would develop as a system is rejected. The deviation from systemness increases between 2001 and 2002.

If the analysis is limited to the three bi-lateral relations (right column of Table 1), the hypothesis of systemness in the data is corroborated. The quality of this latter prediction is worsened by including the trilateral relations (middle column). Similar results were obtained when using the prediction of data for the year 2000 on the basis of the time-series 1993-1999, but the results were then even more pronounced.[93] The systemness in the overlay system of three (or four) categories

---

93

continued >

was disturbed in 2000, but the pattern of before 2000 has nevertheless been continued. This result accords with the patterns visible in Figure 9 above.

In summary, the results suggest that the system of representations of university-industry-government relations at the Internet is developing as a set of bilateral relations. These bilateral relations generate negative entropy and in this sense enable the global system to self-organize the complexity in the data using a virtual overlay of network relations. This development has been slowed down by the dot-com crisis, but the self-organizing dynamics is resuming its pace.

8.3.3 The Triple Helix in the *Science Citation Index*

In the next application of the mutual information in three dimensions on Triple Helix data, I used the 1,432,401 corporate addresses on the CD-Rom version of the *Science Citation Index 2000*. These addresses point to 725,354 records contained in this database on a total of 778,446 items. Only 3.7 % of these records contain no address information.[94] Our research focused on international coauthorship relations in this data, but we report on that project elsewhere (Wagner and Leydesdorff, 2005a, 2005b). Here, I focus on University-Industry-Government relations using the same data set.

prediction of the value in 2000	seven categories (U, I, G, UI, UG, IG, UIG)	four categories (UI, UG, IG, UIG)	three categories (UI, UG, IG)
on the basis of the univariate time series (1993-1999)	1.25	3.14	3.36
on the basis of the previous year (1999) (Markov property)	2.34	0.27	0.30
hypothesis of systemness	**- 0.89** **(rejected)**	**2.87**	**3.06**

Table 8.1a: Testing the hypothesis of systemness in the Triple Helix overlay of University-Industry-Government Relations for the year 2000. (All values are provided in millibits of information.)

[94] The total number of authors in this database is 3,060,436. Thus, on average each record relates to four authors, but at two addresses.

An attempt was made to organize all these (more than one million) addresses automatically in terms of their attribution to university-industry-government relations. The routine first attributed a university label to addresses that contained the abbreviations 'UNIV' or 'COLL.' Once an attribution was made, the record was set aside before further attributions were made. The remaining addresses were subsequently labeled as 'industrial' if they contained one of the following identifiers 'CORP', 'INC', 'LTD', 'SA' or 'AG'. Thereafter, the file was scanned for the identifiers of public research institutions using as identifiers 'NATL', 'NACL', 'NAZL', 'GOVT', 'MINIST', 'ACAD', 'INST', 'NIH', 'HOSP', 'HOP', 'EUROPEAN', 'US', 'CNRS', 'CERN', 'INRA', and 'BUNDES.'

This relatively simple procedure enabled us to identify 1,239,848 or 86.6% of the total number of address records in terms of their origin as 'university,' 'industry,' or 'government.' However, these results remain statistically approximate figures. The distribution is exhibited in Table 2:

	Number of records	*Percentage*
'University'	878,427	61.3
'Industry'	46,952	3.3
'Government'	314,469	22.0
– (not identified)	192,553	13.4
Total	1,432,401	100

Table 8.2: Number of records in the *Science Citation Index 2000* that could be attributed with a Triple Helix label using a routine

The addresses thus refer identified to 676,511 (93.3%) of the 725,354 records in the database that contain address information. Furthermore, the address information also contains country names. For the purpose of this study, records containing an address in England, Scotland, Wales or Northern Ireland were additionally labeled 'UK,' and analogously a dataset for the EU was composed containing all records with addresses in the 15 member states. The label 'Scandinavia' was added to all records containing an address in Norway, Sweden, Denmark, or Finland. A subset of the 120,086 internationally co-authored papers was analogously defined.

For all these subsets a three-dimensional transmission of Triple Helix relations can be calculated. The results of this calculation are shown in Table 3.

	number	% titles retrieved	T_{UIG} in mbits	UI	UG	IG	UIG	Univ.	Ind.	Gov.
All	676511	93.3	**-77.0**	16270	108919	4359	5201	543123	41242	232096
USA	232571	92.5	**-74.4**	7200	37834	1782	2666	200149	18154	66416
EU	257376	93.0	**-50.1**	4455	52112	1485	2028	206747	11192	101545
UK	68404	93.1	**-63.1**	1719	13098	394	690	54823	3970	26202
Germany	61017	94.7	**-43.4**	1028	14003	407	664	51283	2799	23701
France	41112	90.3	**-52.1**	439	11593	452	530	26133	1928	26595
Scandinavia	30939	95.8	**-31.6**	490	8477	162	371	26542	1263	13005
Italy	28958	89.9	**-29.4**	362	7133	87	262	25633	905	10526
Netherlands	18357	95.3	**-25.4**	372	4482	106	259	16379	863	6593
Japan	67715	97.9	**-92.1**	4147	12492	954	1311	56534	9732	21664
PR China	22116	99.5	**-14.9**	237	4610	68	114	18196	480	8583
Taiwan	8390	97.4	**-17.1**	148	2163	19	52	7454	250	3120
Singapore	2931	99.0	**-23.9**	104	476	7	17	2598	145	809
S. Korea	12038	98.3	**-40.1**	351	2341	87	91	10345	676	3978
Russia	22767	98.6	**-24.2**	76	6315	162	138	11507	478	17611
India	10916	89.2	**-78.1**	97	1813	61	55	6099	407	6492
Brazil	9120	91.0	**-22.4**	137	1727	32	52	7968	267	2885
internationally coauthored	120086	98.9	**-21.9**	4550	47054	1349	2545	107569	9422	61138

Table 8.3: University-industry-government relations for various countries and regions using ISI's *Science Citation Index 2000*.[95]

Table 3 suggests a very different pattern for the Triple Helix developments in various world regions. The Triple Helix overlay operates within the U.S.A. and Japan at a much higher level of self-organization than in Europe. Within the European Union, one can observe a scale with the U.K. at the leading end, but the smaller units (e.g., The Netherlands) at much lower levels. Russia and Brazil are

---

[95] The numbers of records under the headings "university," "industry," and "government", respectively, in the three right-hand columns are total numbers of papers with this type of address, that is, including those coauthored with authors from the other sectors.

even less integrated from this perspective, but India exhibits the Asian-Pacific pattern (T < – 0.70).

In terms of the three-dimensional transmission, Japan is far more networked in a Triple Helix mode than the other countries included in this analysis. This can already be seen on visual inspection of the numbers. For example, the number of papers with both university and industry addresses is 4,147 in Japan against 4,455 for the whole EU. This corresponds to 7.3% and 2.2% of all university papers in these two subsets, respectively.

In France the ratio of university papers coauthored with industry is only 1.7%. In this case, the relation between industry and the public sector is even stronger than the one between industry and the university sector. The relations between university research and public sector research are strong everywhere, but in France, Russia, and India, public-sector research is larger than university research in terms of scientific output. The values of the indicators for East Asian countries demonstrate how industrial participation in the network knowledge production system can be a crucial variable for the self-organization of Triple Helix dynamics.

Note that more than 39% of the internationally coauthored papers contain an address of both a university and a government agency. Yet, the relatively low numbers of bilateral coauthorship relations of universities and government agencies with industrial partners indicates a low level of institutional differentiation in this subset. Furthermore there seems to be a size effect of the T_{UIG} indicator among nations, but this correlation is not statistically significant. The main distinction, however, is visible as a pattern of collaboration that is culturally specific. The academic system on the continent in Europe seems much more traditional in its patterns of collaboration than in the U.S.A. and Japan. University-Government relations are more established in the European nations than University-Industry relations. Russia and France are the most extreme cases in this respect. The papers based on international collaborations, however, exhibited the least development in this Triple Helix mode of relations among all the subsets (T = -21.9 mbits).

For validation purposes, I repeated the analysis thereafter using the *Science Citation Index 2002*. The results are exhibited in Table 4. They show first that the analysis can be reproduced using another dataset. On average the values of the T_{UIG} are less negative in 2002 than in 2000. Some smaller systems (e.g., The Netherlands, Singapore, and Taiwan), however, show the opposite tendency.

	number (2000)	% retrieved	titles T_{UIG} in mbits	number (2002)	% retrieved	titles T_{UIG} in mbits
All	676511	93.3	**-77.0**	683222	93.6	**-70.7**
USA	232571	92.5	**-74.4**	238676	92.6	**-71.0**
EU	257376	93.0	**-50.1**	250395	93.4	**-45.3**
UK	68404	93.1	**-63.1**	66544	93.9	**-54.0**
Germany	61017	94.7	**-43.4**	59630	95.2	**-39.6**
France	41112	90.3	**-52.1**	39973	91.1	**-42.5**
Scandinavia	30939	95.8	**-31.6**	30437	95.7	**-32.5**
Italy	28958	89.9	**-29.4**	29795	90.7	**-27.6**
Netherlands	18357	95.3	**-25.4**	17865	95.1	**-32.8**
Japan	67715	97.9	**-92.1**	68338	97.9	**-82.4**
PR China	22116	99.5	**-14.9**	28913	99.5	**-11.0**
Taiwan	8390	97.4	**-17.1**	9572	99.4	**-18.0**
Singapore	2931	99.0	**-23.9**	3411	98.6	**-28.6**
S. Korea	12038	98.3	**-40.1**	14931	98.7	**-33.7**
Russia	22767	98.6	**-24.2**	20723	98.4	**-18.9**
India	10916	89.2	**-78.1**	12570	89.1	**-67.7**
Brazil	9120	91.0	**-22.4**	10888	91.9	**-26.8**

Table 8.4: Comparison of results using data from the *Science Citation Index 2002* and the *Science Citation Index 2000*.

It should be emphasized that these results refer to representations in the *Science Citation Index*, and the above classification into sectors was statistical and therefore approximate. Industry is weakly represented in this data. Collaborations with industry may not lead to this type of scientific publication. The purpose of this study, however, was to demonstrate the use of three-dimensional transmissions as a methodology for data analysis. Data collection may require more care. However, independently of the refinement of the measurement, network data about university-industry-government relations can be written as relative frequency distributions. The indicators of the three-dimensional transmissions can then be applied to a comparison of the state of the Triple Helix configurations under study.

8.4 Two further tests

The above results suggest that the Triple Helix operates strongly as an overlay in the system of global representations, but not similarly at the national level in all the advanced countries. On the contrary, cultural patterns seem to intervene. I shall turn to the issue of the measurement of the knowledge base of geographical units of analysis in the following chapters, but let me first pursue the analysis of national and cultural differences by adding results from two further studies, namely the representation of national systems at the level of an international database (the Internet), and the representation of an international system at the level of a national (U.S.) database. These two tests will enable me to specify the dynamics of globalization and Triple Helix relations in greater detail.

8.4.1 *National subdomains and languages at the Internet*

The Internet can be considered as a global system, but it can also be searched specifically for national domains using the domain name (e.g, '.br' for Brazil) and/or the national language (Portuguese in this case). In a previous study we explored these various dimensions for comparing the Netherlands and Brazil (Leydesdorff and Curran, 2000). In this study, three national domains with their respective languages were analyzed in terms of the Triple Helix indicator of configurational information: Brazil (.br) with Portuguese, Germany (.de) with German, and the Netherlands (.nl) with Dutch. Among the many possibilities, Brazil and the Netherlands were selected for the longitudinal comparison with our previous results (for reasons of validation and control in terms of the descriptive statistics). Germany was added as a third case with a larger economy because Brazil and the Netherlands also exhibited specific similarities in the previous analysis.

After consultation with a number of native speakers, the following search terms were selected:

	University	Industry	Government
Portuguese	Universidade	Indústria	Governo
German	Universit*	Industr*	Bundes*
Dutch	Universit*	Industr*	Overheid

Table 8.5: Search terms for Triple Helix relations in different national languages

The similarity between the English search terms and those in German and Dutch makes it possible to include the terms more globally, possibly disadvantaging Portuguese. However, the results exhibited in Figure 8.10 are clear and robust: the global development of the Internet prevailed over national differences as the Internet developed during the 1990s.[96]

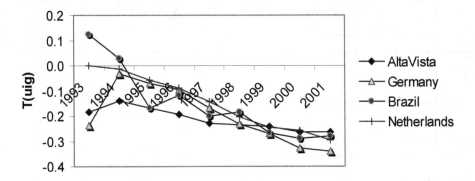

Figure 8.10: The three-dimensional transmission between 'university,' 'industry,' and 'government' in various national systems and languages during the period 1993-2001

Although initially (1993-1995) the 'national' representations of Triple Helix configurations were variously integrated and differentiated at the Internet, the global dynamics harmonized these systems into a similar pattern during the years thereafter. The self-organization of Triple Helix relations at the Internet has prevailed over national differences in terms of domains and languages.

8.4.2 U.S. Patent data

The database of the U.S. Patent and Trademark Office (USPTO) provides us with a nationally organized database which can be used as a window on international developments in patents because it integrates patent applications from around the world at the level of the American market (Narin and Olivastro, 1988; Granstrand, 1999; Leydesdorff, 2004a).

'University,' 'industry,' and 'government,' and their various combinations with Boolean AND operators, can also be used as free text search terms in this database (Black, 2003). As in the case of the Internet, I searched the patent database for the

---

[96] All searches for this analysis were done on March 24, 2002.

number of occurrences of these terms in the file on a year-to-year basis.[97] For reasons of comparison with the Internet analysis in section 7.5, the time series in Table 6 is shown for the period since 1993.

Year	University	Industry	Government	UI	UG	IG	UIG	Total
1993	3063	9716	2619	401	588	334	63	110540
1994	3359	10568	2855	479	684	390	89	114564
1995	3710	10800	2828	529	771	410	93	114864
1996	4552	12147	3149	703	963	488	114	122953
1997	5406	12699	3604	814	1199	583	168	125884
1998	7623	17068	4708	1254	1658	807	266	166801
1999	8326	18553	4856	1352	1735	844	235	170265
2000	8488	19368	4831	1399	1776	865	267	176350
2001	9190	20812	5136	1591	1868	996	296	184172
2002	9228	21089	5242	1619	1928	1047	352	184531

Table 8.6: The number of hits for the search terms 'university,' 'industry,' and 'government' and their combinations in the database of the U.S. Patent and Trade Office.

Note that the number of patents recalled with the search term 'university' has grown steadily over the period, but this growth has declined in recent years. This reversal in the trend can be made even more visible by searching for the term 'university' among the patent assignees, as is shown in Figure 8.11 for the whole period since the introduction of patent rights for universities by the Bayh-Dole Act of 1980. The curve exhibits a sigmoid pattern of growth that has been stabilized more recently.

During the 1980s the value of three-dimensional transmissions among the dimensions 'university,' 'industry,' and 'government' remained stable. (During the period 1976-1992, $T_{uig} = -0.190 \pm 0.008$.) But during the 1990s this value began to rise, indicating a tendency towards a more centrally integrated and systematic word usage (Figure 12). Since 1999, however, the system is stable again. This corresponds with the bending of the upward curve in Figure 11. It seems that the systems innovation induced by the Bay-Dole Act has now come to rest.

---

[97] The use of the word 'industry' in a free-text search means that this word is part of the discourse, but does not refer to the owner or inventor of the patent in question (Debackere *et al.*, 2002). However, the number of patents assigned to corporations is much higher than is indicated by 'industry' as a free-text search term. More than 50% of the patents contains an industrial address (Jaffe and Traitenberg, 2002), whereas only 10-20% are indicated under 'industry' in Table 1.

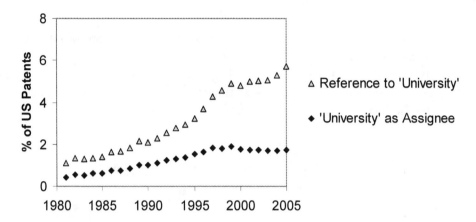

Figure 8.11: Percentage of U.S. Patents (i) with a reference to the word 'university' and (ii) a 'university' among the assignees

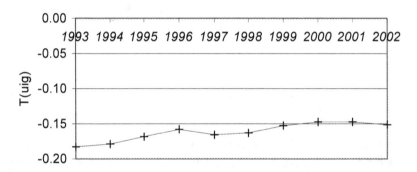

Figure 8.12: Mutual information among 'university,' 'industry,' and 'government' relations in the database of the U.S. Patent and Trade Office

With hindsight, the Bayh-Dole Act of 1980 can be considered as having provided the patent system with one more degree of freedom, that is, by allowing universities increasingly to become players in this institutional field. (The Bayh-Dole Act granted universities the right to patent results from federally funded research.) The patent system, however, has remained a highly institutionalized system of legal control and is therefore under pressure to integrate. New players can be expected to be enrolled within this system in due time. In the initial phase (the 1980s) the new signal was absorbed into the old system, and in the log-phase of the subsequent growth the system found gradually a new equilibrium. Unlike a self-organizing dynamics, this dynamics was first upset and then reorganized.

8.5   Variation and selection

Despite the poor operationalization of the industrial dimension when using the word 'industry' as a search term, the increasing integration into the patent database is not a trivial result. This is demonstrated by the next test: Figure 13 is based on performing precisely the same exercise at the Internet using the *AltaVista Advanced Search Engine*, but now using the searchable fields 'title:' and 'link:' respectively.

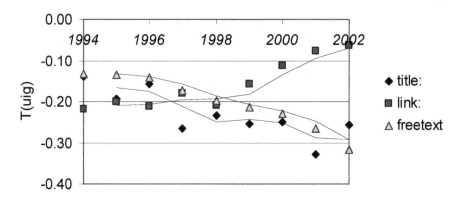

Figure 8.13: The mutual information among 'university,' 'industry,' and 'government' relations as retrieved at the Internet using the *Altavista Advanced Search Engine*. (The curves are based on two-year moving averages.)

The line for the free text search is to a large extent the same as the one for the searches in 2003 provided in Figure 8.9 above. Originally, I wanted only to check whether I would find the same effects with title words as previously with free text searches despite the order of magnitude of difference in the search results. Title words are deliberately provided by the web-authors as meta-tags. Indeed, the resulting values for T_{UIG} are similar in terms of the trend in the indicator. After a period of initial construction of the Internet (1992-1995), the value of the indicator decreases steadily. (The curve based on the two-year moving averages is less smooth because of the lower numbers.) This 'self-organization' of Triple Helix relations in the global dimension at the Internet seems to have flattened in the most recent years.

While the title-words can be considered as variation—provided by the authors—following the hyperlinks enables us to map the selections that the authors of web pages make from the materials previously made available. In this dimension the authors can be expected to integrate references selectively into their text, whereas they are expected to reach out to their audiences in choosing title words (Leydesdorff, 1989). The *AltaVista* search engine enables us to map these hyperlinks to the relevant domains in terms of their institutional affiliation using the extensions '.edu', '.com', and '.gov' as proxies. Note that these proxies are limited to the U.S.A. in the case of the .edu and .gov-domains, whereas the .com-domain is used worldwide.

The resulting trend line in Figure 13 shows a mirror image when compared to the curves for free text and title words. The authors of these documents integrate the hyperlinks by using the available documents as their knowledge base. In other words, the knowledge base is performatively integrated into the texts. The texts can be considered as phenotypical instantiations which take part in the observable knowledge infrastructure (Giddens, 1984). Whereas the title words and other (free text) words show mainly differentiation, this selective integration leads to a less negative value for the mutual information in three dimensions.

Year	.edu	.com	.gov	Edu AND com	edu AND gov	com AND gov	edu AND com AND gov	Link:* (total)
1993	721	753	26	32	16	21	13	140631
1994	10653	5969	5070	1281	454	1657	264	155429
1995	58559	85344	63208	16060	4168	30666	2707	971806
1996	185571	213755	40505	52853	13816	15191	9713	4215445
1997	383999	586804	76767	118249	25447	29842	18723	8410235
1998	714592	1512795	206683	177352	49238	59734	33695	21190676
1999	1410789	3372441	341635	346610	92354	126961	63192	42521722
2000	2212642	10057844	577433	622780	194573	244278	151641	92177426
2001	3722856	30497559	1328142	1344270	373437	599161	305180	196204140
2002	8564790	81698935	4035084	3058198	1159347	1758589	757120	501734312

Table 8.7: The number of hits for the search terms 'link:university,' 'link:industry,' and/or 'link:government' and their combinations using the *AltaVista Advanced Search Engine* (May 15, 2003)

Table 7 shows the number of links involved. The number of links with .com is an order of magnitude larger than the other ones, and among the bilateral links the co-'sitation' of .edu and .com prevails (Rousseau, 1997).[98] Although the more skewed shape of these distributions reduces the values of the entropies in each of the

---

[98] The number of links to .com pages is also an order of magnitude larger than the number of hits using 'industry' as a free text term (Table 2).

dimensions considerably, the interaction effects among the entropies in three dimensions remain invisible on the basis of visual inspection of the values of the different fluxes and their bilateral relations. However, the evaluation of the mutual information in three dimensions requires computation.

8.6   Conclusions

Triple Helix configurations can be measured as network data. The representations need by no means be restricted—as in this study—to the terms 'university,' 'industry,' and 'government' as search terms in a database. However, I have used the results from these relatively straightforward searches in order to explain how the algorithmic indicator of mutual information in three dimensions enables us to distinguish among observable Triple Helix arrangements.

At the global level, the system of representations at the Internet has gone through a rapid phase of expansion and has exhibited a negative transmission in these three dimensions that is further deepening. It could additionally be shown that the self-organization of the probabilistic entropy in this representation was based exclusively on the system of bi-lateral relations. The representations at the national level within this global system followed the trend, and this result confirms the assumption of a global development.

Using the ISI-database, different patterns of integration became visible in various cultural regions of the globe. Industry seems far less integrated into the academic system in Europe than in the U.S.A. and in Asia, in terms of their participation in academic publications. By using the nationally integrated U.S. patent system, I could then show that this *national* system of registration exerts integrative feedback on the otherwise expanding domain. The expansion of the patent system is moderated by the institutional framework.

The *systemness* of the overlay was also evaluated in comparison with the representations of the composing units (e.g., university, industry, and government). In the case of the Internet, the bi-lateral relations between the search terms carried the systemness. The self-organization of the knowledge-based economy can thus be considered as a Triple Helix development at the global level, while nations differ in terms of how they are able to participate in these developments. The value of the mutual information in three dimensions at the national level indicates the extent to which the national systems contain a Triple Helix dynamics. In the next chapters, we zoom in on two national systems (the Netherlands and Germany) as examples.

In this chapter, I used scientometric and webometric representations in order to show how Triple Helix relations work differently at the national and at the global level. But we shall see that the algorithm for measuring the knowledge base as a configurational entropy works equally well on econometric data.

Chapter 9

Measuring the Knowledge Base of the Dutch Economy*

The interrelationships among technology, organization, and territory in an economic system have been considered as a 'holy trinity' (Storper, 1997) from the perspective of regional economics. Can mutual information in three dimensions be used as an indicator of the surplus value (negative entropy) in the configuration of relations? Using micro-data about more than a million companies containing values for these three variables, the indicator will be tested for the Netherlands as a national innovation system. The data contains postal codes (geography), sector codes (proxy for technology), and firm sizes in terms of numbers of employees (proxy for organization). The configurations are mapped at three levels: national (NUTS-1), provincial (NUTS-2), and regional (NUTS-3). The levels are cross-tabled with the knowledge-intensive sectors and services. The results suggest that medium-tech sectors contribute to the knowledge base of an economy more than high-tech ones. Knowledge-intensive services have an uncoupling effect, but less so at the high-tech end of these services.

9.1   The measurement problem in evolutionary economics

Ever since evolutionary economists introduced the concept of a 'knowledge-based economy' (Foray and Lundvall, 1996; Abramowitz and David, 1996), the question of the measurement of this new type of economic configuration has come to the fore (Carter, 1996; OECD, 1996b). Can something as elusive as the knowledge base of a system be measured? (Foray, 2004; Leydesdorff, 2001b; Skolnikoff, 1993). Is a structural transformation of the economy at the global level indicated with potentially different effects in various world regions and nations? In proposing their program of studies at the OECD, David and Foray (1995, at p. 14) argued that the focus on *national* systems of innovation had placed too much emphasis on the organization of institutions and economic growth, and not enough on the

* This chapter is based on a paper, coauthored with Wilfred Dolfsma and Gerben van der Panne, entitled 'Measuring the Knowledge Base of an Economy in terms of Triple Helix Relations among 'Technology, Organization, and Territory,' *Research Policy*, 35(2) (2006) 181-199.

distribution of knowledge itself. However, Lundvall's (1988) argument for considering the nation as a first candidate in defining innovation systems was carefully formulated in terms of a heuristics:

> The interdependency between production and innovation goes both ways. [...] This interdependency between production and innovation makes it legitimate to take the national system of production as a starting point when defining a system of innovation. (Lundvall, 1988, at p. 362)

The choice of the nation as a frame of reference enables the analyst to use national statistics about industrial production and market shares to make systematic comparisons among nations (Lundvall, 1992; Nelson, 1993), and to translate the findings into advice for national governments. The relevant statistics have been made comparable among nations by the OECD and Eurostat (OECD/Eurostat, 1997).

The hypothesis of a transition to a 'knowledge-based economy' implies a systems transformation at the structural level across nations. Following this lead, the focus of efforts at the OECD and Eurostat has been to develop indicators of the relative knowledge-intensity of industrial sectors (OECD, 2001, 2003) and regions (Laafia, 1999, 2002a, 2002b). Alternative frameworks for 'systems of innovation' like technologies (Carlsson and Stankiewicz, 1991) or regions (Braczyk *et al.*, 1998) were also considered (Carlsson, 2006). However, the analysis of the knowledge base of innovation systems (e.g., Cowan *et al.*, 2000) was not made sufficiently relevant for the measurement efforts (David and Foray, 2002). Knowledge was not sufficiently considered as a coordination mechanism of society, but as a public or private good.

Knowledge as a coordination mechanism was initially defined in terms of the qualifications of the labor force. Machlup (1962) argued that in a 'knowledge economy' knowledge-workers would play an increasingly important role in industrial production processes. Employment data has been central to the study of this older concept. For example, employment statistics can be cross-tabled with distinctions among sectors in terms of high- and medium-tech (Cooke, 2002; Schwartz, 2006). However, the concept of a 'knowledge-based economy' refers to a change in the structure of an economy beyond the labor market (Foray and Lundvall, 1996; Cooke and Leydesdorff, 2006). How does the development of science and technology transform economic exchange processes? (Schumpeter, [1939] 1964).

The social organization of knowledge production and control was first considered as a systemic development by Whitley (1984). Dasgupta and David (1994) proposed to consider science as the subject of a new economics. Because of the reputational control mechanisms involved, the dynamics of knowledge production and diffusion differ in important respects from economic market or institutional control mechanisms (Mirowski and Sent, 2001; Whitley, 2001). When a third coordination mechanism is added as a subdynamic to the interactions and potential co-evolution between economic exchange relations and institutional control (Freeman and Perez, 1988), non-linear effects can be expected (Leydesdorff, 1994b). The possible synergies may lead to the envisaged transition to a knowledge-based economy, but not equally or evenly: developments in some geographically defined economies will be more knowledge-based than others.

The geographical setting, the (knowledge-based) technologies as deployed in different sectors, and the organizational structures of the industries constitute three relatively independent sources of variance. One would expect significant differences in the quality of innovation systems among regions and industrial sectors in terms of technological capacities (Fritsch, 2004). The three sources of variance may reinforce one another in a configuration so that uncertainty is reduced at the systems level. A knowledge-based order of the economy can be shaped when technological developments can operate freely on geographical distributions and organizational forms of corporations. The research question is whether one is able to operationalize this configurational order and then also to measure it. I shall use Storper's (1997, at pp. 26 ff.) notion of a 'holy trinity' among technology, organization, and territory from regional economics for the operationalization, and the indicator developed in the previous chapter for the measurement.

9.2   The perspective of regional economics

In his study entitled *The Regional World*, Michael Storper (1997, at pp. 26f.) argued that technology, organization, and territory can be considered as a 'holy trinity' for regional development. Storper emphasized that the holy trinity should not be studied as an aggregate of the composing elements, but in terms of the relations between and among these elements. These relationships shape regional economics. However, his proposal for a 'relational paradigm' was not operationalized in terms which allow for measurement:

> Regional economics, in particular, and integrated territorial economies in general, will be redefined here as *stocks of relational assets*. [...] Technology involves not just the tension between scale and variety, but that between the codifiability or noncodifiability of knowledge; its substantive domain is learning and *becoming*, not just diffusion and deployment. Organizations are knit together, their boundaries defined and changed, and their relations to

each other accomplished not simply as input-output relations or linkages, but as untraded interdependencies subject to a high degree of reflexivity. Territorial economies are not only created, in a globalizing world economy, by proximity in input-output relations, but more so by proximity in the untraded or relational dimensions of organizations and technologies. Their principal assets—because scarce and slow to create and imitate—are no longer material, but relational. (Storper, 1997, at p. 28)

Storper added to his extension of the 'heterodox paradigm' in economics a reflexive turn. The 'holy trinity' is to be understood not only as elements in a network, but as the result of the reflexive dynamics of networks of relations shaping new worlds. The new worlds emerge as densities of links that can be developed into competitive advantages, when and where they materialize by being coupled to regions (Callon, 1986). For example, one would expect the clustering of high-tech services in certain (e.g., metropolitan) areas. The location of such a niche can be considered as a consequence of the self-organization of the interactions (Bathelt, 2003; Cooke and Leydesdorff, 2006).

Elaborating on the model of a Triple Helix of university-industry-government relations, I have argued above in a similar vein for considering an 'overlay' of relations between universities, industries, and governments as emerging potentially as another (sub)dynamics from the interactions. Under certain conditions the feedback from the reflexive overlay can reshape the network relations from which it emerged. Because of this reflexive turn, the parties involved may become increasingly aware of their own and each others' expectations, limitations, and positions. These expectations and interactions can be further informed by relevant knowledge. Thus, the knowledge-based subdynamic may increasingly contribute to the operation of the system.

The knowledge-based overlay and the institutional layer operate upon one another in terms of frictions that provide opportunities for innovation both vertically within each of the helices and horizontally among them. The quality of the knowledge base in the economy depends on the locally specific functioning of the interactions in the knowledge infrastructure and on the interface between this infrastructure and the self-organizing dynamics at the systems level. A knowledge base would operate by diminishing the uncertainty that prevails at the network level, that is, as a structural property of the system.

The correspondence between these two perspectives can be extended to the operationalization. Storper (1997, at p. 49), for example, used the following depiction of 'the economy as a set of intertwined, partially overlapping domains of action' in terms of recursively overlapping Venn-diagrams:

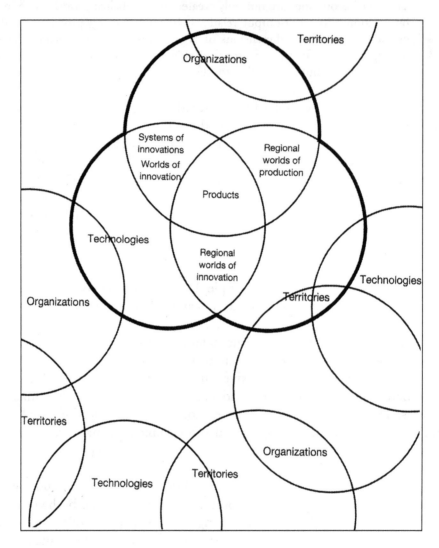

Figure 9.1: Storper's 'holy trinity of technologies, organizations, and territories' provides an overlap in the resulting 'products'.

Using the Triple Helix model, I noted in the previous chapter that the three circles boldfaced in Figure 1 do not necessarily have to overlap in a common zone like the area indicated with 'Products' (see Chapter Eight; Figures 3 and 4). In a networked arrangement an 'overlay' can under certain conditions replace the function of central integration. In this case, a virtual hypercycle (instead of observable products) can close the complex system into a knowledge-based regime.

It could be shown (in Chapter Eight) that a so-called 'interaction information' (McGill, 1954) varies considerably in Triple Helix configurations among nations and world regions (Leydesdorff, 2003b, at p. 460). In this chapter, I extend the scientometric approach in measuring the knowledge base to economic regions at the national and subnational levels by applying this operationalization to data about the distribution of Dutch firms in three dimensions. Thus, the indicator is generalized for the measurement of emergence in terms of three interacting dimensions. The data for indicating 'geography,' 'organization,' and 'technology' was obtained in collaboration with colleagues from Rotterdam and Delft who had used this information extensively in previous studies (Van der Panne and Dolfsma, 2001, 2003).

For example, one would expect high-tech sectors to 'deepen and tighten' the knowledge base of the systems in which they operate (Mokyr, 2002). Firms in these sectors can be expected to act as 'specialized decision-making units whose function it is to improve coordination by structuring information flows' (Casson 1997, at p. 80). The question of which subdynamic prevails, however, remains empirical. Although firms play an important role in constructing the knowledge-based economy, a knowledge-based economy is not a result of the aggregate of individual actions at the firm level, but also of their interactions in a configuration (Dolfsma, 2005).

9.3   Methods and data

9.3.1   Data

The data consists of 1,131,668 records containing information based on the registration of enterprises by the Chambers of Commerce of the Netherlands. The data was collected by Marktselect plc; they specifically correspond to the CD-Rom for the second quarter of 2001 (Van der Panne and Dolfsma, 2003). Because corporations are required to register with the Chamber of Commerce, the dataset covers the entire population. I brought the data under the control of a relational database manager in order to study the relations among these attributes. Dedicated programs were developed for further processing and computation as necessary.

In addition to information at the company level, the data contains three variables which can be used as proxies for the dimensions of technology, organization, and geography at the systems level. Technology will be indicated by sector classification (Pavitt, 1984; Vonortas, 2000), organization by company size in terms of numbers of employees (Pugh *et al.*, 1969a, 1969b; Blau and Schoenherr, 1971), and geographical position by the postal codes in the addresses. Sector classifications are based on the European NACE system. This classification was further elaborated by the Dutch Chambers of Commerce into a five-digit system (BIK-codes).[100] In addition to major activities, most companies also provide information about second and third classification terms. However, I use only the main code at the two-digit level unless otherwise indicated.

Size	Number of employees	Number of companies
1	None	223,231
2	1	453,842
3	2 to 4	279,835
4	5 to 9	88,862
5	10 to 19	42,047
6	20-49	27,246
7	50-99	8,913
8	100-199	4,303
9	200-499	2,313
10	500-749	503
11	750-999	225
12	> 1000	348
		N = 1,131,668

Table 9.1: Distribution of company data by size.

The distribution by company size is provided in Table 1. The data contains a first class of 223,231 companies without employees. We decided to include this category because it contains, among others, spin-off companies which are already on the

---

[100] NACE stands for Nomenclature générale des Activités économiques dans les Communautés Européennes. The NACE code can be translated into the International Standard Industrial Classificiation (ISIC) and into the Dutch national SBI (Standaard Bedrijfsindeling) developed by Statistics Netherlands. The Chambers of Commerce have elaborated this classification into the so-called BIK code (Bedrijfsindeling Kamers van Koophandel). However, these various codes can be translated unambiguously into one another.

market, but whose owners are employed by mother companies or universities. Given the research question, these establishments can be considered as relevant economic activities.

Postal codes are a fine-grained indicator of geographical location. The two-digit level of this code provides us with 90 districts in the Netherlands. Using this information, the data can be aggregated into provinces (NUTS-2) and so-called COROP regions. The Dutch COROP regions correspond with the NUTS-3 level used for the statistics of the OECD and Eurostat.[101] The Netherlands are thus organized in twelve provinces and forty regions, respectively.

9.3.2 Knowledge-intensity and high-tech

The OECD (1986) first defined knowledge-intensity in manufacturing sectors on the basis of R&D intensity. R&D intensity was defined for a given sector as the ratio of R&D expenditure to GDP at the national level, or value added at the level of sectors. Later this method was expanded to take account of the technology embodied in purchases of intermediate and capital goods (Hatzichronoglou, 1997). This new measure could also be applied to service sectors which tend to be technology users rather than technology producers. The discussion continues about how best to delineate knowledge-intensive services (Laafia, 1999, 2002a, 2002b; OECD, 2001, 2003, at p. 140). The classification introduced in the *2001 STI Scoreboard* will be used here (OECD, 2001, at pp. 137 ff.). The relevant NACE categories for high- and medium-tech are as follows:

---

[101] NUTS stands for Nomenclature des Unités Territoriales Statistiques (Nomenclature of Territorial Units for Statistics). COROP is the abbreviation of the Dutch 'Coordinatiecommissie Regionaal Onderzoeksprogramma.'

High-tech Manufacturing	Knowledge-intensive Sectors (KIS)
30 Manufacturing of office machinery and computers **32** Manufacturing of radio, television and communication equipment and apparatus **33** Manufacturing of medical precision and optical instruments, watches and clocks *Medium-high- tech Manufacturing* **24** Manufacture of chemicals and chemical products **29** Manufacture of machinery and equipment n.e.c. **31** Manufacture of electrical machinery and apparatus n.e.c. **34** Manufacture of motor vehicles, trailers and semi-trailers **35** Manufacturing of other transport equipment	**61** Water transport **62** Air transport **64** Post and telecommunications **65** Financial intermediation, except insurance and pension funding **66** Insurance and pension funding, except compulsory social security **67** Activities auxiliary to financial intermediation **70** Real estate activities **71** Renting of machinery and equipment without operator and of personal and household goods **72** Computer and related activities **73** Research and development **74** Other business activities **80** Education **85** Health and social work **92** Recreational, cultural and sporting activities Of these sectors, **64, 72** and **73** are considered *high-tech services.*

Table 9.2: Classification of high-tech and knowledge-intensive sectors according to Eurostat. Source: Laafia, 2002a, at p. 7.

These classifications are based on normalizations across the member states of the European Union and the OECD, respectively. However, the percentages of R&D and therefore the knowledge-intensity at the sectoral level may differ in the Netherlands from the average for the OECD or the EU. In a recent report, Statistics Netherlands (CBS, 2003) provided figures for R&D intensity as percentages of value added in 2001. Unfortunately, the data for the Netherlands is aggregated at a level higher than the categories provided by Eurostat and the OECD. For this reason, and, furthermore because the Dutch economy is heavily internationalized so that knowledge can easily spill over from neighboring countries, we decided to use the Eurostat categories provided in Table 2 to distinguish levels of knowledge-intensity among sectors.

9.3.3 Regional differences in the Netherlands

The reader may need some descriptive statistics to understand the Dutch context, since the geographical make-up of the country is different from its image. The share of employment in high-tech and medium-tech manufacturing in the Netherlands rated only above Luxembourg, Greece, and Portugal in the EU-15 (OECD, 2003, at pp. 140f.). The economically leading provinces of the country, like North- and South-Holland and Utrecht, ranked among the lowest on this indicator in the EU-15.[102] The south-east part of the country is integrated in terms of high- and medium-tech manufacturing with neighboring parts of Belgium and Germany. More than 50% of private R&D in the Netherlands is located in the regions of Southeast North-Brabant and North-Limburg (Wintjes and Cobbenhagen, 2000).

The core of the Dutch economy has traditionally been concentrated on services. These sectors are not necessarily knowledge-intensive, but the situation is somewhat brighter with respect to knowledge-intensive services than in terms of knowledge-based manufacturing. Utrecht and the relatively recently reclaimed province of Flevoland score high on this employment indicator,[103] while both North- and South-Holland are in the middle range. South-Holland is classified as a leading EU region in knowledge-intensive services (in absolute numbers), but the high-tech end of these services has remained underdeveloped. In summary, the country is not homogenous on any of these indicators. On the basis of these employment statistics, the geographical distribution seems almost opposite for high-tech manufacturing and knowledge-intensive services, with provinces specialized in one of the two.[104]

9.3.4 Methodology

Unlike a covariation between two variables, a dynamic interaction among three dimensions can generate a complex pattern (Schumpeter, [1939] 1964, at pp. 174f;

---

[102] Laafia (1999) provides maps of Europe with indication of employment rates in high-tech manufacturing sectors and high-tech service sectors respectively. Laafia (2002a) adds relevant figures.

[103] This newly reclaimed (polder) province is the only Dutch province amenable for EU support through the structural funds.

[104] Employment data have been central in defining the 'knowledge economy' since the term was first introduced (Machlup, 1962; Cooke, 2002; Schwartz, 2005). The concept of a knowledge-based economy, however, refers to the structure of an economy (Foray and Lundvall, 1996; Cooke and Leydesdorff, 2005).

Li &Yorke, 1975). The two configurations possible among three subdynamics were depicted in Figures 8.2 and 8.3 as integrating or differentiating. In the case of overlapping Venn diagrams, the dynamics can be considered as relatively integrated, e.g., in the resulting products (Storper, 1997, at p. 49; see Figure 9.1), while in the absence of overlap the system remains more differentiated. In this latter case, it operates in terms of different systems interfacing each other at the network level. In other words, such a configuration can be considered as a 'failing' center. The overlap among the three domains has become negative, and by using mutual information this can be indicated as negative entropy.[105] The mutual information in three dimensions can be used to measure the extent of integration and differentiation in the interaction among three subsystems. A system without integration in the center reduces uncertainty by providing a differentiated configuration. This differentiation can be reproduced if the dimensions of the complex communication are codified along different axes. The puzzles of integration at the interfaces are then solved in a non-hierarchical, that is, reflexive or knowledge-based mode. The indicator was technically defined in Chapter Eight.

9.4   Results

Let us apply the proposed measure to the data. First, I will provide the descriptive statistics (Table 3). As noted, the data allows us to disaggregate in terms of geographical regions (NUTS-2 and NUTS-3), and one is able to distinguish high-tech, medium-tech sectors, and knowledge-intensive services. The various dimensions can also be combined in order to compute the transmissions in a next step (Table 4).

9.4.1 Descriptive statistics

Table 3 shows the probabilistic entropy values in the three dimensions (G = geography, T = technology/sector, and O = organization) for the Netherlands as a whole and the decomposition at the NUTS-2 level of the provinces.

---

[105] The relation between the geometrical metaphor of overlap or overlay and the algorithmic measure of mutual information is not strictly one-to-one, but the metaphor is helpful for the understanding.

	$H_{Geogr.}$	$H_{Technol.}$	$H_{Organ.}$	H_{GT}	H_{GO}	H_{TO}	H_{GTO}	N
NL	6.205	4.055	2.198	10.189	8.385	6.013	12.094	1131668
% H_{max}	*95.6*	*69.2*	*61.3*	*82.5*	*83.2*	*63.7*	*75.9*	
Drenthe	2.465	4.134	2.225	6.569	4.684	6.039	8.413	26210
Flevoland	1.781	4.107	2.077	5.820	3.852	6.020	7.697	20955
Friesland	3.144	4.202	2.295	7.292	5.431	6.223	9.249	36409
Gelderland	3.935	4.091	2.227	7.986	6.158	6.077	9.925	131050
Groningen	2.215	4.192	2.220	6.342	4.427	6.059	8.157	30324
Limburg	2.838	4.166	2.232	6.956	5.064	6.146	8.898	67636
N-Brabant	3.673	4.048	2.193	7.682	5.851	6.018	9.600	175916
N-Holland	3.154	3.899	2.116	6.988	5.240	5.730	8.772	223690
Overijssel	2.747	4.086	2.259	6.793	5.002	6.081	8.749	64482
Utrecht	2.685	3.956	2.193	6.611	4.873	5.928	8.554	89009
S-Holland	3.651	3.994	2.203	7.582	5.847	5.974	9.528	241648
Zeeland	1.802	4.178	2.106	5.941	3.868	6.049	7.735	24339

Table 9.3: Expected information contents (in bits) of the distributions in the three dimensions and their combinations.

The provinces are very different in terms of numbers of firms. While Flevoland contains only 20,955 units, South-Holland provides the location for 241,648 firms.[106] This size effect is also reflected in the distribution of postal codes: the uncertainty in the geographical distribution—measured as $H_{Geography}$—correlates significantly with the number of firms N ($r = 0.76$; $p = 0.005$). The variance in the probabilistic entropies among the provinces is high (> 0.5) in this geographical dimension, but the variance in the probabilistic entropy among sectors and the size categories is relatively small (< 0.1). Thus, the provinces are relatively similar in terms of the uncertainty in their sector and size distributions,[107] and can thus be meaningfully compared.

The second row of Table 3 informs us that the probabilistic entropy in the postal codes of firms is larger then 95% of the maximum entropy of this distribution at the level of the nation. Since the postal codes are more fine-grained in metropolitan than in rural areas, this indicates that firm-density is not a major source of variance in relation to population density. However, the number of postal-code categories varies among the provinces, and postal codes are nominal variables which cannot be compared across provinces or regions.

---

[106] The standard deviation of this distribution is 80,027.04 with a means of 94,305.7.

[107] The value of H for the country corresponds to the mean of the values for the provinces in these dimensions: $\overline{H}_T = 4.088 \pm 0.097$ and $\overline{H}_O = 2.196 \pm 0.065$.

The corresponding percentages for the technology (sector) and the organization (or size) distributions are 69.2 and 61.3%, respectively. The combined uncertainty of technology and organization (H_{TO}) does not add substantially to the redundancy. In other words, organization and technology have a relatively independent influence on the distribution different from that of postal codes. In the provincial decomposition, however, the highly developed and densely populated provinces (North- and South-Holland, and Utrecht) show a more specialized pattern of sectoral composition (H_T) than Friesland, Groningen, and Limburg. (These latter provinces are more distant from the center of the country.) Flevoland shows the highest redundancy in size distribution (H_O), perhaps because certain traditional formats of middle-sized companies may still be underrepresented in this new province.

The combination of technological and organizational specialization exhibits a specific position for North-Holland (H_{TO} = 5.730 or 60.7% of the maximum entropy) versus Friesland (H_{TO} = 6.223 or 65.9% of the maximum entropy) at the other end of the distribution. Since the mean of the distribution is in this case 63.8% with a standard deviation of 1.3, North-Holland is really an exception in terms of an interaction effect between technological specialization and a relatively low variation in size distribution.

9.4.2 Mutual information

Table 4 provides the values for the transmissions (T) among the various dimensions. These values can be calculated straightforwardly from the values of the probabilistic entropies provided in Table 3 using Equations 1 and 2 provided in Chapter Eight. The first line for the Netherlands as a whole shows that there is more mutual information between the geographical distribution of firms and their technological specialization (T_{GT} = 0.072 bits) than between the geographical distribution and their size (T_{GO} = 0.019). However, the mutual information between technology and organization (T_{TO} = 0.240) is larger than T_{GO} by an order of magnitude. The provinces exhibit a comparable pattern.

	T_{GT}	T_{GO}	T_{TO}	T_{GTO}
NL	0.072	0.019	0.240	-0.034
Drenthe	0.030	0.005	0.320	-0.056
Flevoland	0.068	0.006	0.164	-0.030
Friesland	0.054	0.008	0.274	-0.056
Gelderland	0.040	0.004	0.242	-0.043
Groningen	0.065	0.007	0.353	-0.045
Limburg	0.047	0.006	0.251	-0.033
N-Brabant	0.039	0.016	0.223	-0.036
N-Holland	0.065	0.030	0.285	-0.017
Overijssel	0.040	0.004	0.263	-0.035
Utrecht	0.031	0.005	0.221	-0.024
S-Holland	0.062	0.006	0.223	-0.027
Zeeland	0.038	0.039	0.234	-0.039

Table 9.4: Mutual information in two and three dimensions disaggregated at the NUTS 2-level (provinces).

While the values for T_{GT} and T_{GO} can be considered as indicators of the geographical clustering of economic activities (in terms of technologies and organizational formats, respectively), the T_{TO} provides an indicator for correlation between the maturity of the industry (Anderson and Tushman, 1991) and the specific size of the firms involved (Suárez and Utterback 1995, Utterback and Suárez 1993; cf. Nelson, 1994). The relatively low value of this indicator for Flevoland indicates that the techno-economic structure of this province is less mature than in other provinces. The high values of this indicator for Groningen and Drenthe indicate that the techno-economic structure in these provinces is perhaps relatively over-mature. This indicator can thus be considered as representing a strategic vector (Abernathy and Clark, 1985; Watts and Porter, 2003).

All values for mutual information in three dimensions (T_{TGO}) are negative. When decomposed at the NUTS-3 level of regions, these values are also negative, with the exception of two regions that contain only a single postal code at the two-digit level. (In these two cases the uncertainty is by definition zero.)[108] At first glance, the figures suggest an inverse relationship between mutual information in three dimensions and the intuitively expected knowledge intensity of regions and provinces, with North-Holland, Utrecht, and South-Holland at the one end and Drenthe and Friesland at the other. However, these values cannot be compared

[108] These are the regions Delfzijl and Zeeuwsch-Vlaanderen (COROP / NUTS-3 regions 2 and 31).

among geographical units without a further normalization. As noted, the postal codes are nominal variables. In a next section, I will focus on the relative effects of decompositions in terms of high- and medium-tech sectors on the geographical units of analysis, but let me first turn to the normalization in the geographical dimension because this dimension provides us with recognizable units (like provinces and regions) which may allow us to validate the indicator.

9.4   The regional distribution of the knowledge base

One of the advantages of statistical decomposition analysis is the possibility to specify within-group variances and between-group variances in great detail (Theil, 1972; Leydesdorff, 1995a). However, a full decomposition at the lower level is possible only if the categories for the measurement are similar among the groups. Had we used a different indicator for the regional dimension—for example, percentage 'rural' versus percentage 'metropolitan'—we would have been able to compare and therefore to decompose along this axis, but the unique postal codes cannot be compared among regions like the size or the sectoral distribution of the firms. (I shall use such a scale for the geographic comparison in the next chapter when we discuss the decomposition of the knowledge-based economy in Germany.)

The decomposition algorithm (Theil, 1972) enables us to study the next-order level of the Netherlands as a composed system (NUTS-1) in terms of its lower-level units like the NUTS-2 provinces and the NUTS-3 regions by normalizing in terms of the units of analysis. In this case, the unit of analysis is the individual firm. Using this methodology, the regions and provinces are not compared in terms of their knowledge intensity among themselves, but in terms of their weighted contributions to the knowledge base of the Dutch economy as a whole.

The distributions are weighted in the various dimensions for the numbers of firms in the groups i (e.g., provinces) by first adding the uncertainties within the different groups ($\sum_i (n_i/N) * H_i$; $N = \sum_i n_i$). The in-between group uncertainty H_0 is then defined as the difference between this sum and the uncertainty prevailing at the level of the composed system:

$$H = H_0 + \sum_i (n_i/N) H_i \qquad\qquad (3)$$

Or equivalently for the transmissions:[109]

$$T = T_0 + \sum_i (n_i/N) \, T_i \tag{4}$$

For example, by using for normalization the right-most column of Table 3, which indicates the number of firms in each of the provinces, and given the total number of firms registered (N = 1,131,668), one obtains the following table for the decomposition of mutual information in three dimensions at the level of the provinces:

	ΔT_{GTO} (= $n_i * T_i /N$) in millibits of information	n_i
Drenthe	-1.29	26210
Flevoland	-0.55	20955
Friesland	-1.79	36409
Gelderland	**-4.96**	131050
Groningen	-1.20	30324
Limburg	-1.96	67636
N-Brabant	**-5.56**	175916
N-Holland	**-3.28**	223690
Overijssel	-1.98	64482
Utrecht	-1.86	89009
S-Holland	**-5.84**	241648
Zeeland	-0.83	24339
Sum ($\sum_i P_i \, T_i$)	-31.10	1131668
T_0	**-2.46**	
NL	-33.55	N = 1131668

Table 9.5: Mutual information in three dimensions statistically decomposed at the NUTS 2-level (provinces) in millibits of information.

The table shows that the knowledge base of the country is concentrated in South-Holland ($\Delta T = -$ 5.84 mbits), North-Brabant ($-$ 5.56), and Gelderland ($-$ 4.96). North-Holland follows with a contribution of $-$ 3.28 mbits of information. The other provinces contribute to the knowledge base less than the in-between provinces interaction effect at the national level ($T_0 = -$ 2.46 mbit). Figures 2 and 3

---

[109] The formula is equally valid for the transmissions because these are based on probability distributions in the mutual information between two or more probability distributions. The probability distribution in the transmission T_{ab} can be written as the intersect between the distributions for *a* and *b,* or in formula format as $\sum p_T = \sum (p_a$ AND $p_b)$.

visualize how the knowledge base of the country is geographically organized at the NUTS-2 and the NUTS-3 level, respectively.

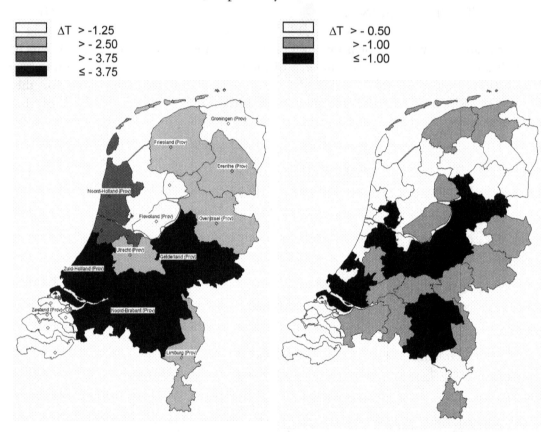

Figure 9.2: Contribution to the knowledge base of the Dutch economy at the provincial (NUTS-2) level.

Figure 9.3: Contribution to the knowledge base of the Dutch economy at the regional (NUTS-3) level.

The further disaggregation in Table 6 shows the contribution of regions at the NUTS-3 level (Figure 3). The contribution of South-Holland is concentrated in the Rotterdam area, the one in North-Brabant in the Eindhoven region, and North-Holland exclusively in the agglomeration of Amsterdam. Utrecht, the Veluwe (Gelderland) and the northern part of Overijssel also show above average contributions on this indicator. However, an important part of the reduction of the uncertainty is provided at a level higher than the NUTS-3 regions ($T_0 = -9.09$ mbit).[110] I shall therefore focus in the next section on the NUTS-2 level.

	NUTS-3 Regions (Corop)	ΔT_{GTO} (= $n_i * T_i /N$) in millibits of information	n_i
1	Oost-Groningen	-0.20	7571
2	Delfzijl en omgeving	0.00	2506
3	Overig Groningen	-0.81	20273
4	Noord-Friesland	-0.99	17498
5	Zuidwest-Friesland	-0.37	7141
6	Zuidoost-Friesland	-0.41	11744
7	Noord-Drenthe	-0.44	9702
8	Zuidoost-Drenthe	-0.39	9121
9	Zuidwest-Drenthe	-0.13	7327
10	**Noord-Overijssel**	**-1.04**	20236
11	Zuidwest-Overijssel	-0.16	7333
12	Twente	-0.57	36971
13	**Veluwe**	**-1.38**	43489
14	Achterhoek	-0.76	24995
15	Arnhem/Nijmegen	-0.85	43388
16	Zuidwest-Gelderland	-0.69	19192
17	**Utrecht**	**-1.86**	88997
18	Kop van Noord-Holland	-0.30	25978
19	Alkmaar en omgeving	-0.39	17145
20	IJmond	-0.07	11017
21	Agglomeratie Haarlem	-0.16	17376
22	Zaanstreek	-0.07	9865
23	**Groot-Amsterdam**	**-1.15**	117518
24	Het Gooi en Vechtstreek	-0.42	24818
25	Agglomeratie Leiden en Bollenstreek	-0.42	26738
26	*Agglomeratie 's-Gravenhage*	*-1.00*	50603
27	Delft en Westland	-0.28	19489
28	Oost-Zuid-Holland	-0.67	25262
29	**Groot-Rijnmond**	**-1.61**	92255
30	Zuidoost-Zuid-Holland	-0.91	27301

[110] More detailed analysis teaches that the provincial structure reduces the uncertainty in the mutual information between the sectoral and the size distribution as two dimensions with -7.79 mbits, while this uncertainty is reduced with -20.06 mbits by the finer-grained structure of COROP regions. Unlike the effect on the mutual information in three dimensions, these reductions of the uncertainty at the NUTS-2 and the NUTS-3 levels are independent of the distribution of postal codes (since these are specified at higher levels of aggregation).

31	Zeeuwsch-Vlaanderen	0.00	6840
32	Overig Zeeland	-0.39	17499
33	West-Noord-Brabant	-0.78	43954
34	Midden-Noord-Brabant	-0.61	32332
35	*Noordoost-Noord-Brabant*	*-1.00*	47214
36	**Zuidoost-Noord-Brabant**	**-1.13**	52416
37	Noord-Limburg	-0.53	16753
38	Midden-Limburg	-0.17	15272
39	Zuid-Limburg	-0.79	35611
40	Flevoland	-0.55	20928
	Sum ($\sum_i P_i T_i$)	-24.46	1131668
	T_0	**-9.09**	
	NL	-33.55	N = 1131668

Table 9.6: Mutual information in three dimensions statistically decomposed at the NUTS-3 level (COROP regions) in millibits of information. Regions with a $\Delta T > 1.00$ mbit are boldfaced; $\Delta T = 1.00$ mbits in italics.

These tables and pictures correspond with common knowledge about the industrial structure of the Netherlands (e.g., Van der Panne and Dolfsma, 2001, 2003). The contribution of northern Overijssel to the knowledge base of the Dutch economy is somewhat surprising because this region has not been recognized previously as an economically active region. Perhaps, it profits from a spill-over effect of knowledge-based activities in the neighboring regions.

As noted, the normalization involves the number of firms in the geographical unit of analysis as a factor in the weighting. Therefore, these results inform us both about the industrial structure of the country and about the knowledge base of the economy,[111] and may differ depending on the aggregation level analyzed. Among the regions, for example, Utrecht (region 17) contributes most to the reduction of the uncertainty at the national level, while as a province the same value for Utrecht ($\Delta T = -1.86$ mbits) remains below the average contribution. In general, mutual information in three dimensions provides a composite measure of the three factors involved in Storper's holy trinity (geography, technology, and organization). These three factors can be decomposed along each axis. We turn in the next section to the sectorial axis, and particularly to the effects of indicating knowledge intensity along this axis.

---

[111] The correlation between the contributions ΔT and the number of firms is high and significant both in the case of analysis at the NUTS-2 level ($r = 0.872$; $p < 0.01$) and the NUTS-3 level ($r = 0.801$; $p < 0.01$).

9.5 The sectorial decomposition

While the geographical comparison is compounded with traditional industrial structure like firm density, all effects of the decomposition in terms of the sectorial classification of high- and medium-tech sectors and knowledge-intensive services can be expressed as a relative effect, that is, as a percentage of increase or decrease in the negative value of the mutual information in three dimensions when a specific selection is compared with the complete population. In the remainder of this study, the categories provided by the OECD and Eurostat (see Table 2 above) will be used as selection criteria for subsets, and the results are compared with those of the full set provided in the previous section as a baseline. A more negative score for the probabilistic entropy as compared to the overall score indicates a reduction of the uncertainty, and can therefore be considered as a more positive condition for a knowledge-based economy.

T_{xyz}	All sectors	High Tech	% increase	N
NL	-0.034	-0.060	80.2	45128
Drenthe	-0.056	-0.093	67.6	786
Flevoland	-0.030	-0.036	20.6	1307
Friesland	-0.056	-0.136	144.9	983
Gelderland	-0.043	-0.094	120.1	4885
Groningen	-0.045	-0.066	48.1	1204
Limburg	-0.033	-0.068	105.9	2191
N-Brabant	-0.036	-0.058	61.2	6375
N-Holland	-0.017	-0.034	103.4	9346
Overijssel	-0.035	-0.079	127.6	2262
Utrecht	-0.024	-0.039	65.9	4843
S-Holland	-0.027	-0.044	61.7	10392
Zeeland	-0.039	-0.067	73.3	554

Table 9.7: Mutual information in three dimensions when comparing high-tech sectors in industrial production and services.

Table 7 provides the results of comparing the subset of enterprises indicated as high-tech manufacturing (sectors 30, 32, and 33) and high-tech services (64, 72, and 73) with the full set. The column headed 'All sectors' corresponds to the right-most column in Table 3. The third column provides the mutual information in three dimensions for the high-tech sectors in both manufacturing and services. In the fourth column the percentage change is indicated in relative terms. This indicates the influence of these high-tech sectors and services on the knowledge base of the economy. The results confirm our hypothesis that the mutual information or entropy that emerges from the interaction between the three dimensions is more negative for high-tech sectors and high-tech services than for the economy as a whole. The dynamics created by these sectors deepen and tighten the knowledge base more than is the case for firms on average.

	All sectors	High and medium tech Manufactur.	% chan ge	N	Knowledge -Intensive Services	% chan ge	N
NL	-0.034	-0.219	553	15838	-0.024	-27.3	581196
Drenthe	-0.056	-0.349	526	406	-0.034	-39.1	11312
Flevoland	-0.030	-0.206	594	401	-0.018	-37.9	10730
Friesland	-0.056	-0.182	227	951	-0.037	-32.6	14947
Gelderland	-0.043	-0.272	536	2096	-0.025	-40.8	65112
Groningen	-0.045	-0.258	479	537	-0.029	-34.0	14127
Limburg	-0.033	-0.245	647	1031	-0.018	-45.1	30040
N-Brabant	-0.036	-0.190	430	2820	-0.030	-16.6	86262
N-Holland	-0.017	-0.173	943	2299	-0.017	1.0	126516
Overijssel	-0.035	-0.207	496	1167	-0.020	-42.8	30104
Utrecht	-0.024	-0.227	859	1020	-0.013	-45.0	52818
S-Holland	-0.027	-0.201	635	2768	-0.015	-45.5	128725
Zeeland	-0.039	-0.180	365	342	-0.028	-27.8	10503

Table 9.8: High-tech and medium-tech manufacturing versus knowledge-intensive services and their effects on mutual information in three dimensions.

Table 8 provides the same figures and normalizations, but now on the basis of selections according to the classifications provided in Table 2 for high- and medium-tech manufacturing combined (middle section of Table 2), and knowledge-intensive services (right-side columns of Table 2), respectively. These results indicate a major effect on the indicator for the sectors of high- and medium-tech manufacturing. The effect is by far the largest in North-Holland with an increase of 943% relative to the benchmark of all sectors combined. Utrecht follows with 859 %. A group of provinces (Limburg, South-Holland, Flevoland) has above average effects of 647, 635, and 594%, respectively. Zeeland has the lowest value on this indicator (365%), but the number of establishments in these categories is also lowest for this province. North-Brabant, however, has the largest number of establishments in these categories, while it does not seem to profit from an additional effect on the configuration.

The number of establishments in knowledge-intensive services is more than half (51.3%) of the total number of companies in the country. These companies are concentrated in North- and South-Holland, with North-Brabant in the third position. With the exception of North-Holland, the effect of knowledge-intensive services on this indicator of the knowledge base is always negative, that is, it leads to a decrease of configurational information. We indicate this with an opposite sign for the change. In the case of North-Holland, the change is marginally positive (+1.0 %), but this is not due to the Amsterdam region.[112] North-Brabant is second on this rank order with a decrease of −16.6%.

These findings accord with a theoretical expectation about the different contributions to the economy of services in general and knowledge-intensive services (KIS) in particular (Bilderbeek *et al.*, 1998; Miles *et al.*, 1995; OECD, 2000; Windrum and Tomlinson 1999). Windrum and Tomlinson (1999) argued that to assess the role of KIS, the degree of integration is more important than the percentage of representation in the economy. Unlike output indicators, the measure adopted here focuses on the degree of integration in the configuration. However, our results indicate that KIS unfavorably affects the synergy between technology, organization, and territory in the techno-economic system of the Netherlands, and its provinces and regions. This indicates a relatively uncoupling effect from the geographically defined knowledge bases of the economy. The effects of KIS spill over geographic boundaries more easily than knowledge-based manufacturing.

This result contrasts with the expectations expressed in much of the relevant literature on the role of knowledge-intensive services in stimulating the knowledge base of an economy. For example, the conclusion of the European Summit in Lisbon (2000) was, among other things, that "the shift to a digital, knowledge-based economy, prompted by new goods and services, will be a powerful engine for growth, competitiveness and jobs. In addition, it will be capable of improving citizens' quality of life and the environment."[113] Our results suggest that the knowledge-based economy and the digital economy are not the same: the manufacturing of goods or the delivering of services can be expected to have other geographical effects and constraints.

---

[112] Only in COROP / NUTS-3 region 18 (North-Holland North) is the value of mutual information in three dimensions is more negative when zooming in on the knowledge-intensive services. However, this region is predominantly rural.

[113] at http://www.europarl.eu.int/summits/lis1_en.htm#b .

Knowledge-intensive services seem to be largely uncoupled from the knowledge flow within a regional or local economy. They contribute negatively to the knowledge-based configuration because of their inherent capacity to deliver these services outside the region. Thus, a locality can be chosen on the basis of considerations other than those relevant for the generation of a knowledge-based economy in the region. For example, the proximity of a well-connected airport (or train station) may be a major factor in the choice of a location.

T_{xyz}	Knowl-intensive services	High-Tech services	% increase	N
NL	-0.024	-0.034	37.3	41002
Drenthe	-0.034	-0.049	45.2	678
Flevoland	-0.018	-0.018	-4.6	1216
Friesland	-0.037	-0.087	131.5	850
Gelderland	-0.025	-0.046	82.3	4380
Groningen	-0.029	-0.044	49.5	1070
Limburg	-0.018	-0.039	118.7	1895
N-Brabant	-0.030	-0.035	16.1	5641
N-Holland	-0.017	-0.020	17.0	8676
Overijssel	-0.020	-0.046	133.1	1999
Utrecht	-0.013	-0.020	49.8	4464
S-Holland	-0.015	-0.025	69.8	9650
Zeeland	-0.028	-0.045	59.7	483

Table 9.9: The subset of high-tech services improves the knowledge base in the service sector.

Table 9 shows the relative deepening of mutual information in three dimensions when the subset of sectors indicated as 'high-tech services' is compared with KIS in general. 'High-tech services' are only 'post and telecommunications' (NACE code 64), 'computer and related activities' (72), and 'research and development' (73). More than knowledge-intensive services in general, high-tech services can be expected to produce and transfer technology-related knowledge (Bilderbeek *et al.*, 1998). These effects of strengthening the knowledge base seem highest in regions which do not have a strong knowledge base in medium and high-tech manufacturing, such as Friesland and Overijssel. The effects of this selection for North-Brabant and North-Holland, for example, are among the lowest. However, this negative relation between high- and medium-tech manufacturing on the one hand, and high-tech services on the other, is not significant ($r = -0.352$; $p = 0.262$). At the NUTS-3 level, the corresponding relation is also not significant. Thus, the effects of high- and medium-tech manufacturing and high-tech services on the knowledge base of the economy are not related to each other.

9.6   Conclusions and discussion

Before I proceed to draw conclusions and consider policy implications, I should emphasize that this research effort was primarily meant to be methodological. On the one hand, I developed an indicator of interaction effects at the network level which provides a quantitative measure for the reduction of the uncertainty that cannot be attributed to the individual players in a network. The reduction of this uncertainty is configurational when a next-order system operates as an overlay. On the other hand, the data and insights from economic geography allowed us to use proxies for the three main dimensions of Storper's 'holy trinity' of technology, organization, and territory, although the operationalization of organization in terms of numbers of employees remains debatable.

Collaboration with evolutionary economists from Delft and Rotterdam provided me with an opportunity to validate and to generalize the scientometric indicator of Triple Helix relations in an economic context. I submit that this indicator can be used to measure the knowledge base of an economy and its decomposition in terms of geographical subunits, and in considerable detail. However, the nominal character of the postal codes made it impossible to compare directly among regions and provinces (but only in terms of their contribution to the national economy). The possible effects of these problems on the data in relation to the indicator and its interpretation made us hesitant to decompose below the NUTS-2 level of the provinces because this may suggest an exactness which cannot be achieved using these data. (I shall test my conclusions in the next chapter using German data without this limitation, but the data in this case will be less fine-grained than the Dutch data.) Nevertheless, the results allow us to formulate the following hypotheses:

1. The knowledge base of a (regional) economy is carried by high-, but more importantly by medium-tech manufacturing; high-tech services contribute favorably to the knowledge-based structuring, but to a smaller extent.
2. Medium-tech manufacturing provides the backbone of the techno-economic structure of the country; this explains why high-tech manufacturing contributes less to the knowledge infrastructure than might be expected, for example, on the basis of patent portfolios (Leydesdorff, 2004b).

3. Knowledge-intensive services which are not high-tech have a relatively unfavorable effect on the territorial knowledge base of an economy. One could say that these services tend to uncouple the knowledge base from its geographical dimension.
4. The Netherlands is highly developed as a knowledge-intensive service economy, but the high-tech end of these services has remained more than an order of magnitude smaller in terms of the numbers of firms.

As noted, these hypotheses are tested in the next chapter using German data. In terms of policy implications, these conclusions suggest that regions which are less developed may wish to strengthen their knowledge infrastructure by trying to attract medium-tech manufacturing and high-tech services. The efforts of firms in medium-tech sectors can be considered as focused on maintaining absorptive capacity (Cohen and Levinthal, 1989) so that knowledge and technologies developed elsewhere can more easily be understood and adapted to particular circumstances. High-tech manufacturing, however, may be more focused on (internal) production and global markets than on local diffusion parameters. High-tech services, however, mediate technological knowledge more than knowledge-intensive services that are medium-tech. The latter services seem to have an unfavorable effect on territorially defined knowledge-based economies.

In the larger context of this monograph, the methodological contribution of this research is the procedure presented for measuring the knowledge base of an economy (Carter, 1996). The indicator captures the knowledge base of an economy as an emerging property at the structural level. The various dimensions correspond to classifications that are readily available from the OECD and Eurostat databases, and the geographical address information of the units is also used. In principle, the dimensionality of the mutual information can further be extended beyond three. Unlike the focus on comparative statics in employment statistics and the *STI Scoreboards* of the OECD (OECD, 2001, 2003; Godin, 2005), the information-theoretical indicator can be considered as a measure of an emergent property (Jakulin and Bratko, 2004; cf. Ulanowicz, 1986, at pp. 142 ff.). Furthermore, the indicator could be specified as an operationalization with reference to two bodies of theorizing, namely regional studies (e.g., Storper, 1997; Van der Panne and Dolfsma, 2003) and the study of knowledge-based systems of innovation (e.g., David and Foray, 2002; Leydesdorff and Etzkowitz, 1998).

Chapter 10

The decomposition of
the German innovation system *

The Triple Helix model of university-industry-government relations has hitherto been developed mainly as a *(neo)institutional* model for studying the knowledge infrastructure in networks of relations (Etzkowitz *et al.*, 2000; Powell and DiMaggio, 1991). From a *(neo)evolutionary* perspective, however, a Triple Helix can be formulated dynamically as the interactions among three (or more) subdynamics of a system (Leydesdorff, 1997d; Leydesdorff and Etzkowitz, 1998). To what extent do the networks allow for a synergy among (1) economic wealth generation, (2) technological novelty production, and (3) institutionally organized retention? How can the economic exchange, the innovation dynamics upsetting the market equilibria, and the locally organized interfaces among these subdynamics be integrated at a systems level?

The dynamics of the links have to be carried by the agents at the nodes, but one can no longer expect a one-to-one correspondence between the development of functions over time and institutional structures at each moment. The functions are based also on the network arrangements among the institutions—which are the subject of study in the neo-institutional approach. More important than the mere presence of agencies in the networks is the quality of their relations in a configuration. Since the functions are distributed among different agents and relations, one expects an uncertainty which can be measured as probabilistic entropy. Systemic effects may occur that can no longer be traced back directly to specific exchanges. The interaction effects in the mutual information among more than two dimensions cannot be attributed to elements of the network (nodes and links), but emerge in the configuration.

The research question thus becomes to what degree an emerging dynamics is conducive to the development of specific regions and nations. The data enables us to compare 438 districts (*Kreise*) in Germany with the conclusions from the study of the Netherlands (Chapter Nine). The results confirm the conclusion that regional differences in the configurations are determined almost exclusively by high- and medium-tech *manufacturing*. The economic benefits of knowledge-intensive *services* are not provided at the level of the regional innovation system but at the national level, while knowledge-based manufacturing tends to remain geographically embedded. Secondly, we are able to test the hypothesis that medium-tech manufacturing contributes more than high-tech production to the knowledge-based configuration. Corroboration of these two hypotheses may have important implications for industrial development policies. Thirdly, the results for the whole of Germany are compared with those for the former Eastern and Western parts of the country, respectively, and at the level of the Federal States (*Länder*). At the level of regions (NUTS-2) the knowledge-based economy is no longer structured by the previous East-West divide, while this divide has remained the main structure at the level of the states (NUTS-1) which constitute the Federal Republic. However, the effects of high and medium-tech are not specific for the Western or Eastern parts of the country. Some regions in the former East Germany have been successful in profiting from the coupling at the high-tech end of the knowledge-intensive services.

10.1   Methods and materials

The data for this study was collected from the German Social Insurance Statistics (*Statistik der sozialversicherungspflichtig Beschäftigten*). These statistics are generated by the Federal Employment Office (*Bundesagentur für Arbeit*) (Fritsch and Brixy, 2004). In Germany, all public and private employers are required by law to register their employees with this office for enrollment in the social insurance and pension systems. In the case of composed (e.g., international) corporations with multiple locations, data is collected at the level of local establishments, and thus the geographical dimension is preserved. However, employees who are not obliged by law to contribute to these insurance systems are (by definition) excluded from the statistics. These include, among others, civil servants, army personnel, the self-employed, and the unemployed.[1]

The statistics were made available to us at the NUTS-3 level of the Eurostat classification of regions (Eurostat, 2003). (NUTS is an abbreviation of *Nomenclature des Unités Territoriales Statistiques*.)[2] In the German Federal Republic the NUTS-3 level coincides with the district or *Kreis*. Eurostat (2003) distinguished 440 of these

---

[1] In manufacturing, the Social Insurance Statistics cover more than 90 percent of all employees. In the service sector, this share is about 80 percent. Coverage is relatively low in agriculture (less than 24 percent) and in the public sector (about 50 percent).

[2] The Nomenclature of Territorial Units for Statistics (NUTS) was established by Eurostat more than 25 years ago in order to provide a single uniform breakdown of territorial units for the production of regional statistics for the European Union; at http://europa.eu.int/comm/eurostat/ramon/nuts/introduction_regions_en.html

districts. One of these is an unclassified category entitled 'extra region.' Two regions (Eisenach and Wartburg) have not always been distinguished in the German statistics and were merged for the purpose of this study.[3] Thus, we assume 438 districts as the units of analysis. These districts are organized in 41 regions at the NUTS-2 level which are called in German *Regierungsbezirke*. The NUTS-1 level is defined as the 16 Federal States or *Länder* that compose the German Federal Republic. Bavaria, for example, is one of these states (Figure 1).

Figure 10.1: The political administration of the German Federal Republic at the NUTS-1 and NUTS-2 levels of *Länder* and *Regierungsbezirke*, respectively.

For historical reasons, the cities of Berlin, Hamburg, and Bremen have been considered administratively as NUTS-1 categories (*Länder*). Berlin and Hamburg consist only of single districts which are defined under the same name at the NUTS-3, NUTS-2, and NUTS-1 levels. Bremen is subdivided at the NUTS-3 level into two

---

[3] The two districts 16056 (the city of Eisenach) and 16063 (the district of Wartburg) have been distinguished administratively only since 1998. They are considered in this study as a single unit because of comparisons along the time line which we envisage in future studies.

districts (Bremen and Bremerhaven). Other large cities, like Munich, Cologne, and Frankfurt, are defined as districts at the NUTS-3 level within their respective regions and states. For the purpose of this study, we decided to modify the data by adding Berlin as a district (at the NUTS-3 level) to Brandenburg – South-East (NUTS-2: DE42), Hamburg to the region Schleswig-Holstein (NUTS-2: DEF0), and the two districts Bremen and Bremerhaven to the region of Lüneburg (NUTS-2: DE93). At the NUTS-1 level Berlin will thus be considered as part of Brandenburg (DE4), Hamburg as part of Schleswig-Holstein (DEF), and Bremen/Bremerhaven belongs to Lower Saxony (DE9).

	Administratively	for the purpose of this study
NUTS-3 (districts)	439	438
NUTS-2 (regions)	41	38
NUTS-3 (states)	16	13

Table 10.1: Reorganization of NUTS definitions for the purpose of this study.

The German Federal Office for Building and Regional Planning (*Bundesamt für Bauwesen und Raumordnung*, BBR, 2002) has attributed categories to these districts using the following scheme:

Type of district	Classification number	Number of districts
Agglomerations		
Core cities	1	43
Districts with high density	2	44
Districts with average density	3	39
Rural districts	4	23
Urbanized regions		
Core cities	5	29
Districts with average density	6	91
Rural districts	7	68
Rural areas		
Rural districts with relatively high density	8	58
Rural districts with relatively low density	9	43
		N = 438

Table 10.2: Classification of districts into district types (Source: BBR, 2002).

Not surprisingly, this classification is negatively correlated with the population density (population/area) of the districts at the level of Spearman's $\varrho = -.67$ (p < 0.01; N = 438). However, the category numbers do not indicate ranks in a spatial hierarchy, since some core cities of the urbanized regions (in class 5) can be ranked higher than the rural districts of the agglomerations (class 4). However, the classification will not be used as a rank order, but as a scheme only in order to generate a distribution containing an uncertainty in the geographical dimension. As in the Dutch case, the geographical units themselves are unique (that is, variables at the nominal scale), and therefore do not contain uncertainty.[4]

In addition to information at the level of each district, such as the population and the size of the district, the data contains the numbers of establishments and employees in each district at the three-digit level of the NACE classification (Audretsch and Fritsch, 1994). The NACE classifications for medium- and high-tech will be used as in the previous chapter (Table 9.2). The 222 NACE categories present in this data at the three-digit level can be subsumed for that purpose under 60 NACE categories at the two-digit level. The computations are based on the information at the three-digit level, but the two-digit level will be used for making appropriate selections according to the definitions of the OECD (2001, at pp. 137 ff.) and Eurostat (Laafia, 2002a, at p. 7).

For reasons of comparison with the Dutch study, the same classification for the average sizes of establishments is used (Table 10.3). While the Dutch data was micro-data at the level of individual firms, the German data allows us to compute a comparable business indicator (average firm size) per NACE-category and per district, since we have the number of employees and the number of firms in each category. However, the Dutch data included a first category for firms with zero employment, but this category is not contained in the German statistics because self-employed persons are not obliged to contribute to the social insurance scheme.

---

[4] Although we could have used population density as a classifier, we considered this informed classification as the better choice.

Number of employees	Frequency	Percent	Cumulative Percent
1	4721	7.0	7.0
2 to 4	16117	24.0	31.0
5 to 9	17416	25.9	56.9
10 to 19	12690	18.9	75.7
20-49	9745	14.5	90.2
50-99	3501	5.2	95.4
100-199	1775	2.6	98.1
200-499	912	1.4	99.4
500-749	186	.3	99.7
750-999	70	.1	99.8
> 1000	132	.2	100.0
	67265	100.0	

Table 10.3: Distribution of company sizes in the German data.

In summary, the maximum entropy of the system under study is determined by 222 NACE categories, 9 district types, and 11 size categories of firms, that is, $H_{max} = {}^2\log (222 * 9 * 11) = 14.42$ bits of information.

10.2   Results

10.2.1 The regional decomposition

Figure 2 shows the results of the computations using the specification of the data and methods above for the whole of Germany, aggregated at both the NUTS-1 level (*Länder*) and the NUTS-2 level of *Regierungsbezirke*.

The left-hand figure (at the NUTS-1 level) exhibits mainly the different dynamics in the former Eastern and Western parts of the country. This is not surprising given the need for radical reorganization of the East-German innovation system after unification. The socialist type of innovation regime that existed in the former German Democratic Republic until the fall of the Iron Curtain in 1989 was so different from a market-based system that the transition between these two regime types can be expected to take considerable time (Fritsch and Werker, 1999). It is, however, remarkable that the weakest knowledge base is found for the West-German region of Saarland, and that the East-German NUTS-1 level unit Saxony seems already to perform better on this indicator than the West-German state of Schleswig-Holstein (Table 4).

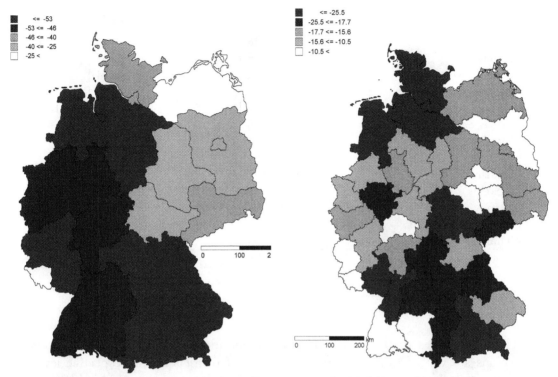

Figure 10.2: Mutual information in three dimensions at the NUTS-1 and NUTS-2 levels, respectively

The right-hand figure (at the NUTS-2 level) shows a more differentiated picture. The metropolitan areas of Munich and Hamburg are highlighted. The decomposition at the NUTS-2 level shows that in addition to Saarland the regions of Trier, Gießen, Freiburg, and Tübingen have similarly low values in the Western part of Germany. In East Germany the weakest knowledge base is found in rather sparsely populated Northeast Brandenburg, as well as in the neighboring regions of Leipzig, Halle, and Dessau. While the region of Northeast Brandenburg is nearly bare of R&D resources the regions of Leipzig, Halle, and Dessau are old industrialized areas in which the need for radical change has been particularly strong.

NUTS 1 (Länder)	T_{GTO} in mbits before normalization	ΔT_{GTO} (= $n_i * T_i$ /N) in mbits of information	n_i
Baden-Württemberg	-474.91	-47.71	44
Bavaria	-412.48	-90.41	96
Brandenburg	-583.86	-25.33	19
Hesse	-778.93	-46.24	26
Mecklenburg-Western Pomerania	-430.28	-17.68	18
Lower Saxony	-632.35	-69.30	48
North Rhine-Westphalia	-404.10	-49.82	54
Rhineland-Palatinate	-647.76	-53.24	36
Saarland	-639.67	-8.76	6
Saxony	-649.83	-43.03	29
Saxony-Anhalt	-600.14	-32.88	24
Schleswig-Holstein	-1102.75	-40.28	16
Thuringia	-619.48	-31.12	22
Germany	-180.08	-180.08	438

Table 10.4: Mutual information in three dimensions statistically decomposed at the NUTS-1 level of the German states (*Länder*)

The two pictures are based on different normalizations because the contributions of regions are weighed in terms of the number of districts at the respective level of aggregation, but with reference to the values for Germany as a whole (that is, N = 438). The districts (at the NUTS-3 level) are our units of analysis, and the NUTS-2 level and the NUTS-1 level are levels of aggregation. In addition to the aggregation, however, one would expect in-between group interaction effects among the higher-order units at the national level. Given the different normalizations at the NUTS-2 or NUTS-1 level, the two representations cannot be compared in terms of the absolute values of the indicator.

For example, the states of Schleswig-Holstein (formerly part of Western Germany) and Mecklenburg-Western Pomerania (formerly part of Eastern Germany) are defined both at the NUTS-1 and the NUTS-2 level, and thus these units are comparatively large when compared with other (NUTS-2 level) regions in the right-hand picture, while the same values are compared with the other (NUTS-1 level) states in the left-hand figure. In both figures, the contribution of each part of the country is normalized with reference to the country (that is, Germany; N = 438) as the baseline using ΔT_{GTO} = $n_i * T_i$ /N (Equation 3 in Chapter Nine). Since the districts are our units of analysis, n_i in this formula stands for the number of districts in the unit under study and T_i for the mutual information in the three dimensions (G)eography, (T)echnology, and (O)rganization at this level of aggregation. Table 10.5 provides these values for the *Länder* (that is, at the NUTS-1 level). At the NUTS-2 level the values for n_i are lower except for those NUTS-1 level units which are not further decomposed (e.g., Schleswig-Holstein and Mecklenburg-Western Pomerania). The values at the NUTS-2 level are provided in an Appendix to this chapter.

Unlike the previous results for the Netherlands, the value of the indicator for Germany as a whole is less negative than the sum of the values for the *Länder*. This means that there is configurational synergy at the local levels of NUTS-1 and NUTS-2 which is no longer retrieved when the distributions are aggregated at the national level. This negative entropy is a local attribute. When decomposed, the additional synergy is generated mainly by the mutual information between the NACE-codes and the size categories of the business. The type of district (rural versus urban) has less influence on the potential synergy than the interplay between the organizational format and the technological structure of the industry.

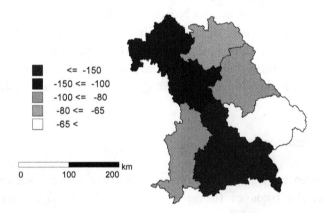

Figure 10.3: Mutual information in three dimensions normalized for the seven regions (*Regierungsbezirke*) of Bavaria.

Should the Netherlands as a country be compared with the separate states of the Federal Republic? This question cannot be answered on the basis of this data because the results for the Netherlands were based on micro-data, and in the previous study we did not characterize the districts as rural, urban, etc., but only in terms of postal codes. However, Figure 3 shows the results of limiting the analysis to Bavaria as an example of such a lower-level decomposition at the level of a single state.

The picture that we obtain for Bavaria (Figure 3) corresponds well with the commonly assumed quality of the innovation system in the different regions of this state. Unfortunately, information about the quality of regional innovation systems is hitherto available only for certain regions, often in the form of case studies that do not allow for a systematic interregional assessment and comparison with our indicator. According to such case studies, the innovation system of the Munich region has been said to be highly productive in recent times, while the Ruhr area and some of the East-German regions are lagging behind, with the exception of Saxony and Thuringia (Sternberg and Tamasy, 1999; Krauss and Wolff, 2002). This corresponds with our findings at the NUTS-2 level (Figure 2).

The pronounced position of the metropolis of Munich in Figure 3 contrasts with the lowest rank for the innovation system in the region of Lower Bavaria (east of Munich). This region, as well as Upper Palatinate and Upper Franconia, were located on the border with the Czech Republic and the former German Democratic Republic, respectively. The Iron Curtain that divided Eastern and Western Europe for a long period of time may have left a longer lasting imprint on these regions. Particularly Upper Franconia is peripheral and distanced from any larger centre. The region of Middle Franconia contains Nuremberg, the second largest city in the state of Bavaria, while the region of Lower Franconia is adjacent to the dynamic Frankfurt area. According to our calculations, both regions are in the second highest category. One may assume that Swabia draws some benefits from its geographical closeness to Munich and to Nuremberg, so that it maintains a middle-range position.

10.2.2 Sectorial decomposition

As noted, the main purpose of this study was to test two conclusions that were hypothesized on the basis of the analysis of the knowledge base of the Dutch economy (in Chapter Nine). These hypotheses were:

1. Medium-tech manufacturing generates more configurational information in a geographical unit than high-tech establishments;
2. Knowledge-intensive services uncouple the knowledge base from its geographical location, while high- and medium-tech manufacturing remain geographically embedded.

The interpretation of these two predictions could be that the sectors assume different roles in the division of innovative labor (Fritsch, 2004). Medium-tech manufacturing can be expected to focus on maintaining absorptive capacity, so that knowledge and technologies developed elsewhere can more easily be understood and adapted to local circumstances (Cohen and Levinthal, 1989). From the perspective of the organization of technological knowledge, high-tech manufacturing may be focused on (internal) production within the transnational corporation, take place as spin-offs of research institutions, and involve global markets more than local environments. From an industrial perspective, one could assume that medium-tech manufacturing may function as a seedbed for high-tech.

Knowledge-intensive services can be expected to uncouple from their geographical locations because these services can be offered across regional boundaries, for example, by using communication media or traveling consultants. It is not uncommon for knowledge-intensive services to be offered on the site of the customer by someone brought in from elsewhere. Unlike manufacturing, knowledge-intensive services can be offered throughout the country and abroad without necessary links to local production facilities like factories. Thus, the geographical location can be chosen by these establishments on grounds different from their local configurations in terms of Triple Helix dynamics. Note that this reasoning can be expected to hold less for knowledge-intensive sectors which are also high-tech, because in this case a local production component (e.g., R&D laboratories) may be needed for support.

Table 5 compares the relevant numbers of units (e.g., establishments) according to the respective NACE categories (as provided in Table 9.2 above). While in the Netherlands 51.3% of the establishments were knowledge-intensive services, this percentage is only 33.2% for Germany. Note that in accordance with the OECD/Eurostat classifications the high-tech services are considered as a subclass of knowledge-intensive services, while high- and medium-tech manufacturing are considered as two different classes. The ratio between high- and medium-tech manufacturing establishments is $23,912/39,281 = 0.61$ for Germany versus $4,126/11,712 = 0.35$ for the Netherlands.[5] This confirms that Germany is relatively more high-tech in manufacturing, but less knowledge-intensive in the service sectors.

---

[5] Unfortunately, the Dutch data does not allow us to make this comparison in terms of the numbers of employees in the different sectors because the respondents indicated only the size categories. However, more than 71.8% of high-tech manufacturing involves firms with fewer than five employees, while this is only 61.2% for medium-tech. For Germany, the ratio of 663,210 employees in high-tech versus 2,820,436 in medium-tech manufacturing is 0.23.

2002	Nr of records	Nr of establishments	Nr of employees	NACE categories
The full database	67,265	2,119,028	27,596,100	
High-tech manufacturing	2,606 *3.9%*	23,912 *1.1%*	663,210 *2.4%*	30, 32, 33
Medium-tech manufacturing	7,127 *10.6%*	39,281 *1.9%*	2,820,436 *10.2%*	24, 29, 31, 34, 35
Knowledge-intensive services	17,271 *25.7%*	703,817 *33.2%*	9,619,657 *34.9%*	61, 62, 64, 65, 66, 67, 70, 71, 72, 73, 74, 80, 85, 92
High-tech services	3,097 *4.6%*	45,485 *2.1%*	817,305 *3.0%*	64, 72, 73

Table 10.5: The distribution of records and establishments in the database across sectors given different selections using NACE codes.

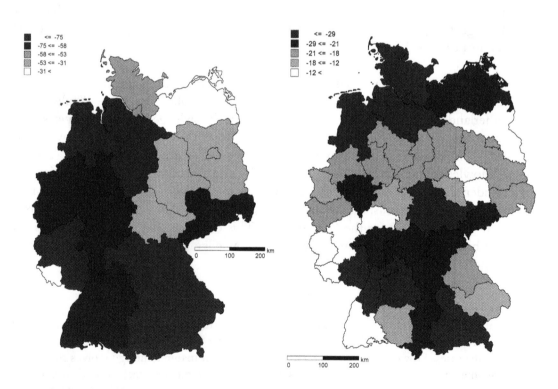

Figure 10.4: Medium-tech manufacturing generates the knowledge base in Germany

Figure 4 provides visualizations of the results when the analysis is limited to medium-tech manufacturing, that is, approximately 1.9 % of the total number of establishments included in the data. The pictures are virtually identical with those in Figure 2 which were based on 100% of the data. As expected, some regions are ranked higher when we focus on this selection, but the pattern is the same. In other words, the quality of these regional innovation systems is determined more or less completely by medium-tech manufacturing. The tables in the Appendix teach us that the high-tech manufacturing reduces the (negative) configurational information more often than not, while the effects of medium-tech always make the configurational information more negative. Therefore, the configuration of medium-tech manufacturing can be considered a better indicator of the knowledge-based economy than that of high-tech manufacturing.

The relation between high- and medium-tech manufacturing thus exhibits the patterns that were predicted on the basis of the study for the Netherlands. With the exception of Mecklenburg-Western Pomerania, the configurational information gain is always larger for medium-tech than for high-tech manufacturing at the NUTS-1 level. At the NUTS-2 level high-tech manufacturing provides a decrease in the configurational information in 26 of the 38 regions, while medium-tech manufacturing always diminishes the prevailing uncertainty. These effects are not specific for the western or eastern parts of Germany.

The tables in the Appendix further teach us that knowledge-intensive services *always* have the effect of making the configurational information less pronounced. This conclusion is confirmed for all states and all regions. With the single exception of Hesse, however, all states (at the NUTS-1 level) are further coupled geographically when from the knowledge-intensive services only the high-tech ones are selected. For Mecklenburg-Western Pomerania and Saxony-Anhalt (both parts of the former GDR) these couplings even make a positive contribution to the knowledge-based economy. At the NUTS-2 level, such a positive contribution of high-tech services is also found in certain West-German regions (e.g., Koblenz), but this effect is more pronounced in East-German regions like Magdeburg.

Table 6 expresses these conclusions in quantitative terms by using the respective variances as a measure of the synergy. The variances clearly show that the levels of regional difference are considerably smaller for high-tech manufacturing than for medium-tech manufacturing, but as we have seen above, both have a structuring effect on the economy. The knowledge-intensive services do not contribute to structuring the knowledge-based economy differently among regions, but this is less the case at the high-tech end of these services. As noted, this latter effect is enhanced in less-developed regions like Eastern Germany.

	NUTS-1	NUTS-2
All sectors	458.277	83.763
knowledge intensive services	256.176	57.624
high-tech services	357.369	75.007
medium-tech manufacturing	1133.959	161.110
high-tech manufacturing	744.390	91.898
high and medium-tech manufacturing	1058.008	106.112
Number of regions	13	38

Table 10.6: Variances in the ΔT across knowledge-based sectors of the economy at the NUTS-1 and NUTS-2 levels.

10.3   Conclusions and policy implications

This analysis indicates that the federal structure of Germany makes the states (*Länder*) a more important unit of analysis in studying the knowledge-based economy than the Federal Republic as a whole. This suggests that innovation processes indeed have a regional dimension. Using the mutual information in three dimensions as an indicator, the former division of the country between East and West was reproduced at the NUTS-1 level of the states, but at the lower (NUTS-2) level of districts (*Regierungsbezirke*) the picture has in the meantime become more complex. Several dynamics are indicated as different for East and West—for example, the function of high-tech knowledge-intensive services seems to function more locally in the Eastern part of Germany—but one can also note a further merging together of the two parts of the country in terms of its knowledge-based dynamics. One should keep in mind that globalization and the very emergence of a knowledge-based economy were partly effects of the demise of the Soviet Union and the subsequent integration of Germany (Leydesdorff, 2000c).

The Netherlands has been a nation-state since the time of Napoleon. Nevertheless, we found as much variation in the Netherlands as in Germany in terms of mutual information among technology indicators, business indicators, and geographical locations. One technical reason for this is, perhaps, that the data for the Netherlands was finer-grained than for Germany. From the perspective of evolution theory, however, an emerging feedback operating as an additional selection mechanism—albeit in this case a notional one (Dosi, 1982)—can be expected to produce a skewed distribution in the underlying dimensions of the (potentially random) variation. Thus, one can expect for evolutionary reasons that some regions will tend to become more knowledge-based in their economy than others despite efforts by national and regional governments to redistribute resources proportionally (Danell and Persson, 2003). In an increasingly globalized environment, mechanisms other than political control become more important than traditional policies (Bathelt, 2003; Cooke and Leydesdorff, 2006). The non-equilibrium dynamics of the knowledge base can be expected to counteract the equilibrium-seeking mechanisms of the market and the quasi-equilibrium of redistribution by institutional policies (Aoki, 2001).

It has been my argument throughout this study that knowledge-based innovations add a third dynamics of organized knowledge production and control to the political dynamics of institutionalization and regulation, and the equilibrating forces of the market: This interaction among three subdynamics can be captured by using a neo-evolutionary version of the Triple Helix model and can then be measured by using the mutual information among the three subdynamics. The results of the measurements confirmed the hypothesis that the quality of a regional innovation system—as measured here—is determined almost exclusively by medium- and high-tech manufacturing. The contribution of medium-tech manufacturing to the configuration can be used as a predictor of the properties of the innovation system in a given region. High-tech manufacturing adds to the pattern, but the size of high-tech manufacturing is smaller and its relative effect is also small. Because high-tech is so thinly spread across the country, its distribution may be more specific than for larger sectors.

Knowledge-intensive services seem to be largely uncoupled from the knowledge flow within a regional or local economy. They contribute negatively to the knowledge-based configuration because of their inherent capacity to deliver services outside the region. Thus, a locality can be chosen on the basis of considerations other than those relevant for the generation of a knowledge-based economy within the region. For example, the proximity of a well-connected airport (or train station) may be a major factor in the choice of a location. This conclusion of the globalizing effect of knowledge-intensive services holds true for all regions both in the Netherlands and in Germany.

The high-tech component of the knowledge-intensive services sometimes exhibits a coupling with the regional economy. This effect was particularly strong in some of the formerly East-German regions (e.g., Dessau, Magdeburg, Mecklenburg, and

Western Pomerania). However, given the prevailing pattern in more developed parts of the economy, this effect may disappear in the longer run because it may be specific to the developmental stage of the economy in these parts of Eastern Germany. Note that the non-localized character of knowledge-intensive services does not necessarily mean that they are unimportant for a regional innovation system. In addition to providing potentially high-quality employment, knowledge-intensive service providers that operate at an inter-regional level may be an important medium for knowledge spillovers across regions.

Appendix 1: Decomposition in terms of medium- and high-tech manufacturing versus high-tech and knowledge-intensive services

Table A1: T in mbits and change of T-values at the NUTS-1 level

	All sectors	Manufacturing						Services			
		High-tech	Change (%)	Medium-tech	Change (%)	High- and medium-tech	Change (%)	Knowledge intensive	Change (%)	High-tech	Change (%)
Germany	-180.08	-163.337	-9.3	-202.135	12.2	-199.013	10.5	-161.912	-10.1	-164.037	-18.8
Baden-Württemberg	-47.71	-52.672	10.4	-62.893	31.8	-63.281	32.6	-41.168	-13.7	-46.155	-3.3
Bavaria	-90.41	-110.363	22.1	-142.965	58.1	-137.331	51.9	-67.983	-24.8	-79.023	-12.9
Brandenburg	-25.33	-20.696	-18.3	-30.564	20.7	-29.213	15.3	-21.06	-16.8	-22.447	-11.4
Hessen	-46.24	-44.662	-3.4	-58.114	25.7	-56.669	22.6	-36.101	-21.9	-35.146	-24.0
Mecklenburg-Western Pomerania	-17.68	-10.692	-39.5	-22.514	27.3	-22.71	28.4	-16.944	-4.2	-19.429	9.9
Lower Saxony	-69.3	-72.053	4.0	-94.14	35.8	-94.219	36	-54.223	-21.8	-66.376	-4.2
North Rhine-Westphalia	-49.82	-46.531	-6.6	-63.765	28.0	-61.668	23.8	-38.333	-23.1	-43.291	-13.1
Rhineland-Palatinate	-53.24	-48.53	-8.8	-75.113	41.1	-72.715	36.6	-44.538	-16.3	-50.665	-4.8
Saarland	-8.76	-9.123	4.1	-8.792	0.4	-9.721	10.9	-7.951	-9.3	-8.712	-0.5
Saxony	-43.03	-40.379	-6.2	-58.074	35.0	-56.217	30.7	-31.644	-26.5	-36.931	-14.2
Saxony-Anhalt	-32.88	-22.845	-30.5	-46.793	42.3	-43.659	32.8	-26.831	-18.4	-33.386	1.5
Schleswig-Holstein	-40.28	-41.331	2.6	-53.345	32.4	-54.838	36.1	-33.144	-17.7	-34.15	-15.2
Thuringia	-31.12	-25.059	-19.5	-45.461	46.1	-43.412	39.5	-22.593	-27.4	-29.887	-4.0

Table A2: T in mbits and change of T-values at the NUTS-2 level

	All sectors	Manufacturing						Services			
		High-tech	Change (%)	Medium-tech	Change (%)	High- and medium-tech	Change (%)	Knowledge intensive	Change (%)	High-tech	Change (%)
Germany	-180.08	-163.337	-9.3	-202.135	12.2	-199.013	10.5	-161.912	-10.1	-164.037	-8.9
Arnsberg	-17.93	-18.711	4.4	-23.859	33.1	-23.822	32.9	-11.947	-33.4	-14.806	-17.4
Brandenburg — Northeast	-5.52	-4.042	-26.8	-5.878	6.5	-5.607	1.6	-4.801	-13	-5.25	-4.9
Brandenburg — Southwest	-17.62	-15.759	-10.6	-19.135	8.6	-19.18	8.9	-15.036	-14.7	-16.32	-7.4
Brunswick	-13.81	-19.051	38.0	-18.087	31.0	-19.649	42.3	-10.506	-23.9	-15.534	12.5
Chemnitz	-21.92	-15.495	-29.3	-26.262	19.8	-25.845	17.9	-17.426	-20.5	-19.132	-12.7
Darmstadt	-17.06	-16.374	-4.0	-21.064	23.5	-20.881	22.4	-13.578	-20.4	-12.381	-27.4
Dessau	-5.34	-1.427	-73.3	-8.109	51.9	-7.713	44.4	-4.551	-14.8	-6.017	12.7
Detmold	-15.78	-11.895	-24.6	-17.794	12.8	-17.389	10.2	-13.608	-13.7	-15.21	-3.6
Dresden	-16.61	-15.325	-7.7	-19.385	16.7	-20.062	20.8	-12.858	-22.6	-15.162	-8.7
Duesseldorf	-12.63	-12.134	-3.9	-15.055	19.2	-14.968	18.5	-10.713	-15.2	-13.547	7.3
Freiburg	-8.58	-8.754	2.0	-8.983	4.7	-9.856	14.9	-7.621	-11.1	-9.094	6.0
Giessen	-3.67	-2.806	-23.5	-4.582	24.9	-4.342	18.3	-3.032	-17.4	-3.204	-12.7
Halle	-10.31	-4.612	-55.3	-12.306	19.4	-11.307	9.6	-8.788	-14.8	-4.795	-53.5
Hanover	-15.58	-10.946	-29.7	-18.66	19.8	-18.49	18.7	-12.162	-21.9	-9.756	-37.4
Karlsruhe	-25.51	-26.348	3.3	-28.749	12.7	-30.567	19.8	-22.15	-13.2	-24.036	-5.8
Kassel	-13.71	-5.462	-60.2	-13.975	1.9	-13.681	-0.2	-10.933	-20.2	-11.801	-13.9
Koblenz	-11.08	-9.439	-14.8	-11.302	2.0	-11.744	6	-9.761	-11.9	-11.991	8.2
Cologne	-16.52	-11.029	-33.2	-19.042	15.3	-18.708	13.3	-14.123	-14.5	-14.717	-10.9
Leipzig	-9.2	-6.301	-31.5	-10.196	10.8	-9.932	8	-6.958	-24.4	-8.593	-6.6
Lüneburg	-29.69	-19.320	-34.9	-38.109	28.4	-36.888	24.2	-26.414	-11	-28.161	-5.1

305

Magdeburg	-17.28	-14.664	-15.1	-17.65	2.1	-17.705	2.5	-15.558	-10	-20.052	16.0
Mecklenburg-Western Pomerania	-17.68	-10.692	-39.5	-22.514	27.3	-22.71	28.4	-16.944	-4.2	-19.429	9.9
Middle Franconia	-23.4	-23.846	1.9	-26.82	14.6	-27.4	17.1	-18.897	-19.2	-16.221	-30.7
Muenster	-13.84	-13.632	-1.5	-17.577	27.0	-17.551	26.8	-12.35	-10.8	-11.838	-14.5
Lower Bavaria	-11.2	-9.780	-12.7	-15.275	36.4	-15.228	36	-7.598	-32.2	-7.634	-31.8
Upper Bavaria	-41.88	-40.463	-3.4	-54.101	29.2	-53.566	27.9	-34.495	-17.6	-34.719	-17.1
Upper Frankonia	-14.16	-16.318	15.2	-20.542	45.1	-20.387	44	-10.643	-24.8	-11.732	-17.1
Upper Palatinate	-17.92	-15.371	-14.2	-20.145	12.4	-20.367	13.6	-14.145	-21.1	-15.118	-15.6
Rheinhessen-Palatinate	-33.07	-34.937	5.6	-49.102	48.5	-48.831	47.6	-28.737	-13.1	-34.158	3.3
Saarland	-8.76	-9.123	4.1	-8.792	0.4	-9.721	10.9	-7.951	-9.3	-8.712	-0.5
Schleswig-Holstein	-40.28	-41.331	2.6	-53.345	32.4	-54.838	36.1	-33.144	-17.7	-34.15	-15.2
Swabia	-19.04	-22.383	17.6	-26.878	41.2	-27.671	45.3	-13.094	-31.2	-16.286	-14.5
Stuttgart	-23.61	-24.511	3.8	-28.782	21.9	-29.855	26.4	-20.072	-15	-23.589	-0.1
Thuringia	-31.12	-25.059	-19.5	-45.461	46.1	-43.412	39.5	-22.593	-27.4	-29.887	-4.0
Trier	-4.78	-1.416	-70.4	-5.737	20.0	-5.256	9.9	-4.568	-4.5	-3.392	-29.0
Tuebingen	-10.47	-12.039	15.0	-12.639	20.7	-13.375	27.7	-9.12	-12.9	-6.735	-35.7
Lower Franconia	-22.94	-14.503	-36.8	-26.163	14.0	-26.572	15.8	-18.563	-19.1	-19.201	-16.3
Weser-Ems	-26.72	-21.168	-20.8	-34.547	29.3	-33.875	26.8	-21.611	-19.1	-28.17	5.4

Chapter 11

Summary and Conclusions: The foundation of the knowledge base in Husserl's *Cogitatum*

One of the main ideas behind the concept of innovation *systems* is that innovation takes place both within firms and across the interfaces among institutional agents like universities, industries, and government agencies. In the preceding chapters I have shown that the concept of a knowledge-based economy or, more generally, a knowledge-based system can be specified in terms of the non-linear dynamics generated when the various subdynamics of the social system interact. The subdynamics which prevail at each moment of time (e.g., market clearing) and those which operate over time (e.g., novelty production) were cross-tabled with two operations along the time axis: a recursive one following the axis of time and an incursive one which operates against the axis of time. Meaning is provided with hindsight; the hindsight perspective enables us to specify expectations. Using language, meaning can be communicated in addition to information.

The exchange of knowledge further codifies the processing of meaning at the level of the social system by considering some meaning as more meaningful for the exchange than others. Codified knowledge can additionally be black-boxed and used from other perspectives. Bodies of knowledge can thus be considered as attributes of organizations or agents. A knowledge base as a coordination mechanism, however, emerges at the systems level when discursive knowledge is systematically used within a network. The new coordination mechanism operates differently from older ones like the market or decision-making and authority. New technologies and knowledge-based innovations upset both the market mechanism and existing institutional settings.

11.1 Knowledge production, circulation, and control

The social system can be considered as a complex dynamics: a complex dynamics is composed of several subdynamics. The relative weights of the different subdynamics can be expected to change not only historically, but also evolutionarily. For example, when the system becomes so complex that it can no longer be controlled hierarchically from a center, the reduction and absorption of uncertainty over time may become more important for its further development than coordination by exchange mechanisms at each moment of time. Anticipations enable us to reduce uncertainty over time by specifying expectations.

In a belief system, the anticipations and expectations can be integrated normatively, but the social system of coordination allows for one more degree of freedom when the expectations can circulate as hypotheses. Knowledge then becomes a complex medium with a meaning within local groups that is potentially different from its meaning at the (global) systems level. When central control increasingly fails, knowledge production organized as in science and technology can become a coordination mechanism alongside and in competition with other social coordination mechanisms (e.g., the market). In principle, this allows for functional optimization among the coordination mechanisms of society and thus for differentiation, but the new arrangements have to be invented historically. When central steering and control become a specific function of the political subsystem, functional differentiation has to be developed further by the communicative operations of the subsystems in relation to each other, that is, autopoietically.

The various axes of the functionally differentiated system of communication and control develop uncertainly because the axes remain based in flows of communication. However, the differentiation among the various subdynamics spans the capacity of the system to process uncertainty. In Chapter One, the subdynamics were modeled as different dimensions which are *analytically* orthogonal. Note that this orthogonality in the analytical model does not preclude interactions. Interactions can be first-order (between two axes) or higher-order (among more than two axes). The knowledge base of an economy, for example, was characterized as a second-order interaction effect among three first-order interaction effects: (1) the innovative dynamics between economic exchange processes and knowledge production; (2) the political economy as an interaction between economic exchanges and normative control; and (3) the knowledge infrastructure as the result of an interaction between organized knowledge production and institutions at geographical locations. Thus, the model could be grounded in three micro-foundations: positions at geographic locations, exchange relations, and reflexive learning.

Since the subdynamics are analytically different (and, therefore, orthogonal in the model), one can expect reflections from different perspectives to develop incommensurably. Furthermore, the weight of the various interactions and subdynamics can be expected to vary historically, and these changes are evaluated differently from the various perspectives. For example, neo-classical economists tend to consider the market by definition as the leading perspective, while evolutionary economists focus programmatically on how markets are continuously upset by innovations. Both schools of thought are able to provide convincing arguments for their respective perspectives (e.g., David, 1985, 1999; Liebowitz and Margolis, 1999; Lewin, 2003). One can expect incommensurabilities between these two paradigms because economic theorizing in the neo-classical tradition focuses on variation and selection (by the market) at each moment, while evolutionary economists are mainly interested in change and stabilization over time. Each discourse organizes and stabilizes a specific perspective on the system(s) under study. As these perspectives become more orthogonal, more complexity can be processed at the systems level, albeit at the price of losing common ground for understanding across (inter)disciplinary boundaries.

In Chapter One, the subdynamics of organized knowledge production and control were first distinguished from the economic and social environments in which this historically later subdynamic operates. Three subdynamics were provided with their respective micro-foundations: (1) agents at nodes with geographical positions and sets of preferences guiding decisions, (2) economic exchange processes in the network of links among agents, and (3) the dynamics of learning and innovation over time. The latter mechanism is reflexive and generates the tension between historical construction and 'creative destruction' (Schumpeter, 1943). The knowledge base of an economy can then be considered as a second-order interaction effect because it is no longer based on the historical co-evolutions between two subdynamics—along trajectories—but on the interactions of these interactions from a third perspective. The next-order regime is developed as a reflexive perspective at the supra-individual level *given* the historical contingencies and trajectories. The regime guides and limits the choice among the viable trajectories.

The historical specificity of a system can be reflected from an external (third) perspective. While containing reflexivity at the level of the social system, the second-order interaction effect may induce an order of expectations at the regime level on top of the historical trajectories. The trajectories are based on mutual adjustments in co-evolutions, but the reflexive context disturbs and potentially erodes the historical stability in existing patterns of behavior. In Chapter Two, I used the mathematical theory of communication because a more abstract perspective is needed for the specification of the dynamics of expectations (as different from observable events). For example, one tends intuitively to think of reflection as a mirroring, but the abstract model enables us to understand the importance of reflection at ninety degrees.

Meaning processing cannot be observed directly although one is able to understand observables with reference to expectations if the expectations are specified and integrated into a (proto-)theory. In other words, a theory of meaning is needed as an extension of the mathematical theory of communication. The latter focused on information (Shannon, 1948), but Weaver (1949, at p. 116) soon noted the need for this extension (Chapter Two). Using Maturana and Varela's (1980) concept of autopoiesis (self-organization), semantic domains of the first and second order can be considered as probabilistic operations and thus imported into information theory (Maturana, 1978). Unlike biological systems—for which the meaning of a sign or signal is fixed and can only be changed by wear and tear along a life-cycle[1]—meaning can be exchanged and changed reflexively by communication among human beings using language. Human language can be considered as the evolutionary achievement which allows us to exchange both information and meaning. Language as a medium can further be codified at the level of the social system in terms of symbolically generalized media of communication (Künzler, 1987, 1989; Parsons and Smelser, 1966). The systemic differences among these generalized media can be used to organize a new, that is, functional, differentiation of society (Luhmann, 1977, 1984).

In summary, invoking the formal perspective enables us to understand that 'variation and selection' take place at each moment of time, while the same operation can be appreciated over time as 'change and stabilization.' The semantics for the appreciation are developed along orthogonal axes, and therefore one can expect the reflexive discourses to be incommensurate. Stabilization of meaning over time is based on two (sub)dynamics operating selectively upon each other. First, the incoming information is selected at a specific moment in time by positioning it with reference to the structure of the system of reference. This operation is momentary and may be volatile. The stabilization implies a reflection of the instantaneous selections along the time axis.

Since stabilizations are historical, they can also be considered as second-order variations. However, these variants are constructed by and within systems, and the uncertainty in the distribution can therefore no longer be considered as meaningless information. Analogously, second-order selection corresponds with globalization: some stabilizations can be selected for globalization. Three systemic operations are then involved: selection, stabilization, and globalization. Globalization remains pending as a (second-order) selection pressure upon historical realizations. This

---

[1] In population dynamics, the cycles do not refer to an individual performing a life-cycle, but to collectives performing cycles. However, the epistemological status of these two types of cycles is the same, as both are part of biological discourse.

selection pressure can in turn be stabilized by subsystems which not only provide meaning, but can also codify meaning in a knowledge base.

Luhmann's (1984) social systems theory added to these insights from biological and general systems theory the idea that meaning can also be communicated. Of course, this has been a central premise of symbolic interactionism (Blumer, 1969; Glaser and Strauss, 1967), but in this intellectual tradition the relation with the evolutionary and systemic perspectives had been ignored or even denied (Grathof, 1978; Leydesdorff, 1993a, 2001b). Knowledge further codifies meaning, and knowledge can also be communicated, for example, as discursive knowledge. These next-order communication processes add other dimensions to the probabilistic entropy generated by the underlying exchange processes on which they build and to which they remain coupled. For example, one can pursue a scientific exchange using emails or in interactions over lunch.

Because providing meaning is an anticipatory mechanism, one also needs a theory of anticipatory systems (Rosen, 1985; Dubois, 1998) for the specification. Using this theory, it could be made clear how the anticipatory production of probabilistic entropy is different from its historical production (that is, with the axis of time). For example, one can specify how 'global meaning' is different from 'local meaning' by distinguishing between incursion and hyper-incursion. These specifications are urgent if one wishes to understand a 'knowledge-based economy' as a second-order interaction effect.

The agents remain structurally coupled to local communications as the carriers of next-order communications, but identifiable agents have only reflexive access to the further dynamics of communications among other agents, that is, by learning and thus improving their communicative competencies. The communications have to be understood not only as linguistic utterances, but also with reference to their contexts. The dynamics thus become complex. The heuristics of this study have been to specify the various subdynamics of the composed system analytically—that is, in the model—as independent dimensions of communication. Because of this analytical independence, developments along the orthogonal axes and in the different spaces between the axes can be codified differently. Unlike the strong couplings among the various operations which one might expect at the level of an individual person, the couplings are relaxed at the level of the social system. This system has one more degree of freedom because of its inherent *distributedness*. The distributions among agents contain an uncertainty which can be structured by the differentiation at the level of the distributed (social) system.

The social communication system operates by redistributing whatever is distributed among the agents, i.e., by communicating this substance both spatially and over time along the different axes of the system, but without *ex ante* coordination. For example, power, money, and affection can be distributed and communicated on a daily basis, while the distribution of personal property among people changes only over generations. The uncoupling of distributedness from a center of control allows for the reorganization of the communication in terms of its functionality for processing information and meaning. The carriers of functional differentiation at the systems level are then no longer primarily the individual agents (vectors) who carry the system, but the codes of the communication (eigenvectors) which span the network by grouping the carriers into specific configurations. The effect is an interaction between the grouped agents and the grouping rules.

When the network loses its common medium (e.g., language) as a single dimension of the coordination of meaning, the next-order (that is, symbolically generalized) media of communication can self-organize a knowledge-based system. These media are able to convey 'hyper-meaning,' that is, meaning among possible alternatives, while language was suited to convey both information and meaning. The research question thus became the specification of the conditions under which a probabilistic entropy among three relevant subdynamics can be negative at the systems level or, in other words, the conditions under which the emergence of a knowledge base reduces the uncertainty that prevails at the systems level. This negative entropy can only be generated by interactions among the coordination mechanisms.

In the empirical design, this operationalization required the substantive specification of three independent subdynamics as sources of variation. First, I illustrated the advantage of a model that assumes the analytical independence of different sources of variation (in Chapter One), using the orthogonality between factor substitution and technological change in the production function model. While these two subdynamics of the system can interact in techno-economic co-evolutions, the assumption of their analytical independence has been very fruitful for the theorizing about technological trajectories and regimes (e.g., Sahal, 1981b; Dosi, 1982; Freeman and Perez, 1988). The assumption of three independent subdynamics makes it possible to use the third axis for the reflection of historical developments between each two. Reflection was then specified in Chapter Two as an incursive mechanism.

In summary, the same formal mechanism can be projected on orthogonal dimensions and therefore appreciated differently. The reasoning becomes mathematical because one has to abstract from observable phenomena which are provided with different (and potentially incommensurable) interpretations along each axis. However, after distinguishing the mechanisms formally, each of them has to be provided with another interpretation. For example, along the axis of incursion, knowledge is generated as a second-order process of communication on the basis of meaning processing in communication. This process is second-order because meaning-processing is itself reflexive on the processing of information. Knowledge codifies meaning, while meaning codifies information. The second-order process, however, operates on the first-order configuration of both meaning and information processing because the new axis only adds another dimension at ninety degrees and all lower-level interactions therefore remain possible. Knowledge, for example, may not only be meaningful, but also be informed, and to a variable extent.

11.2   Codification and globalization

The communication of knowledge adds a next-order layer of communication on top of the 'natural' codification processes that are ongoing in the exchanges. In the case of scientific knowledge, for example, this layer is no longer mediated only by natural language, but more importantly by a symbolically generalized medium of communication which guides and restricts the use of natural language. 'Quality control' on the use of language presumes standards which have emerged and been stabilized in the communication. Once this next-order codification has been stabilized in the fluid organization of the scientific community, the sciences can—under certain historical conditions—operate as globalizers on other previously stabilized layers of meaning processing in cultural formations.

Although the layers can be distinguished analytically, the various layers can be expected to continue to interact, for example, in informal communication like face-to-face meetings and telephone conversations. These interactions are geographically constrained (Bernstein, 1971). However, the scientific discourses develop at various levels (e.g., the local and the global level) at the same time, and can therefore be characterized as both hyper- and infra-reflexive (Mulkay *et al.*, 1983; Gilbert and Mulkay, 1984; Ashmore, 1989). Formal and informal communications, restricted and elaborate discourses can be intertwined in each (series of) events, but be distinguished analytically. Specific communication layers can be relatively suppressed or enhanced depending on the historical configurations and/or the state of the discipline. Globalization adds another layer of expectations (of future selections) to the communication: some contributions will fit into the globalizing systems more than others.

The option of developing incursive mechanisms at the level of the social system emerged historically after the invention of the printing press. The printing press made it possible to generate the circulation of human knowledge in communication with orders of magnitude larger than the local production of hand-written texts (e.g., in scriptoria and cloisters). While the oral and literal tradition required human-based transcription and human-based messaging for the diffusion—implying thus a direct link to the sources which produced the communication—a pamphlet and in later stages a newspaper could be circulated in huge numbers of copies during short periods of time. Electronic communication further accelerates this diffusion process. Analogously, but along a differently codified axis of the differentiated system of social coordination, the printing of banknotes accelerated the economic exchange processes by orders of magnitude. An electronic transfer system which uses credit cards for payments instead of tangible banknotes reinforces the globalization of the market. Credit is based on a knowledgeable *expectation* of future payments.

The puzzles of interfacing the various possible subdynamics of anticipation (e.g., credit, knowledge) in communication with the historical (that is, traditional) ones were resolved during the centuries after the bifurcation of production and diffusion by proliferating meanings and values other than religiously fixed ones at the network level. For example, the truth of a scientific statement can only be validated *ex post*, and can eventually no longer be based on an authoritative text like the Bible or Aristotle. Of course, the truth remains rooted in a tradition, but the added value of the new statement is precisely the innovation on the locus where the traditional interpretation is gradually changed with reference to puzzles formulated in the present and from the perspective of hindsight. The gradual changes in series of innovations may in the longer run add up to a more fundamental revision of the meaning of a communication (Fujigaki, 1998). If the revision is globalized, it becomes difficult for future generations to reconstruct the meaning of a concept under a previous regime.

For example, it is difficult for us to explain why doctors believed for a very long period that letting sick people bleed would improve their health, or how one interpreted the theory of phlogiston in the 18th century. Processes analogous to the codification processes in scientific communication have taken place in other function systems like the economy. However, the coding was different and consequently one can expect different reflections. For example, prices codify the exchange system by providing every commodity with an expected value. The value of commodities on the market (*Tauschwert*) can be distinguished from their intrinsic value in the historical process of production (*Gebrauchswert*; Marx, 1867). The diffusion dynamics entertains a model of production in terms of prices and can, therefore, be considered as incursive.

In the historical interactions among these very different codification processes running in parallel, a more complex (since composed) system of communications and expectations could gradually be stabilized and globalized. I used the thesis of functional differentiation in the communication (Luhmann, 1984) as a first approach to the sociological understanding of the structure in these macro-sociological processes: the developments of modern science, capitalism, democracy, etc., were not synchronized *ex ante* or the results of a common cause. These differently codified coordination mechanisms were developed largely in parallel. However, I added the notion of incursion over time from the theory of anticipatory systems in order to distinguish the social system from a biological perspective. The processing of meaning at the level of the social system generates a distributed, but yet structured intentionality at the supra-individual level which can be considered as the knowledge base of this system. This cultural order of expectations can be considered the *differentia specifica* of the (inter-human) social system.

Expectations operate as incursions and hyper-incursions because they are based on providing meaning to the past. The specification of incursion enabled us to understand first how meaning can be changed operationally by being exchanged, and secondly, how meaning can be translated between differently coded domains. Hyper-incursion generates uncertainty by interfacing differently coded communications. This induces decision-making and thus the recombination of differently coded meanings along historical trajectories. The incursive operation is reflexive: incursion upon meaning-processing may change the codification of meaning in addition to changing the underlying meaning itself. However, one can expect structural change to evolve at a lower pace than the reflexive operations generating change.

11.3   The triple contingency of communication

Luther's writings were probably the first which profited fully from the newly invented printing press. The translation of the Bible conveyed an already meaningful message (that is, the Gospel) with new meaning. From the perspective of hindsight, the schismatization in the religious order which followed can be considered as a bifurcation induced by the increased diffusion rate of Luther's writings. For example, Luther's thirty publications presumably sold over 300,000 copies between 1517 and 1520 (Strydom, 1999). The printing of Luther's writings generated an avalanche which was made possible by the removal of a technical bottleneck in the communication system. The new subdynamics of diffusion thus could be bifurcated from local production. However, the retention mechanisms of these new subdynamics of communication had still to be constructed and stabilized reflexively.

More than a century later, for example, Galileo's (1683) *Discorsi* were printed in Leiden after the *Dialogo* (1632) had been placed on the Index by the Inquisition in Catholic countries. New forms for dealing with such opportunities were gradually invented. First, the new technology was used primarily to print the Bible (e.g., the Gutenberg Bible of 1455). Historians have distinguished between this initial period of printing with *incunabula* (1450-1500) and the period thereafter when type-setting became common (Eisenstein, 1979, 1983). It seems that only the latter technology allowed for globalization of the medium by sufficiently accelerating the pace of the reproduction and diffusion of the communication.[2]

The bifurcation between the manufacture and local production of communication, on the one hand, and the diffusion of texts (potentially containing new knowledge) through more abstract mechanisms like markets, on the other, changed the system not only historically, but also more fundamentally in terms of its cultural dynamics (Dupree and Parsons, 1976; Parsons and Dupree, 1976). Luhmann (e.g., 1982a) elaborated Parsons's concept of the functional differentiation of the social system in terms of functionally different types of communication. The codes of the communication are different, and this is functional for development at the systems level because a differentiated system can process more complexity. For example, one can attach a price to a scientific communication, but this external perspective no longer has to indicate the intrinsic quality of this communication. Economic utility can be distinguished from theoretical meaning although the two dimensions may co-vary. Note that the model of functional differentiation remains analytical when the social system is considered as a system of communications. In historical practices, one expects interactions among the differently codified communications. How the subdynamics couple remains a domain for empirical investigations. The mathematical foundation of the model in terms of uncertainties here pays off: the substantive specifications remain also uncertain or, in other words, hypotheses. These hypotheses are embedded in theories which reflect a historical and consequently provisional state of the art.

---

[2] Gouldner (1976) shows a similar diffusion of the newspaper as a new communications technology when cotton became available as a source for textiles, and old textiles could become a source for paper production at a price much lower than before.

In Chapter Seven, I used the word 'translation' for changing the meaning of a communication from one functional domain to another.[3] For example, in economic terms 'high oil prices' mean shortages of oil supplies on the market, but these same terms can also be provided with a political meaning. The two meanings are not unrelated and can be translated into each other (to a variable and asymmetrical extent). Translations at interfaces may over time stabilize into translation systems which can be supported by hybrid institutions. I also argued that these co-evolutions between differently coded communications can be bifurcated in a next stage when a previous balance between the two subdynamics is upset, for example, by strong interactions with a third one. For example, if alternative energy sources were increasingly available, the previous relation between the economic and political concern about the oil prices could be changed, and the organization of Oil Producing and Exporting Countries (OPEC) might lose its current position in translating between the political and the economic domains.

Because of these possible alterations between bifurcations and co-evolutions among subdynamics, the relatively uncontrolled and uncoordinated ('free') development of the various networks alongside one another can be expected to lead gradually to the transformation of the hierarchically organized communication structures of a high culture into a modern and differentiated system of social communication and control. During such deep transformations in the dynamics of social coordination, the carrying agents have to go through learning processes that may take several generations. The reflexive use of different codes for communication by the carrying persons and institutions may offer advantages, but these advantages can be enjoyed only if one has learned to translate among the structurally different codes. Thus, a transformation of all spheres can be expected after a phase transition, but only in the longer run. The agents follow the developments of their social systems reflexively, that is, by learning.

The functional differentiation of communication in terms of different codes can be expected to transform all spheres within society. In a critique of Habermas's (1974) thesis of the transformation of the public sphere, Strydom (1999, at p. 5) argued that 'once communication processes are uncoupled from the physical presence of the public, a completely yet by no means untypical situation under modern conditions ensues':

---

[3] Luhmann (1984) excluded this mechanism because functional subsystems, in his opinion, are operationally closed and therefore can only be *disturbed* by the operation of other subsystems (see Chapter Five).

> If institutionalized gatherings are a remove away from talk or encounter, this new situation is characterized by a still higher degree of abstraction. This quality is explicable by reference to the absence of the public. Generalized communication processes come into operation which presuppose a complex institutional and technical infrastructure and are oriented towards an unlimited body of absent and anonymous addressees. [...] The institutionalization of the absent and anonymous public profoundly changed the structure and process of public communication and thereby transformed the conditions of reproduction of modern societies. They now definitively became communication societies.

Although Strydom's argument moves historically with large steps—given the centuries that were needed for these transformations—the crucial point from the perspective of evolution theory is the new mechanism of the *expectation* of a potentially absent audience. The anticipation of this audience incurs on the local situation as a pending selection by a third-person observer. Its incursive dynamics operates reflexively by raising the question of the possible alternatives to what hitherto has happened 'naturally' (that is, following the axis of historical time).

In other words, another (third) subdynamics can be generated endogenously to the system. The third position is configured by the network of relations. Despite the tight coupling between action and structure in initial stages—as in 'actor-networks' (Callon *et al.*, 1986)—a bifurcation makes possible a dynamic that is different from the system's historical progression in terms of actions, namely one of the reconstruction of all given ('natural') environments in terms of possible recombinations of codes in innovations. This new subdynamic, however, does not necessarily operate with the same clock. Thus, the subdynamics can also become differentiated over time. Institutions other than those previously available may be invented and prove to be more viable for carrying the new subdynamics because they are less rooted in previous stages. It remains an empirical question whether and where the systems can adapt. The constructed subdynamic feeds back on its historical construction insofar as the new code is able to gain control relative to the previous ones. The newly added code, however, increases the capacity to process complexity.

In the longer term, the old conditions are reshaped by this continuous process of 'creative destruction.' The forces of change in the modern reconstruction are no longer based on individual reflection or aggregate action along the time axes, but on reconstructions made possible by the structural parameters of the emerging network of social relations when the networked system can be stabilized as a new social order. As Marx (1848) put it: 'All that is solid melts into air' (Berman, 1982). For example, the techno-economic co-evolutions develop along trajectories which may lead the system from one basin of attraction into another (Freeman and Perez, 1988). New mechanisms of exclusion and inclusion at the level of organizations and institutions are among the consequences of this evolution (Luhmann, 1997b, 2000).

Decisive for inclusion or exclusion are the speed of learning communicative competences by the carriers of the communication. In a functionally differentiated order of expectations, inter-human communications can be provided with meanings different from the meanings intended by the sender and/or provided by the receiver. In the tradition of symbolic interactionism, this 'situational meaning' is called (Thomas and Thomas, 1928). However, a situation is structured by its latent dimensions. These dimensions are instantiated by events. Some interaction terms (but not others) will be stabilized by selection over time, for example, as market structures, national states, or scientific disciplines. These next-order structures feed back on the 'double contingencies' that continuously emerge in each interaction among human beings. Inter-human 'interaction' thus becomes increasingly a *specific* level of communication. This level ('double contingency') can be distinguished from organized communication ('triple contingency') and symbolically mediated communication (as in the generalized Triple Helix model elaborated in previous chapters).

While organized communication can be stabilized, symbolically mediated communication can also be globalized. Inter-human communications tend to remain localized. Note that the independence is analytical because in the practices of the communicators the different dimensions can be expected to interact and to resonate to variable degrees. The next-order levels of communication feed back on the wealth of these interactions by selecting some communications as more important than others. Subjectively, one is able to refine one's communication by recognizing the different frames of reference. The contexts codetermine the meaning of communications. For example, in some contexts one can ask about the price of a transaction, while in other contexts raising this question would be considered a transgression.

Unlike the 'double contingency' between *Ego* and *Alter* in inter-human interaction (Parsons, 1968; Parsons and Shils, 1951, at pp. 3-39; Habermas, 1981; Luhmann, 1984, at pp. 148 ff.), the 'triple contingency' among two agents and a structured context assumes the analytically independent position of a third-person observer or 'a public' (Strydom, 1999). This third-person observer can technically be considered as another (parallel) communication channel. One can communicate either directly or through this medium. However, as the channel is further developed into a different system, this other dynamic may become an independent source of variation which feeds back on the communication between the sender and receiver.

For example, the telephone line has been the prime example of a (Shannon-type) communication channel. But as the telephone system developed by allowing for data transfer, sms messages, etc., the choice of which channels to use becomes increasingly relevant for the quality of the communication. Henceforth, the uncertainty generated in the communication can be attributed to the sending or receiving end or to the communication system as 'a third person' (Leydesdorff, 1993a). Each communication channel can be expected to be noisy, but in a triple contingency the third system can under certain—but not under all—conditions also reduce the uncertainty for the participants in the communication at the systems level, that is, behind their backs. I have argued that this reduction (or increase) of the uncertainty can be measured using entropy statistics.

In Chapters Eight, Nine, and Ten, historical configurations were analyzed in terms of the progression of this process of inverting the time axis using the generalized Triple Helix model. The complex system of communication needs both historical stabilization (that is, retention), and further development by generating new options at the interfaces among differently codified communications. This latter mechanism generates uncertainty, and this source of variation can be strengthened by making it more knowledge-intensive. Reflexivity about the interface, however, drives the system into the hyper-incursive mode and then decisions are needed at the organizational level to move the system forward. Thus, the action perspective becomes increasingly dependent on the communication perspective. The neo-classical criterion of subjects deciding on the basis of their 'natural preferences' is transformed into informed decision-making at the level of organizations (Chapter Five).

In summary, the social system of communications is historically constructed in layers. Insofar as the interactions between differently codified meanings can be retained, the codes can be stabilized in organizational formats. However, the codification of meaning in communication occurs with hindsight and therefore takes time. The historical process of monetary unification in Burgundy and the Netherlands during the period 1450-1550 was used as an example in Chapter Five. The processes of the constitutional stabilization of nations during the Dutch and English revolutions of the period 1570-1690 (e.g., Hobbes, 1651)[4] were reflected

---

[4] More precisely, the Dutch Revolution is usually said to have begun in 1568, and the Glorious Revolution came to an end in 1689.

during the 18th century in the writings of the French *philosophes* which provided the intellectual basis for drafting the constitutions of modern states during the American and French revolutions (Luhmann, 1989, at pp. 399 ff.).

Analogously to these developments in political communication, the Republic of Letters in science was organized into a scientific journal system from 1665 onwards (Price, 1961; Elkana *et al.*, 1978; Garfield, 1979). The format of scientific reporting initially remained similar to the format of personal correspondence (Bazerman, 1988; Leydesdorff, 1998). Only after the Napoleonic reforms, and the subsequent construction of the Humboldt university in Germany, could institutional mechanisms for the reproduction of scientific communication could be organized at the supra-individual level (e.g., in university departments). However, it would take until the end of the 19th century before the modern citation emerged (Leydesdorff and Wouters, 1999). A scientific citation (unlike an acknowledgement to an individual) enables a reader to choose reflexively between considering a reference in relation to a text or an author. Thus, the subsystem of communication could become more complex because of this invention.

11.4   The anticipatory operation of structure

While a weakly anticipatory system (e.g., an individual) can anticipate on the future in a predictive mode, the social system of communication can additionally develop strong anticipation using the degree of freedom provided by the distribution of individuals. This degree of freedom can be used for grouping and functional differentiation along the codes of the communication. Unlike a weakly anticipatory system, however, the next state of a strongly anticipatory system cannot be predicted because the next stages of this system are co-constructed by the system in its current state. Hyper-incursive routines at the interfaces between (asynchronous) subsystems enable the carriers to participate in this co-construction by making relevant decisions. The social system cannot be developed without this structural coupling: the decisions synchronize the subsystems again. This operation of updating by a decision across an interface can be considered as a translation.

The incursion (in the operation of providing meaning) is first organized along the time-axis in both social and psychological systems (Chapter Three). The differentiations in the social system of communications provide the second update mechanism (Chapter Four). The asynchronicity between the operations (e.g., between invention in a research laboratory and innovation on the market place) provides room for decentralized decision-making and therewith a second update mechanism. This transversal update is analytically orthogonal to the self-reference over time in each updated system.

The operation of the two anticipatory mechanisms upon each other potentially closes the communication (in co-evolutions along trajectories which exclude third parties), but it also generates structural pressures for increasingly informed decisions at the interfaces (Chapter Five). It could be shown that the hyper-incursive formulation of the relevant equations generates an uncertainty within the communication system which loops the communication back into taking reflexive action. This loop can also be considered as a formalization of Giddens's (1979, 1984) 'duality of structure.' However, Giddens did not specify this operation from a systems perspective, but introduced it only as a methodological postulate from the perspective of action theory (Leydesdorff, 1993a).

From the theory of anticipatory systems, action can be considered as a consequence of the reflexive need to take decisions. Note that 'action' is then a dependent variable; action reinforces decisions reflexively. The *distribution* of actions generates variation which enables the selective structures—which remain hypothetical constructs—further to develop (or not) in terms of their specific codes. However uncertain the axes remain because of the inherent distributedness of the social system, the operation is determined by the specificity of the code, that is, at the level of the selecting (sub)systems. The specification of the code by an analyst remains reflexive on the observable construction, and therefore continues to have the epistemological status of a hypothesis.

In the sciences, for example, the exclusive jargon of a paradigm may close the communications when both its differentiation from other discourses and its codification within this subsystem are sufficiently developed. At the interfaces with other subsystems (e.g., economic development), knowledge-based innovations, however, require careful and reflexive reconstruction of the new insights in elaborate discourses (Coser, 1975; Bernstein, 1971; Blauwhof, 1995). Because of these investments at the interfaces, a third-person (or 'objectifying') perspective can be stabilized as analytically different. This incursive perspective of the third person is needed as a feedback for managing the translation of the historically generated dynamics into new combinations.

Since human agents are reflexive, they are also able to internalize this external perspective and themselves act as participant-observers or even 'translation spokespersons' who take the lead in performative actions (Callon, 1986). However, the structural presence of this third dimension can be perceived also in the case of non-decisions (Bachratz and Baratz, 1963). In general, one does not need a focus on the special case of a specific agent, but the distribution of actions and non-actions is decisive. Since the distribution contains an uncertainty, action thus becomes an expectation instead of a fact: what action may mean requires specification of the relevant system(s) of reference. In the semiotic tradition, this reinterpretation of action as a function of the communication is sometimes expressed by using the word 'actant' instead of 'actor' for the agent of change (Greimas, 1983, pp. 49 ff.).

The configuration cannot determine who takes the decisions and actions. The formalized layers operate upon the informal communications, and *vice versa*. The multi-layered networks can be expected to reinforce action at some places more than others. For example, a communication outside a prevailing paradigm disqualifies the author of the message as an outsider. The system filters the distributions of proposals using its code(s). Reflexively hypothesized structures operate as selection mechanisms and thus determine the effectiveness of actions in a knowledge-based system. Actions provide the necessary variation; selection mechanisms tend to operate deterministically while remaining fragile constructs of the communication. It may be easiest to consider them as feedback mechanisms, but the feedback operates on the basis of a distribution. The distribution spans an orthogonal dimension. The variation is grouped by this grouping variable. The latter cannot be observed, but it can be specified as an expectation with the epistemological status of a hypothesis.

In other words, the functionalist model has to be handled reflexively. Functional differentiation becomes itself a hypothesis and one would expect changes due to further differentiations at interfaces. Consequently, the differentiated codes transform the public as a general audience into functional audiences or—to use a current word—stakeholders. The functionally differentiated codes of communication generate their respective publics with different update cycles, their organizations, and accordingly relevant actions (Leydesdorff, 1993c). For example, one can give a paper at a conference, and also publish this paper as an article in a journal. The communication dynamics of these two processes are predictably different. Specific functions can be attributed to the instantiations reflexively. One can participate in the respective systems according to one's communicative competencies.[5]

---

[5] Under certain conditions, one can expect this functionalization to include individual actions and interactions to a such degree that the pressure of the social system results in alienation and oppression (Horkheimer and Adorno, 1969 [1947]; Serres, 1980, 1982; Knorr-Cetina, 1999).

11.5   The Triple Helix and 'the duality of structure'

When the triple contingency is reproduced as a structural configuration of functional differentiation, a Triple Helix can increasingly be generated. (I developed the model for three subdynamics for reasons of parsimony, but the extension to more than three subdynamics is straightforward.) Three subdynamics can be expected to disturb one another in the communication to such an extent that the closure in a process of mutual shaping between two of them can be eroded. Thus, any hierarchical organization within a differentiated system can be expected to perish sooner or later along a trajectory. The trajectory leads into a regime different from the one in which it was generated. There remains no expectation of a long-term return to a previous configuration of hierarchical stabilization or homeostasis after the phase transition of reflexive modernization (Leydesdorff, 1997e). The fluxes of communications can no longer be completed and fixed when the system of communications is functionally differentiated because the functions develop within a system that remains under reconstruction. The temporarily stable organizations function as stepping stones for moving the self-organizing dynamics at the systems level.

The social system is thus propelled by a dynamics of variation and selection in recursive and incursive layers of operations. The trajectories guide the system from one basin of attraction to another, but neither the trajectories nor the regimes are historically 'given.' They remain historically constructed and in need of legitimacy within the social contexts of communication. Legitimacy can come from different sources because social systems are differentiated. Each audience can be expected to contain a discourse. These discourses are specific among other possible discourses. The various discourses operate upon one another incursively, that is, they provide meaning to the substance of communication in other discourses using their own codes of communication. Although these incursive operations are *ex ante* symmetrical in the formal model, the symmetry is broken historically because the substantive communications are different on both sides of an interface. The progression along the time axis breaks the *ex ante* symmetry in the expectations into a historical order *ex post*.

The sequencing of decisions can be reinforced by decision-rules, but even without the formalization of such rules the decisions generate path dependencies and consequently lock-ins. This process enables the social system to retain 'wealth' from these interactions by shaping historical trajectories. The materialization in institutional formats and social roles historicizes the evolutionary development.

However, these dynamics can no longer be considered as a Darwinian evolution of random variation and 'natural selection' or the 'survival of the fittest.' The selective mechanisms of communication are generated by processing meaning. Meaning is specific to the code of the communication. Thus, what is 'fittest' can be reflected as a matter of decision-making, as is the delineation of the collective making these decisions. Decisions about inclusion and exclusion are endemic to organizations (Luhmann, 2000).

The decision rules and the underlying communities can vary, but the two levels can also be expected to interact. If the analyst approaches this interaction from the material side of the 'instantiations' by focusing on historical actions and institutions as observable units of analysis, one is able to specify the aggregation, but one can no longer explain the interaction effects among aggregates of communication with different functions. Giddens (1979, 1984), for example, declared these interaction effects to be a consequence of the 'duality of structure,' but using his historistic framework, one can no longer specify the 'duality of structure' as an operation of the system. Without the specification of the grouping variable as a hypothesis, the interaction effects can be considered as 'unintended consequences' emerging at the systems level, but they cannot be provided with a theoretical appreciation (cf. Callon, 1998). Throughout Giddens's œuvre, this 'duality of structure' therefore remained a methodological postulate which could not be specified substantively (Leydesdorff, 1993a).

The evolutionary perspective, which specifies the grouping variable as a process of functional differentiation of the code of the communications, enables us to take another reflexive turn. The focus is on the constructed system as an operative unit rather than on its historical construction by action. The constructed system can be expected to contain (selective) structures which operate both historically and in an anticipatory mode. First, aggregated *relations* among agents span a network that can be expected to contain architecture. In this architecture the relating agents have *positions* (Burt, 1982). These positions can be unintended. The structural dimensions of the network thus gain independence in directions tangential to the historical construction. In formal terms, the network develops a so-called 'eigen-structure,' that is, a 'structure of itself.' However, human beings are not themselves a social network. They have no access to the network other than reflexively. Thus, the specification of an eigen-structure remains a hypothesis in a discourse. The question becomes whether and how this hypothesis and the sociological theory it implies can be made fruitful for the explanation.

In Chapter Four, I showed that *interaction* and *aggregation* can be considered parsimoniously as the two incursive operations of the social system. In a next step, the aggregation and interaction of incursive operations provided me with the two options of stabilization (in an organization at each moment of time or along a trajectory over time), and globalization as a hyper-incursive operation. The hyper-incursion recombines two anticipatory operations in a specific format that was provided with an interpretation in terms of the need to take a decision. The structural coupling between stabilization and globalization was thus formalized as the uncertainty in this hyper-incursive operation: the uncertainty requires decision-making because otherwise the complexity can be expected to explode (Chapter Five). A next-order control structure can come into place insofar as the historical layer is able to take relevant decisions bottom-up. Historically, decisions lead to organization and then potentially to stabilization along a trajectory. Thus, the system is able to reinforce itself in an autocatalytic loop. This autocatalytic loop was further modeled as a hypercycle in Chapters Six and Seven.

In addition to being a prerequisite for the formation of an institution, organization can also be considered as another function of the complex system. From a functional perspective, organization provides a retention mechanism. Note that functions are understood in this context dynamically as being carried by specifically coded communication structures. Decisions can be considered as the specific type of communications which organize the communications by including and excluding communications at specific moments (Luhmann, 2000). Decisions can further be codified into decision-rules. This next-order functioning of a decision rule as code can be entertained reflexively in a knowledge-based organization. Decisions are then no longer based upon 'natural preferences,' but stabilized against idiosyncratic wishes over time. In other words, the processes of organization and self-organization are not nested hierarchically, but holographically: the subdynamics which at one moment in time serve integration (by organizing the relevant functions into an organization) may from another perspective or at a next moment serve differentiation since each specific organization can be expected to disturb differently codified subdynamics.

For example, decisions within the intellectual organization of the sciences may lead to specific formats in the institutionalization of university departments in national contexts. National legislation in turn modifies the options for the economic exploitation of knowledge-based resources and decision-making about the sciences. Figure 8.5 pictured how such a complex dynamics of interlocking decisions can be represented as a tetrahedron of communication systems operating upon one another. A tetrahedron can be tumbled in all directions without being distorted topographically. Thus, the system operating 'on top' can be changed historically and in accordance with one's perspective. However, one should keep in mind that the hypercycle cannot be closed historically because the three (or more) subdynamics

326   *Chapter Eleven*

continue to disturb one another in addition to selecting upon each other's disturbances. Each next-order position remains fragile.

In other words, uncertainty about the configuration cannot be dissolved from any of the perspectives. The interactions among the perspectives generate a non-linear dynamics among the perspectives while the latter continue to operate in parallel. An uncertainty which cannot be dissolved, however, can be measured by using information theory. The hypothesis of self-organization among the fluxes of communication in the Triple Helix dynamics enabled me (in Chapters Eight and Nine) to specify research designs for investigating the extent to which specific social systems dynamics had become knowledge-based. The measurement indicates the degree to which a configuration can be expected to exist historically or, in other words, to operate in terms of synergies among expectations.

Knowledge-based dynamics 'exist' only negatively, that is, by reducing the uncertainty in a configuration because an order of expectations prevails. On the measurement scale of the mutual information in more than two dimensions, this order of expectations was indicated as an alternative (with a negative value) to observable existence (with a positive value). The question about existence (fact) and expectation (meaning) could thus be made the subject of empirical research. For example, the Triple Helix configuration of university-industry-government relations made a difference in the various countries measured using data from the *Science Citation Index* about coauthorship relations among the three sectors (Chapter Eight). Hypotheses about the mechanisms of variation, selection, codification/stabilization, and globalization in links and hyperlinks could thereafter be tested in webometric analysis. In Chapters Nine and Ten, this model was elaborated for the measurement of the knowledge base of the national economies in the Netherlands and Germany, respectively.

11.6   Hyper-incursive models of cultural evolution

The theoretical implications of the model were elaborated mainly in Chapters One and Seven. Chapter Seven introduced the transition to the empirical part of these studies, while in Chapter One I focused first in general on how the specification of expectations differs from the theorizing hitherto prevalent in evolutionary economics. Evolutionary economists have tended to begin with historical 'facts' and observable trajectories of firms. The observables are then explained by using a theory of the firm (e.g., Casson, 1997). This focus on historical firm behavior has turned evolutionary economics into a 'heterodoxy' from neo-classical economics (Storper, 1997).

The neo-classical tradition begins with the specification of *counter-factuals* in a model. In Chapter One, I followed Andersen's (1994) critique of the dominant (Nelson and Winter) model in evolutionary economics. Andersen specified the difference between an approach that begins with the specification of (game-theoretical) expectations and one that begins with observable firm behavior. Some evolutionary economists have even called their models 'history-friendly' (e.g., Malerba *et al.*, 1999), but consequently historicism could not be avoided (Popper, 1967). For example, the models become sector-specific and one is no longer able to explain differences among sectors other than in terms of historical aggregations. Although the game-theoretical approaches are analytical, they share with evolutionary models the meta-biological assumption of a competition for survival at the systems level given scarce resources.

The specification of how the sociological categories of meaning and the communication of meaning add to the meta-biological model of evolutionary economics and evolutionary game-theory made it necessary to specify reflection from a communication-theoretical perspective (in Chapter Two). How is meaning provided to historical exchange processes? The processing of meaning was substantiated as the specific operation of the social system (Chapters Three, Four, and Five). Let us now radicalize this approach and specify the elements of cultural evolution which can introduced from an anticipatory perspective.

Three hyper-incursive models can be derived from the logistic equation:

$$x_t = ax_t (1 - x_{t+1}) \tag{1a}$$
$$x_t = ax_{t+1} (1 - x_t) \tag{1b}$$
$$x_t = ax_{t+1} (1 - x_{t+1})$$
$$[1c]$$

- Equation 1a evolves into $x = (a - 1)/a =$ Constant. I submit that this evolution towards a constant through anticipation can be considered as modeling the self-reference of an (individual) identity. At the level of the social system, a group or an organization can also maintain an identity;
- Equation 1b evolves into $x_{t+1} = (1/a) \{x_t / (1 - x_t)\}$. Since the latter term approaches -1 as its limit value and the former term is a constant $(1/a)$, this representation can alternate between itself and its mirror image. This subdynamic thus formalizes the reflexive operation. Reflection is relevant both

in the case of an identity (e.g., an organization or an individual). However, in addition to aggregation a social system contains also interaction terms;

- Equation 1c is only possible on the basis of interaction between and among systems which process representations, because this system (x_t) has lost any reference to its present state. It refers only to its own future state and its being selected in this future state, but this system cannot exist otherwise than in terms of expectations.

The intersubjective intentionality modeled by Equation 1c has been theorized in sociology as the 'double contingency' between *Ego* and *Alter* (Parsons, 1968). Using this mechanism for the anticipation, the *Ego* in the present (x_t) no longer has a reference to itself, but only to itself in a future state (x_{t+1}), that is, as an *Alter Ego*. The orientation of providing meaning with reference to other possible meanings thus constitutes the social world as a system different from psychological ones (Schutz, 1932). Unlike social systems, psychological systems cannot avoid containing a reference to themselves as an identity in the present (Equations 1a). The social system of expectations remains structurally coupled to psychological systems because it would otherwise not be manifest historically (Luhmann, 1984). The social system is only perceptible after a reflexive turn, that is, on the basis of an expectation of an *Alter Ego*.

The coupling between the social system and agents carrying it is provided by the reflexivity formalized in Equation 1b. Because of this reflexivity, the social system can be entertained by individuals as a notional order of expectations. *Vice versa*, the individuals or other agents are reflected in the social system as addresses at nodes ('actants'). While both systems can contain the reflexive operation expressed in Equation 1b, a co-evolution ('mutual adjustment') between the social and the psychological systems can also be expected. This co-evolution requires and shapes language as a medium sufficiently rich for shaping and communicating meaning. However, the co-evolution can temporarily be interrupted when expectations are further codified on either side.

For example, an eigendynamics at the level of the social system may lead to 'alienation,' while the recursive application of the reflexive operation provides discretionary room for private thinking and tacit knowledge on the side of psychological systems. In summary, both systems can also apply their reflexivity to themselves and thus develop hyper-reflexivity. Under pre-modern conditions, however, the social system was not yet sufficiently free to use this degree of freedom as a differentiation because of the need for centralized control. This has changed during the past centuries, albeit to variable extents. The next-order systems contain a representation of the lower-order subdynamics on which they rest, at the respective interfaces.

The non-linear dynamics of meaning at the level of the social system includes its manifestations in social institutions as historical footprints of the system. The reflexive layers of psychological and social dynamics are evolutionary achievements which could be added to and integrated into these systems because of the development of language. The reflexive layer first allows for the selection by the system of an identity (by delineating the system from an environment; Equation 1b), but then also for the expectation of an identity over time (Equation 1a). This *Ego* is further reaffirmed by the selection by *Alter*—that is, $(1 - x_{t+1})$—or, in other words, by providing a mutual (or 'double') contingency. Equation 1b affirms the identity by providing the mirror image as a negative that transcends the positive *Ego* as in Descartes's original *Cogito*. The expectation of an identity in the future (Equation 1c) presumes an *Alter Ego* (or the expectation of a future *Ego*) to take part in an intersubjective intentionality (Husserl, 1929). This can also be discussed in terms of 'trust' or 'social capital.'

At the level of the social system, the diffusion of meaning can further be accelerated when the symbolically generalized media of communication are functionally differentiated. The system can then go through a phase transition because of a bifurcation between the local production of meaning and the potential globalization of meaning by diffusion following another subdynamics. The reaction-diffusion mechanism was explained in Chapter Five for the case of techno-economic co-evolutions, but it can be used analogously as a model for understanding the differentiation between 'situational meaning' and the 'horizon of meaning' emphasized by authors like Husserl, Habermas, and Luhmann.

Although the systems are constructed bottom-up, control operates top-down. Thus, the globalizing dynamic tends to select on the stabilizing one. In a distributed system, however, control can only be differentiated. Thus, once the social system of inter-human communication is in place as an order of intersubjective intentionality, the reflection of future states at the psychological level is increasingly controlled by this next-order level, albeit in an uncertain way. Unlike a social system, an individual identity can reflect on the future given its current state in history. However, an individual needs interactions with others to co-reconstruct parts of the social system under reflection; psychological systems are only weakly anticipatory. One's historical continuity, however, provides room for decisions and actions on the basis of expectations and discretionary trade-offs in the reflexive domain (like private meaning and tacit knowledge). In other words, one can solve one's own problems, but one cannot solve social problems psychologically.

At the level of the individual, the solutions found hitherto can sometimes be retained and stabilized at the (biological) level of one's individual' body (which is structurally coupled to the mind by the chemo-physics of biology). Analogously, the social system can be considered as 'embodied' in the social institutions. Institutions provide the system with physical continuity. Like individuals, institutions and organized collectives have room for agency and tacit knowledge. The hyperreflexive uncertainty can thus be black-boxed during potentially long periods of time because of the continuity and the reflexivity contained at the respective systems level. However, the subdynamics at the network level add to these historical continuities an order of expectations. Such an order can only be entertained by systems which are able to communicate meaning.

11.7 The sociological and communication-theoretical foundations

The difference between the substantive (sociological) model and the formal (mathematical) theory of communication was further specified in Chapter Two with reference to the problem of how one can model the exchange of meaning. I had to pursue this abstract road because—as more fully explained in Chapter Seven—Luhmann's communication-theoretical approach in sociology can still be read as a meta-biological model. While biologists take the development of life as a given, Luhmann tends to treat the development of meaning as a cultural *given*;[6] meaning is no longer considered as constructed in communication, but meaning processing precedes and controls communication as an independent variable. Habermas (1987) made the argument about this meta-biological foundation of Luhmann's systems theory most forcefully:

> In this way, subject-centered reason is replaced by systems rationality. As a result, the critique of reason carried out as a critique of metaphysics and a critique of power, which we have considered in these lectures, is deprived

---

[6] Luhmann alternates between this meta-biological model using concepts of functional differentiation and structural coupling for the explanation, and a meta-theological one where meaning seems to be given transcendentally as a substance analogous to life (Luhmann, 1986a). The meta-theological metaphor is pursued by Luhmann by grounding the theory on the operation of the distinction (that is, on a paradox). The *first* distinction is then Lucifer's breaking away from God as the devil (Luhmann, 1990, at pp. 118 ff.) or, in other words, the problem of the Theodicy, that is, the origin of evil in the world (Leibniz, 1710).

of its object. To the degree that systems theory does not merely make its specific disciplinary contribution with the system of the sciences but also penetrates the lifeworld with its claim to universality, it replaces metaphysical background convictions with metabiological ones. Hence, the conflict between objectivists and subjectivists loses its point. (Habermas, 1987, at p. 385).

In other words, Habermas appreciates Luhmann's distinction between psychic and social systems, but he challenges us to bring the critique of metaphysical issues (of providing meaning to events in a dialectics) back into a metabiological perspective that processes meaning without intentionality, that is, as a scientistic objectivation. How can one think both these metaphysical and metabiological perspectives?

I agree with Habermas that the sociological enterprise needs the reflexive specification of both the role of the participant and the analytical position of the observer. However, the perspective of a metabiological system and the one of a metaphysically based intentionality can be considered as the two sides of the interface between social systems and psychological systems. If the social system is distinguished from the psychological units carrying this system, the intentionality at the level of the social system cannot easily be defined, and therefore the social system tends to be objectified. As long as society is considered as integrated in persons (e.g., a King), the tensions between the two types of meaning processing (that is, of the social and psychic systems, respectively) could be resolved in meaning shared *ex ante* within a community, but not necessarily as the result of interaction. However, the subdynamics on both sides of the interface contain feedback loops, and thus a non-linear dynamics of meaning processing can be expected when the two systems are bifurcated. The angles of the reflections are ninety degrees, and thus 'meaning' at the level of the social system can become increasingly incommensurable with 'meaning' at the subjective level. However, meanings can be communicated between reflexive systems.

This formalization has provided us with an opportunity for distinguishing between the reflections among systems and the (hyper-)reflections within systems as different operations. One can expect this distinction to work differently for the social system than for the psychic system because one more degree of freedom is available for the differentiation. (This degree of freedom is provided by the distributedness of any social system among human beings.) I shall now proceed by arguing that the mathematical perspective can help bridge the gap between the meta-biological and the meta-physical perspectives without resolving the tension between the two, because an additional degree of freedom can be specified and then used for the reflection. This reflection is different from the substantive reflections, since it is formal, that is, yet without meaning, and therefore cannot substantively support the construction of a meta-level. The additional axis which is used for the reflection is only spanned at ninety degrees (across the distribution) and not as a mirror at 180 degrees. Consequently, this formal reflection is not 'meta'—that is, at a next level—but it remains 'epi': the added dimension opens a space of alternative possibilities for recombining the substantive dynamics in the previous communications of meaning. The historical operation of the system remains substantive.

I turn to Husserl's (1929) *Cartesian Meditations* for epistemological specification and foundation of this reflection in *inter*subjectivity. The *Cogito* of Descartes and Shannon's mathematization of uncertainty provide us with tools to understand the uncertainty in communication as a *cogitatum*, that is, a subject of doubt. The mathematization of anticipation (Rosen, 1985; Dubois, 1998) enables us to relate the uncertainty at each moment of time with expectation and anticipation over time without having to resort to a single—that is, undifferentiated—transcendentality. (Descartes's contingent *Cogito* is delineated from God as the Transcendency.) A system of social relations, however, can be specified as a *cogitatum* which transcends individual minds but remains structurally coupled to them as their distribution. An individual mind cannot specify this system without entertaining a discourse. However, its possibility can fruitfully be hypothesized. A program of empirical studies and simulations can thus be formulated.

11.7.1 Anticipation, uncertainty, and the intentionality of communication

I noted in Chapter Seven that both Luhmann and Habermas make references to Husserl's reflections on intersubjectivity (Husserl, 1929, 1936, 1962; Derrida, 1964). It has been claimed in the literature (Schutz, 1952, at p. 105; cf. Habermas, 1981, at p. 178f.; Luhmann, 1995b, at p. 170) that Husserl failed to ground the concept of 'intersubjectivity,' but I follow Luhmann's (1995b) interpretation that this was never Husserl's argument or intention.

The *locus classicus* for the alleged failure of Husserl is Alfred Schutz's (1952) study entitled 'Das Problem der transzendentalen Intersubjektivität bei Husserl' (The problem of intersubjectivity with Husserl; Schutz, 1975). Schutz formulated:

> All communication, whether by so-called expressive movements, deictic gestures, or the use of visual or acoustic signs, already presupposes an external event in that common surrounding world which, according to

Husserl, is not constituted except by communication. (Schutz, 1975, at p. 72).[7]

Schutz wished to ground the communication in the 'life-world' as a common frame of reference for the communication. He criticized Husserl for explaining this ground as a *result* of communication. However, Husserl considered the external referent of communication as a horizon of a potential variety of meanings. Husserl's intersubjectivity remains intentional, whereas Schutz argued in favor of an existential grounding of intersubjectivity in a 'we,' for example, when he went on to say: 'As long as man is born from woman, intersubjectivity and the we-relationship will be the foundation for all other categories of human existence.' (*ibid.*, at p. 82).[8]

In other words, Schutz disagreed with Husserl about the possibility of *deriving* social relations from communication. Social relations, in Schutz's opinion, are prior to communications, while Husserl argued that social relations are embedded in communication or—as he put it—'transcendental intersubjectivity.' It has been argued in previous chapters that the question of what 'prior' means in these contexts depends on recursive or incursive perspectives. 'Prior' can have a theoretical meaning very different from historical priority if one turns to an evolutionary perspective. In the latter case the focus is on the present as a basis for reconstructing the past. The past thus is reconstructed and therefore analytically later.

Husserl abstracted from the historical given (that is, the modeled system) by putting the latter between brackets in what he called an ἐποχη (epoché). What is left when one abstracts from what is given? These non-material traces can be provided with meaning as the subject of a meditation. The meditation gives access to an *a priori* domain for which no discursive concepts are available to the Ego. In this meditation Husserl not only questions what it means to be 'human,' but also asks about the referent of human intentionality. While the first question refers back to Descartes' '*cogito ergo sum*,' the latter addresses the subject of doubt in the *cogito*, that is, the *cogitata*. In the *Cartesian Meditations* of 1929, this quest is elaborated by extending on Descartes' (1637) category of the *cogito*. In addition to oneself as the

---

[7] 'Alle Kommunikation, ob es sich um eine sogenannte Ausdrucksbewegung, eine Zeigegeste, oder den Gebrauch visueller oder akustischer Zeichen handelt, setzt bereits einen äußeren Vorgang in eben jener gemeinsamen Umwelt voraus, die nach Husserl erst durch die Kommunikation konstituiert werden soll.' (Schutz, 1952, at p. 97).

[8] 'Solange Menschen von Müttern geboren warden, fundiert Intersubjektivität und Wirbeziehung alle anderen Kategorien des Menschseins.' (Schutz, 1952, at p. 105).

subject of doubt, one can also raise the question of the substance about which one is in doubt, that is, the *cogitatum*: the external referent or the subject of one's doubting.

For Descartes this *cogitatum* could be distinguished only negatively from the *cogito* as that which transcends the contingency of one's *cogito* at each moment of time. From this perspective, the Other in the act of doubting is defined as God. God transcends the contingency of the *cogito*, and therefore one can expect this Other to be eternal. While the *cogito* knows itself to be mortal and incomplete, God as the Other is necessarily complete. Because of His completeness, the world as His creation is given to us transcendentally. According to Descartes, it would contradict the completeness of God (not to mention His veracity) if the transcendental dimension of the world were a continuous deception. This *ex ante* correspondence between our ideas and experiental uncertainties was elaborated by Leibniz (1686) into the idea of an *harmonie préétablie*. Leibniz ([3]1966, at p. 272) acknowledged that this idea has the status of a hypothesis among other possible arrangements, but entertaining this hypothesis was the only option for explaining the perfection of Nature as God's creation (Leydesdorff, 1994c, at p. 36). Kant agreed with this superior likelihood of Leibniz's explanation above others, and designated it as the cosmopolitan proof of the existence of God. (Descartes's position was characterized by Kant as the ontological proof of the existence of God. Both proofs, however, were rejected by Kant as insufficient evidence for the existence of God.)[9]

Husserl proposed in the *Meditations* to consider the *cogitatum* as a self-reinforcing ground for the meditation. It provides the *cogito* with a reference to a horizon of meanings (unlike the single Transcendency of Descartes). We are uncertain about

---

[9] In the terminology of the 17th century, the issue was formulated in terms of how the substances communicate. Descartes distinguished between two substances (e.g., Leibniz, 1686): matter (*res extensa*) and thought (*res cogitans*). In the Catholic religion the two are mediated in the miracle of transubstantiation. But how can the mind know about the world using scientific reasoning about uncertainties? Leibniz assumed an *a priori* correspondence originating from God's creation. Others (e.g., Huygens) argued that one has to distinguish analytically between mathematical clarity and experimental uncertainty. Hypotheses then can be tested (Huygens [1690], 1888-1950, Vol. XXI, at p. 541; Elzinga, 1972, at p. 37). From our sociological perspective, the question remains of what generates the hypotheses? Are these individual ideas, transpersonal mathematics, or intersubjective discourses? For Leibniz these three possible sources of variation were harmonized at a single (transcendental) origin (Leydesdorff, 1994c). The evolutionary dynamics among these three dimensions were addressed from philosophical perspectives by Popper (1972) and Hull (2001), among others.

what things mean, and this generates an intersubjectivity which transcends individual subjectivity. Although meanings are structured at the supra-individual level, these structures are no longer necessarily identified with a personal God.[10] On the contrary, meaning can be constructed, enriched, and reproduced among human beings by using language. Husserl acknowledged this function of language for the generation of meaning when he formulated for example: 'The beginning is the pure and one might say still mute experience which first has to be brought into the articulation of its meaning' (*ibid.*, p. 40).

Unlike Habermas who proposed to ground (Schutz's) 'lifeworld' in language, Husserl grounds the act of doubt in *noesis*, that is, a knowledgeable awareness of the structuredness of experiences. This formal awareness generates an intentionality in the present which can be communicated among human beings as meaningful. Husserl calls this intentionality transcendental because it precedes its articulation in language. Language can then be considered as a first-order ('natural') medium for the communication. However, the *noesis* abstracts from everyday language by adding the reflexivity of the knowing subject who can remain aware of his/her intentionality in communicating. Note that this awareness accompanies the expression in communication at a level which remains 'epi' rather than 'meta.'

By using language one is able to relate meanings to one another, but within language the world is resurrected as an architecture in which the words additionally can be provided with a position as concepts. This *cogitatum* can only be grasped by a reflexive agent in an intentional performance analogous to capturing the operation of one's own *cogito*. Husserl emphasized that the substance of the social system ('intersubjectivity') is different because one knows it *ex ante* as transcending the domain of the individual. The study of this new domain would provide us with 'a concrete ontology and a theory of science' (*ibid.*, at p. 159). However, Husserl concedes that he has no instruments beyond the transcendental apperception of this domain and therefore he has to refrain from empirical investigation:

> We must forgo a more precise investigation of the layer of meaning which provides the human world and culture, as such, with a specific meaning and therewith provides this world with specifically "mental" predicates. (Husserl, 1929, at p. 138; my translation).

---

[10] I leave the relation with Spinoza's philosophy out of consideration here. For Spinoza, all structure is transcendental and therefore within God. This leads to pantheism.

Intersubjectivity precedes objectivity in the world (*ibid.*, at p. 160) because the world is represented within it, for example, by using language. Phenomena remain an instantiation. First, the experience of the phenomenological world may be common sense (for example, using natural languages), but the meanings provided to what is represented can further be codified as in scientific discourse. Thus, the system is grounded in inter-subjective knowledge that is generated historically within the system. As noted, intersubjective knowledge can further be codified into discursive knowledge under historically specifiable conditions.

The order of priority itself changes with Husserl's reflection: the *cogitatum* provides a necessary condition for the *cogito*, although the latter remains a historical condition for the former. Husserl used the word 'rooting' for the historical origins, but he emphasized that the intentionality develops in the present. As noted, Husserl was not able to specify the 'mental' predicates which he hypothesized other than as an analogy to the categories of philosophical reflection within the *cogito*. I submitted in this study that the mathematical theory of communication provides us with these categories, and the theory of anticipatory systems provides us with categories for studying their evolution.[11]

First, Shannon's (1948) theory of communication can be elaborated for systems which communicate in more than a single dimension at the same time (Chapter Two; Theil, 1972). Human language can be considered as the evolutionary step that enables us to communicate both (Shannon-type) information and meaning. Meaningful information was distinguished from Shannon-type information as an interaction term between these two layers of processing. However, meaning is provided from the perspective of hindsight. Thus, the arrow of time is locally inverted. This was modeled using Rosen's (1985) theory of anticipatory systems. Although Rosen's model was developed within theoretical biology, the model can be made more general by mathematization in terms of incursive routines (Dubois, 1998; 2000). The incursive operation is recursive: some meanings can be provided with meaning in a scientific discourse and thus be further codified.

---

[11] Künzler (1987, at p. 331) formulated that 'between Luhmann's marginalization of language (cf. Habermas, 1985, at p. 438) and Habermas's foundation of sociology in the theory of language, one should be able to find the comparatively innocent consideration of meaning as the *ratio essendi* of language and language as the *ratio cognoscendi* of meaning' (my translation). My argument, however, goes beyond this position because I argue that codified knowledge in a functionally differentiated configuration can only be analyzed by invoking codes of communication generalized at a level beyond human language.

Two anticipatory mechanisms at a systems level can co-evolve hyper-incursively into a strongly anticipatory system. The one anticipation is contained, for example, in the demarcation of scientific communications from differently coded ones (e.g., on the market), and the other precedes differentiation and is inherent to specifying meaning among human beings using language. Thus, the formal and informal layers of communication are always intertwined. However, they can be distinguished analytically. The analytical dimensions abstract from the observable world. One might say that the models provide us with a 'genomenology' in which we are able to specify the 'genotypes' as analytically different routines without a one-to-one relation with observable phenomena. The models remain our constructs in language and *noesis*.

11.7.2 *Husserl's phenomenology and social genomenologies*

The formal perspective of mathematics which abstracts from the contents of respective models enables us to think of inter-subjectivity as an interaction effect grounded in an inter-textuality or even an inter-disciplinarity among perspectives. Phenomena can be expected to contain interaction terms among the genomena. The subdynamics of the genomenological organization of the complex system are first abstracted analytically from the substantive categories that have been made available to us in the positive sciences (e.g., variation and selection) by appreciating these substantive insights as the specifications of subdynamics. The historical phenomena can then be reconstructed as the results of interactions among the reflections. Culture and civilization thus remain constructs that feed back on what is 'naturally' or previously given. The feedbacks operate in an anticipatory mode. The sciences are part and parcel of the knowledge bases of this transformative culture. The external references of the communication can be considered as a reality 'out there,' but these 'realities' have been constructed reflexively and therefore invested with meaning.

In economics, for example, this new meaning provided by the reconstruction can be appreciated as the value of commodities on the market. The values are shaped by market forces (under the conditions of modernity). Thus, in addition to commodities, capital and shares can also be traded. Since Newton the concepts of physics (like centers of gravity and gravitation) have been theoretical constructs that can be provided with an interpretation by the experiment. These concepts have highly codified meanings. Maturana (2000, at p. 169) formulated this as an 'interobjectivity that we observers in language live as operations in the flow of languaging in which we observers exist.' Our frame of reference, in my opinion, is not the 'we' of the aggregate of living subjects, but the interactive development of this 'interobjectivity' as a *cogitatum*.

The phenomena in this 'interobjectivity' can be considered as stabilizations based on quasi-equilibria among the fluxes of communications. The stabilizations occur historically as instantiations among other potentially possible ones. How can the knowledge-based operations which reproduce the phenomena as a knowledge-based system be specified? Let me quote Husserl one more time:

> This, the *cogitatum as cogitatum* can never be imagined as a readily available given; it becomes clear by the specification of the horizon and the continuously regenerated horizons. The specification itself is yet always imperfect, but because of its uncertainty to be considered as a structure of determination. For example, the cube leaves perspectives open on the sides which cannot be seen, and nevertheless as a cube conceptualized [...]. This openness precedes the real specification in more detail. [...] Real observing—unlike abstract clarification in the anticipating imagination—leads to more precise specification and perhaps differentiation, but with new horizons opening. (*ibid.*, at pp. 47f.; my translation).

Note the emphasis on 'anticipating imagination' and the analogy between the metaphor of a cube and Hofstadter's triplet Gödel-Escher-Bach provided in Figure 4.3 above. I have argued (in Chapter Two) that the positive sciences (e.g., biology) tend to begin with observations, but in sociology this approach has led to positivism. On the basis of *a priori* decisions, the stabilization of facts would then be given priority over the meanings of these facts. This generates only one perspective among other possible ones. When this configuration is reflected, observations in the past can be turned into expectations about the future provided that a code in the communication is stabilized for making the inference.

Sociological specification is neither able nor allowed to forget that the 'facts' contain meanings and thus already imply a perspective. This double perspective is the very subject of methodological reflection in the discipline. Next-order, symbolic, and global horizons can be expected to resonate within hitherto stabilized meanings. Further reflections bring the meanings and the tensions among them to the fore. Meanings can be subjective and/or intersubjective. Intersubjective meanings can further be codified, for example, by using symbolically generalized media of communication in addition to everyday languages. For example, science can be considered in a sociology of science as the specific subsystem of communication in which truth-finding operates as a symbolically generalized medium of communication.

The meaning of intersubjectivity could be specified by Husserl only from the perspective of the subjective *cogito*, but nevertheless as a genomenon—a monade—that transcends the individual *cogito*. Other authors, e.g. Levinas (1953, 1963), have argued in favor of the foundation of intersubjectivity in the relation with the other human being ('Thou') as a transcendental instance. In sociology, however, the contingent other provides an instance of a double contingency, while—as was argued above—the configuration can modulate this relation as a third source of the uncertainty. Three sources of uncertainty can no longer be envisaged within a single metaphor. Since the metaphors are then no longer 'natural,' the systems under study tend to become visible as knowledge-based constructions that remain under reconstruction.

In summary, the hyper-incursive routine of a knowledge-based system remains the result of the intentionality of the carriers, but this is not a sufficient condition for the emergence of an order of expectations at the systems level. The groupings and the interactions of weak anticipations in social formations need first to be developed into a differentiated communication structure that contains another asynchronicity and, therefore, potential incursion endogenously. Insofar as this second incursion resonates with our weak anticipations and predictions, the intersubjectivity can become an interobjectivity. This remains always a matter of degree because the strongly anticipatory system *co*-constructs our future on the basis of organizational formats that are entertained in knowledge-based representations.

Because of the expectation of incompleteness and fragmentation of the codifications in the differentiated system, the formal reflection cannot guide us as a grandiose meta-theory. However, it is available and needed at the *epi*-level (that is, around) to increase the clarity of the substantive reflections. Simulations inform expectations in quasi-experiments in measuring the knowledge bases of historically stabilized systems. The models no longer need to be 'history friendly' or grounded in the evolutionary metaphor of survival. The emerging knowledge base is not a living system, but a social system. It rests like a hyper-network on the networks on which it builds. As a hypercycle, the knowledge-based subdynamics transform 'the ship while a storm is raging on the open sea.' In the resulting economy this reconstruction is no longer a mission only for the scientists involved (Leydesdorff, 2006a). The matching of knowledge-based anticipations and innovative reconstruction on this basis has been woven into the complex dynamics of the social system and its economy as one of its coordination mechanisms.

References

Abbate, J. (1999). *Inventing the Internet*. Cambridge, MA: MIT Press.

Abernathy, W. J., and J. Utterback (1978). Patterns of Industrial Innovation. *Technology Review*, 50, 41-47.

Abernathy, W. J., and K. B. Clark (1985). Innovation: Mapping the Winds of Creative Destruction. *Research Policy*, 14(1), 3-22.

Abramowitz, M. (1956). Resource and Output Trends in the United States since 1870. *American Economic Review*, 46, 5-23.

Abramowitz, M., and P. A. David (1996). Measuring Performance of Knowledge-Based Economy. In *Employment and Growth in the Knowledge-Based Economy* (pp. 35-60). Paris: OECD.

Abramson, N. (1963). *Information Theory and Coding*. New York, etc.: McGraw-Hill.

Aczel, P. (1987). Lectures in Nonwellfounded Sets. *CLSI Lecture Notes*, 9.

Ahrweiler, P. (1995). *Künstliche Intelligenz-Forschung in Deutschland. Die Etablierung eines Hochtechnologie-Fachs [Artificial Intelligence Research in Germany: The Establishment of a High-Tech Field]*. Münster and New York: Waxmann.

Alchian, A. A. (1950). Uncertainty, Evolution, and Economic Theory. *Journal of Political Economy*, 58, 211-221.

Alexander, P. J. (1996) Entropy and Popular Culture: Product diversity in the popular music recording industry. *American Sociological Review*, 61(1), 171-174.

Allen, P. M. (1994). Evolutionary Complex Systems: Models of Technology Change. In L. Leydesdorff and P. Van den Besselaar (Eds.), *Evolutionary Economic and Chaos Theory: New Directions in Technology Studies* (pp. 1-18). London and New York: Pinter.

Amsterdamska, O., and L. Leydesdorff (1989). Citations: Indicators of Significance? *Scientometrics*, 15, 449-471.

Andersen, E. S. (1994). *Evolutionary Economics: Post-Schumpeterian Contributions*. London: Pinter.

Anderson, P. W., K. J. Arrow, and D. Pines (Eds.). (1988). *The Economy as a Complex Evolving System*. Reading, MA: Addison-Wesley.

Anderson, P., and M. L. Tushman (1990). Technological Discontinuities and Dominant Designs: A Cyclical Model of Technological Change. *Administrative Science Quarterly*, 35, 604-633.

Anderson, P., and M. L. Tushman (1991). Managing through cycles of technological change, *Research-Technology Management*, 34(3), 26-31.

Aoki, M. (2001). *Towards a Comparative Institutional Analysis*. Cambridge, MA: MIT Press.

Archer, M. S. (1995). *Realist Social Theory: The Morphogenetic Approach*. Cambridge, UK: Cambridge University Press.

Arrow, K. J. (1962). The Economic Implications of Learning by Doing. *Review of Economic Studies*, 29, 155-173.

Arthur, W. B. (1988). Competing Technologies. In G. Dosi, C. Freeman, R. Nelson, G. Silverberg, and L. Soete (Ed.), *Technical Change and Economic Theory* (pp. 590-607.). London: Pinter.

Arthur, W. B. (1989). Competing Technologies, Increasing Returns, and Lock-in by Historical Events. *Economic Journal,* 99 (116-131.

Arthur, W. B. (1994). *Increasing Returns and Path Dependence in the Economy.* Ann Arbor: University of Michigan Press.

Arthur, W. B., S. N. Durlauf, and D. A. Lane (Eds.). (1997). *The Economy as an Evolving Complex System II.* Redwood, CA: Addison-Wesley.

Ashby, R. (1958). Requisite Variety and Its Implications for the Control of Complex Systems. *Cybernetica,* 1 (2), 1-17.

Ashmore, M. (1989). *The Reflexivity Thesis: Wrighting Sociology of Scientific Knowledge.* Chicago and London: Chicago University Press.

Audretsch, D. B., and M. Fritsch (1994). On the Measurement of Entry Rates, *Empirica,* 21, 105-113.

Axelrod, R. (1997). *The Complexity of Cooperation: agent-based models of competition and collaboration.* Princeton: Princeton University Press.

Bachratz, P., and M. S. Baratz (1963). Decisions and Nondecisions: An Analytical Framework. *American Political Science Review,* 57, 641-651.

Baecker, D. (Ed.) (1993). *Kalkül der Form.* Frankfurt a. M.: Suhrkamp [English translation: *Problems of Form.* Stanford: Stanford University Press, 1999].

Baecker, D. (1999). *Organisation als System.* Frankfurt a.M.: Suhrkamp.

Baecker, D. (2002). *Wozu Systeme?* Berlin: Kulturverlag Kadmos.

Baecker, D. (2005). *Form und Formen der Kommunikation.* Frankfurt a.M.: Suhrkamp.

Bailey, K. D. (1994). *Sociology and the New Systems Theory.* New York: State University of New York Press.

Bailey, N. T. J. (1957). *The Mathematical Theory of Infectious Diseases and Its Applications.* London: Charles Giffin and Co.

Bak, P., and K. Chen (1991). Self-Organized Criticality,. *Scientific American,* January 1991, 1926-1933.

Barabási, A.-L. (2002). *Linked: The New Science of Networks.* Cambridge, MA: Perseus Publishing.

Bar-Hillel, Y. (1955). An Examination of Information Theory. *Phil. Sci.,* 22, 86-105.

Bar-Ilan, J. (2001). Data collection methods on the Web for informetric purposes—A review and analysis. *Scientometrics, 50(1),* 7-32.

Barnes, B., and D. Edge (Eds.). (1982). *Science in Context.* Cambridge, MA: MIT Press.

Barras, R. (1990). Interactive Innovation in Financial and Business Services: The Vanguard of the Service Revolution. *Research Policy,* 19, 215-237.

Barwise, J., and L. Moss (1991). Hypersets. *Mathematical Intelligencer,* 13 (4), 31-41.

Bateson, G. (1972). *Steps to an Ecology of Mind.* New York: Ballantine.

Bathelt, H. (2003). Growth Regimes in Spatial Perspective 1: Innovation, Institutions and Social Systems. *Progress in Human Geography,* 27(6), 789-804.

Bazerman, C. (1988). *Shaping Written Knowledge: The Genre and Activity of the Experimental Article in Science.* Madison, WI: University of Wisconsin Press.

Beccatini, G., M. Bellandi, G. Dei Ottati, and F. Sforzi (2003). *From Industrial Districts to Local Development: An Itinerary of Research.* Cheltenham, UK; Northhampton, MA: Edward Elgar.

Beck, U. (1992a). *Risk Society. Towards a New Modernity*. London, etc.: Sage.

Beck, U. (1992b). From Industrial Society to the Risk Society: Questions of Survival, Social Structure and Ecological Enlightenment. *Theory, Culture and Society*, 9, 97-123.

Beck, U., W. Bonns, and C. Lau (2003). The Theory of Reflexive Modernization: Problematic, Hypotheses and Research Program, *Theory, Culture and Society*, 20 (2), 1-33.

Bell, D. (1973). *The Coming of the Post-Industrial Society*. New York: Basic Books.

Benjamin, W. ([1936], 1963). *Das Kunstwerk im Zeitalter seiner technischen Reproduzierbarkeit : drei Studien zur Kunstsoziologie*. Frankfurt a.M.: Suhrkamp.

Berger, P. L., and T. Luckmann (1966). *The Social Construction of Reality: A Treatise in the Sociology of Knowledge*. Garden City: Doubleday.

Berman, M. (1982). *All That Is Solid Melts into Air: The Experience of Modernity*. New York: Simon and Schuster.

Bernstein, B. (1971). *Class, Codes and Control, Vol. 1: Theoretical Studies in the Sociology of Language*. London: Routledge and Kegan Paul.

Bernstein, R. B. (1995). *The New Constellation: The ethical-political horizons of modernity/postmodernity*. Cambridge, MA: MIT Press.

Bernstein, R. L., C. Rossier, R. v. Driel, M. Brunner, and G. Gerisch (1981). Folate Deaminase and Cyclic AMP Phosphodiesterase in Dictyostelium Discoideum: Their Regulation by Extracellular Cyclic AMP and Folic Acid. *Cell Differentiation*, 10, 79-86.

Bhaskar, R. (1975). *A Realist Theory of Science*. Leeds: Leeds Books Ltd.

Bhaskar, R. (1997). On the Ontological Status of Ideas, *Journal for the Theory of Social Behavior* 27(3), 139-147.

Bhaskar, R. (1998). Societies. In M. Archer, R. Bhaskar, A. Collier, T. Lawson and A. Norrie (Eds.), *Critical Realism: Essential Readings* (pp. 206-257). London and New York: Routledge.

Biagioli, M., and P. Galison (Eds.). (2003). *Scientific Authorship: Credit and Intellectual Property in Science*. New York: Routledge.

Biggiero, L. (1998). Italian Industrial Districts: A Triple Helix Pattern of Problem Solving. *Industry and Higher Eductation*, 12 (4), 227-234.

Biggiero, L. (2001). Self-organizing processes in building entrepreneurial networks: a theoretical and empirical investigation, *Human Systems Management*, 20, 209-222.

Bijker, W. E., T. P. Hughes, and T. J. Pinch (1987). *The Social Construction of Technological Systems. New Directions in the Sociology and History of Technology*. Cambridge, MA: MIT Press

Bilderbeek, R., P. den Hertog, G. Marklund, and I. Miles (1998). *Services in Innovation: Knowledge Intensive Business Services (KIBS) as C-producers of innovation*. STEP report no. S14S.

Black, G. R. (2003). *Keyword Patent Searching Online*, at http://www.keypatent.net/.

Blau, P. M., and R. Schoenherr (1971). *The Structure of Organizations*. New York: Basic Books

Blauwhof, G. (1994). Non-Equilibria Dynamics and the Sociology of Technology. In L. Leydesdorff and P. van den Besselaar (Eds.), *Evolutionary Economics and Chaos Theory: New Directions in Technology Studies* (pp. 152-166). London, etc.: Pinter.

Blauwhof, G. (1995). *The Non-Linear Dynamics of Technological Developments: An Exploration of Telecommunications Technology.* University of Amsterdam, Amsterdam.

Bloor, D. (1976). Knowledge and Social Imagery London, etc.: Routledge and Kegan Paul).

Blumer, H. (1969). *Symbolic Interactionism. Perspective and Method.* Englewood Cliffs: Prentice Hall.

Boerlijst, M., and P. Hogeweg (1992). Self-Structuring and Selection: Spiral Waves as a Substrate for Prebiotic Evolution. In C. G. Langton, C. Taylor, J. D. Farmer and S. Rasmussen (Eds.), *Artificial Life II* (Vol. II, pp. 255-276). Redwood City, CA: Addison-Wesley.

Boshouwers, S. (1997). *In-Formare: De Wereld van het Kensysteem,* Unpublished MA Thesis, Cognitive Artificial Intelligence, Utrecht University.

Braczyk, H.-J., P. Cooke, and M. Heidenreich (Eds.) (1998). *Regional Innovation Systems.* London and Bristol PA: University College London Press.

Braverman, H. (1974). *Labor and Monopoly Capital. The Degradation of Work in the Twentieth Century.* New York and London: Monthly Review Press.

Brillouin, L. (1962). *Science and Information Theory.* New York: Academic Press.

Brookes, B.C. (1979). The Bradford Law: A new calculus for the social sciences? *Journal of the American Society for Information Science,* 30, 233-234.

Brookman, F. H. (1983). The Development of Science Policy in the Netherlands, 1945-1975. *Science and Public Policy,* 10(3), 134-141.

Brooks, Daniel R., and E. O. Wiley (1986). *Evolution as Entropy.* Chicago and London: University of Chicago Press.

Brown, G. S. (1969). *Laws of Form.* London: George Allen and Unwin.

Brown, G. S. (1993/94), Self-reference, Distinctions and Time, *Teoria Sociologica,* 2-3(1), 47-53.

Bruckner, E., W. Ebeling, M. A. J. Montaño, and A. Scharnhorst (1994). Hyperselection and Innovation Described by a Stochastic Model of Technological Evolution. In L. Leydesdorff and P. van den Besselaar (Eds.), *Evolutionary Economics and Chaos Theory: New Directions in Technology Studies* (pp. 79-90). London: Pinter.

Brusoni, S., A. Prencipe, and K. Pavitt (2000). Knowledge Specialization and the Boundaries of the Firm: Why Do Firms Know More Than They Make? *Administrative Science Quarterly,* 46, 597-621.

Bundesamt für Bauwesen und Raumordnung (BBR) (2002) *Aktuelle Daten zur Entwicklung der Städte, Kreise und Gemeinden, Ausgabe 2002,* Berichte, Band 14, Bonn: Federal Office for Building and Regional Planning.

Burt, R. S. (1982). *Toward a Structural Theory of Action.* New York, etc.: Academic Press.

Bush, V. (1945). *The Endless Frontier: A Report to the President.* Reprinted New York: Arno Press, 1980.

Butler, D. (2000). Souped-up search engines,. *Nature,* Vol. 405, 11 May 2000, 2112-2115.

Callon, M. (1986). The Sociology of an Actor Network: The Case of the Electric Vehicle. In M. Callon, J. Law and A. Rip (Eds.), *Mapping the Dynamics of Science and Technology* (pp. 19-34). London: Macmillan.

Callon, M. (1998). *The Laws of the Market.* Oxford and Malden, MA: Blackwell.

Callon, M., and B. Latour (1981). Unscrewing the big Leviathan: how actors macro-structure reality and how sociologists help them to do so. In K. D. Knorr-Cetina and A. V. Cicourel (Eds.), *Advances in Social Theory and Methodology.Toward an Integration of Micro- and Macro-Sociologies* (pp. 277-303). London: Routledge and Kegan Paul.

Callon, M., C. Méadel, and V. Rabeharisoa (2002). The Economy of Qualities. *Economy and Society*, 31 (2), 194-217.

Camacho, E. F., and C. Bordons (1999). *Model Predictive Control*. London: Springer Verlag.

Carlsson, B. (Ed.). (2002). *New Technological Systems in the Bio Industries -- an International Study*. Boston/Dordrecht/London: Kluwer Academic Publishers.

Carlsson, B. (2006). Internationalization of Innovation Systems: A Survey of the Literature. *Research Policy*, 35(1), 56-67.

Carlsson, B., and R. Stankiewicz (1991). On the Nature, Function, and Composition of Technological Systems. *Journal of Evolutionary Economics*, 1 (2), 93-118.

Carter, A. P. (1996). Measuring the Performance of a Knowledge-Based Economy. In D. Foray and B. A. Lundvall (Eds.), *Employment and Growth in the Knowledge-Based Economy* (pp. 61-68). Paris: OECD.

Casson, M. (1997). *Information and Organization: A New Perspective on the Theory of the Firm*. Oxford: Clarendon Press.

Castells, M. (1996). *The Rise of the Network Society*. Oxford and Malden, MA: Blackwell.

Casti, J. L. (1989). *Alternate Realities*. New York, etc.: Wiley.

Casti, J. L. (1990). *Paradigms Lost: Images of Man in the Mirror of Science*. London: Scribners.

CBS (2003). *Kennis en Economie 2003: Onderzoek en innovatie in Nederland*. Voorburg/Heerlen: Centraal Bureau voor de Statistiek.

Chandler, A. D. (1962). *Strategy and Structure*. Cambridge, MA: MIT Press.

Cimoli, M. (Ed.). (2000). *Developing Innovation Systems: Mexico in a Global Context*. London: Continuum.

Cohen, H. F. (1994). *The Scientific Revolution: A Historiographical Inquiry*. Chicago, IL: University of Chicago Press.

Cohen, W. M., and D. A. Levinthal (1989). Innovation and Learning: The two faces of R&D, *The Economic Journal*, 99, 569-596.

Comte, A. ([1838], 1864). *Cours de Philosophie Positive* (Vol. IV). Paris: Ballière.

Cook, T., and D. Campbell (1979). *Quasi-Experimentations: Design and Analysis Issues for Field-Settings*. Boston: Houghton Mifflin Company.

Cooke, P. (2002). *Knowledge Economies*. London: Routledge.

Cooke, P., and L. Leydesdorff (2006). Regional Development in the Knowledge-Based Economy: The Construction of Advantages. *Journal of Technology Transfer*, 31(1), 5-15.

Coser, R. L. (1975). The Complexity of Roles as a Seedbed of Individual Autonomy. In L. A. Coser (Ed.), *The Idea of Social Structure. Papers in Honor of Robert K. Merton* (pp. 237-264). New York and Chicago: Harcourt Brace Jovanovich.

Council of the European Communities, and Commission of the European Communities (1992) *Treaty on European Union*. Luxemburg: Office for Official Publications of the European Communities.

Coveney, P., and R. Highfield (1990). *The Arrow of Time*. London: Allen.

Cowan, R., and D. Foray (1997). The Economics of Codification and the Diffusion of Knowledge. *Industrial and Corporate Change*, 6, 595-622.

Cowan, R., P. David, and D. Foray (2000). The Explicit Economics of Knowledge Codification and Tacitness. *Industrial and Corporate Change*, 9(2), 211-253.

Cowan, R., and D. Foray (2002). Evolutionary Economics and the Counterfactual Threat: On the Nature and Role of Counterfactual History as an Empirical Tool in Economics. *Journal of Evolutionary Economics*, 12 (5), 539-562.

ČSSR (1968). *Action Programme of the Communist Party of Czechoslovakia*. Prague: Svoboda.

Danell, R., and O. Persson (2003). Regional R&D Activities and Interaction in the Swedish Triple Helix. *Scientometrics*, 58(2), 205-218.

Dasgupta, P., and P. David (1994). Towards a New Economics of Science. *Research Policy*, 23(5), 487-522.

David, P. A. (1985). Clio and the Economics of QWERTY. *American Economic Review*, 75, 332-337.

David, P. A. (1999). *At Last, a Remedy for Chronic QWERTY-Skepticism!* Paper presented at the European Summer School in Industrial Dynamics (ESSID), held at the Institute d'Étude Scientifique de Cargèse, Cargèse (Corse), 5-12 September.

David, P. A. (2000). Path Dependence and Varieties of Learning in the Evolution of Technological Practice. In J. Ziman (Ed.), *Technological Innovation as an Evolutionary Process* (pp. 118-133). Cambridge and New York: Cambridge University Press.

David, P. A., and D. Foray (2002). An Introduction to the Economy of the Knowledge Society. *International Social Science Journal*, 54 (171), 9-23.

De Gregori, T. R. (1986) Technology and Negative Entropy: Continuity or Catastrophy? *Journal of Economic Issues*, 20(2), 463-469.

De Rosa Pires, A., and E. A. de Castro (1997). Can a Strategic Project for a University Be Strategic to Regional Development? *Science and Public Policy*, 24 (1), 15-20.

De Zeeuw, G. (1993). Improvement and Research: A Paskian Evolution. *Systems Research*, 10(3), 193-203.

Dei Ottati, G. (2003). Local Governance and Industrial Districts' Competitive Advantage. In G. Beccatini, M. Bellandi, G. D. Ottati and F. Sforzi (Eds.), *From Industrial Districts to Local Development: An Itinerary of Research* (pp. 108-130). Cheltenham, UK and Northhampton, MA: Edward Elgar.

Depew, D. J., and B. H. Weber (1994). *Darwinism Evolving: Systems Dynamics and the Genealogy of Natural Selection*. Cambridge, MA: MIT Press.

Derrida, J. (1974). *Edmund Husserl's origine de la géometrie*. Paris: Presses Universitaires de France.

Descartes, R. (1637). *Discours de la méthode*. Amsterdam.

Devaney, R. (2003). *An Introduction to Chaotic Dynamical Systems* (2nd edition). Boulder, CO: Westview.

Dits, H., and G. Berkhout (1999). Towards a Policy Framework for the Use of Knowledge in Innovation Systems. *Journal of Technology Transfer*, 14, 211-221.

Dittrich, P., T. Kron, & W. Banzhaf (2003). On the Scalability of Social Order: Modeling the Problem of Double and Multi Contingency Following Luhmann. *Journal of Artificial Societies and Social Simulation*, 6(1), at

<http://jasss.soc.surrey.ac.uk/6/1/3.html>.

Dosi, G. (1982). Technological Paradigms and Technological Trajectories: A Suggested Interpretation of the Determinants and Directions of Technical Change. *Research Policy*, 11, 147-162.

Douglas, M. (1982). *Essays in the Sociology of Perception*. London: Routledge and Kegan Paul.

Dubois, D. M. (1998). Computing Anticipatory Systems with Incursion and Hyperincursion. In D. M. Dubois (Ed.), *Computing Anticipatory Systems: CASYS'97*, AIP Proceedings Volume 437, pp. 3-29. American Institute of Physics, New York: Woodbury.

Dubois, D. M. (2000). Review of Incursive, Hyperincursive and Anticipatory Systems — Foundation of Anticipation in Electromagnetism. In D. M. Dubois (Ed.), *Computing Anticipatory Systems CASYS'99*. AIP Proceedings Vol. 517, pp. 3-30. Melville, NY: American Institute of Physics.

Dubois, D. M. (2001). Theory of Incursive Synchronization and Application of a Chaotic Epidemic. *International Journal of Computing Anticipatory Ssystems*, 10, 3-18.

Dubois, D. M. (2002). Theory of Incursive Synchronization of Delayed Systems and Anticipatory Computing of Chaos. In R. Trappl (Ed.), *Cybernetics and Systems* (Vol. 1, pp. 17-22). Vienna: Austrian Society for Cybernetic Studies.

Dubois, D. M. (2003). Mathematical Foundation of Discrete and Functional Systems with Strong and Weak Anticipation. In M. V. Butz, O. Sigaud and P. Gérard (Eds.), *Anticipatory Behavior in Adaptive Learning Systems*. Lecture Notes in Computer Science 2684. Heidelberg: Springer.

Dubois, D. M., and Ph. Sabatier (1998). Morphogenesis by Diffuse Chaos in Epidemiological Systems, In D. M. Dubois (Ed.), *Computing Anticipatory Systems CASYS – First International Conference* (Vol. 437, pp.295-308). Woodbury, NY: Amercian Institute of Physics.

Dubois, D., and G. Resconi (1992). *Hyperincursivity: A New Mathematical Inquiry*. Liège: Presses Universitaires de Liège.

Dupree, A. H., and T. Parsons (1976). The Relations between Biological and Sociocultural Theory. *Zygon: journal of religion and science*, 11(3), 163.

Durkheim, E. (1930). *De la division du travail social*. Paris.

Ebeling, W., and A. Scharnhorst (2000). Evolutionary Models of Innovation Dynamics. In D. Helbing, H. J. Herrmann, M. Schreckenberg, D. E. Wolf (Eds.), *Traffic and Granular Flow '99 – Social, Traffic, and Granular Dynamics* (pp. 43–56). Berlin: Springer.

Ebeling, W., T. Poeschel, and K.-F. Albrecht (1995). Entropy, Transinformation and Word Distribution of Information-Carrying Sequences. *Int. J. Bifurcation and Chaos*, 5, 51; at http://arxiv.org/abs/cond-mat/?0204045

Edelman, G. M. (1989). *The Remembered Present: A Biological Theory of Consciousness*. New York: Basic Books.

Edqvist, C. (Ed.) (1997). *Systems of Innovation: Technologies, Institutions and Organizations*. London: Pinter.

Edwards, P. (1996). *The Closed World, Computers and the Politics of Discourses in Cold War America*, Cambridge, MA: MIT Press.

Eigen, M., and P. Schuster (1979). *The Hypercycle: A Principle of Natural Self-Organization*. Berlin: Springer.

Eisenstein, E. L. (1979). *The Printing Press as an Agent of Change.* Cambridge: Cambridge University Press.

Eisenstein, E. L. (1983). *The Printing Revolution in Early Modern Europe.* Cambridge: Cambridge University Press.

Elkana, Y., J. Lederberg, R. K. Merton, A. Thackray, and H. Zuckerman (1978). *Toward a Metric of Science: The Advent of Science Indicators.* New York, etc.: Wiley.

Elmer, J. (1995). Blind Me with Science: Motifs of Observation and Temporality in Lacan and Luhmann. *Cultural Critique,* 30, 101-136.

Elzinga, A. (1972). *On a Research Program in Early Modern Physics.* Gothenburg: Akademiförlaget.

Elzinga, A. (1985). Research, Bureaucracy and the Drift of Epistemic Criteria. In B. Wittrock and A. Elzinga (Eds.), *The University Research System* (pp. 191-217). Stockholm: Almqvist and Wiksell.

Elzinga, A. (1992). The Theory of Epistemic Drift: A Way of Relating the Social and the Epistemic. *Revue Roumaine de Philosophie,* 36, 45-61.

Epstein, J. M., and R. Axtell (1996). *Growing Artificial Societies: Social Science from the Bottom Up.* Cambridge, MA: MIT Press.

Etzkowitz, H. (1994). Technology Centers and Industrial Policy: The Emergence of the Interventionist State in the USA. *Science and Public Policy,* 21(2), 79-87.

Etzkowitz, H. (1996). Losing Our Bearings: The Science Policy Crisis in Post-Cold War Eastern Europe, Former Soviet Union and USA. *Science and Public Policy,* 23(1), 13-26.

Etzkowitz, H. (2002). *MIT and the Rise of Entrepreneurial Science.* London: Routledge.

Etzkowitz, H., and L. Leydesdorff (1995). The Triple Helix---University-Industry-Government Relations: A Laboratory for Knowledge Based Economic Development. *EASST Review 14,* 14-19.

Etzkowitz, H., and L. Leydesdorff (Eds.) (1997). *Universities in the Global Knowledge Economy: A Triple Helix of University-Industry-Government Relations.* London: Pinter.

Etzkowitz, H., and L. Leydesdorff (1998). The Endless Transition: A "Triple Helix" of University-Industry-Government Relations. *Minerva,* 36, 203-208.

Etzkowitz, H., and L. Leydesdorff (2000). The Dynamics of Innovation: From National Systems and 'Mode 2' to a Triple Helix of University-Industry-Government Relations. *Research Policy,* 29 (2), 109-123.

Etzkowitz, H., A. Webster, C. Gebhardt, and B. R. C. Terra (2000). The Future of the University and the University of the Future: Evolution of Ivory Tower to Entrepreneurial Paradigm. *Research Policy,* 29 (2), 313-330.

European Commission (1997). *Targeted Socio-Economic Research (TSER): Work Programme Edition 1997.* Brussels, 1996.

European Commission (2000). *Towards a European research area.* Brussels, 18 January 2000; at http://europa.eu.int/comm/research/era/pdf/com2000-6-en.pdf .

European Commission (2005). *Working together for growth and jobs. A new start for the Lisbon Strategy;* at http://europa.eu.int/growthandjobs/pdf/COM2005_024_en.pdf

Eurostat (2003). Regulation (EC) No 1059/2003 of the European Parliament and of the Council of 26 May 2003 on the establishment of a common classification of territorial units for statistics (NUTS). *Official Journal of the European Union,* L 154, 21/06/2003; at http://europa.eu.int/eur-lex/pri/en/oj/dat/2003/l_154/l_15420030621en00010041.pdf.

Febvre, L., and H.-J. Martin (1950). *L'apparition du livre.* Paris: Albin Michel.

Federal Office for Building and Regional Planning (Bundesamt für Bauwesen und Raumordnung) (2002) *Aktuelle Daten zur Entwicklung der Städte, Kreise und Gemeinden, Ausgabe 2002*, Berichte, Band 14, Bonn: Federal Office for Building and Regional Planning.

Fisher, J. C., and R. H. Pry (1971). A Simple Substitution Model of Technological Change. *Technological Forecasting and Social Change*, 3, 75-88.

Foray, D. (2004). *The Economics of Knowledge.* Cambridge, MA/London: MIT Press.

Foray, D., and B.-A. Lundvall (1996). The Knowledge-Based Economy: From the Economics of Knowledge to the Learning Economy. In *OECD Documents: Employment and Growth in the Knowledge-Based Economy* (pp. 11-32). Paris: OECD.

Foucault, M. (1966). *Les mots et les choses: archéologie des sciences humaines.* Paris: Gallimard.

Foucault, M. (1972 [1969]). *The Archaeology of Knowledge.* New York: Pantheon.

Freeman, C. (1982). *The Economics of Industrial Innovation.* Harmondsworth: Penguin.

Freeman, C. (1987). *Technology Policy and Economic Performance: Lessons from Japan.* London: Pinter.

Freeman, C. (1988). Japan, a New System of Innovation. In G. Dosi, C. Freeman, R. R. Nelson, G. Silverberg and L. Soete (Eds.), *Technical Change and Economic Theory* (pp. 31-54). London: Pinter.

Freeman, C., and C. Perez (1988). Structural Crises of Adjustment, Business Cycles and Investment Behavior. In G. Dosi, C. Freeman, R. N. G. Silverberg and L. Soete (Eds.), *Technical Change and Economic Theory* (pp. 38-66). London: Pinter.

Frenken, K. (2000). A Complexity Approach to Innovation Networks. The Case of the Aircraft Industry (1909-1997), *Research Policy*, 29(2), 257-272.

Frenken, K. (2001). *Understanding Product Innovation Using Complex Systems Theory.* Amsterdam: Unpublished Ph. D. Thesis, University of Amsterdam.

Frenken, K. (2006). *Innovation, Evolution and Complexity Theory.* Cheltenham UK and Northampton MA: Edward Elgar.

Frenken, K., and L. Leydesdorff (2000). Scaling Trajectories in Civil Aircraft (1913-1970). *Research Policy*, 29 (3), 331-348.

Frenken, K., and L. Leydesdorff (2004). Scientometrics and the Evaluation of European Integration. Pp. 87-102 in J. Ulijn and T. Brown (Eds.), *Innovation, Entrepreneurship and Culture: The Interaction between Technology, Progress and Economic Growth.* Cheltenham, UK and Northhampton, MA: Edward Elgar Publishing.

Fritsch, M. (2004). R&D-Cooperation and the Efficiency of Regional Innovation Activities, *Cambridge Journal of Economics*, 28, 829-846.

Fritsch, M., and U. Brixy (2004): The Establishment File of the German Social Insurance Statistics, *Schmollers Jahrbuch / Journal of Applied Social Science Studies*, 124, 183-190.

Fritsch, M., and A. Stephan (2005). Regionalization of Innovation Policy – Introduction to the Special Issue, *Research Policy*, 34(8), 1123-1127.

Fritsch, M and C. Werker (1999). Systems of Innovation in Transition. In M. Fritsch and H. Brezinski (Eds.), *Innovation and Technological Change in Eastern Europe – Pathways to Industrial Recovery* (5-22). Cheltenham: Edward Elgar.

Fry, J. (2006). Scholarly Research and Information Practices: A Domain Analytic Approach. *Information Processing and Management*, 42(1), 299-316.

Fuchs, P. (2004). *Der Sinn der Beobachtung: Begriffliche Untersuchungen.* Velbrück: Weilerswist.

Fujigaki, Y. (1998). Filling the Gap between Discussions on Science and Scientists' Everyday Activities: Applying the Autopoiesis System Theory to Scientific Knowledge. *Social Science Information*, 37 (1), 5-22.

Fukuyama, F. (1992). *The End of History and the Last Man.* London: Hamilton.

Fukuyama, F. (2002). *Our Posthuman Future: Political Consequences of the Biotechnology Revolution.* New York: Farrar Straus and Giroux.

Galbraith, J. K. (1967). *The New Industrial State.* Penguin: Harmondsworth.

Galbraith, J. R., and D. A. Nathanson (1978). *Strategy Implementation: The Role of Structure and Process.* St. Paul, etc.: West Publishing Company.

Garfield, E. (1979). *Citation Indexing: Its Theory and Application in Science, Technology, and Humanities.* New York: John Wiley.

Geertz, C. (1973). *The Interpretation of Cultures.* New York: Basic Books.

Georgescu-Roegen, N. (1971). *The Entropy Law and the Economic Process.* Cambridge, MA: Harvard University Press.

Gerisch, G. (1968). Cell Aggregation and Differentiation in *Dictyostelium Discoideum*, *Developmental Biology* 3, 157-197.

Gibbons, M., C. Limoges, H. Nowotny, S. Schwartzman, P. Scott, and M. Trow (1994). *The New Production of Knowledge: The Dynamics of Science and Research in Contemporary Societies.* London: Sage.

Gibson, B. (2000). Practical Applications of Luhmann's Work: Observations from a Grounded Theory Perspective. *Luhmann On-Line*, 1 (4), at http://www.sociocyberforum.org/newsletter/lol_nwsltr_1n4.pdf

Giddens, A. (1976). *New Rules of Sociological Method.* London: Hutchinson.

Giddens, A. (1979). *Central Problems in Social Theory.* London, etc.: Macmillan.

Giddens, A. (1981). Agency, Institution, and Time-Space Analysis. In K. D. Knorr-Cetina and A. V. Cicourel (Eds.), *Advances in Social Theory and Methodology. Toward an Integration of Micro- and Macro-Sociologies* (pp. 161-174). London: Routledge and Kegan Paul.

Giddens, A. (1984). *The Constitution of Society.* Cambridge: Polity Press.

Giddens, A. (1992). *The Transformation of Intimacy: Sexuality, Love and Eroticism in Modern Societies.* Stanford, CA: Stanford University Press.

Gilbert, G. N. (1997). A Simulation of the Structure of Academic Science. *Sociological Research Online*, 2(2), http://www.socresonline.org.uk/socresonline/2/2/3.html.

Gilbert, G. Nigel, and Michael J. Mulkay (1984). *Opening Pandora's Box. A Sociological Analysis of Scientists' Discourse.* Cambridge: Cambridge University Press.

Glanville, R. (Ed.) (1996). Heinz von Foerster, a Festschrift. *Systems Research*, 13 (3), 191-432.

Glaser, B. G. (1992). *Emergence Vs Forcing: Basics of Grounded Theory Analysis.* Mill Valley, CA: Sociology Press.

Glaser, B. G., and A. Strauss (1967). *Discovery of Grounded Theory: Strategies for Qualitative Research.* Chicago: Aldine de Gruyter.

Godin, B. (2006). The Knowledge-Based Economy: Conceptual Framework or Buzzword. *Journal of Technology Transfer*, 31(1), 17-30; at http://www.csiic.ca/Pubs_Histoire.html .

Godin, B., and Y. Gingras (2000). The Place of Universities in the System of Knowledge Production. *Research Policy*, 29 (2), 273-278.

Goffman, E. M. (1959). *The Presentation of Self in Everyday Life.* Garden City, NY: Doubleday.

Goguen, J. A., and F. J. Varela (1979). Systems and distinctions: duality and complementarity, *International Journal of General Systems 5*, 31- 43.

Gouldner, A. W. (1976). *The Dialectic of Ideology and Technology.* London: Macmillan.

Graham, L. R. (1974). *Science and Philosophy in the Soviet Union.* New York: Vintage Books.

Granstrand, O. (1999). *The Economics and Management of Intellectual Property: Towards Intellectual Capitalism.* Cheltenham, UK: Edward Elgar.

Granstrand, O., P. Patel, and K. Pavitt (1997). Multitechnology Corporations: Why They Have 'Distributed' Rather Than 'Distinctive' Core Capabilities. *California Management Review*, 39, 8-25.

Grant, C. B. (2003). Complexities of Self and Social Communication. In C. B. Grant (Ed.), *Rethinking Communicative Interaction.* Amsterdam and Philadelphia: John Benjamins.

Grathoff, R. (Ed.) (1978). *The Theory of Social Action. The Correspondence of Alfred Schutz and Talcott Parsons.* Bloomington and London: Indiana University Press.

Greimas, A. J. (1983). *Du sens II: Essais sémiotiques.* Paris: Éditions du Seuil.

Groustra, I. (1995). *Monetaire Unie in de Habsburg-Bourgondische Nederlanden tussen 1489-1556.* Amsterdam: Faculty of Economics and Econometrics, University of Amsterdam.

Gumbrecht, H. U. (2003). *What Will Remain of Niklas Luhmann's Philosophy? A Daring (and Loving) Speculation.* Paper presented at The Opening of Systems Theory, Copenhagen, 23-25 May 2003.

Gunasekara, C. (2006). Reframing the Role of Universities in the Development of Regional Innovation Systems. *Journal of Technology Transfer* 31(1), 101-113.

Guston, D. (2000). *Between Politics and Science.* Cambridge, UK, etc.: Cambridge University Press.

Habermas, J. (1968). Technik und Wissenschaft als 'Ideologie'. *Technik und Wissenschaft als 'Ideologie'* (pp. 48-103). Frankfurt a.M.:Suhrkamp.

Habermas, J. (1974). *Strukturwandel der Öffentlichkeit.* Frankfurt a.M.: Suhrkamp.

Habermas, J. (1981). *Theorie des kommunikativen Handelns.* Frankfurt a.M.: Suhrkamp.

Habermas, J. (1987). Excursus on Luhmann's Appropriation of the Philosophy of the Subject through Systems Theory. In: *The Philosophical Discourse of Modernity: Twelve Lectures*, pp. 368-85. Cambridge, MA: MIT Press. [*Der philosophische Diskurs der Moderne: Zwölf Vorlesungen.* Frankfurt a.M.: Suhrkamp, 1985.]

Habermas, J., and N. Luhmann (1971). *Theorie der Gesellschaft oder Sozialtechnologie.* Frankfurt a.M.: Suhrkamp.

Hajer, M. (1993). Discourse-Coalitions and the Institutionalisation of Practice - the Case of Acid Rain in Britain. In J. Forester and F. Fischer (Eds.), *The Argumentative Turn in Policy Sciences and Planning* (pp. 43-76). Durham, NC: Duke University Press.

Hall, P. A., and D. W. Soskice (Eds.) (2001). *Varieties of Capitalism: The Institutional Foundations of Comparative Advantage*. Oxford, etc.: Oxford University Press.

Han, T. S. (1980). Multiple Mutual Information and Multiple Interactions in Frequency Data. *Informaiton and Control*, 46(1), 26-45.

Hanneman, R. (1988). *Computer-Assisted Theory Building: Modeling Dynamic Social Systems*. Newbury Park, CA.: Sage.

Hanneman, R. A., and Collins, R (1986). A dynamic simulation of Marx. In N. Wiley (Ed.), *The Marx/Weber Debate*. Newbury Park, CA.: Sage.

Haraway, D. (1988). Situated Knowledges: The Science Question in Feminism and the Privilege of Partial Perspective,. *Feminist Studies 14*, 575-599.

Hatzichronoglou, T. (1997). *Revision of the High-Technology Sector and Product Classification*. Paris: OECD; at

  http://www.olis.oecd.org/olis/1997doc.nsf/LinkTo/OCDE-GD(97)216 .

Hayles, N. K. (1990). *Chaos Bound; Orderly Disorder in Contemporary Literature and Science*. Ithaca, etc.: Cornell University.

Heertje, A. (1973). *Economie en Technische Ontwikkeling*. Leiden: Stenfert Kroese.

Hegel, G. W. F. (1952 [1807]). *Phänomenologie des Geistes*. Hamburg: Felix Meiner.

Heidegger, M. (1962). *Die Frage nach dem Ding* Tübingen: Max Niemeyer.

Hellsten, I., L. Leydesdorff, and P. Wouters (forthcoming). Multiple Presents: How Search Engines Re-write the Past, *New Media and Society* (In print).

Herrmann, T. (2001). *Kommunikation von Jugend. Analysen zur Jugend der Gesellschaft*. Kiel: Unpublished Ph.D. Thesis, Faculty of Philosophy, Christian-Albrechts-Universität.

Hesse, M. (1980). *Revolutions and Reconstructions in the Philosophy of Science*. London: Harvester Press.

Hesse, M. (1988). The Cognitive Claims of Metaphor, *The Journal of Speculative Philosophy*, 2(1), 1-16.

Hobbes, T. (1651). *The Leviathan*. New York: Prometheus Books, 1988.

Hollak, J. (1963). Hegel, Marx en de Cybernetica. *Tijdschrift voor Philosophie*, 25, 270-294.

Horkheimer, M., and T. W. Adorno (1969 [1947]). *Dialektik der Aufklärung*. Frankfurt a.M.: Fischer Verlag.

Hughes, T. P. (1987). The Evolution of Large Technological Systems. In W. Bijker, T. P. Hughes and T. Pinch (Eds.), *The Social Construction of Technological Systems* (pp. 51-82). Cambridge, MA: MIT Press.

Hull, D. L. (2001). *Science and Selection: Essays on Biological Evolution and the Philosophy of Science*. Cambridge, UK: Cambridge University Press.

Husserl, E. ([1929] 1973). *Cartesianische Meditationen und Pariser Vorträge*. [Cartesian meditations and the Paris lectures.] Edited by S. Strasser. The Hague: Martinus Nijhoff.

Husserl, E. (1936). Der Ursprung der Geometrie als Intentional-Historisches Problem. *Revue internationale de philosophie*, 1(2), 203-225.

Husserl, E. (1939). *Erfahrung und Urteil: Untersuchungen zur Genealogie der Logik*. Prag and Hamburg: Claassens and Goverts, 1948.

Husserl, E. (1962). *Die Krisis der Europäischen Wissenschaften und die Transzendentale Phänomenologie*. Den Haag: Martinus Nijhoff.

Huygens, C. (1888-1950). *Oeuvres Complètes*. Publ. Soc. Holl. des Sciences, 22 Vols. The Hague: Nijhoff.

Innis, H. A. (1950). *Empire and Communications*. Oxford: Clarendon Press.

Irvine, J., and B. R. Martin (1984). *Foresight in Science: Picking the Winners*. London: Frances Pinter.

Jaffe, A. B., and M. Trajtenberg (2002). *Patents, Citations, and Innovations: A Window on the Knowledge Economy*. Cambridge, MA and London: MIT Press.

Jakulin, A., and I. Bratko (2004). *Quantifying and Visualizing Attribute Interactions: An Approach Based on Entropy*, from http://arxiv.org/abs/cs.AI/0308002

Jensen, S. (1978). Interpenetration--Zum Verhältnis Personaler Und Sozialer Systeme? *Zeitschrift für Soziologie*, 7, 116-129.

Kampmann, C., C. Haxholdt, E. Mosekilde, and J. D. Sterman (1994). Entrainment in a Disaggregated Long-Wave Model. In L. Leydesdorff and P. van den Besselaar (Eds.), *Evolutionary Economics and Chaos Theory: New Directions in Technology Studies* (pp. 109-124). London and New York: Pinter.

Kaufer, D. S., and K. M. Carley (1993). *Communication at a Distance: The Influence of Print on Sociocultural Organization and Change*. Hillsdale NJ: Erlbaum.

Kauffman, L. H. (2001). The Mathematics of Charles Sanders Pierce. *Cybernetics and Human Knowing*, 8 (1-2), 79-110.

Kauffman, S. A. (1993). *The Origins of Order: Self-Organization and Selection in Evolution*. New York: Oxford University Press.

Kauffman, S. A. (2000). *Investigations*. Oxford, etc.: Oxford University Press.

Kemp, R., J. Schot, and R. Hoogma (1998). Regime Shifts to Sustainability through Processes of Niche Formation. The Approach of Strategic Niche Management. *Technology Analysis and Strategic Management*, 10 (2), 175-195.

Kermak, W. O., and A. G. McKendrick (1927). Contribution to the Mathematical Theory of Epidemics. *Proc. Roy. Soc. A*, 115 (700-721.

Khalil, E.L. (2004). The Three Laws of Thermodynamics and the Theory of Production, *Journal of Economic Issues*, 38(1), 201-226.

Khalil, E. L., and K. E. Boulding (Eds.) (1996). *Evolution, Order and Complexity*. London and New York: Routledge.

Kingston, W. (2003). *Innovation: The Creative Impulse in Human Progress*. Washington, DC: Leonard R. Sugerman Press.

Klepper, S. (1997). Industry Life-Cycles. *Industrial and Corporate Change*, 6, 145-182.

Kline, S., and N. Rosenberg (1986). An Overview of Innovation. In R. Landau and N. Rosenberg (Eds.), *The Positive Sum Strategy: Harnessing Technology for Economic Growth* (pp. 275-306). Washington, DC: National Academy Press.

Knorr-Cetina, K. D. (1982). Scientific Communities or Transepistemic Arenas of Research? A Critique of Quasi-Economic Models of Science. *Social Studies of Science*, 12, 101-130.

Knorr-Cetina, K. D. (1997). Sociality with Objects: Social Relations in Postsocial Knowledge Societies. *Theory, Culture and Society*, 14(4), 1-30.

Knorr-Cetina, K. D. (1999). *Epistemic Cultures: How the Sciences Make Knowledge*. Cambridge, MA: Harvard University Press.

Knorr-Cetina, K. D., and A. V. Cicourel (Eds.) (1981). *Advances in Social Theory and Methodology. Toward an Integration of Micro- and Macro-Sociologies* London: Routledge and Kegan Paul.

Kobayashi, S.-I. (2000). Applying Audition Systems from the Performing Arts to R&D Funding Mechanisms: Quality Control in Collaboration among the Academic, Public, and Private Sectors in Japan. *Research Policy*, 29(2), 181-192.

Krauss, G., and H.-G. Wolff (2002). Technological Strengths in Mature Sectors--an Impediment of an Asset of Regional Economic Restructuring? The Case of Multimedia and Biotechnology in Baden-Württemberg. *Journal of Technology Transfer,* 27 (1), 39-50.

Kristeva, J. (1980). *Desire in Language.* New York: Columbia University Press.

Krohn, W., G. Küppers, and H. Nowotny (Eds.) (1990). *Selforganization. Portrait of a Scientific Revolution.* Dordrecht: Reidel.

Kron, T. (Ed.). (2002). *Luhmann Modelliert: Sozionische Ansätze zur Simulation von Kommunikationssystemen.* Opladen: Leske and Budrich.

Krugman, P. (1996). *The Self-Organizing Economy.* Malden, MA, and Oxford: Blackwell.

Kuhn, T. S. (1962). *The Structure of Scientific Revolutions.* Chicago: University of Chicago Press.

Künzler, J. (1987). Grundlagenprobleme der Theorie Symbolisch Generalisierter Kommunikationsmedien bei Niklas Luhmann. *Zeitschrift für Soziologie,* 16(5), 317-333.

Künzler, J. (1989). *Medien und Gesellschaft: Die Medienkonzepte von Talcott Parsons, Jürgen Habermas und Niklas Luhmann.* Stuttgart: Ferdinand Enke Verlag.

Laafia, I. (1999). *Regional Employment in High Technology*: Eurostat; at http://europa.eu.int/comm/eurostat/Public/datashop/print-product/EN?catalogue=Eurostat&product=CA-NS-99-001-___-I-EN&mode=download .

Laafia, I. (2002a). Employment in High Tech and Knowledge Intensive Sectors in the EU Continued to Grow in 2001. *Statistics in Focus: Science and Technology,* Theme, 9(4), at http://europa.eu.int/comm/eurostat/Public/datashop/print-product/EN?catalogue=Eurostat&product=KS-NS-02-004-___-N-EN&mode=download .

Laafia, I. (2002b). National and Regional Employment in High Tech and Knowledge Intesive Sectors in the EU – 1995-2000. *Statistics in Focus: Science and Technology,* Theme 9(3), at http://europa.eu.int/comm/eurostat/Public/datashop/print-product/EN?catalogue=Eurostat&product=KS-NS-02-003-___-N-EN&mode=download .

Lancaster, K. J. (1979). *Variety, Equity and Efficiency.* New York: Columbia University Press.

Langford, C. H., R. D. Burch, and M. W. Langford (1997). The 'Well-Stirred Reactor': Evolution of Industry-Government- University Relations in Canada. *Science and Public Policy* 24(1), 21-27.

Langford, C., and M. Langford (2001). Funding Strategic University Research in Canada. *Paper presented at the Annual Meeting of the Society for the Social Studies of Science (4S),* Boston, MA, November 2001.

Langton, C. G. (1989). Artificial Life. In C. G. Langton (Ed.), *Artificial Life*. Redwood, etc.: Addison-Wesley, pp. 1-47.

Larédo, P. (2003). Six Major Challenges Facing Public Intervention in Higher Education, Science, Technology and Innovation. *Science and Public Policy*, 30 (1), 4-12.

Latour, B. (1987). *Science in Action*. Milton Keynes: Open University Press.

Latour, B. (1988). *The Pasteurization of France*. Cambridge, MA, and London: Harvard University Press.

Latour, B. (2003). Is *Re*-Modernization Occurring—And If So, How to Prove It? *Theory, Culture and Society*, 20(2), 35-48.

Lawrence, P. R., and J. W. Lorsch (1967). *Organization and Environment: Managing Differentiation and Integration*. Boston: Graduate School of Business Administration, Harvard University.

Lazarsfeld, P. F. (1995). Analyzing the Relations between Variables. In B. G. Barnes (Ed.), *Grounded Theory 1984-1994* (pp. 83-102). Mill Valley, CA: Sociology Press.

Lazarsfeld, P. F., and N. W. Henry (1968). *Latent Structure Analysis*. New York: Houghton Mifflin.

Lecourt, D. (1976). *Lyssenko: Histoire réelle d'une "science prolétarienne"*. Paris: Maspero.

Leibniz, G. W. (1692). Letter to Christiaan Huygens, 8 January 1692. In *Oeuvres Complètes* (Vol. X, p. 227). The Hague: Nijhoff, 1888-1950.

Leibniz, G. W. (1695). New Systems of the Nature and of the Communication of Substances, and of the Union between the Soul and the Body. *Journal des Savants*, June 1695.

Leibniz, G. W. (1710). *Essais de Théodicée sur la bonté de Dieu, la liberté de l'homme et l'origine du mal*. Paris: Aubier, 1962.

Leibniz, G. W. (^{3}1966). *Hauptschriften zur Grundlegung der Philosophie*. E. Cassirer (Ed.), Hamburg: Meiner.

Levinas, E. (1953). Liberté et Comandement. *Revue de Métaphysique et de Morale*, 58, 264-272.

Levinas, E. (1963). La Trace de l'Autre. *Tijdschrift voor Filosofie*, 25, 605-623.

Lewin, P. (Ed.) (2003). *The Economics of QWERTY: History, Theory, and Policy -- Essays by Stan J. Liebowitz and Stephen E. Margolis*. New York: New York University Press.

Lewontin, R. (2000). *The Triple Helix: Gene, Organism, and Environment*. Cambridge, MA/London: Harvard University Press.

Lewy, C. P. (1976). *Studies in Business Policy, Structure and Control in a Major Dutch Diversified Industrial Company*. Unpublished Ph.D. Thesis, Écoles des Hautes Études Commerciales, Université de Lausanne, Lausanne.

Leydesdorff, L. (1980). The Dutch Science Shops. *Trends in Biochemical Sciences*, 5(5), 1-2.

Leydesdorff, L. (1984). *Werknemers en het Technologisch Vernieuwingsbeleid*. Amersfoort: De Horstink.

Leydesdorff, L. (1986). The Development of Frames of References,. *Scientometrics*, 9, 103-125.

Leydesdorff, L. (1989). Words and Co-Words as Indicators of Intellectual Organization. *Research Policy*, 18, 209-223.

Leydesdorff, L. (1991). The Static and Dynamic Analysis of Network Data Using Information Theory. *Social Networks*, 13, 301-345.

Leydesdorff, L. (1992). "Self-Organization" as a Theme for Technology Studies. *EASST Newsletter*, 11(1), 10-13.

Leydesdorff, L. (1993a). 'Structure'/'Action' Contingencies and the Model of Parallel Distributed Processing, *Journal for the Theory of Social Behavior*, 23, 47-77.

Leydesdorff, L. (1993b). Is Society a Self-Organizing System? *Journal of Social and Evolutionary Systems* 16, 331-349.

Leydesdorff, L. (1993c). Why the Statement "Plasma-membrane Transport is Rate-limiting for its Metabolism in Rat-liver Parenchymal Cells" Cannot Meet the Public, *Public Understanding of Science*, 2, 351-364.

Leydesdorff, L. (1994a). The Evolution of Communication Systems, *Int. J. Systems Research and Information Science*, 6, 219-230.

Leydesdorff, L. (1994b). Epilogue. In L. Leydesdorff and P. van den Besselaar (Eds.), *Evoluticonary Economics and Chaos Theory: New Directions for Technology Studies* (pp. 180-192). London and New York: Pinter.

Leydesdorff, L. (1994c). Uncertainty and the Communication of Time, *Systems Research*, 11, 31-51.

Leydesdorff, L. (1995a). *The Challenge of Scientometrics: The Development, Measurement, and Self-Organization of Scientific Communications.* Leiden: DSWO Press, Leiden University; at http://www.upublish.com/books/leydesdorff-sci.htm.

Leydesdorff, L. (1995b). The Operation of the Social System in a Model based on Cellular Automata. *Social Science Information, 34*(3), 413-441.

Leydesdorff, L. (1996a). Luhmann's Sociological Theory: Its Operationalization and Future Perspectives. *Social Science Information*, 35, 283-306.

Leydesdorff, L. (1996b). The Possibility of a Mathematical Sociology of Scientific Communications. *Journal for General Philosophy of Science* 27, 243-265.

Leydesdorff, L. (1996c). *Is a General Theory of Communications Emerging?* Paper presented at the Emergence - Complexité Hiérarchique - Organisation: Modèles de la boucle évolutive. Actes du Symposium ECHO, Amiens.

Leydesdorff, L. (1997a). The Non-linear Dynamics of Sociological Reflections. *International Sociology*, 12 (1), 25-45.

Leydesdorff, L. (1997b). The 'Post-Institutional' Perspective: Society as an Emerging System with Dynamically Changing Boundaries. *Soziale Systeme*, 3, 361-378.

Leydesdorff, L. (1997c). Why Words and Co-Words Cannot Map the Development of the Sciences, *Journal of the American Society for Information Science*, 48(5), 418-427.

Leydesdorff, L. (1997d). The New Communication Regime of University-Industry-Government Relations. In H. Etzkowitz and L. Leydesdorff (Eds.), *Universities and the Global Knowledge Economy* (pp. 106-117). London and Washington: Pinter.

Leydesdorff, L. (1997e). Sustainable Technological Developments and Second-Order Cybernetics. *Technology Analysis and Strategic Management*, 9(3), 329-341.

Leydesdorff, L. (1998). Theories of Citation? *Scientometrics*, 43 (1), 5-25.

Leydesdorff, L. (2000a). Are EU Networks Anticipatory Systems? An Empirical and Analytical Approach. In D. M. Dubois (Ed.), *Computing Anticipatory Systems—Casys'99*. Woodbury, NY: American Institute of Physics.

Leydesdorff, L. (2000b). The Triple Helix: An Evolutionary Model of Innovations. *Research Policy*, 29(2), 243-255.

Leydesdorff, L. (2000c). Is the European Union Becoming a Single Publication System? *Scientometrics*, 47 (2), 265-280.

Leydesdorff, L. (2000d). Luhmann, Habermas, and the Theory of Communication, *Systems Research and Behavioral Science* 17, 273-288.

Leydesdorff, L. (2000e). A Triple Helix of University-Industry-Government Relations, *Scipolicy—The Journal of Science and Health Policy*, Vol. 1, No. 1 (2000), 51-60

Leydesdorff, L. (2001a). Technology and Culture: The Dissemination and the Potential 'Lock-in' of New Technologies. *Journal of Artificial Societies and Social Simulation*, 4 (3), Paper 5, at http://jasss.soc.surrey.ac.uk/4/3/5.html.

Leydesdorff, L. (2001b). *A Sociological Theory of Communication: The Self- Organization of the Knowledge-Based Society*. Parkland, FL: Universal Publishers; at http://www.upublish.com/books/leydesdorff.htm.

Leydesdorff, L. (2001c). Indicators of Innovation in a Knowledge-based Economy. *Cybermetrics*, 5 (Issue 1), Paper 2, at http://www.cindoc.csic.es/cybermetrics/articles/v5i1p2.html.

Leydesdorff, L. (2002a). The Complex Dynamics of Technological Innovation: A Comparison of Models Using Cellular Automata. *Systems Research and Behavioral Science*, 19 (6), 563-575.

Leydesdorff, L. (2002b). Some Epistemological Implications of Semiosis in the Social Domain. *Semiotics, Evolution, Energy, and Development (SEED) Journal*, 2 (3), 60-83; at http://www.library.utoronto.ca/see/SEED/Vol62-63/62-63%20resolved/Leydesdorff.htm.

Leydesdorff, L. (2002c). The Communication Turn in the Theory of Social Systems. *Systems Research and Behavioral Science*, 19 (2), 129-136.

Leydesdorff, L. (2003a). The Mutual Information of University-Industry-Government Relations: An Indicator of the Triple Helix Dynamics. *Scientometrics*, 58 (2), 445-467.

Leydesdorff, L. (2003b). The Construction and Globalization of the Knowledge Base in Inter-Human Communication Systems. *Canadian Journal of Communication*, 28 (3), 267-289.

Leydesdorff, L. (2003c). Interaction versus Action in Luhmann's Sociology of Communication. In C. B. Grant (Ed.), *Rethinking Communicative Interaction* (pp. 163-186). Amsterdam and Philadelphia: John Benjamins.

Leydesdorff, L. (2004a). The University-Industry Knowledge Relationship: Analyzing Patents and the Science Base of Technologies. *Journal of the American Society for Information Science and Technology* (forthcoming).

Leydesdorff, L. (2004b). The University-Industry Knowlege Relationship: Analyzing Patents and the Science Base of Technologies. *Journal of the American Society for Information Science and Technology*, forthcoming.

Leydesdorff, L. (2005a). Anticipatory Systems and the Processing of Meaning: A Simulation Inspired by Luhmann's Theory of Social Systems. *Journal of Artificial Societies and Social Simulation*, 8(2), Paper 7, at http://jasss.soc.surrey.ac.uk/8/2/7.html .

Leydesdorff, L. (2005b). Similarity Measures, Author Cocitation Analysis, and Information Theory. *Journal of the American Society for Information Science and Technology*, 56(7), 769-772.

Leydesdorff, L. (2006a). 'While a Storm Is Raging on the Open Sea:' Regional Development in a Knowledge-Based Economy. *Journal of Technology Transfer*, 31(1), 189-203.

Leydesdorff, L. (2006b). The Biological Metaphor of a (Second-Order) Observer and the Sociological Discourse. *Kybernetes*, 35 (3/4), 531-546.

Leydesdorff, L. (2006c). Meaning, Anticipation, and Codification in Functionally Differentiated Systems of Communication. In T. Kron, U. Schimank and L. Winter (Eds.), *Luhmann Simulated – Computer Simulations to the Theory of Social Systems*. forthcoming.

Leydesdorff, L. (2006d), Unlocking the Lock-In: Co-evolution and Bifurcation in Technological Trajectories and Regimes. Paper presented at the Workshop Knowledge Economies: Innovation, Organization and Location. NIAS, Wassenaar, May 29-30, 2006.

Leydesdorff, L. (2006e). Hyperincursion and the Globalization of a Knowledge-Based Economy, Proceedings of the 7th International Conference on *Computing Anticipatory Systems, CASYS'05*. Melville, NY: American Institute of Physics, Vol. 839, pp. 560-569.

Leydesdorff, L. *et al.* (1980). *Philips en de Wetenschap*. Amsterdam: SUA.

Leydesdorff, L., and O. Amsterdamska (1990). Dimensions of Citation Analysis. *Science, Technology and Human Values*, 15, 305-335.

Leydesdorff, L., P. Cooke, and M. Olazaran (Eds.) (2002). Regional Innovation Systems in Europe (Special Issue). *Journal of Technology Transfer*, 27 (1), 5-145.

Leydesdorff, L., S. E. Cozzens, and P. van den Besselaar (1994). Tracking Areas of Strategic Importance Using Scientometric Journal Mappings. *Research Policy*, 23, 217-229.

Leydesdorff, L., and M. Curran (2000). Mapping University-Industry-Government Relations on the Internet: An Exploration of Indicators for a Knowledge-Based Economy. *Cybermetrics 4 Issue 1*, Paper 2 at

http://www.cindoc.csic.es/cybermetrics/articles/v4i1p2.html.

Leydesdorff, L., W. Dolfsma, and G. van der Panne (2004). Measuring the Knowledge Base of an Economy in Terms of Triple-Helix Relations among 'Technology, Organization, and Territory.' *Research Policy*, 35(2), 181-199.

Leydesdorff, L., and D. M. Dubois (2004). Anticipation in Social Systems: The Incursion and Communication of Meaning. *International Journal of Computing Anticipatory Systems*, 15, 203-216.

Leydesdorff, L., and H. Etzkowitz (1998). The Triple Helix as a Model for Innovation Studies. *Science and Public Policy*, 25 (3), 195-203.

Leydesdorff, L., and H. Etzkowitz (2003). Can "the Public" Be Considered as a Fourth Helix in University-Industry-Government Relations? Report of the Fourth Triple Helix Conference. *Science and Public Policy*, 30(1), 55-61.

Leydesdorff, L., and É. Gauthier (1996). The Evaluation of National Performance in Selected Priority Areas Using Scientometric Methods. *Research Policy*, 25, 431-450.

Leydesdorff, L., and Z. Guoping (2001). University-Industry-Government Relations in China: An Emergent National System of Innovations. *Industry and Higher Education*, 15(3), 179-182.

Leydesdorff, L., and G. Heimeriks (2001). The Self-Organization of the European Information Society: The Case of "Biotechnology". *Journal of the American Society for Information Science and Technology*, 52(14), 1262-1274.

Leydesdorff, L., and M. Meyer (2003). The Triple Helix of University-Industry-Government Relations: Introduction to the Topical Issue. *Scientometrics*, 58 (2), 191-203.

Leydesdorff, L., and N. Oomes (1999). Is the European Monetary System Converging to Integration? *Social Science Information*, 38(1), 57-86.

Leydesdorff, L., and A. Scharnhorst (2003). *Measuring the Knowledge Base: A Program of Innovation Studies. Report to "Förderinitiative Science Policy Studies" of the German Bundesministerium für Bildung und Forschung.* Berlin: Berlin-Brandenburgische Akademie der Wissenschaften; at http://www.sciencepolicystudies.de/dok/expertise-leydesdorff-scharnhorst.pdf

Leydesdorff, L., P. Ulenbelt, and A. Teulings (1984). Trade Union Participation in University Research Policies. *Journal of Institutional Management in Higher Education*, 8, 135-146.

Leydesdorff, L., and P. van den Besselaar (1987a). What We Have Learned from the Amsterdam Science Shop. In S. Blume, J. Bunders, L. Leydesdorff, and R. D. Whitley (Eds.), *The Social Direction of the Public Sciences. Sociology of the Sciences Yearbook* (Vol. XI, pp. 135-160). Dordrecht, etc.: Reidel.

Leydesdorff, L., and P. van den Besselaar (1987b). Squeezed between Capital and Technology: On the Participation of Labour in the Knowledge Society. *Acta Sociologica*, 30, 339-353.

Leydesdorff, L., and P. van den Besselaar (Eds.) (1994). *Evolutionary Economics and Chaos Theory: New Directions in Technology Studies.* London and New York: Pinter.

Leydesdorff, L., and P. van den Besselaar (1998a). Technological Development and Factor Substitution in a Non-Linear Model. *Journal of Social and Evolutionary Systems*, 21, 173-192.

Leydesdorff, L., and P. van den Besselaar (1998b). Competing Technologies: Lock-Ins and Lock-Outs. In D. M. Dubois (Ed.), *Computing Anticipatory Systems: CASYS'97, AIP Proceedings Volume 437*, pp. 309-323. American Institute of Physics, New York: Woodbury.

Leydesdorff, L., and P. van der Schaar (1987). The Use of Scientometric Indicators for Evaluating National Research Programmes. *Science and Technology Studies*, 5, 22-31.

Leydesdorff, L., and H. van Erkelens (1981). Some Social-Psychological Aspects of Becoming a Physicist. *Scientometrics*, 3, 27-46.

Leydesdorff, L., and J. Ward (2005). Science Shops: A Kaleidoscope of Science-Society Collaborations in Europe. *Public Understanding of Science* 14(4), 353-372.

Leydesdorff, L., and P. Wouters (1999). Between Texts and Contexts: Advances in Theories of Citation? *Scientometrics*, 44(2), 169-182.

Leydesdorff, L., and S. Zeldenrust (1984). Technological Change and Trade-Unions. *Research Policy,* 13, 153-164.

Li, T.-Y., and J. A. Yorke (1975). Period Three Implies Chaos. *American Mathematical Monthly,* 82, 985-992.

Li, Z., and G. Zeng (1999). *Zhongguo Chuangxin Xitong Yanjiu: Jishu, Zhidu He Zhishi Ji'Nan [A Study of the Chinese Innovation System: Technology, Institution and Knowledge].* Shandong: Shandong Education Publishing House.

Liebowitz, S. J., and S. E. Margolis (1999). *Winners, Losers and Microsoft: Competition and Antitrust in High Technology.* Oakland, CA: The Independent Institute.

Lindesmith, A. R., A. L. Strauss, and N. K. Denzin (1949, 4 1975). *Social Psychology.* Hinsdale: Dryden.

List, F. (1841). *The National Systems of Political Economy.* London: Longman, 1904.

Löbl, E. (1968). *Geistige Arbeit: Die wahre Quelle des Reichtums. Entwurf eines neuen sozialistischen Ordnungsbildes.* Vienna and Düsseldorf: Econ Verlag.

Luhmann, N. (1964). *Funktion und Folgen formaler Organisation.* Berlin: Duncker and Humblot.

Luhmann, N. (1971). Sinn als Grundbegriff der Soziologie. In Habermas and Luhmann (1971), pp. 25-100.

Luhmann, N. (1975a). Einführende Bemerkungen Zu einer Theorie symbolisch generalisierter Kommunikationsmedien. In *Soziologische Aufklärung* (pp. 170-192). Vol. 2. Opladen: Westdeutscher Verlag.

Luhmann, N. (1975b). Interaktion, Organisation, Gesellschaft: Anwendungen der Systemtheorie. In M. Gerhardt (Ed.), *Die Zukunft der Philosophie* (pp. 85-107). München. [*Soziologische Aufklärung 3.* Opladen: Westdeutscher Verlag, 1975, pp. 9-20.]

Luhmann, N. (1977). Differentiation of Society. *Canadian Journal of Sociology,* 2, 29-53.

Luhmann, N. (1978a). Interpenetration bei Parsons. *Zeitschrift für Soziologie,* 7, 299-302.

Luhmann, N. (1978b). *Organisation und Entscheidung.* Opladen: Westdeutscher Verlag. [reprinted in *Soziologische Aufklärung 3.* Opladen: Westdeutscher Verlag, 1981, pp. 335-389.]

Luhmann, N. (1981). Gesellschaftsstrukturelle Bedingungen und Folgeprobleme der Naturwissenschaftlich-Technischen Fortschirtts. In R. Löw, P. Koslowski and P. Kreuzer (Eds.), *Fortschritt ohne Maß: Eine Ortsbestimmung der Wissenschaftlich-Technischen Zivilisation* (pp. 112-131). München. [Reprinted in *Soziologische Aufklärung 4.* Opladen: Westdeutscher Verlag, 1987, pp. 49-63.]

Luhmann, N. (1982a). *Liebe als Passion.* Frankfurt a.M.: Suhrkamp.

Luhmann, N. (1982b). Systems Theory, Evolution Theory, and Communication Theory. In *The Differentiation of Society* (pp. 255-270). New York: Columbia University Press.

Luhmann, N. (1984). *Soziale Systeme. Grundriß einer allgemeinen Theorie.* Frankfurt a. M.: Suhrkamp [*Social Systems.* Stanford: Stanford University Press, 1995].

Luhmann, N. (1986a). The autopoiesis of social systems. In F. Geyer and J. Van Der Zouwen (Eds.), *Sociocybernetic Paradoxes.* London: Sage, pp. 172-192.

Luhmann, N. (1986b). *Ökologische Kommunikation: Kann die moderne Gesellschaft sich auf ökologische Gefährdungen einstellen?* Opladen: Westdeutscher Verlag.

Luhmann, N. (1989). *Gesellschaftsstruktur und Semantik III.* Frankfurt a.M: Suhrkamp.

Luhmann, N. (1990a). *Die Wissenschaft der Gesellschaft.* Frankfurt a.M.: Suhrkamp.

Luhmann, N. (1990b). The Cognitive Program of Constructivism and a Reality that Remains Unknown. In W. Krohn, G. Küppers and H. Nowotny (Eds.), *Selforganization. Portrait of a Scientific Revolution* (pp. 64-85). Dordrecht: Reidel

Luhmann, N. (1993a). Die Paradoxie der Form. In D. Baecker (Hrsg.), *Kalkül der Form* (pp. 197-212). Frankfurt a. M.: Suhrkamp. [Engl. translation: Baecker, 1999, pp. 15-26.]

Luhmann, N. (1993b). *Das Recht der Gesellschaft.* Frankfurt a.M.: Suhrkamp.

Luhmann, N. (1994). The Modernity of Science. *New German Critique*, 61, 9-23.

Luhmann, N. (1995a). *Die neuzeitlichen Wissenschaften und die Phänomenologie.* Picus: Wiener Vorlesungen.

Luhmann, N. (1995b). Intersubjektivität oder Kommunkation: Unterschiedliche Ausgangspunkte Soziologischer Theoriebildung. In *Soziologische Aufklärung.* Opladen: Westdeutscher Verlag.

Luhmann, N. (1996). On the Scientific Context of the Concept of Communication. *Social Science Information*, 35 (2), 257-267.

Luhmann, N. (1997a). *Die Gesellschaft der Gesellschaft.* Frankfurt a.M.: Surhkamp.

Luhmann, N. (1997b). Globalization of World Society: How to Conceive of Modern Society? *International Review of Sociology*, 7(1), 67-79.

Luhmann, N. (1999). The Paradox of Form. In D. Baecker (Ed.), *Problems of Form* (pp. 15-26). Stanford, CA: Stanford University Press.

Luhmann, N. (2000). *Organization und Entscheidung.* Opladen: Westdeutscher Verlag.

Luhmann, N. (2002a). The Modern Sciences and Phenomenology. In W. Rasch (Ed.), *Theories of Distinction: Redescribing the descriptions of modernity* (pp. 33-60). Stanford, CA: Stanford University Press.

Luhmann, N. (2002b). The Modernity of Science. In W. Rasch (Ed.), *Theories of Distinction: Redescribing the Descriptions of Modernity* (pp. 61-75). Stanford, CA: Stanford University Press.

Luhmann, N., H. Maturana, M. Namiki, V. Redder, and F. Varela (1990). *Beobachter. Konvergenz der Erkenntnistheorieen?* München: Wilhelm Fink Verlag.

Lundvall, B.-Å. (1988). Innovation as an Interactive Process: From User-Producer Interaction to the National System of Innovation. In G. Dosi, C. Freeman, R. Nelson, G. Silverberg and L. Soete (Eds.), *Technical Change and Economic Theory* (pp. 349-369). London: Pinter.

Lundvall, B.-Å. (Ed.) (1992). *National Systems of Innovation.* London: Pinter.

Lundvall, B.-Å., and S. Borras (1997). *The Globalising Learning Economy: Implication for Innovation Policy.* Luxembourg: European Commission.

Lynch, M. E. (1988). Sacrifice and the Transformation of the Animal Body into a Scientific Object: Laboratory Culture and Ritual Practice in the Neurosciences. *Social Studies of Science*, 18, 265-289.

Machlup, F. (1962). *The Production and Distribution of Knowledge in the United States.* Princeton: Princeton University Press.

MacKay, D. M. (1969). *Information, Mechanism and Meaning.* Cambridge and London: MIT Press.

Mackenzie, A. (2001). The Technicity of Time. *Time and Society*, 10(2/3), 235-257.

Maddox, B. (2002). *Rosalind Franklin: The Dark Lady of DNA*. London: Harper Collins.

Malerba, F., R. Nelson, L. Orsenigo, and S. Winter (1999). 'History-Firendly' Models of Industry Evolution: The Computer Industry. *Industrial and Corporate Change*, 8 (1), 3-35.

March, J. G., and H. A. Simon (1958). *Organizations*. New York and London: Wiley.

March, J. G., and J. P. Olsen (1976). *Ambiguity and Choice in Organization*. Bergen: Universitetsforlaget.

Marx, K. (1848). *The Communist Manifesto*. Paris. (Translated by Samuel Moore in 1888.) Harmondsworth: Penguin (1967 edn.).

Marx, K. (1857). *Grundriße der Kritik der politischen Oekonomie*. Moscow: Marx-Engels-Lenin Institute (1939 edn.).

Marx, K. (1867). *Das Kapital I*. Hamburg: Meisner.

Maryanski, A., and J. H. Turner (1992). *The Social Cage: Human Nature and the Evolution of Society*. Stanford, CA: Stanford University Press.

Mason, S. F. (1992). *Chemical Evolution: Origins of the Elements, Molecules and Living Systems*. Oxford: Oxford University Press.

Matsuno, K. (2003). Quantum Mechanics in First, Second and Third Person Descriptions. *BioSystems*, 68, 107-118.

Maturana, H. R. (1978). Biology of Language: The Epistemology of Reality. In G. A. Miller and E. Lenneberg (Eds.), , *Psychology and Biology of Language and Thought. Essays in Honor of Eric Lenneberg* (pp. 27-63.). New York: Academic Press.

Maturana, H. R. (2000). The Nature of the Laws of Nature. *Systems Research and Behavioral Science*, 17, 459-468.

Maturana, H. R., and F. J. Varela (1980). *Autopoiesis and Cognition: The Realization of the Living*. Dordrecht, etc.: Reidel.

Maturana, H. R., and F. J. Varela (1984). *The Tree of Knowledge*. Boston: New Science Library.

May, R. M. (1973). *Stability and Complexity in Model Ecosystems*. Princeton, NJ: Princeton University Press.

May, R. M., and W. J. Leonard (1975). Nonlinear Aspects of Competition between Three Species. *SIAM Journal of Applied Mathematics*, 29(2), 243-253.

Maynard-Smith, J. (1979). Hypercycles and the Origin of Life. *Nature*, 280, 445.

McGill, W. J. (1954). Multivariate Information Transmission. *Psychometrika*, 19(2), 97-116.

McLuhan, M. (1962). *The Gutenberg Galaxy*. Toronto: Toronto University Press.

McLuhan, M. (1964). *Understanding Media: The Extension of Man*. New York: McGraw-Hill.

Mead, G. H. (1934). The Point of View of Social Behaviorism. In C. H. Morris (Ed.), *Mind, Self, and Society from the Standpoint of a Social Behaviorist. Works of G. H. Mead* (Vol. 1, pp. 1-41). Chicago and London: University of Chicago Press.

Merton, R. K. (1938). *Science, Technology and Society in Seventeenth-Century England*. Bruges, Belgium: Saint Catherine Press.

Merton, R. K. (1948). The Self-Fulfilling Prophecy. *Antioch Review*, 8, 193-210.

Merton, R. K. (1968). The Matthew Effect in Science. *Science*, 159, 56-63.

Merton, R. K. (1973). *The Sociology of Science: Theoretical and Empirical Investigations*. Chicago and London: University of Chicago Press.

Meyrowitz, J. (1994). Medium Theory. In D. Crowley and D. Mitchell (Eds.), *Communication Theory Today* (pp. 50-77). Stanford, CA: Stanford University Press.

Miles, I., N. Kastrinos, K. Flanagan, R. Bilderbeek, P. den Hertog, W. Huitink, and M. Bouman (1995). *Knowledge-Intensive Business Services: Users, Carriers and Sources of Innovation.* Luxembourg, European Innovation Monitoring Service, No. 15.

Mokyr, J. (2002). *The Gifts of Athena – Historical Origins of the Knowledge Economy.* Princeton, NJ: Princeton University Press.

Monge, P. R., and N. S. Contractor (2003). *Theories of Communication Networks.* New York, etc.: Oxford University Press.

Montesquieu, C. de Sécondat, Baron de (1748). *De l'esprit des lois.* Paris.

Moso, M., and M. Olazaran (2002). Regional Technology Policy and the Emergence of an R&D System in the Basque Country. *Journal of Technology Transfer,* 27 (1), 61-75.

Mowery, D. C., and N. Rosenberg (1979). The Influence of Market Demand upon Innovation: A Critical Reveiw of Some Empirical Studies. *Research Policy,* 8 (102-153.

Mowery, D. C., and N. Rosenberg (1989). *Technology and the Pursuit of Economic Growth.* Cambridge: Cambridge University Press.

Mulkay, M. J. (1976). The mediating role of the scientific elite, *Social Studies of Science,* 6: 445-470.

Mulkay, M., J. Potter, and S. Yearley (1983). Why an Analysis of Scientific Discourse Is Needed. In K. D. Knorr and M. J. Mulkay (Eds.), *Science Observed: Perspectives on the Social Study of Science* (pp. 171-204.). London: Sage.

Münch, R. (1982). *Theorie des Handelns* (Understanding Modernity. London and New York: Routledge, 1988 ed.). Frankfurt a.M.: Suhrkamp.

Myers, G. (1985). Texts as Knowledge Claims: The Social Construction of Two Biology Articles. *Social Studies of Science,* 15, 593-630.

Narin, F. (1976). *Evaluative Bibliometrics: The Use of Publication and Citation Analysis in the Evaluation of Scientific Activity.* Washington, DC: National Science Foundation.

Narin, F., and E., Noma (1985). Is Technology Becoming Science? *Scientometrics,* 7, 369-381.

Narin, F., and D. Olivastro (1988). Technology Indicators Based on Patents and Patent Citations. In A. F. J. v. Raan (Ed.), *Handbook of Quantitative Studies of Science and Technology.* Amsterdam: Elsevier, pp. 465-507.

National Science Board (1987). *Science and Engineering Indicators - 1987.* Washington, DC: National Science Foundation.

Nelson, R. R. (1994). Economic Growth Via the Co-evolution of Technology and Institutions. In L. Leydesdorff and P. van den Besselaar (Eds.), *Evolutionary Economic and Chaos Theory: New Directions in Technology Studies* (pp. 21-32). London and New York: Pinter.

Nelson, R. R. (1995). Recent Evolutionary Theorizing About Economic Change. *Journal of Economic Literature,* 33 (1), 48-90.

Nelson, R. R. (Ed.) (1982). *Government and Technical Progress: A Cross-Industry Analysis.* New York: Pergamon.

Nelson, R. R. (Ed.) (1993). *National Innovation Systems: A Comparative Analysis.* New York: Oxford University Press.

Nelson, R. R., and S. G. Winter (1975). Growth Theory from an Evolutionary Perspective: The Differential Productivity Growth Puzzle. *American Economic Review*, 65, 338-344.

Nelson, R. R., and S. G. Winter (1977). In Search of Useful Theory of Innovation. *Research Policy*, 6, 35-76.

Nelson, R. R., and S. G. Winter (1982). *An Evolutionary Theory of Economic Change.* Cambridge, MA: Belknap Press of Harvard University Press.

Neurath, O. (1933). Protokollsätze. *Erkenntnis*, 3, 204-214.

Neurath, O., R. Carnap, and H. Hahn (1929) *Wissenschaftliche Weltauffassung — Der Wiener Kreis.* Vienna: Veröffentlichungen des Vereins Ernst Mach.

Newman, W. H., and J. P. Logan (1981). *Strategy, Policy and Central Management.* Cincinatti, OH: South-Western Publishing Cy.

Nonaka, I., and H. Takeuchi (1995). *The Knowledge Creating Company.* Oxford and New York: Oxford University Press.

Nooteboom, B. (1999). Innovation, learning and industrial organization. *Cambridge Journal of Economics*, 23, 127-150.

Nowotny, H. (1989). *Eigenzeit: Entstehung und Strukturierung eines Zeitgefühls.* Frankfurt A.M.: Suhrkamp. [English Translation: *Time: The Modern and Postmodern Experience.* Cambridge, UK: Polity Press, 1994.]

Nowotny, H., P. Scott, and M. Gibbons (2001). *Re-Thinking Science: Knowledge and the Public in an Age of Uncertainty.* Cambridge, etc: Polity.

NSF (2000). *Science and Technology Then and Now.* NSF Fact Sheet at http://www.nsf.gov/od/lpa/news/media/2000/bckgrdrst.htm (last visited Sep. 8, 2003).

O'Malley, M., G. McOuat, and W. F. Doolittle (forthcoming). The Triple Helix Account of Innovation: A Critical Appraisal. *Science, Technology and Human Values* (in preparation).

OECD (1963, ³1976). *The Measurement of Scientific and Technical Activities: 'Frascati Manual'.* Paris: OECD.

OECD (1964). *The Residual Factor and Economic Growth.* Paris: OECD.

OECD (1980). *Technical Change and Economic Policy.* Paris: OECD.

OECD (1986). *OECD Science and Technology Indicators: R&D, Invention and Competitiveness.* Paris: OECD.

OECD. (1988). *Biotechnology and the Changing Role of Government.* Paris: OECD.

OECD (1996a). *OECD Documents: Employment and Growth in the Knowledge-Based Economy.* Paris: OECD.

OECD (1996b). *OECD Economic Outlook, No. 60.* Paris: OECD.

OECD (2000). *Promoting Innovation and Growth in Services.* Paris: OECD.

OECD (2001). *Science, Technology and Industry Scoreboard: Towards a Knowledge-based Economy.* Paris: OECD.

OECD (2003). *Science, Technology and Industry Scoreboard; 2003 Edition..* Paris: OECD.

OECD/Eurostat (1997). *Proposed Guidelines for Collecting and Interpreting Innovation Data, 'Oslo Manual'.* Paris: OECD.

Park, H. W., H. D. Hong, and L. Leydesdorff (2005). A Comparison of the Knowledge-Based Innovation Systems in the Economies of South Korea and the Netherlands Using Triple Helix Indicators. *Scientometrics*, 65(1), 3-27.

Parsons, T. (1937). *The Structure of Social Action*. Glencoe, IL: The Free Press.

Parsons, T. (1951). *The Social System*. New York: The Free Press.

Parsons, T. (1953). The Theory of Symbolism in Relation to Action. In T. Parsons, R. Bales and E. Shills (Eds.), *Working Papers in the Theory of Action*. New York: The Free Press.

Parsons, T. (1963a). On the Concept of Political Power,. *Proceedings of the American Philosophical Society 107 (3)* 232-262.

Parsons, T. (1963b). On the Concept of Influence. *Public Opinion Quarterly 27 (Spring)*, 37-62.

Parsons, T. (1968). Social Interaction. In David L. Sills (editor), *International Encyclopedia of the Social Sciences*, Vol. 7 (pp. 429-441). New York: MacGraw-Hill.

Parsons, T., and A. H. Dupree (1976). The Relations between Biological and Socio-Cultural Theory. *Bulletin of the American Academy of Arts and Sciences*, 29(8).

Pask, G. (1975). *Conversation, Cognition and Learning*. Elsevier: Amsterdam.

Pauling, L., and R. B. Corey (1953). A proposed structure for the nucleic acids. *Proc. Natl. Acad. Sci. USA, 89*, 84-97.

Pavitt, K. (1984). Sectoral Patterns of Technical Change: Towards a Theory and a Taxonomy. *Research Policy*, 13, 343-373.

Pearl, J. (1988). *Probabilistic Reasoning and Artificial Intelligence: Networks of Plausible Inference*. San Mateo, CA: Morgan Kaufman.

Pearl, R. (1924). *Studies in Human Biology*. Baltimore: William and Wilkins.

Persson, O., W. Glänzel, and R. Danell (2004). Inflationary Bibliometric Values: The Role of Scientific Collaboration and the Need for Relative Indicators in Evaluative Studies, *Scientometrics*, 60(3), 421-432.

Pinch, T. J., and W. E. Bijker (1984). The Social Construction of Facts and Artifacts: Or how the sociology of science and the sociology of technology might benefit from each other. *Social Studies of Science*, 14, 399-442.

Pinker, S. (1994). *The Language Instinct: The New Science of Language and Mind*. London, etc: Penguin.

Poincaré, H. (1905). *Leçons de mécanique céleste* (1905 vol. I, 1907 vol. II part I, 1909 vol. II part II, 1911 vol. III). Paris: Gauthier-Villars.

Popper, K. R. ([1935] 1959). The Logic of Scientific Discovery. London: Hutchinson.

Popper, K. R. (1967). *The Poverty of Historicism*. London: Routledge and Kegan Paul.

Popper, K. R. (1972). *Objective Knowledge. An Evolutionary Approach*. Oxford: Oxford University Press.

Porter, M. E. (1990). *The Competitive Advantage of Nations*. London: Macmillan.

Price, D. de Solla (1961). *Science since Babylon*. New Haven: Yale University Press.

Prigogine, I., and I. Stengers (1984). *Order out of Chaos*. New York: Bantam.

Prigogine, I., and I. Stengers (1988). *Entre le temps et l'éternité*. Paris: Fayard.

Pugh, D. S., and D. J. Hickson (1969a) The Context of Organization Structures, *Administrative Science Quarterly*, 14(1), 91-114.

Pugh, D. S., D. J. Hickson and C. R. Hinings (1969b) An empirical taxonomy of structures of work organizations, *Administrative Science Quarterly*, 14(1), 115-126.

Quine, W. V. O. (1953). *From a Logical Point of View*. Cambridge, MA: Harvard University Press.

Quine, W. V. O. (1962). Carnap and Logical Truth. In *Logic and Language: Studies dedicated to Professor Rudolf Carnap on the Occasion of his Seventieth Birthday* (pp. 39-63). Dordrecht: Reidel.

Rabeharisoa, V., and M. Callon (2002). The Involvement of Patients' Associations in Research. *International Social Science Journal*, 54 (171), 57-65.

Raju, C. K. (2003). *The Eleven Pictures of Time: The Physics, Philosophy and Politics of Time Beliefs*. New Delhi, etc.: Sage.

Ramachandran, G. N., and G. Kartha (1955). Structure of Collagen. *Nature*, 176(4482), 593-595.

Rashevsky, N. (1940). *Bull. Math. Biophys.*, 1, 15-20.

Reggiani, A., and P. Nijkamp (1994). Evolutionary Dynamics in Technological Systems: A Multi-layer Niche Approach. In L. Leydesdorff and P. Van den Besselaar (Eds.), *Evolutionary Economics and Chaos Theory: New directions in technology studies* (pp. 93-108). London: Pinter.

Riba-Vilanova, M., and L. Leydesdorff (2001). Why Catalonia cannot be considered as a Regional Innovation System. *Scientometrics, 50*(2), 215-240.

Richta, R. *et al.* (1968). *Politische Oekonomie des 20. Jahrhunderts*. Prague and Frankfurt a.M.: Makol.

Rorty, R. M. (1988). The Priority of Democracy to Philosophy. In M. D. Peterson and R. C. Vaughan (Eds.), *The Virginia Statute for Religious Freedom: Its Evolution and Consequences in American History* (pp. 257-288). Cambridge: Cambridge University Press.

Rosen, R. (1985). *Anticipatory Systems: Philosophical, Mathematical and Methodological Foundations*. New York: Pergamon Press.

Rosenberg, A. (1994). *Instrumental Biology, or, the Disunity of Science*. Chicago: Chicago University Press.

Rosenberg, N. (1976a). *Perspectives on Technology*. Cambridge: Cambridge University Press.

Rosenberg, N. (1976b). The Direction of Technological Change: Inducement Mechanisms and Focusing Devices. In *Perspectives on Technology* (pp. 108-125). Cambridge: Cambridge University Press.

Rosenberg, N. (1982). Learning by Using. In *Inside the Black Box: Technology and Economics* (pp. 120-140). Cambridge, etc.: Cambridge University Press.

Rothwell, R., and W. Zegveld (1981). *Industrial Innovation and Public Policy*. London: Pinter.

Rousseau, R. (1999). Daily time series of common single word searches in AltaVista and NorthernLight,. *Cybermetrics   2/3,   Paper   2   at* <http://www.cindoc.csic.es/cybermetrics/articles/v2i1p2.html>.

Sahal, D. (1979). A Unified Theory of Self-Organization. *Journal of Cybernetics*, 9, 127-142.

Sahal, D. (1981a). *Patterns of Technological Innovation*. Reading, MA: Addison Wesley.

Sahal, D. (1981b). Alternative Conceptions of Technology, *Research Policy* 10, 2- 24.

Sahal, D. (1985). Technological Guideposts and Innovation Avenues. *Research Policy*, 14, 61-82.

Salter, W. E. G. (1960). *Productivity and Technical Change*. New York: Cambridge University Press.

Saviotti, P. P. (1996). *Technological Evolution, Variety and the Economy*. Cheltenham and Brookfield: Edward Elgar.

Sayer, A. (2000). *Realism and Social Science*. London, etc.: Sage.

Scharnhorst, A. (1998). Citation-Networks, Science Landscapes and Evolutionary Strategies. *Scientometrics*, 43 (1), 95-106.

Schmitt, M. (2002). Ist Luhmann in Der Unified Modeling Language Darstellbar? Soziologische Beobachtung Eines Informatischen Kommikationsmediums. In T. Kron (Ed.), *Luhmann Modelliert: Sozionische Ansätze Zur Simulation Von Kommunikationssystemen.* (pp. 27-53). Opladen: Leske and Budrich.

Schrödinger, E. (1944). *What Is Life?* Cambridge: Cambridge University Press.

Schumpeter, J. ([1911], 1949). *The Theory of Economic Development*. Cambridge, MA: Harvard University Press.

Schumpeter, J. ([1939], 1964). *Business Cycles: A Theoretical, Historical and Statistical Analysis of Capitalist Process*. New York: McGraw-Hill.

Schumpeter, J. (1943). *Socialism, Capitalism and Democracy*. London: Allen and Unwin.

Schutz, A. (1951). Making Music Together. *Social Research*, 18 (1), 76-97.

Schutz, A. (1975). *Collected Papers III. Studies in Phenomenological Philosophy*. The Hague: Martinus Nijhoff.

Schütz, A. (1932). *Der Sinnhafte Aufbau der Sozialen Welt*. Vienna: Springer. [*The Penomenology of the Social World*, trans. G. Walsh and F. Lehnert. Evanston, IL: Northwestern University Press, 1967.]

Schütz, A. (1952). Das Problem der Transzendentalen Intersubjectivität bei Husserl. *Philosophische Rundschau*, 5(2), 81-107.

Schwartz, D. (2005). The Regional Location of Knowledge-Based Economy Activities in Israel. *Journal of Technology Transfer*, 30(3), forthcoming.

Searle, J. R. (1998). *Mind, Language and Society: Philosophy in the Real World*. New York: Basic Books.

Serres, M. (1980). *Le Parasite*. Paris: B. Grasset.

Serres, M. (1982). *Hermes: Literature, Science, Philosophy*. Baltimore and London: Johns Hopkins University Press.

Sforzi, F. (2003). The 'Tuscan Model' and Recent Trends. In G. Beccatini, M. Bellandi, G. dei Ottati and F. Sforzi (Eds.), *From Industrial Districts to Local Developments: An Itinerary of Research* (pp. 29-61). Cheltenham, UK and Northhampton, MA: Edward Elgar.

Shannon, C. E. (1948). A Mathematical Theory of Communication I and II. *Bell System Technical Journal*, 27, 379-423 and 623-656.

Shannon, C. E., and Warren Weaver (1949). *The Mathematical Theory of Communication*. Urbana: University of Illinois Press.

Shapin, S., and S. Shaffer (1985). *Leviathan and the Air-Pump: Hobbes, Boyle and the Experimental Life*. Princeton, NJ: Princeton University Press.

Shinn, T. (1987). Géometrie et Langage: La Structure des Modèles en Sciences Sociales et en Sciences Physiques. *Bulletin de Méthodologie Sociologique*, 1(16), 5-38.

Shinn, T. (2002). The Triple Helix and New Production of Knowledge : Prepackaged Thinking on Science and Technology. *Social Studies of Science*, 32 (4), 599-614.

Simon, H. A. (1955). A Behavioral Model of Rational Choice. *Quarterly Journal of Economics*, 69, 99-118.

Simon, H. A. (1969). *The Sciences of the Artificial*. Cambridge, MA and London: MIT Press.

Simon, H. A. (1973). The Organization of Complex Systems. In Howard H. Pattee (Ed.), *Hierarchy Theory: The Challenge of Complex Systems* (pp. 1-27). New York: George Braziller Inc.

Skolnikoff, E. B. (1993). *The Elusive Transformation: Science, technology and the evolution of international politics*. Princeton, NJ: Princeton University Press.

Smolensky, P. (1986). Information Processing in Dynamical Systems: Foundation of Harmony Theory. In D. E. Rumelhart, J. L. McClelland, and the PDP Research Group (Eds.), *Parallel Distributed Processing* (Vol. I, pp. 194-281). Cambridge, MA and London: MIT Press.

Solow, R. M. (1957). Technical Progress and the Aggregate Production Function. *Review of Economics and Statistics*, 39, 312-320.

Sonis, M. (1992). Innovation Diffusion, Schupeterian Competition and Dynamic Choice: A new synthesis. *Journal of Scientific and Industrial Research*, 51, 172-186.

Sonis, M. (2000). Nonlinear Socio-Ecological Dynamics and First Principles of Collective Choice Behavior of "Homo Socialis". *Progress of Theoretical Physics*, 139 (Supplement No. 139), 257-269.

Spencer, H. (1897). *The Principles of Sociology, 2* Vols. New York: D. Appleton.

Spencer Brown, G. (1969), *Laws of Form*. London: George Allen and Unwin.

Spencer Brown, G. (1993/94), Self-reference, Distinctions and Time, *Teoria Sociologica*, 2-3(1), 47-53.

Steinmueller, W. E. (2002). Knowledge-Based Economies and Information and Communication Technologies. *International Social Science Journal*, 54(171), 141-153.

Sterman, J. D. (1985). The Growth of Knowledge: Testing a Theory of Scientific Revolutions with a Formal Model. *Technological forecasting and social change*, 28 (2), 93-122.

Sterman, J. D. (1999). Path Dependence, Competitions, and Succession in the Dynamics of Scientific Revolutions. *Organization Science*, 10 (3), 322-341.

Stewart, I., and J. Cohen (1997). *Figments of Reality: The Evolution of the Curious Mind*. Cambrige and New York: Cambridge University Press.

Stichweh, R. (1984). *Zur Entstehung des Modernen Systems Wissenschaftlicher Disziplinen. Physik in Deutschland, 1740-1890*. Frankfurt A.M: Suhrkamp.

Stichweh, R. (2000). Semantik und Sozialstruktur: Zur Logik einer Systemtheoretischen Unterscheidung. *Soziale Systeme*, 6, 237-250.

Sternberg, R., and C. Tamasy (1999). Munich as Germany's No. 1 high technology region: empirical evidence, theoretical explanations and the role of small firm – large firm relationships. *Regional Studies*, 33, 367-377.

Storper, M. (1997). *The Regional World - Territorial Development in a Global Economy*. New York: Guilford Press.

Strydom, P. (1999). Triple Contingency: The Theoretical Problem of the Public in Communication Societies. *Philosoph and Social Criticism*, 25(2), 1-25.

Studer, K. E., and D. E. Chubin (1980). *The Cancer Mission. Social Contexts of Biomedical Research.* Beverly Hills, etc.: Sage.

Suárez, F. F., and J.M. Utterback (1995). Dominant design and the survival of firms. *Strategic Management Journal,* 16, 415-430.
    Technological Forecasting and Social Change 70: 735-758.

Teubal, M. (1979). On User Needs and Need Determination. Aspects of a Theory of Technological Innovation. In M. J. Baker (Ed.), *Industrial Innovation. Technology, Policy and Diffusion* (pp. 266-289). London: Macmillan Press.

Theil, H. (1972). *Statistical Decomposition Analysis.* Amsterdam and London: North-Holland.

Theil, H., and D. G. Fiebig (1984). *Exploiting Continuity: Maximum Entropy Estimation of Continuous Distributions.* Cambridge, MA: Ballinger Publishing Company.

Thellwall, M. (2001). The Responsiveness of Search Engine Indexes. *Cybermetrics,* 5(1), http://www.cindoc.csic.es/cybermetrics/articles/v5i1p1.html.

Thom, R. (1972). *Stabilité structurelle et morphogénèse: essai d'une théorie générale des modèles.* Reading, MA: Benjamin.

Thomas, W. I., and D. S. Thomas (1928). *The Child in America: Behavior Problems and Programs.* New York: A. A. Knopf.

Tong, J. (1996). Reflections on Human Capital Theory and Niche Theory in Evolutionary Economics. *Paper presented at the First Triple Helix Conference,* Amsterdam: University of Amsterdam.

Turing, A. M. (1952). *Philos. Trans. R. Soc. B.,* 237, 5-72.

Turner, S. P. (1990). Forms of Patronage. In S. E. Cozzens and T. F. Gieryn (Eds.), *Theories of Science in Society* (pp. 185-211). Bloomington: Indiana University Press.

Turner, J. H., and A. Maryanski (1979). *Functionalism.* Menlo Park, CA: Benjamin and Cummings Pub. Co.

Ulanowicz, R. E. (1986). *Growth and Development: Ecosystems Phenomenology.* San Jose, etc.: toExcel.

Ulanowicz, R. E. (1996). The Propensities of Evolving Systems. In E. L. Khalil and K. E. Boulding (Eds.), *Evolution, Order and Complexity* (pp. 217-233). London and New York: Routledge.

Ulanowicz, R. E. (1997). *Ecology, the Ascendent Perspective.* New York: Columbia University Press.

Urry, J. (2000). *Sociology Beyond Societies: Mobilities for the twenty-first century.* London and New York: Routledge.

Urry, J. (2003). *Global Complexity.* Cambridge, UK: Polity Press.

Utterback, J. M., and F. F. Suárez (1993). Innovation, Competition, and Industry Structure. *Research Policy,* 22, 1-21.

Van den Belt, H., and A. Rip (1987). The Nelson-Winter-Dosi Model and Synthetic Dye Chemistry. In W. E. Bijker, T. P. Hughes and T. J. Pinch (Eds.), *The Social Construction of Technological Systems. New Directions in the Sociology and History of Technology* (pp. 135-158.). Cambridge MA: MIT Press.

Van den Besselaar, P. (1998). Technology and democracy, the limits to steering. In R. H. Chatfield, S. Kuhn, M. Muller (Eds.), *Broadening Participation - 5th PDC* (pp. 1-10). Seattle: CPSR.

Van den Besselaar, P., and L. Leydesdorff (1993). Research Performance in Artificial Intelligence and Robotics. An International Comparison,. *AI Communications*, 6, 83-91.

Van den Besselaar, P., and L. Leydesdorff (1996). Mapping Change in Scientific Specialties: A Scientometric Reconstruction of the Development of Artificial Intelligence. *Journal of the American Society for Information Science*, 47, 415-436.

Van den Daele, W., W. Krohn, and P. Weingart (Eds.) (1977). *Geplante Forschung: Vergleichende Studien über den Einfluss politischer Programme auf die Wissenschaftsentwicklung*. Frankfurt a.M.: Suhrkamp.

Van der Meulen, B. (1998). Science Policies as Principal-Agent Games; Institutionalization and Path Dependency in the Relation between Government and Science. *Research Policy*, 27, 397-414.

Van der Panne, G., and W. Dolfsma (2001). Hightech door Nederland, *Economisch Statistische Berichten*, 86(4318), 584-586.

Van der Panne, G., and W. Dolfsma (2003). The Odd Role of Proximity in Knowledge Relations: High-Tech in the Netherlands. *Journal of Economic and Social Geography*, 94(4), 451-460.

Van Lente, H., and A. Rip (1998). Expectations in Technological Developments: An example of prospective structures to be filled in by agency. In Cornelis Disco and Barend van der Meulen (Eds.), *Getting new technologies together: Studies in making sociotechnological order* (pp. 203-229). Berlin: Walter de Gruyter.

Varela, F. (1975), A Calculus for Self-Reference, *International Journal of General Systems*, 2(1), 5-24.

Varela, F. J., and J. A. Goguen (1978), The Arithmetic of Closure, *Journal of Cybernetics*, 8, 291-324.

Varela, F. J., E. Thompson, and E. Rosch (1991). *The Embodied Mind: Cognitive Science and Human Experience*. Cambridge, MA: MIT Press.

Vavakova, B. (2000). *La science de la nation? Paradoxes politiques de la logique économique*. Paris: l'Harmattan.

Verhulst, P.-F. (1847). Deuxième mémoire sur la loi d'accroissement de la population. *Mém. de l'Academie Royale des Sci., des Lettres et des Beaux-Arts de Belgique*, 20, 1-32.

Viale, R., and S. Campodall'Orto (2002). An Evolutionary Triple Helix to Strengthen Academy-Industry Relations: Suggestions from European Regions. *Science and Public Policy*, 29 (3), 154-168.

Von Foerster, H. (1982). *Observing Systems* (with an introduction of Francisco Varela ed.). Seaside, CA: Intersystems Publications.

Von Foerster, H. (1993a). Für Niklas Luhmann: Wie rekursiv ist Kommunikation? In: *Teoria Sociologica*, 2, 61-85.

Von Foerster, H. (1993b). Über selbstorganisierende Systeme und ihre Umwelten. In S. J. Schmidt (Ed.), *Wissen und Gewissen: Versuch einer Brücke* (pp. 211-232). Frankfurt am Main: Suhrkamp.

Vonortas, N.S. (2000) Multimarket Contact and Inter-firm Cooperation in R&D. *Journal of Evolutionary Economics* 10(1-2), 243-271.

Waddington, C. H. (1957). *The Strategy of Genes*. London: Allen and Unwin.

Wagner, C. S., and L. Leydesdorff (2003). Seismology as a Dynamic, Distributed Area of Scientific Research. *Scientometrics*, 58(1), 91-114.

Wagner, C. S., and L. Leydesdorff (2005a) Mapping the Network of Global Science: Comparing International Co-Authorships from 1990 to 2000. *International Journal of Technology and Globalization*, 1(2), 185-208.

Wagner, C. S., and L. Leydesdorff (2005b). Network Structure, Self-Organization and the Growth of International Collaboration in Science. *Research Policy*, 34(10), 1608-1618.

Wagner, P., B. Wittrock, and H. Wollmann (1991). Social Science and the Modern State: Knowledge, Institutions, and Societal Transformations. In P. Wagner, C. Weiss, B. Wittrock and H. Wollmann (Eds.), *Social Science and Modern States: National Experiences and Theoretical Crossroads*. Cambridge: Cambridge University Press.

Wallerstein, I. (1974). *The Modern World System: Capitalist Agriculture and the Origins of the European World Economy in the Sixteenth Century*. New York: Academic Press.

Walsh, J. P., and T. Bayma (1996). Computer Networks and Scientific Work. *Social Studies of Science*, 26(3), 661-703.

Watkins, J. W. N. (1952). Ideal Types and Historical Explanation. *British Journal for the Philosophy of Science*, 3(9), 22-43.

Watson, J. (1970). *The Double Helix: A Personal Account of the Discovery of the Structure of DNA*. Harmondsworth: Penguin.

Watson, J., and F. Crick (1953). A structure for Deoxyribose Nucleic Acid. *Nature* 171 (25 April) 737-738.

Watts, R. J., and A.L. Porter (2003). R&D cluster quality measures and technology maturity.

Weaver, W. (1949). Some Recent Contributions to the Mathematical Theory of Communication. In C. E. Shannon and W. Weaver, *The Mathematical Theory of Communication* (pp. 93-117). Urbana: University of Illinois Press.

Weber, M. (1904). Die Objektivität sozialwissenschaftlicher und sozialpolitischer Erkenntnis, *Gesammelte Aufsätze zur Wissenschaftslehre* (pp. 146-214). Tübingen: Mohr, ³1968.

Weber, M. (1917). Der Sinn der 'Wertfreiheit' der soziologischen und ökonomischen Wissenschaften (pp. 489-540). Tübingen: Mohr, ³1968.

Weber, M. (1920). *Gesammelte Aufsätze zur Religionssoziologie III*. Tübingen: Mohr.

Weinstein, F., and G. M. Platt (1969). *The Wish to Be Free: Society, Psyche, and Value Change*. Berkeley, etc.: University of California Press.

Weinstein, F., and G. M. Platt (1973). *Psychoanalytic Sociology*. Baltimore and London: Johns Hopkins University Press.

Whitley, R. D. (1984). *The Intellectual and Social Organization of the Sciences*. Oxford: Oxford University Press.

Whitley, R. D. (1999). *Divergent Capitalisms: The Social Structuring and Change of Business Systems*. New York: Oxford University Press.

Whitley, R. D. (2001). National Innovation Systems. In N. J. Smelser and P. B. Baltes (Eds.), *International Encyclopedia of the Social and Behavioral Sciences* (pp. 10303-10309). Oxford, UK: Elsevier.

Wiener, N. (1948). *Cybernetics: Or Control and Communication in the Animal and the Machine*. Cambridge, MA: MIT Press.

Williamson, O. (1985). *The Economic Institutions of Capitalism*. New York: Free Press.

Windrum, P. (1999). Simulation Models of Technological Innovation: A Review. *American Behavioral Scientist*, 42 (10), 1531-1550.

Windrum, P., and M. Tomlinson (1999). Knowledge-Intensive Services and International Competitiveness: A Four Country Comparison. *Technology Analysis and Strategic Management*, 11(3), 391-408.

Wintjes, R., and J. Cobbenhagen (2000), Knowledge intensive Industrial Clustering around Océ; Embedding a vertical disintegrated codification process into the Eindhoven-Venlo region. *MERIT Research Memorandum*, nr. 00-06. MERIT, University of Maastricht.

Wolfram, S. (2002). *A New Kind of Science*. Champaign, IL: Wolfram Media.

Wouters, P., I. Hellsten, and L. Leydesdorff (2004). Internet Time and the Reliability of Search Engines. *First Monday*, 9(10); at <http://www.firstmonday.org/issues/issue9_10/wouters/index.html>.

Yoder, J. G. (1988). *Unrolling Time. Christiaan Huygens and the Mathematization of Nature*. Cambridge, Etc: Cambridge University Press.

York, H. F. (1970). *Race to Oblivion: A Participants View of the Arms Race*, New York: Simon and Schuster; at http://www.learnworld.com/ZNW/LWText.York.Race.Access.html

Zaal, R., and L. Leydesdorff (1987). The Amsterdam Science Shop and Its Influence on University Research: The Effects of Ten Years Dealing with Non-Academic Questions. *Science and Public Policy*, 14(6), 310-316.

Zeeman, E. C. (1976). Catastrophe Theory. *Scientific American*. 234(4), 65-83.

Zhou, P., and L. Leydesdorff (2006). The Emergence of China as a Leading Nation in Science. *Research Policy*, 35(1), 83-104.

Zilsel, E. (1976). *Ursprünge der neuzeitlichen Wissenschaft*. (Wolfgang Krohn, Hrsg.) Frankfurt A.M: Suhrkamp.

List of Figures

List of Tables

Appendices

Author Index

Subject Index